Digital Transformation Management

This book addresses key topics related to organization design and knowledge management in the digital economy with organizational context, particularly in Asia. Asian nations are moving fast toward the digital economy, within which the role of organization design and knowledge management is crucial to support innovative and creative ideas for meeting huge market opportunities where customers are ready for digitalization.

The book conceptualizes organization design into three dimensions, people, information and technology, and offers readers a unique valued insight, bringing new perspectives to understanding emerging business opportunities and challenges in Asia. It presents a valuable collection of 14 chapters with empirical studies from leading researchers. The book addresses digital transformation in companies and organizations in Asia, analysing how disruptive technologies can help them have more efficient organization processes, create innovative products and services, be more resilient and achieve sustainable goals in the post-pandemic time. It fills a gap in the market, offering a valuable collection of chapters that combines strategic topics for companies, organizations and nations today, such as digital economy, disruptive technologies, big data and knowledge management, with a specific focus on the Asian region, providing rich examples and studies focused in countries and regions within Asia.

Written for scholars, researchers and other specialists in digitalization, this book offers a unique collection of insights into the current and future situation in Asia.

Mohammad Nabil Almunawar is Associate Professor at the School of Business and Economics, Universiti Brunei Darussalam (UBDSBE), Brunei Darussalam. His overall research interests include applications of IT in management, e-business/commerce, digital marketplace/platform, digital business ecosystem, health informatics, information security and cloud computing. Currently, he focuses his research on digital platforms and the digital business ecosystem. He has published more than 100 papers in refereed journals, books and book chapters. He is an associate editor of *Asian Business and Information Management* (*IJABIM*) and a member of many editorial boards of international journals.

Md Zahidul Islam is Associate Professor at the School of Business and Economics at Universiti Brunei Darussalam (UBD). His teaching and research interests focus on strategic management, human resource management and knowledge management. His research work has appeared in such journals as *International Journal of Information Management*, *Management Decision*, *Journal of Database Management*, *Corporate Social Responsibility and Environmental Management* and *VINE: The Journal of Information and Knowledge Management Systems*.

Patricia Ordóñez de Pablos is Professor in the Department of Business Administration in the Faculty of Economics and Business of the University of Oviedo, Spain. Her teaching and research interests focus on the areas of strategic management, knowledge management, intellectual capital, human resources management and IT. She is Editor in Chief of the *International Journal of Asian Business and Information Management* and also serves as Executive Editor of the *International Journal of Learning and Intellectual*. She is the Editor-in-Chief of the book series titled *Routledge Advances in Organizational Learning and Knowledge Management*.

Routledge Advances in Organizational Learning and Knowledge Management
Edited by Patricia Ordóñez de Pablos

Key topics such as Organizational Learning (OL), Knowledge Management (KM), and Intellectual Capital (IC) are of increasing interest to both the academic community and organisations operating globally, in this post-crisis situation. They have a bearing on innovation and learning and can influence the achievement of competitive advantage for institutions, universities, organizations and regions. The existing literature on knowledge management and intellectual capital suggests that competitive advantage flows from the creation, ownership, protection, storage and use of certain knowledge-based organisational resources. Superior organisational performance depends on firms/universities/regions' ability to be good at innovation, learning, protecting, deploying, amplifying and measuring these strategic yet intangible resources.

This series brings together a selection of new perspectives from leading researchers from around the world, on topics such as knowledge management and learning in cities and regions, knowledge management and intellectual capital reporting in universities, research centres and cities, to name but a few. Not only are the volumes of the series supported by quantitative and qualitative analysis, but they are reinforced by the experiences of practitioners as well.

The series gives readers the chance to explore cutting-edge research in the fields of knowledge management, intellectual capital and organizational learning not only from Europe and the USA, but also from Asia, an area which has been largely overlooked.

Digitalisation and Organization Design
Knowledge Management in the Asian Digital Economy
Edited by Mohammad Nabil Almunawar, Md Zahidul Islam and Patricia Ordóñez de Pablos

Digital Transformation Management
Challenges and Futures in the Asian Digital Economy
Edited by Mohammad Nabil Almunawar, Md Zahidul Islam and Patricia Ordóñez de Pablos

For more information about this series, please visit: *www.routledge.com/Routledge-Advances-in-Organizational-Learning-and-Knowledge-Management/book-series/RAOLKM*

Digital Transformation Management

Challenges and Futures in the Asian Digital Economy

Edited by Mohammad Nabil Almunawar, Md Zahidul Islam and Patricia Ordóñez de Pablos

Routledge
Taylor & Francis Group
LONDON AND NEW YORK

First published 2022
by Routledge
2 Park Square, Milton Park, Abingdon, Oxon OX14 4RN

and by Routledge
605 Third Avenue, New York, NY 10158

Routledge is an imprint of the Taylor & Francis Group, an informa business

British Library Cataloguing-in-Publication Data
A catalogue record for this book is available from the British Library

Library of Congress Cataloging-in-Publication Data
A catalog record for this book has been requested

ISBN: 978-1-032-12434-6 (hbk)
ISBN: 978-1-032-12436-0 (pbk)
ISBN: 978-1-003-22453-2 (ebk)

DOI: 10.4324/9781003224532

Typeset in Times New Roman
by Apex CoVantage, LLC

Contents

Contributors

Norazillah Abdullah is a lecturer at the UTB School of Business, Universiti Teknologi Brunei (UTB), Brunei. She has vast experience in teaching at the Higher National Diploma (HND) and undergraduate levels at UTB. Her academic background is in business information technology, for both masters and BSc (Hons) from Aston University, United Kingdom. Her research interests are in the areas of business information systems, information management and social media.

Ani Safwanah Bakar is a postgraduate student of Universiti Brunei Darussalam pursuing a master of management. She has received her bachelor's degree in business administration (Hons) in 2018 from Kolej International Graduate Studies, Brunei Darussalam. She also has a National Diploma in interior design, graduating in 2010 from Sultan Saiful Rijal Technical College of Brunei Darussalam. Currently she is working as marketing assistant at one of the leading security services providers in Brunei Darussalam.

Subhanil Banerjee is an economist working in Amity University Chhattisgarh as Assistant Professor. His specialisations include digital economics, econometrics, growth and development, business economics, international trade, environmental economics, history of economics, bank merger and so on. He has been published in many reputed Scopus indexed journals, including *Economic and Political Weekly*, *Journal of Health Management* and many others.

Chukiat Chaiboonsri is Associate Professor of Economics at Chiang Mai University, Chiang Mai, Thailand. He is also a director of the Modern Quantitative Economic Research Centre (MQERC) at this faculty as well. His research focuses on the field of quantitative analysis in economics and statistics approach in economics, respectively. He has taught economic and business forecasting, business cycle theory, econometrics and quantitative analysis in economics for both graduate and undergraduate students.

Harish Chandan is an independent researcher and business consultant. He was Professor of Business at Argosy University, Atlanta. He was interim chair of the business program in 2011. He received the President's award for excellence in teaching in 2007, 2008 and 2009. His teaching philosophy is grounded in learner needs and lifelong learning. His research interests include applied social psychology, multiculturalism, research methods, leadership, marketing and organisational behaviour. He has published 20 peer-reviewed articles in business journals and 19 book chapters in business reference books. He has co-edited four business reference books and is working on the fifth one. He has presented conference papers at the Academy of Management, International Academy of Business and Management, Southeast Association of Information Systems, and Academy of International Business. Prior to joining Argosy, he managed optical fibre and cable product qualification laboratories for Lucent Technologies, Bell Laboratories. During his career with Lucent, he had 40 technical publications, a chapter in a book and five patents. He serves on the Board of Trustees at Down Syndrome of Louisville. He also teaches Sunday school at the Hindu School of Kentucky.

Alfina Damayanti is a researcher in the Industrial Engineering Department, University of Muhammadiyah Malang, Indonesia. Her research interests are industrial system optimisation, usability, system modelling and operations management.

Mononita Kundu Das is Professor at Amity University, Kolkata. Her prior associations are Lal Bahadur Shastri National Academy of Administration and National Law University. Her areas include jurisprudence, banking law, environmental law and public policy. She has 20 years of teaching experience in law in several premier institutions in India. She has been regularly writing for journals and books at both national and international levels.

Rituparna Das is Life Member of the Council of Indian Statistical Institute. He completed the academic cycle from lecturer to professor over two decades. His academic associations include the Centre of Risk Management and Derivatives at National Law University, National Institute of Bank Management, Indian Institute of Social Welfare and Business Management and Adamas University School of Business and Economics. His PhD in econometrics was preceded by dual masters in economics and management. His areas include strategies, bank risk management, financial economics, microeconomics and policy research. He is Life Member of Indian Statistical Institute, the Indian Econometric Society and Indian Economic Association. He received the honour of being named "One of the IBC's Leading Educators of the World" from the International Biographical Centre and a Lifetime Achievement Award from Marquis Who's Who. His complete profile is available at https://vidwan.inflibnet.ac.in/profile/163636.

Manlio Del Giudice is Full Professor of Management at the University of Rome "Link Campus," where he serves as delegate for Erasmus+ Program and a director for the master in smart public administration. He holds a PhD in Management at the University of Milano-Bicocca. His scholarly profile shows more than 150 peer-reviewed contributions. His researches have been published or are forthcoming on such flagship journals like *MIS Quarterly*, *Journal of*

Product Innovation Management, *Journal of Organizational Behavior*, *Journal of World Business*, *Long Range Planning*, *IEEE Transactions on Engineering Management*, *Journal of Technology Transfer*, *R&D Management*, *Technological Forecasting and Social Change*, *Production Planning & Control* and *International Marketing Review*. His main research interests deal with knowledge management, technology transfer, foresight management, innovation and technology management. He was the first Italian scholar to be appointed as associate editor for the *Journal of Business Research*.

Dayang Fatzainalutfiah Awang Ahmad is a postgraduate student enrolled in the master in management programme under UBD's School of Business and Economics, which she completed in early 2021. She received her bachelor of arts (Hons) degree in sociology and anthropology under UBD's Faculty of Arts and Social Science in 2018. As a part of a requisite for her undergraduate degree, under the supervision of Dr. Magne Knudsen, she wrote a dissertation focusing on the prohibitions or "*pantang larang*" related to Brunei-Malay marriage ceremonies. It mainly explores the nature and rationale behind Brunei-Malay marriage prohibitions, identifying the reasons behind youth's decision in forgoing them and investigating the implications of Islamisation on the practice of such prohibitions.

Chai Lee Goi is a senior lecturer at the Faculty of Business, Curtin University, Malaysia campus. Goi holds a PhD in management and business, specialisation in Internet marketing (Management and Science University, Malaysia), a master's in information technology management and a bachelor's in computer science (University of Wollongong, Australia). In addition to teaching, he has held several positions at the faculty and university levels, such as Head of Department – Marketing and Management, Associate Dean of R&D, Chair of Graduate Studies and Deputy Dean of R&D. His research interests include Internet marketing, consumer behaviour, sustainable development and big data.

Shilpi Gupta is an ICWA, earned an MBA in finance and is pursuing a PhD in behavioural finance. Her specialisations include behavioural finance and stock market decision-making. She was a member of Confederation of Indian Industries (CII) in the year 2016 in the Taxation Panel.

Muhamad Sanusi Hussin holds an MSc in management and technology from the Universiti Teknologi Brunei (UTB) School of Business. Currently, he works in the Science, Technology and Innovation Division at the Ministry of Technology, Information Communication (MTIC), Brunei.

Yeoul Hwangbo is a director of Asian affairs of the Yong Consulting Service as well as a professor at Tashkent University, Uzbekistan. He has experience in working as (i) a senior adviser for the Prime Minister's Office, a director general of Brunei Economic Development Board (BEDB) and a professor of the e-Government Innovation Centre of Universiti Brunei Darussalam (UBD) in Brunei and (ii) a professor of e-government innovation Centre of Korea Advanced Institute of Science and Technology (KAIST) in the Republic of Korea (ROK). Meanwhile, he conducted the government services in the area of e-government and e-business promotion as an international consultant of Asian Development Bank (ADB) and as a government adviser. His working areas include science and technology innovation (STI) policy, e-business and e-government. He received his bachelor's degree in public administration with a minor in physics from Sungkyungkwan (SKK) University in 1985, a master's in public administration from Seoul National University (SNU) in 1987, and a PhD in management information systems from Korea Advanced Institute of Science and Technology (KAIST) in 1999.

Fahmi Ibrahim (PhD) is Assistant Professor of the School of Business, Universiti Teknologi Brunei (UTB), Brunei Darussalam. He earned his PhD from Glasgow Caledonian University, Glasgow, UK, and his MSc in business information technology systems (BITS) from University of Strathclyde, Glasgow, UK. He has a wide range of academic experience gained in higher education establishments in the Brunei Darussalam and UK. His current teaching and research areas are in the field of strategic management, knowledge management, management information systems (MIS), human resource management, operations management and tourism management-development within public, private, and small and medium-sized enterprise (SME) organisations. His consultancy experience is in the area of business transformation, particularly in SMEs. The consultancy expertise is supported by and complemented by his research interests. His research output includes book chapters, journal articles and conference papers. In recent years, his research interest has evolved to be contextualised around the strategic development of organisations in complex and transitional environments.

Ilyas Masudin is Professor in the Industrial Engineering Department, University of Muhammadiyah Malang, Indonesia. He holds a PhD in logistics from RMIT University, Australia. His research interests include logistics optimisation, supply chain management, multi-criteria decision-making and operations management.

Muhammad Mahreza Maulana received his master's degree in information technology (IT) from Bandung Institute of Technology (ITB) Indonesia in 2006 and is now a doctoral student in computer science at IPB University Indonesia. He has worked for more than 14 years in one of the telecommunications companies in Indonesia and currently as an IT manager and trainer. His research interests are enterprise architecture, IT governance and smart cities.

Khairunnisa Musari is Assistant Professor in the Department of Islamic Economics, Postgraduate Program and Faculty of Islamic Business Economics, KH Achmad Shiddiq State Islamic University (UIN KHAS), Jember, Indonesia. She is a member of the Indonesian Association of Islamic Economists

(IAEI) and a member of the Expert Board of the Islamic Economic Society (MES) of Lumajang. She is also a lead independent associate ambassador of VentureEthica. Her concerns include sukuk, waqf, esham, fiscal and monetary policies, circular economy, halal logistics, climate change, and microfinance and nanofinance. Her writings and papers are published in local and national daily newspapers, magazines, international journals and book chapters. She also has experience as a senior specialist for Islamic finance of United Nations Development Programme (UNDP) Indonesia and is listed as the Top 150 Most Influential Women in Islamic Business & Finance 2020 by Cambridge-IFA.

Bình Nghiêm-Phú is currently an assistant professor at the School of Economics and Management, University of Hyogo, Japan. He is doing research in the fields of applied psychology, marketing and tourism.

Thành Hưng Nguyễn is currently a lecturer at Thuongmai University, Vietnam. The focus of his research is accounting and auditing in Vietnam.

Armando Papa, PhD, is currently Associate Professor of Management at the Faculty of Communication Sciences, University of Teramo. He earned the Italian national qualification as full professor in 2020. Earlier, he joined the Universitas Mercatorum of Rome. He was formerly a research fellow at ICxT Innovation Center, University of Turin. He holds a PhD in management from the University of Naples Federico II and a postgraduate master's in finance (2011). He is skilled in knowledge management, open innovation and technology entrepreneurship, corporate governance and family business. He is an associate editor of the *Journal of Knowledge Economy* (Springer) and an assistant managing editor of the *Journal of Knowledge Management* (Emerald). He is listed as an innovation manager at the Italian Ministry of Economic Development. He is engaged as editorial board member for the *Journal of Intellectual Capital, British Food Journal, Management Research Review* and other international journals. He is member of the I.P.E. Business School of Naples.

Rossana Piccolo is Research Fellow at the Department of Economics of the University of Campania-Vanvitelli. She holds a European PhD in entrepreneurship and innovation at the University of Campania-Vanvitelli, discussing a thesis on behavioural finance in the credit sector. In 2012, she earned a master's degree in finance and markets at the Second University of Naples, discussing an experimental thesis in advanced corporate finance. Her studies and research interest are focused around behavioural finance, innovation and knowledge management. Likewise, she is currently involved in research studies on the soft dimension of technological innovation and the role of knowledge management in fintech. She is also involved in several peer review processes for international journals. She has participated in many international conferences as key speaker as well as president. Since 2014, she has been a lecturer in corporate finance and advanced corporate finance at the Department of Economics of the University of Campania-Vanvitelli.

Ahmad Rafiki is Assistant Professor in the Faculty of Economics and Business of Universitas Medan Area, Indonesia. He obtained his BBA degree with a major in marketing from MARA University of Technology and his master's in management from the International Islamic University of Malaysia. In March 2014, he was awarded a Doctor of Philosophy from Islamic Science University of Malaysia. He also holds an Islamic marketing associate (IMA) certificate from the International Islamic Marketing Association (IIMA). His research interest is on Islamic entrepreneurship, management and marketing. He has authored many book chapters and books and articles related to Islamic management, entrepreneurship, SMEs, leadership and halal industry by international publishers such as IBA-MacMillan, IGI Global, Emerald Publishing, Springer, IntechOpen, Routledge and more. He also joined the editorial advisory board of and became a reviewer for Emerald and Elsevier publishers, and he has presented academic papers in various international conferences. He recently won the Outstanding Reviewer of Literati Awards 2020 by Emerald Publishing.

Dian Palupi Restuputri is a lecturer and researcher in the Industrial Engineering Department at the University of Muhammadiyah Malang. Her research interests are in the area of ergonomics and human factor engineering. She received her bachelor's degree in industrial engineering from Diponegoro University, Indonesia (2007). She holds a master's degree in industrial engineering from the Institute of Technology Bandung, Indonesia (2013).

Norhafizzah Abdullah Sali is currently pursuing her Master of Management at Universiti Brunei Darussalam (UBDSBE). She graduated from the University of Hull, Scarborough Campus, United Kingdom, earning a Bachelor of Arts (Hons) in tourism management in 2013 and a Higher National Diploma (HND) in travel and tourism management from Loughborough College in 2011. Currently she is a business lecturer at Kolej International Graduate Studies and a former extracurricular activities (ECA) coordinator, Kiulap Brunei Darussalam.

Anuphak Saosaovaphak is an assistant professor who works as an experienced lecturer at the Faculty of Economics, Chiang Mai University, Chiang Mai, Thailand. He graduated from Victoria University, Australia, with a doctoral degree in logistics and supply chain and has written for many international publications. His research topics are mainly based on logistics and supply chain economy, tourism management, political economy and digital economy.

Veronica Scuotto, PhD, joined the University Federico II of Naples after working at the University of Turin and the Pôle Universitaire Léonard de Vinci in Paris (France) as an associate professor in entrepreneurship and innovation. She obtained the Italian national qualification as Full Professor in 2020. She received a PhD in marketing and management from Milan Bicocca University. Her research interests are focused on SMEs, entrepreneurship, knowledge management, intellectual capital and digital technologies. She has been published in several top-quality research journals such as the *Journal of Product Innovation Management*, *Journal of World Business*, *Journal of Organizational Behaviour*, *Journal of Business Research*, *Forecasting and Social Change*, and more. She serves as an editorial assistant for the *Journal of Intellectual Capital* and editorial board member of the *Journal of Knowledge Management*. She is a member of the International Council for Small Business and mentors for the Techstars Smart Mobility Accelerator in Turin, Italy.

Arif Imam Suroso was born in Tuban in 1961. He obtained an MSc in computer science from the University of New Brunswick, Canada, and a doctoral degree in agricultural economics from IPB University, Indonesia. He currently works as Associate Professor at the School of Business, IPB University. His interest of research are in business intelligence and analytics, decision support systems, economics and business modelling, and agricultural economics.

Heru Susanto is currently Assistant Professor in the School of Business, Universiti Technologi of Brunei, and Researcher at the Research Center for Informatics, the Indonesian Institute of Sciences. He has worked as an IT professional in several roles, including Web Division head of IT Strategic at Indomobil Group and Prince Muqrin Chair for Information Security Technologies. His research interests are in the areas of information security, 5G technologies, grid application, big data, business process re-engineering, and e-marketing. He received a BSc in computer science and an MBA in marketing management, an MSc in information systems, and a PhD in information security, from IPB University, King Saud University and Tunghai University, respectively. He has authored more than 35 books published by Francis & Taylor Group, including eight full authored books and 30 book chapters, and has published more than 60 articles in international peer reviewed and high-impact journals.

Mun Heng Toh is Honorary Fellow of the National University of Singapore (NUS). He was former Associate Professor at NUS Business School and holds a doctorate degree from the London School of Economics. He is an economist with more than 30 years of experience and has consulted for international organisations and local enterprises. He had been economic consultant for several ministries and statutory boards in Singapore, including Ministry of Trade and Industry, Ministry of Finance, Ministry of Manpower, InfoComm Media Development Authority and National Secretariat of Climate Change at the Prime Minister Office. His main areas of expertise are in the area of public policies and strategies for economic development, economic impact analysis, productivity improvement, digitalisation and environment-related policies. He has authored, co-authored and edited several titles, the latest being *Productivity in Singapore's Retail and Food Services Sectors: Contemporary Issues* and *Lifting Productivity in Singapore Retail & Food Services Sectors: Role of Technology, Manpower & Marketing*.

Satawat Wannapan is a researcher working at the Modern Quantitative Economic Research Center (MEQRC). His PhD in economics is a comprehensive application of modern econometrics, such as Bayesian inference and simulations, economic hypothesis testing without p-value, and alternative econometric analyses with machine learning. He is very keen to study applied economic researches, and his works try to sensibly explain real situations using modern econometric approaches.

Preface

Introduction

The notion of digital transformation is not novel – such a phenomenon is believed to have been underway for decades since the mainframe era in the 1950s. Digital technologies – including smartphones, cloud computing, the Internet of Things (IoT), big data and artificial intelligence (AI) – have opened up new possibilities that we could not even envisage several years ago. Such technologies have inevitably reshaped one industry after another at a massive scale across the world. Consequently, many businesses are jumping into digital transformation to capture the perks of these trends or solely to keep up with competitors. Such large-scale change efforts are particularly prevalent in the Asia Pacific region, the global frontrunner in the digital transformation wave.

As businesses begin to explore their digital transformation pathway, the strategic path and destination towards such initiatives are notoriously difficult and have been portrayed as akin to "changing flight in mid-air." These businesses may face various challenges during the execution and implementation stages, including organisational barriers, socio-technical inertia and cybersecurity risk. To ensure digital transformation initiatives deliver the expected results at every step, it is crucial to identify the potential challenges and develop effective ways to overcome them.

Notwithstanding, we are living in a world where technologies continue to develop at a very accelerated pace. What is of relevance now can become obsolete rapidly or abruptly, due either to innovation or imitation by competitors. In this view, digital transformation is anticipated to remain as technology advances. From a future perspective, it is essential to recognise, conceptualise and validate the next emerging phenomenon long before it becomes significant in the real world. The book is designed for readers to grab various aspects of digital transformation in Asia.

This book encompasses a wide array of conceptual and practical viewpoints associated with digital transformation. Its collection of 14 chapters provides valuable insights to readers, specifically in the Asian context. Potential readers are students, academics, researchers, policymakers and practitioners. This book can be used as a primary or supplementary textbook for undergraduate and postgraduate students in business management or related areas.

Contents of the book

Chapter 1, titled "Science, Technology and Innovation (STI) in ASEAN in the Context of Digital Economy" (by Yeoul Hwangbo), states that " 'digital economy has continuously been changing and formulating various activities of the ASEAN science, technology and innovation (STI) and its ecosystem under the ever-changing ICT environment. This chapter suggests a futuristic STI platform and the STI thrusts for the ASEAN countries in the context of the digital economy. These include (i) the STI digital platform, (ii) STI and R&D policy, (iii) liaison with academia and industry on the global value chain, (iv) facilitating technology transfer, and (v) promoting young entrepreneurs and start-ups in the digital economy. This chapter reviews how the digital economy relates to the STI thrusts. In order for the digital economy to be a game changer for ASEAN STI initiatives, we need to develop such strategies as (i) establishing diplomatic relationships in an official way, (ii) engaging with the private sector in STI initiatives, (iii) applying official development assistance effectively, and (iv) facilitating open innovation' ".

Chapter 2, titled "Identifying Success Factors of Digital Transformation" (by Ani Safwanah Bakar, Dayang Fatzainalutfiah Awang Ahmad, Norhafizzah Abdullah Sali and Mohammad Nabil Almunawar), argues that " 'digital transformation (DT) is an important trend for all businesses, including small and medium-sized enterprises (SMEs), as the whole business is influenced by the digitalisation of the value chain. Nowadays, technology is one of the main factors that helps businesses thrive in the competitive marketplace. The emergence of digital technology helps businesses to grow, innovate and address development challenges to sustain businesses and secure their future. The temptation to pursue DT is increasing for SMEs; however, most remain unclear and ill-prepared in engaging the proper way to achieve successful DT. The insufficient research on success factors of DT may contribute to this as SMEs are lacking proper guidelines in successfully achieving DT. This would implicate high failure rates among not only SMEs but start-up digital businesses as well, as they are not able to fully utilise digital technology, resulting in them lagging behind the competition. The research presented in this chapter attempts to identify success factors that contribute to DT to assist SMEs, especially in Brunei Darussalam, to properly transform their businesses digitally. The study is in the form of qualitative research, and both primary data and secondary data are utilised. Data was collected through survey questionnaires from 25 SMEs of different industries, and articles on DT were also compiled and analysed' ".

Chapter 3, titled "How Digital Transformation Connects Knowledge Exploration and Exploitation with Business Model Innovation: A Fintech Perspective" (by Rossana Piccolo, Armando Papa, Veronica Scuotto and Manlio Del Giudice), explains that " 'despite the Covid-19 pandemic, digital transformation is changing society's *modus operandi* of doing business from the "old" to the "new" knowledge-driven economy, where organisations must have the right organisational design to ensure they are competitive. In particular, the banking and finance ecosystem has been revolutionised by technology, where fintech has brought technological innovation to financial services by transforming how customers access financial services. Asia seems to possess great potential in technology, and several companies are revolutionising all financial sectors, including banking services. WeChat represents a successful product of the company, demonstrating how a society changes and develops new entrepreneurial and business opportunities through technology. WeChat, developed by the Chinese company Tencent, has multiplied in the Asian market, where it may soon have no rivals, given that China is at the forefront of Asia's economic development. This chapter shows how Asia as an innovation ecosystem is continuously transforming towards digital through its dynamic capabilities. It also exposes the benefits associated with the use of digital technologies in the Asian economy, highlighting how the interaction between business model innovation and knowledge exploration and exploitation mechanisms foster and improve human and social well-being. The originality of the chapter consists of a changing perspective grounded on fintech that explores the impact of digital transformation on value creation'".

Chapter 4, titled "Is Digital Money an Alternative to Conventional Money in Pandemic in the Asian Emerging Economy Context?" (by Rituparna Das, Harish Chandan and Mononita Kundu Das), states that "'scant opportunity for using money during the period of the corona pandemic has prompted the public to search for an alternative to conventional or fiat money. Digital money can be an alternative for those few with adequate purchasing power and education. However, the inability of the conventional monetary system to track the use of every coin and paper note of fiat money in an emerging economy causes cavities in the database of transactions in a sizable informal sector. As a result, the use of digital money and its associated tools may not be able to yield the desired results in the absence of computer literacy, financial inclusion and technology-oriented mindset of the entire population in a continent like Asia. Here, only half of the population can afford to use mobile Internet, though the pandemic has stimulated digital banking and payments. This chapter offers an overview of the nature and use of cryptocurrency and its compatibility with the smooth functioning of macroeconomic systems of some of the Asian emerging economies, such as Cambodia'".

Chapter 5, titled "Impact of Digital Connectivity on Ease of Doing Business: The Asian Experience" (by Subhanil Banerjee and Shilpi Gupta), states that "'the advent of information technology and its subsequent adaptation to human life and nature gave a new impetus to business. It created a timeless and spaceless society in which time and geographic barriers were no longer a hindrance to the flourishing of business. The symmetric and real-time information that flowed to the producers and consumers equally reduced the deadweight loss for both of them and helped them to make informative decisions. However, these logical explanations lack the empirical rigour in the existing literature. Given this background, the present chapter focuses on the impact of digital connectivity on the ease of doing business. Considering the huge growth of information and technology in the last few years in Asia, the impact has been assessed for the continent". 42 countries of the continent, and their ease of doing business ranking has been chosen as the dependent variable. On the other hand, per 100 mobile subscriptions and per 100 fixed broadband subscriptions along with air transport freight have been taken as the independent variables."

Chapter 6, titled "Application of Knowledge Management and Digitalization in an Islamic View" (by Ahmad Rafiki), discusses "'knowledge management and digitalisation in an Islamic view, which may have different perspectives than do other religions. Islam encourages the implementation of knowledge management for an individual or an organisation that could improve personal or organisational competencies and development. These have been highlighted and emphasised by the verses in the Al-Qur'an and other Muslim scholars' opinions. Meanwhile, digitalisation in Islam is a crucial element that could expedite the learning process, creativity and innovativeness. Both knowledge management and digitalisation are meant to obtain the blessing of God Almighty (Allah SWT) and achieve a better life in the world and the hereafter. This chapter adopts a content descriptive analysis that elaborates on and discusses knowledge management and digitalisation in Islam and the issues that arise. This shows that Islam, in general, governs everything in life, including matters related to science and technology'".

Chapter 7, titled "Designing a Simple House of Knowledge Management" (by Muhammad Mahreza Maulana and Arif Imam Suroso), affirms that "'managing data, information and knowledge is a challenge for every company or organisation, and the biggest challenge is how to make those things provide the maximum benefit for the organisation. Every organisation has different targets, capabilities and resources. Therefore, we need knowledge management design that includes all those aspects. In conducting knowledge management, components of house design are used. There are at least three components – foundation, pillars and roof. First, organisations must understand the definition of data, information, knowledge and learning organisation as their assets. The function is understanding their current position and taking steps to achieve the desired position. In knowledge foundations, there are the organisation, leadership and management models assisted by technology. Setting the knowledge management process starts from the creation, sharing, transfer and innovation of knowledge. The ultimate goal is achieving competitive advantage by transitioning from an information society of data, information, pieces of knowledge and competence knowledge to a data-driven society'".

Chapter 8, titled "Enterprise Social Media as Knowledge Management System in Higher Education Institutions (HEIs)" (by Fahmi Ibrahim, Muhamad Sanusi Hussin, Heru Susanto and Norazillah Abdullah), addresses "higher education institutions (HEIs) and their role in "'knowledge creation and production through research, learning and teaching. In fact, knowledge management (KM) has gained acceptance in academia and has a major role to play in the knowledge economy, bringing new challenges for HEIs. The educational landscape has evolved from a traditional teaching environment to a highly open and dynamic knowledge-based environment due to the large adoption of computers, Internet, intranet, and instructional software applications, including social media. However, the studies on the utilisation of social media within HEIs are still limited. Upon realising the importance of the concept of knowledge sharing through social media, the aim of this chapter is to extend the knowledge within the literature and explore KM practices through enterprise social media (ESM) while identifying the contributing factors that may facilitate and hinder the implementation. The findings highlight issues involving conceptual understanding, knowledge-sharing culture and perceived usefulness. The study further contributes with the development of a conceptual framework for adopting and effectively implementing ESM as a KM system in HEIs'".

Chapter 9, titled "The Risk Management of Cryptocurrencies Based on the Prediction of VaR and ES under the Quantum Wave: Outlook for ASEAN Countries" (by Anuphak Saosaovaphak, Chukiat Chaiboonsri and Satawat Wannapan), states that "'suspicious information and chaotic situations caused by the Covid-19 pandemic are the main issues in recent economic predictions. The ASEAN community is a group of member countries trying to decentralise restricted systems, especially financial sectors. The huge gap in the investigation in ASEAN economies is obscure information. To deal with this issue, an example of applying a novel tool for exploring invisible factors forcing fluctuations in ASEAN economies is empirically presented in this paper. Cryptocurrencies – the indexes that are intentionally defined as a decentralised market – are chosen. Four major digital currencies – Bitcoin (BTC), Ethereum (ETH), Tether (USDT) and Ripple (XRP) – have been collected as a daily time-series sample from 1 January 2018 to 27 December 2020. The main objective is to present the outlook of risk management by using quantum formalism in parts of data transformation, extreme analysis and risk foresight. The result provides strong evidence that a quantum mechanism not only can be applied in a computational lab, but also can be a predominant alternative for studying ASEAN in terms of big data analyses'".

Chapter 10, titled "Developing a Digital Business Ecosystem in Singapore" (by Mun Heng Toh), proposes that "'in recent years, the aim to transform into a smart nation together with the drive towards ubiquitous digitalisation of the economy has provided the hope and conduit to launch the economy into a new phase of growth. In this chapter, we trace the evolution of Singapore's journey in the digital transformation of the economy. Starting from encouraging greater use of ICT in industries and the computerisation drive in the civil services to increase labour productivity and service quality, the many national IT plans launched over the years had laid a solid foundation for the establishment of a SMART nation and digital economy. The chapter describes and analyses the strategies adopted by the Singapore government to develop a digital business ecosystem to transform the economy into a new phase of growth. In particular, we consider the various schemes, incentives and action plans crafted to help small and medium-sized enterprises, which make up 99% of total enterprises in the economy, to transform their business models into one that makes the best use of digital technologies. Digitalisation is part of Singapore game plan to be a global-Asia node for technology, innovation and enterprise'".

Chapter 11, titled "P2P Lending and Philanthropy Platform: A New Face of Asian Digital Financial Inclusion (Evidence from Indonesia)" (by Khairunnisa Musari), states that "'financial inclusion becomes a global agenda to achieve sustainable development goals. In Asia, many countries are engaging in financial inclusion as a strategy to reach inclusive growth. Digitalisation now brings digital financial inclusion. Peer-to-peer (P2P) lending and philanthropy platforms have become a new face of digital financial inclusion in Asia. As the third-largest population in Asia and Southeast Asia's biggest economy, Indonesia has remarkable untapped financial technology prospects in P2P lending and philanthropy platforms. Indonesia represents a major global economy in Asia, where financial inclusion works and the digital economy has begun to arise, and has become the most generous country through Islamic philanthropy. Therefore, by using Indonesia as a case study, this chapter describes the P2P lending and philanthropy platform by focusing on three issues: (1) entry barriers; (2) developing digital financial inclusion ecosystems; and (3) social and economic impacts. Overall, this chapter has a mission to invite the public to be involved in financial inclusion as a form of shared social responsibility through digital financial inclusion. The aim is not oriented for commercial financing to the people who are the target of financial inclusion, but as social financing for empowering them to reach a better living standard'".

Chapter 12, titled "Antecedents of User Acceptance of Digital Banking Service: A Qualitative Study in Vietnam" (by Bình Nghiêm-Phú and Thành Hưng Nguyễn), addresses "'digital banking in Vietnam. It affirms that digital banking is the next generation of online banking. Digital banks, which are totally virtual units, are preparing to start their operations soon. Understanding the factors that may affect user adoption behaviour at this early stage will provide important insights for bank managers and administrative agents. The purpose of this study, therefore, is to examine the antecedents of user acceptance of digital banking products and services in the Vietnam context. Five discussions with 22 participants in Hanoi were implemented both online and onsite over a one-year period (March 2020–February 2021) to gather information. The analysis of the qualitative data helped identify three categories and eight main subcategories of factors that can affect customers' adoption of digital banking products and services. Although there may be certain differences, these factors can either facilitate and encourage or hinder and discourage customers from adopting digital banking products and services, depending on who the customers are and what stage of development the digital banks are in. Based on these observations, implications for banks and administrative bodies are proposed to further assist the development of digital banking'".

Chapter 13, titled "The Role of Usability in Business-to-Customer Digital Transaction on Multiservice Platform in Indonesian E-Money Providers" (by Dian Palupi Restuputri, Ilyas Masudin and Alfina Damayanti), states that "'the rapid development of Internet technology has also provided social changes, one of which is e-payment as a paying feature. E-payment is growing and increasingly being used by Indonesians to make transactions, in the form of both cards (e-money) and applications (e-wallets). Gojek and Grab are multiservice platform companies in Indonesia that use e-money as one of their payment features. The ease of use is one of the main factors in consumer acceptance of e-payments. This study aims to assess the ease of use, especially concerning payments using electronic money on mobile phone applications. Gojek and Grab both use e-money as their payment system; Gojek uses Gopay while Grab uses OVO. Based on the usability metric calculation results, it can be seen that OVO always gets higher usability than Gopay. OVO excels in the influential factor, but Gopay's usability value for the learnability aspect is better'".

Finally, the last chapter of the book, Chapter 14, titled "The Next Frontier towards Digital Sarawak: Advancing into the Future" (by Chai Lee Goi), states that as "'urbanisation speeds up, five of the biggest challenges confronting the future of cities are environmental threats, resources, inequality, technology, and governance. Digital transformation is the answer for helping to solve some of the current and future challenges of urbanisation. Malaysia is one of the countries in Southeast Asia that responds to digital and technological change challenges. Not only has this development benefited Malaysia as a country, but the digital transformation and innovation have also spilled over to other states in Malaysia, including Sarawak. Currently, the rapid growth of digital technologies has not yet been fully translated into digital dividends, even as access to the Internet by businesses has tripled. The Sarawak government has carried out new efforts to address these gaps through a major paradigm shift in the development of Sarawak Digital. The Sarawak government embarked on a journey towards digital transformation and developed a state with the concept of "Digital Sarawak." On 13 December 2017, Sarawak's chief minister, Datuk Patinggi Abang Johari Tun Openg, launched the Sarawak Multimedia Board and, at the same time, launched the first version of the Sarawak Digital Economic Strategy Book 2018–2022, which marks the start of the digitalisation transformation in Sarawak'".

Acknowledgements

This book is composed of the hard work and dedication of the authors, who are academics, researchers or practitioners in Asia. The editors would like to sincerely thank all the authors for their valuable contributions to this book.

The editors would also like to extend heartfelt appreciation to all reviewers who had participated in the reviewing process. Their time and expertise in evaluating the suitability of submitted chapters for publication contributed significantly to the completion of this edited book.

Moreover, we are also profoundly thankful to our colleagues at the School of Business and Economics (UBDSBE), Universiti Brunei Darussalam, for their continuous support.

Finally, we also like to express our sincere gratitude to the editorial team from Routledge, CRC Press and Taylor & Francis Group for their wise feedback, advice and support in publishing this book.

Mohammad Nabil Almunawar
UBD School of Business and Economics,
Universiti Brunei Darussalam, Brunei Darussalam
Md Zahidul Islam
UBD School of Business and Economics,
Universiti Brunei Darussalam, Brunei Darussalam
Patricia Ordóñez de Pablos
Faculty of Economics and Business of
the University of Oviedo, Spain

1 Science, Technology and Innovation (STI) in ASEAN in the context of digital economy

Yeoul Hwangbo

Introduction

A national innovation system (NIS) was introduced as a new conceptual framework in science, technology, and innovation studies in the 1980s and has been developed by the Organisation for Economic Co-operation and Development (OECD) to put into practice.[1] The NIS has been considered as a system approach in view of a macro system consisting of government, university, industry, and their environment, emphasising their relationships. The NIS framework has been developed by Freeman, Nelson, and Lundvall.[2] According to UNESCO, science, technology, and innovation (STI) play a pivotal role in sustainable development, highlighting a proper policy framework.[3] In this context, STI emphasises a creativity, which thereby constitutes a core component for the NIS.

Meanwhile, it has been observed that the relationships between/among entities constituting the NIS have been closely linked under the ever-changing information and communication technology (ICT) environment in an era of a digital economy, which incorporates all economic activities enhanced by the use of digital technologies, digital infrastructure, digital services, and data.[4] The digital economy is accordingly underpinned by the spread of ICTs across all business sectors to enhance its productivity,[5] and STI activities function in the all sectors of knowledge-based society. As such, all sectors have been interlinked in a way that (i) NIS vitalises the entities' interactions and relationships, (ii) STI facilitates knowledge activities, and (iii) the digital economy provides ICT enablers as the platform. While the digital economy has currently been a global trend to form the emerging innovation ecosystem and laid the foundation for all sectors, STI continues to generate new products and services and thereby promote technology-intensive industries as a new growth engine in a knowledge-based society. Likewise, the digital economy should be so aligned with STI that the lack of concerted endeavours might otherwise make it difficult for (i) the digital economy to find new solutions and services with more benefits and less effort and (ii) STI to be implemented in an effective and efficient manner.

The Association of Southeast Asian Nations (ASEAN) member countries, consisting of various ethnic groups, religions, cultures, and industry development status, have dramatically achieved economic development, indicating (i) 5.7%

DOI: 10.4324/9781003224532-1

economic growth rate between 2010 and 2020 and (ii) around 3 billion of GDP, 2 billion in trade, and 170 million in foreign direct investment (FDI) in U.S. dollars as of 2019.[6] Particularly, the FDI growth rate was 15% between 2008 and 2015, which means that the ASEAN member countries will be positioned as a global economic growth engine in the near future. However, the ASEAN member countries are confronted with insufficient STI initiatives in the digital economy era. In spite of the recent successful national development by ASEAN member countries, they might be caught in a middle-income trap without STI efforts. As the digital economy has increasingly been influencing all sectors in the ASEAN, particularly industries, ASEAN member countries have to seek out STI and ICT initiatives that would induce more technology-intensive industries.

This chapter addresses the following questions: (i) what is the relationship between STI and the digital economy; (ii) what are the major STI thrusts and how are they identified in the digital economy; and (iii) what are the strategies to achieve this endeavour effectively?

The methodology of this chapter is mainly based on a qualitative approach through discussions with the Ministry of Science and ICT in Korea, ASEAN-Korea Centre, Asian Development Bank (ADB), and related agencies/academy associations. The interviews have been carried out through (i) official workings and tasks such as drafting a memorandum of understanding (MoU) for bilateral collaboration, (ii) conducting the project as an international consultant for ADB, and (iii) official visits to related agencies of research institutes.

ASEAN STI thrusts in accordance with the advent of the digital economy

Industry-oriented innovation

ASEAN leaders recognised the need for the ASEAN to be prepared to maximise digital economy opportunities[7] with the advent of the Fourth Industrial Revolution (4IR), from the perspective of industry development. In initiating the 4IR, crucial steps have been taken by the ASEAN, including an 'Assessment of ASEAN Readiness for 4IR' which discusses (i) the diversity of readiness levels among the ASEAN member states and (ii) the need to strengthen cross-pillar sectorial coordination and transform various frameworks and guidelines into implementation.[8]

The ASEAN Secretariat released the 'ASEAN Economic Community Blueprint 2025' highlighting digital technology as leverage to enhance trade and investments to provide an e-based business platform, promote micro, small, and medium enterprises (MSMEs), and facilitate the use of green technology.[9]

ASEAN STI and ICT initiatives

The ASEAN telecommunication and IT ministers (TELMIN) have mapped out the ICT Masterplan (AIM) 2020 with eight strategic thrusts, including (i) Economic Development and Transformation; (ii) People Integration and Empowerment

Through ICT; (iii) Innovation; (iv) ICT Infrastructure Development; (v) Human Resource Development; (vi) ICT in the ASEAN Single Market; (vii) New Media and Content; and (viii) Information Security and Assurance,[10] while at the same time, the ASEAN Committee of Science and Technology (COST) released the 'ASEAN Plan of Action on Science, Technology and Innovation (APASTI) 2016–2025'[11] with the visions of science, technology, and innovation-enabled ASEAN, which is innovative, competitive, vibrant, sustainable, and economically integrated. APASTI's goals include (i) ASEAN STI addressing the grand challenges of the new millennium; (ii) an economically integrated ASEAN that actively collaborates with the public and private sectors, especially SMEs, and enhances mobility of talents; (iii) deep awareness of STI and the beneficial impacts of STI on the bottom of the pyramid that refers to economic development that promises to alleviate widespread poverty;[12] (iv) an innovation-driven economy with deep STI enculturation and a system of seeding and sustaining STI by leveraging ICT and the resources of the talented young, women, and private sectors; (v) active research and development collaboration, technology commercialisation and entrepreneurship and network of centres of excellence; and (vi) an enhanced STI management system that supports ASEAN innovation reaching global markets and promotes innovation, integration and narrowing of development gaps across the ASEAN members countries.

As such, the ASEAN has been implementing both STI and ICT initiatives, recognising STI's potential to bring huge benefits to its member countries. If STI and ICT had not been developed separately, they would have maximised the synergy effect in a mutually related and coordinated way.

Official Development Assistant (ODA)

There have been collaborative programmes and projects to facilitate knowledge flow across the ASEAN countries, particularly ASEAN and Plus 3 comprising China, Japan, and Korea, beyond the ASEAN regional collaboration. Korea has been assisting science and technology and R&D for the ASEAN member countries as part of official development assistance (ODA).[13] ODA projects have usually been decided through (i) official discussions between donor country and recipient country and (ii) international organisation such as the Asian Development Bank and the World Bank.

Korea's ODA flagship projects are variously designed and implemented, ranging from S&T infrastructure to human resource development.[14] These Korean ODA projects for STI are considered to be applied to the ASEAN member countries, given that their requirements are on the rise in the fields of appropriate technologies, human resource development, joint use of research equipment, technology transfer, and promoting industrial R&D.

Identification of STI thrusts

In order to identify the appropriate STI thrusts for the ASEAN member countries, this chapter uses five different sources through reviewing policy documents and

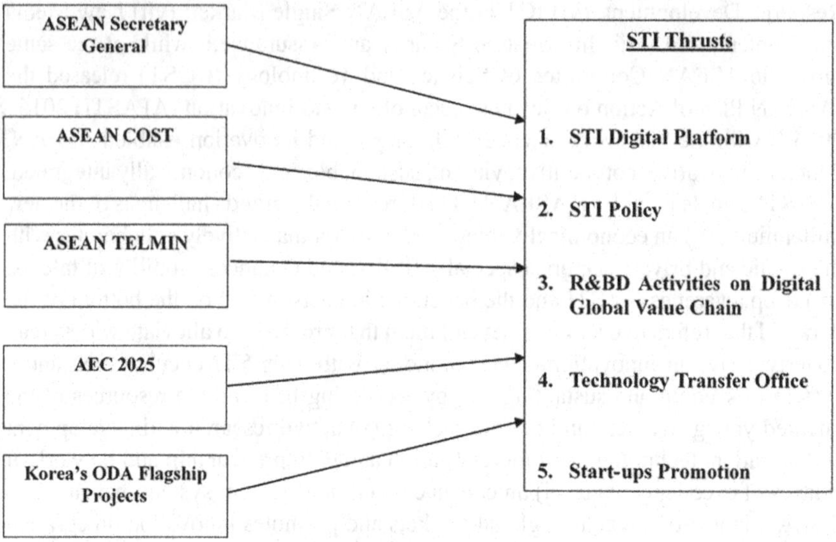

Figure 1.1 Identification of STI thrusts

interviewing related officials. The sources are from (i) ASEAN Secretary General, (ii) ASEAN COST (iii) ASEAN TELMIN, (iv) ASEAN Economic Community (AEC), and (v) Korea's ODA flagship projects discussed earlier (refer to Figure 1.1).

STI thrusts are drawn with aims to:

- i develop the ASEAN S&T and R&D policy based on big data and thereby identify R&D programmes/projects suitable for the ASEAN member countries;
- ii promote collaborative innovation activities and foster the liaison of industries, academia and research institutes through the ASEAN global value chain (GVC);[15]
- iii develop the ASEAN Technology Transfer Office (TTO) services to facilitate combining technology suppliers with their demanders;
- iv promote the technology-intensive starts-ups of ASEAN entrepreneurs so they can efficiently tap into global technology markets using ICT enablers; and
- v develop an ICT enabler-based digital platform for the ASEAN with STI cooperation.

ASEAN STI thrusts in the digital economy

STI digital platform

ICT forms the core part of the digital economy, and conventional technologies – such as cloud computing, automation, traditional enterprise resource planning (ERP) systems – could be leveraged to improve current processes and build transparency between the relevant stakeholders. A variety of technologies are required to be analysed for use in particular domains or applications.[16] STI can provide futuristic solutions through intangible intellectual property (IP) management, creative outputs, and innovation of products and process.[17]

The platform would act as a basic framework for S&T and research and business development (R&BD) activities to be performed in line with (i) a front-office integration functioning as a single window to improve the accessibility and convenience of users and stakeholders and (ii) a back-office integration combining various ICT systems beyond individual country's silo ICT. From the perspective of system implementation, back-office integration is more difficult and complicated to achieve than front-office integration. Because of this, challenges remain over streamlined services rendered, because individual organisations may be reluctant to integrate their system. Back-office integration can be implemented through information sharing, necessitating database consolidation and technology standards, integrated procedures, and common services. This integration, however, usually requires some sort of agreements and contracts among/between individual ASEAN member countries or agencies.

The chapter outlines technologies, business applications which have been surveyed by Gartner,[18] and information communication technology of OECD.[19] Potential technologies can be identified as appropriate for the ASEAN regional countries to establish an STI digital platform. This can be seen as the domain-specific technologies that act as ICT enablers for STI in the digital economy. Relevant technologies are screened to establish the STI platform and roll out its services in the context level. These include (i) knowledge base (KB), (ii) virtual reality (VR), (iii) artificial intelligence (AI), (iv) big data analysis, (v) Internet of Things (IoT), (vi) blockchain, (v) cryptography, (vi) fintech, and (vii) other relevant technologies. Although off-the-shelf software has been applied to various businesses, the STI digital platform needs to be newly developed for their particular R&BD activities (e.g., gentic technologies using big data, 3D printing for research prototypes, and AI virtual researchers) in some cases if needed.

Flagship programmes – called killer applications – for the ASEAN STI platform can bring broader benefits with fewer resources and less effort from the countries by concentrating on certain programmes. The flagship programmes need to be designed in accordance with the purports that (i) the ASEAN STI initiatives have effectively carried out industrialisation and commercialisation through exploiting R&BD outputs/outcomes[20] and (ii) the digital economy can provide an opportunity for the ASEAN member countries to leapfrog industrial development by promoting STI activities. Flagship programmes are identified in Figure 1.2.

S&T and R&D policy supporting system

Governments or related agencies used to rely on data and information to manipulate STI policy adequate to their situations, resources, and national/regional policy goals: STI information can be classified as codified and un-codified types: Survey results of S&T and R&D activities are regarded as a kind of codified information, whereas new volatile information can be viewed as un-codified information. In this regard, knowledge base has evolved from database (DB) and is able to manage both

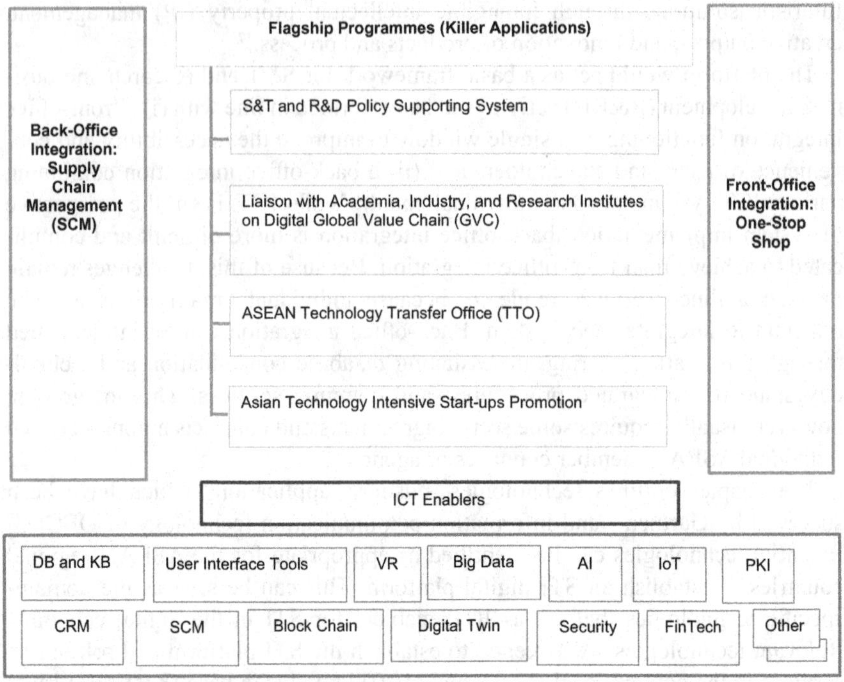

Figure 1.2 STI digital platform

codified data and un-codified information. As such, the ASEAN member countries have been exploiting both types of information for their STI policy-making.

ICT should be a pillar of the digital economy that (i) supports digitalised surveys for R&D activity, (ii) manages data and information more intelligently, and (iii) supports STI policymakers in making appropriate decisions. The online survey of 'S&T and R&D' activities need to be conducted at the ASEAN level to enable comparison with countries anytime and anywhere. The survey of R&D and S&T activities is necessary for appropriate STI initiatives: R&D activities should basically be surveyed with a standard form and manner such as the Frascati manual[21] at the national or regional level, enabling the comparisons between/among countries and thereby making their own proper policy for achieving national and/or regional STI goals. Likewise, the database of 'S&T and R&D Survey' contains relevant data for the decision supporting system (DSS) that can provide STI policy appropriate for its country (refer to Figure 1.3). However, the ASEAN member countries are unlikely to manage R&D data systematically. Even worse, some ASEAN member countries have not conducted the survey on a regular basis and have not accumulated S&T and R&D information systematically.

Table 1.1 shows the results of the ASEAN R&D financing and human resources survey. The survey results can be utilised by the public as well as by officially related agencies in a digital way.

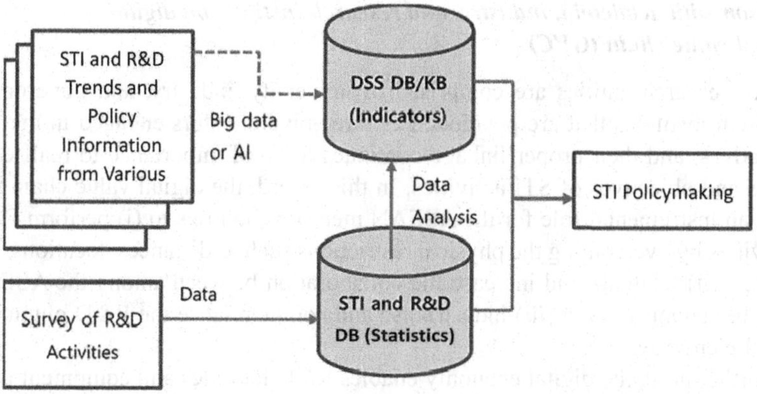

Figure 1.3 Database for STI policy-making

Table 1.1 ASEAN indicators of S&T and R&D activities

Country	*R&D expenditure (% of GDP)*	*Researchers per million persons*	*Tertiary enrolment (%)*	*Champion ministry or agency*
Brunei	0.04 (2004)	287 (2004)	33 (2016)	Ministry of Energy, Manpower, and Industry
Cambodia	0.05 (2002)	30 (2002)	13 (2015)	Ministry of Industry and Handicraft
Indonesia	0.08 (2012)	90 (2009)	36 (2017)	Ministry of Research, Technology, and Higher Education (RISTEKDIKI)
Korea	4.23 (2015)	7,087 (2015)	94 (2016)	Ministry of Science and ICT
Lao PDR	0.04 (2002)	16 (2002)	16 (2017)	Ministry of Science and Technology
Malaysia	1.30 (2015)	2,261 (2015)	42 (2017)	Ministry of Science, Technology and Innovation
Myanmar	0.16 (2002)	12 (2002)	16 (2017)	Ministry of Education
Philippines	0.14 (2013)	189 (2014)	35 (2017)	Research and Development Department of Science and Technology
Singapore	2.2 (2014)	6,658 (2012)	84 (2016)	Agency for Science, Technology and Research (A-STAR)
Thailand	0.63 (2015)	874 (2015)	40 (2016)	Ministry of Science and Technology
Vietnam	0.37 (2013)	675 (2013)	28 (2016)	Ministry of Science and Technology

Source: Compiled from individual countries statistics

Liaison with academia, industry, and research institute on digital global value chain (GVC)

Major research entities are comprised of university, industry, and government research institutes that are positioned as three pivotal actors engaged in the STI initiatives, and their proper linkage continues to be of importance to realise the goals and objectives of STI activities. In this regard, the digital value chain will play an instrumental role for the ASEAN member countries to (i) perform R&D activities by overcoming the physical restrictions such as distances, locations, and spaces, (ii) facilitate and increase the collaboration between/among the ASEAN member countries, and (iii) industrialise and commercialise the R&D outputs in an efficient way.

Furthermore, the digital economy enables R&D facilities and equipment to be shared online and on the value chain network across the ASEAN member countries. It is worth establishing a common facilities and equipment sharing centre – tentatively named – as one of the STI platforms in the digital ASEAN value chain. The common services provided by the sharing centre are able to support the ASEAN member countries struggling with a vulnerable R&D infrastructure or the lack of R&D facilities and equipment. As such, the digital GVC is a useful instrument for the ASEAN member countries to continue to conduct their R&D, so that developing countries suffering from limited S&T funds do not necessarily purchase equipment and building facilities that may generate large costs. In this way, R&D facilities and equipment can be shared across the ASEAN countries in the digital economy, leaving no ASEAN member countries lagging behind in their R&D activities. Bilateral and multilateral agreements on common services for the use of facilities and equipment can help developing countries conduct their R&D activities by collaborating with advanced Asian countries.

Vietnam KIST (VKIST) is one case of liaison collaboration. VKIST is a new public agency on science and technology under the Ministry of Science and Technology (MOST) in Vietnam. It was established through a joint project between the Vietnamese and Korean governments following the Presidential Agreement on September 9, 2013.[22] VKIST is a new agency on science and technology that is positioned to propel the NIS with the following identities of (i) public science and technology agency, (ii) R&D institute of industrial technologies, (iii) a contract R&D institute, and (iv) accredit agency for full leverage of the financial autonomy.[23] With the digital economy deployment, VKIST is expected to embrace ICT and move the digital economy forward so as to effectively perform the collaborative R&D activities and facilitate technology transfer between Vietnam and Korea.

ASEAN Technology Transfer Office

The ASEAN countries emphasise industrialisation and commercialisation of their R&D outputs and outcomes. In spite of the STI imperatives to exploit the R&D outputs needed for their economic development, there have been significant obstacles

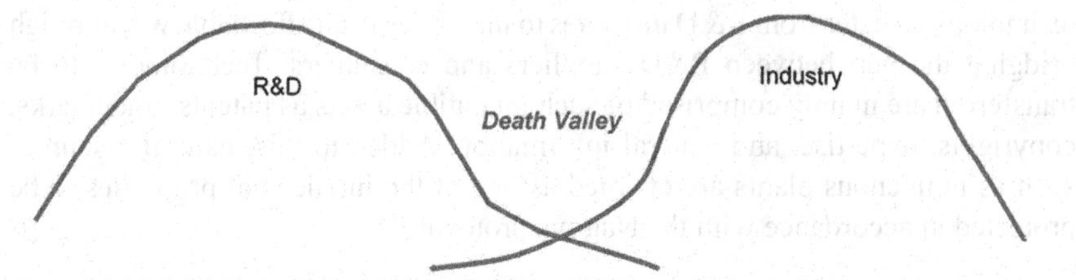

Figure 1.4 Death valley between R&D and industrialisation

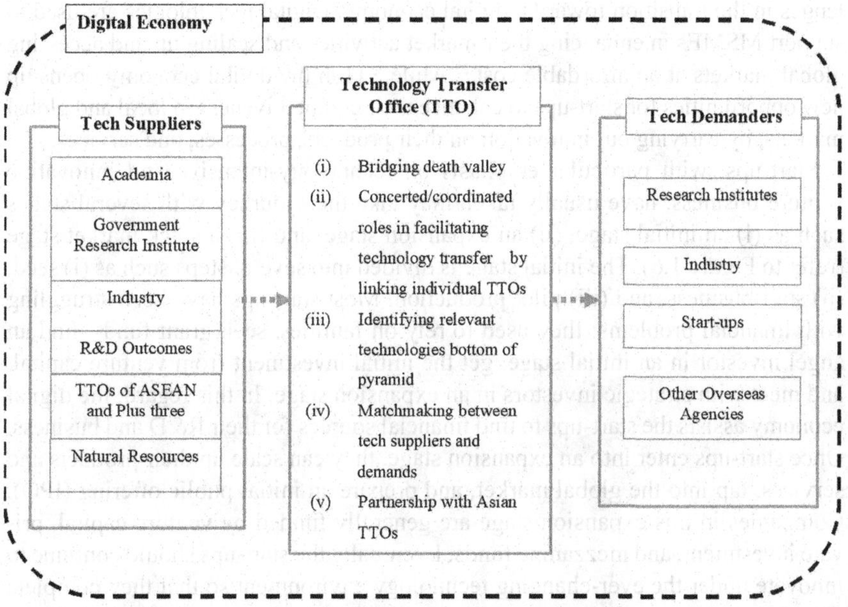

Figure 1.5 Technology Transfer Office in the digital economy

on the flows from R&D institutes to industries. This gap can be expressed metaphorically as a death valley between the R&D mountain and the industrial mountain (refer to Figure 1.4). The death valley makes it hard to transfer R&D outputs and outcomes from research institutes as the supplier to industries as the consumers.

In the backdrop of technology transfer, the ASEAN Technology Transfer Office – tentatively named – is able to act as the bridge to streamline R&BD activities and facilitate industrialisation by (i) bridging death valley, (ii) playing a concerted role in facilitating technology transfer by coordinating every single TTO located in the ASEAN member countries, (iii) identifying intellectual properties and technologies appropriate for ASEAN, (iv) matchmaking technology suppliers and demanders, and (v) providing information and knowledge for research institutes as well as industries.

The digital economy will increasingly provide more opportunities to promote technology transfer from R&D institutes to industries in an affordable way through bridging the gap between R&D suppliers and consumers. Technologies to be transferred are mainly comprised of such intangible assets as patents, trademarks, copyrights, expertise, and general information. Added to this, natural resources such as indigenous plants are claimed as one of the intellectual properties to be protected in accordance with the Nagoya protocol.[24]

Promoting start-ups in the digital economy

Micro, small, and medium enterprises have been facing both opportunities and challenges in the transition toward a digital economy. Digital technologies are used to support MSMEs in enhancing their market activities and scaling up and accessing global markets at an affordable cost,[25] while STI in the digital economy opens up new opportunities for start-ups to enhance their competitiveness in local and global markets, by carrying out innovation on their products, processes, and services.

Start-ups, with particular emphasis on technology-intensive and innovative venture business, have usually taken/may take their journey with several stages such as (i) an initial stage, (ii) an expansion stage, and (iii) a stock market stage (refer to Figure 1.6). The initial stage is divided into several steps such as (i) seed, (ii) start business, and (iii) pilot production. Most start-ups have been struggling with financial problems: they used to rely on families, seek grant funds, find an angel investor in an initial stage, get the initial investment from venture capital, and meet with strategic investors in an expansion stage. In this regard, the digital economy assists the start-ups to find financial sources for their R&D and business. Once start-ups enter into an expansion stage, they can scale up their products and services, tap into the global market, and prepare an initial public offering (IPO). Companies in this expansion stage are generally funded by venture capital, private investment, and mezzanine funds. Eventually the start-ups should continue to innovate under the ever-changing technology environment so that they complete their journey successfully.

It is no wonder that start-ups used to encounter formidable obstacles between (i) the initial stage and the expansion stage and (ii) the expansion stage and the stock market stage (refer to Figure 1.6). The digital economy is able to lower the barriers by providing relevant knowledge appropriate for the start-ups. The digital economy is thus able to facilitate start-ups to successfully take their journey by supporting the creations of new ideas, ensuring accessibility to financing sources, and finding potential business partners in a way that provides relevant information in every stage of business and supports start-ups in developing strategies to complete their innovative business routes. The digital economy, with its agile software development and beta version release strategy, can also affordably establish the test beds to help start-ups enter the market earlier and facilitate their rapid scale-up and innovation.

Figure 1.6 shows that the shortened journey in the digital economy is in stark contrast to the long linear journey that was previously regarded as usual. It is

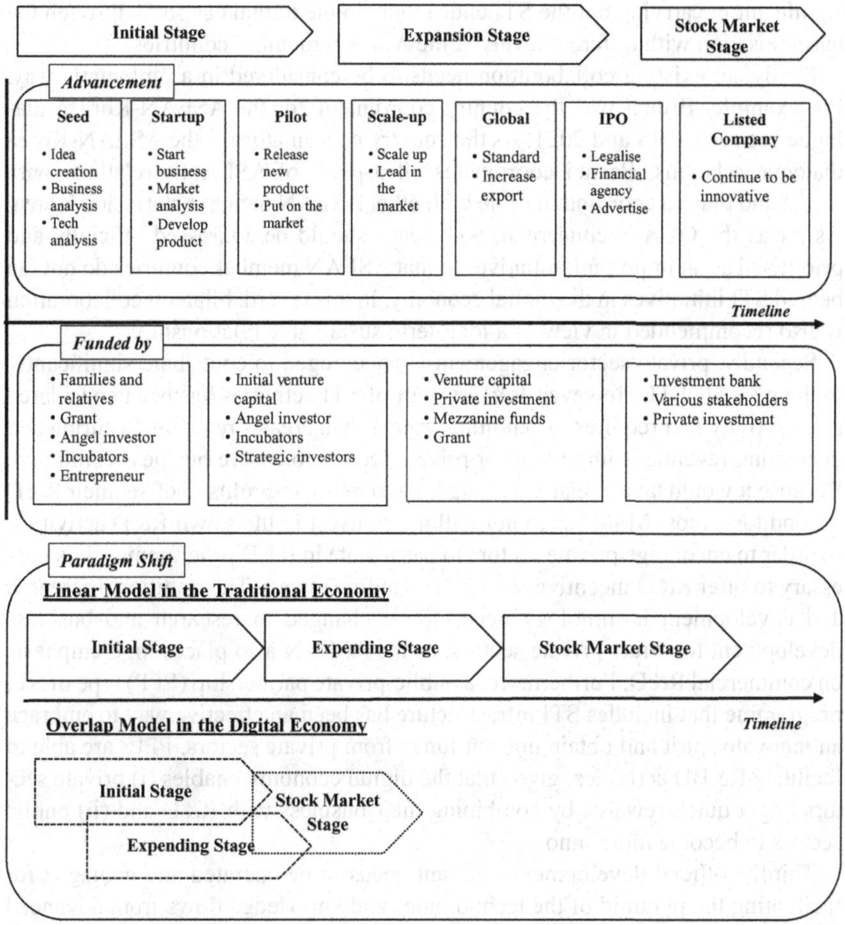

Figure 1.6 Start-ups' journey in the digital economy

therefore worth noting that the digital economy can reduce the timeline of the start-ups' journey by overlapping their stages, so that they can achieve their objectives in a rapidly changing business environment.

ASEAN STI strategies in the digital economy era

The STI strategies are drawn from discussions with officials and researchers working for STI and ICT to identify potential strategic approaches appropriate for the ASEAN member countries. The ASEAN member countries, however, have different political systems, economic conditions, cultures, religions, and ethnic groups, resulting in differing levels of STI and digital economy maturity, from an initial stage to an advanced stage. The following strategies are regarded as significant in carrying out the STI endeavours in the digital economy through the harmonisation with different levels of the ASEAN member countries.

Firstly, an existing collaboration needs to be considered in a diplomatic way. For example, Brunei was the country coordinator for the ASEAN-Korean dialogue between 2018 and 2021. As the country coordinator for the ASEAN-Korea dialogue relations, Brunei coordinates all aspects of ASEAN's relations with Korea and plays a coordinating role with other ASEAN member states and Korea. As far as the ODA is concerned, STI issues should be addressed officially and prioritised as an important initiative, so that ASEAN member countries do not lag behind STI initiatives in the digital economy. In this regard, bilateral collaboration is also recommended in view of a long-term sustainable relationship.[26]

Secondly, private sector engagement is encouraged to contribute significantly to the ASEAN STI. However, R&D as part of STI activities has been considered as an activity that requires expenditures rather than creates revenue. Securing and generating revenue is important for private sectors to ensure business continuity. Because it would take a relatively long time to return to profits to offset their R&D expenditure, most MSMEs are not willing to invest in their own R&D activities. In order to encourage private sectors to participate in R&D programmes, it is necessary to offer R&D incentives in direct or indirect ways. The traditional research and development terminology needs to be changed to research and business development to attract private sectors, as the ASEAN also places high emphasis on commercial R&D. Furthermore, a public-private partnership (PPP) type of STI programme that includes STI infrastructure has been an effective way to embrace an innovate spirit and obtain upfront funds from private sectors. PPPs are able to facilitate R&BD activities, given that the digital economy enables (i) private sectors to get quick rewards by combining their business with R&D and (ii) public sectors to become more innovative.

Thirdly, official development assistant needs to be operated and managed for facilitating the pyramid of the technologies and knowledge flows from advanced countries to developing countries. ODA programmes should be assessed from the viewpoint of beneficiary countries, not donor countries, in the beginning stage prior to identifying ODA projects. ICT enablers in the digital economy are believed to play a pivotal role in achieving the goals and objectives of ODA, and it is therefore recommended that ASEAN ODA programmes be designed and implemented in the areas where STI, ICT, and the digital economy are mutually correlated.

Fourthly, an online STI awareness programme needs to be created at the regional level of the ASEAN or at subregional levels, such as the 'Brunei Darussalam-Indonesia-Malaysia-the Philippines' – the East ASEAN Growth Area (BIMP-EAGA). The programmes are able to provide not only to STI-related agencies, but also to the public, the relevant skills and knowledge on the digital economy trends which is helpful in doing their tasks. As a result, the awareness programmes can create an environment conductive to open innovation by organising technology exhibition events, including online seminars and forums for ASEAN knowledge sharing. Furthermore, open innovation can easily obtain user feedback through the living labs in the digital economy and incorporate users into the R&BD and STI activities.

Conclusion

Most of the ASEAN member countries have been implementing STI initiatives with a view to developing their economy by emphasising industrial R&BD. Meanwhile, ICT has been accordingly exploited as an enabler in the digital economy with particular emphasis on digital transformation. In brief, the digital economy is closely related with various platforms. The platform is based on a centralised architecture, thereby providing more chances for the participants to do their business efficiently. However, the digital economy might create a 'copy and paste economy', in which everybody could easily start a business by copying from the existing services provided without their own creativity, resulting in non-sustainable business. The digital economy can be shabby without the creativity where the STI sets high value. The lack of STI may make it difficult for ASEAN member countries to escape the middle-income trap. So, the digital economy should be enhanced by STI initiatives.

This chapter also identified the five STI thrusts comprised of (i) an STI digital platform, (ii) an S&T and R&D policy supporting system, (iii) an ASEAN digital GVC, (iv) an ASEAN TTO, and (v) the promotion of innovative start-ups in the digital economy. These thrusts are likely to be eligible for the ASEAN to implement their R&BD initiatives for the time being and should be expanded in a timely manner in the near future in accordance with the digital economy. In order to proceed with the STI thrusts effectively, the STI strategies are enumerated as (i) enhancing a bilateral collaboration, (ii) engaging private sectors into the STU, (iii) applying ODA programmes to the STI, and (iv) creating open innovation.

Notes

1 OECD (1997), *National innovation systems*. OECD Publications.

2 Freeman (1987), *Technology and economic performance: Lessons from Japan*. Pinter; Nelson (1993), *National innovation systems: A comparative analysis*. Oxford University Press; Lundvall (1992), *National innovation systems: Towards a theory of innovation and interactive learning*. Pinter.

3 UNESCO (2020), www.unesco.org/new/en/natural-sciences/science-technology/sti-policy/

4 OECD (2020a), *Roadmap toward a common framework for measuring the digital economy, Report for the G20 Digital Economy Task force, Saudi Arabia 2020.*

5 OECD (2014), *The digital economy, new business models and key features*. Addressing the Tax Challenges of the Digital Economy; OECD (2014). *OECD/G20 base erosion and profit shifting project*. OECD Publishing.

6 The World Bank (2020), data.worldbank.org/.

7 ASEAN (2019), https://asean.org/consultative-meetings-discuss-aseans-fourth-industrial-revolution-strategy/.

8 Congratulatory remarks by H.E. Dato Lim Jock Hoi, Secretary-General of ASEAN in anniversary for ASEAN-Korea Centre.

9 ASEAN (2015), *ASEAN Economic Community Blueprint 2025*.
10 ASEAN (2015), *The ASEAN ICT Masterplan (AIM) 2020*.
11 ASEAN (2017), *ASEAN Plan of Action on Science, Technology and Innovation (APASTI) 2016–2025*.
12 The bottom of the pyramid can create ASEAN businesses and markets that mutually benefit the companies and the communities through partnerships with ASEAN in developing countries.
13 OECD (2020b), What-is-ODA, www.oecd.org/dac/financing-sustainable-development/development-finance-standards/What-is-ODA.pdf: The OECD Development Assistance Committee (DAC) defined official development assistance (ODA) as government aid that promotes and specifically targets the economic development and welfare of developing countries. The DAC adopted ODA as the 'gold standard' of foreign aid and it remains the main source of financing for development aid.
14 Korea's ODA projects are summarised as establishing STI governance, building government research institutes modelled after the Korea Institute of Science & Technology (KIST), supporting appropriate technologies for developing countries, developing human S&T resources, establishing S&T infrastructure, building Korea's model of science park, supporting science universities, linking with industry, academy, and research institutes, modernising research equipment and facilities, creating a favourable environment for industry, supporting health care research, diffusing intellectual properties (IPs), fostering young talents, spreading S&T culture to the public, establishing national S&T information systems, and improving the rural environment by providing satellite services.
15 World Bank, Trade and Development (2020) Global Value Chain (GVC) can continue to boost growth, create better jobs, and reduce poverty provided that developing countries implement deeper reforms to promote GVC participation, industrial countries pursue open, predictable policies, and all countries revive multilateral cooperation', www.worldbank.org/en/publication/wdr2020.
16 OECD (2019), *Blockchain technologies as a digital enabler for sustainable infrastructure: OECD Environment Policy Paper No. 16*, www.oecd-ilibrary.org/docserver/0ec26947-en.pdf?expires=1634802099&id=id&accname=guest&checksum=F80D9B62270D9BFC7214A85A7608EFC2.
17 OECD (2018), *Oslo Manual, Guidelines for collecting, reporting and using data on innovation,* 4th Edition, OECD Publishing: innovation is classified as (i) product innovation, (ii) process innovation, (iii) organisation innovation, and (iv) market innovation.
18 Gartner (2020), *Gartner top 10 strategic technology trends*, www.gartner.com/smarterwithgartner/gartner-top-10-strategic-technology-trends-for-2020/
19 OECD (2021), information communication technology is classified as (i) ICT Access and Usage by Households and Individuals, (ii) ICT Access and Usage by Businesses, (iii) Broadband Indicators, and (iv) Telecommunication Indicators, Information communication technology. www.oecd.org/statistics/data-collection/informationandcommunicationtechnology.htm.
20 Industrial R&D has been prioritized in ASEAN member countries.
21 OECD (2015), *Frascati manual 2015:* Several manuals addressing this topic have been released by OECD and UNESCO including Frascati manual.
22 www.vjsonline.org/news/vietnam-korea-institiute-science-and-technology-new-dynamic-and-advanced-institute-research, 2021.
23 VKIST (2021), Overview, https://www.vkist.gov.vn/en/page/tong-quan-vkist.
24 On October 29, 2010, the Nagoya Protocol on Access to Genetic Resources and the Fair and Equitable Sharing of Benefits Arising from their Utilization to the Convention on Biological Diversity was adopted in Nagoya, Japan.
25 OECD (2017), *Level enhancing the contributions of SMEs in a global and digitalised economy: Meeting of the OECD Council at Ministerial Level, Paris 7–8, June 2017*, www.oecd.org/industry/C-MIN-2017-8-EN.pdf.

26 Examples are the bilateral STI collaborations between organization of STI and R&D in the ASEAN member countries and Korea that include Scinece and Technology Policy Institute, Korean Institute of S&T Evaluation and Planning, and Vietnam-KIST.

References

ASEAN. (2015). *The ASEAN ICT masterplan (AIM) 2020*. ASEAN.

ASEAN. (2017). *ASEAN plan of action on science, technology and innovation (APASTI), 2016–2025*. ASEAN.

ASEAN. (2019). https://asean.org/asean-discusses-next-steps-fourth-industrial-revolution/?highlight=4IR

ASEAN Secretariat. (2015). *ASEAN economic community blueprint 2025*. ASEAN.

Freeman, C. (1987). *Technology and economic performance: Lessons from Japan*. Pinter.

Gartner. (2020). *Gartner top 10 strategic technology trends*. www.gartner.com/smarterwithgartner/gartner-top-10-strategic-technology-trends-for-2020/.

Lundvall, B. Å. (1992). *National innovation systems: Towards a theory of innovation and interactive learning*. Pinter.

Nelson, R. (1993). *National innovation systems: A comparative analysis*. Oxford University Press.

OECD. (2014). *The digital economy, new business models and key features*. Addressing the Tax Challenges of the Digital Economy. OECD/G20 Base Erosion and Profit Shifting Project. OECD.

OECD. (2015). *Frascati manual 2015*. OECD.

OECD. (2017). *Enhancing the contributions of SMEs in a global and digitalised economy*. OECD.

OECD. (2018). *Oslo manual 2018*. OECD.

OECD. (2019). *OECD environment policy paper no. 16, blockchain technologies as a digital enabler for sustainable infrastructure*. OECD.

OECD. (2020a). *Roadmap toward a common framework for measuring the digital economy*. OECD.

OECD. (2020b). *What-is-ODA*. www.oecd.org/dac/financing-sustainable-development/development-finance-standards/What-is-ODA.pdf

OECD. (2021). *Information communication technology*. www.oecd.org/statistics/data-collection/informationandcommunicationtechnology.htm

UNESCO. www.unesco.org/new/en/natural-sciences/science-technology/sti-policy/

Vietnam KIST. (2020). https://vkist.gov.vn/c3/en-US/gioi-thieu-f/Research-strategy-1–1300

The World Bank. (2020). *The world bank*. https://data.worldbank.org/

2 Identifying success factors of digital transformation

Ani Safwanah Bakar, Dayang Fatzainalutfiah Awang Ahmad, Norhafizzah Abdullah Sali and Mohammad Nabil Almunawar

Introduction

Rapid development of digital technology has changed the environment of businesses and organisations throughout all industries by means of radically altering business procedures, products, services, and relationships, which consequently suggest the need for firms to change the way their businesses are conducted, that is, by undergoing digital transformation (Karimi & Walter, 2015; Hartl & Hess, 2017). Recently, the idea of digital transformation has been a significant and influential aspect of the discourse about whether it could affect the growth and sustainability of organisations. According to Boulton, citing from a 2016 Harvard Business School study, organisations that engage in digital transformation experienced three years of an average increase of 55% in gross margins. Yet, in spite of this, digital transformation success rates among firms and organisations are relatively poor (Boutetière et al., 2018). It is further stated that the success rate in digital transformation was relatively lower than the findings of the previous study, which revealed that less than a third of the organisational transformations have succeeded in enhancing the performance and sustainability of organisations. These findings are quite daunting as organisations, especially small and medium-sized enterprises (SMEs), are becoming increasingly interested in engaging in and pursuing digital transformation.

There is a growing urgency for SMEs today to pursue digital transformation given the increasing competition from rivals and non-industry entrants, as they attempt to stay relevant and competitive by keeping pace with the digital shifts that emerged in their respective industries. In addition, by engaging in digital transformation, SMEs could potentially gain competitive advantage over multinational companies (MNCs) and penetrate the global market efficiently and cost-effectively. Yet, the guarantee of achieving successful digital transformation is concerningly low, as concluded from Boutetière et al.'s study and McKinsey's 2018 Global Survey, especially among SMEs because they have relatively fewer resources and capabilities compared to larger organisations, in addition to the ill-prepared and ill-informed SME manager concerning the proper way to achieve successful digital transformation. What is more, the lack of sufficient research being conducted on identifying the factors of successful digital transformation may also greatly contribute to the failure rates among SMEs.

DOI: 10.4324/9781003224532-2

This chapter explores and analyses some factors that may potentially lead to successful digital transformation among Brunei SMEs. The main objective of our research is to investigate the factors that contribute to the success of Brunei SMEs' digital transformation. Hence, in relation to this, the research question to be answered in this study is, what is essential or required for Brunei SMEs to accomplish digital transformation?

Literature review

Digital transformation

Digital transformation is defined as an iterative process that involves progressive and disruptive makeover as a means to computerise business processes Barann et al. (2019), as cited in Lombardi (2019). Lu (2017) states that digital transformation is altering the existing administrative and managerial company that reinforces daily activities to be more operative, potentially and ultimately increasing the firms' business viability. Meanwhile, Frank et al. outlined digital transformation as the need for skills or capability to adjust business models with emerging technology or technological advances in the socio-technical climate to direct technological developments, which affects customer experiences and business operations (as cited in Barann et al. (2019).

Reis et al. (2018), on the other hand, outlines digital transformation quite differently. He defined it based on three different categories: (1) technological digital transformation which involves using new digital technologies that enhances business transformation; (2) organisational digital transformation, which is based on the digitisation of the organisational process and the use of a new business model; and (3) social digital transformation, which is a phenomenon by which technology influences the way people live their lives. However, Reis et al. (2018) further note that digital transformation is involved not only in adapting new digital technologies for the improvement of business processes but also in addressing different managerial issues in the business world, such as management of human capital, improving business efficiency and redesigning business processes.

Matt et al. (2015) have also echoed similar sentiments, mentioning that digital transformation often implies the modification of central business operations that could impact not just the products, but also the business processes. This, in turn, changes how organisations are structured and how they should be managed. Hence, it is important to first develop a strategy that could act as a blueprint for effectively coordinating, prioritising and implementing digital transformation. A digital transformation framework is introduced beforehand to help organisations formulate such digital transformation strategies, and this framework contains dependent relationships of four transformational dimensions: technology usage, changes in value creation, changes in structure and financial aspects. Another framework introduced by Vial (2019) describes digital transformation as a process by which digital technologies could cause disruptions that prompt organisations to create a strategy that would alter their value creation path, simultaneously ensuring that the structural changes and organisational barriers that could potentially influence the outcome are managed effectively.

Furthermore, Verhoef et al. (2019) initiated a multidisciplinary discourse on digital transformation, in which they describe it as the revision in the way digital technology is utilised by organisations to establish a new digital business model that contributes to the creation and securing of more value for the company. From analysis of past research, they establish three levels of digital transformation: (1) digitisation, which refers to converting analogue data into digital information that allows for storing and transmission of information, (2) digitalisation, which refers to the change of business processes via usage of digital technology or IT and (3) digital transformation, which refers to a process that involves the whole organisation in the move to form new business models. Verhoef et al.'s research has also determined the types of assets and capabilities that are needed in digital transformation and further claim that such transformation requires a particular organisational structure to be successful.

Digital transformation, according to Zott and Amit (2008), impacts an organisation as a whole. It affects the organisation's ways of conducting business by means of transforming simple and conventional tasks and processes of its operations. Digital transformation entails the rearrangement of a business's internal processes to change the organisation's business logic and its process of value creation (Li et al., 2018; Gölzer & Fritzsche, 2017). Furthermore, digital transformation involves the adoption and integration of digital technologies to facilitate interactions across borders with competitors, suppliers and customers (Singh & Hess, 2017). According to Liu et al. (2011), digital technologies also assist in establishing competitive advantage via transforming the firms to leverage current core competencies or improve upon new ones. Hence, digital transformation is constitutionally connected to strategic changes in the organisation's business model due to the implementation of digital technology (Sebastian et al., 2017).

Given how beneficial digital transformation is for organisations in general to pursue, it is believed that SMEs can yield the most benefit from this process, especially considering how they lack the relevant resources and capabilities to contend with larger organisations in the increasingly competitive market.

Small and Medium-Sized Enterprises

SMEs play an important role in the growth and represent the backbone of a nation's economy, as it creates job opportunities and enhances economic growth, in addition to providing an alternative source of income to the public sector.

In the case of Brunei, Polsaram et al. (2011) mention that SMEs created job opportunities for local Bruneians, where the SMEs manage to contribute more than 50% to Brunei employment, specifically in the private sector. According to Azimah and Kamariah (2019), food and beverage (F&B) industries are quite predominant in Brunei, with more than 60% of business in Brunei SMEs operating under F&B industries in 2015 managed by local entrepreneurs. Azimah and

Kamariah (2019) further asserted that F&B industries have an impactful role in economic growth, boosting economic efficiency and productivity to improve GDP growth. Wasil (2018) states that SMEs contributed about 38% of the sultanate's GDP by 2015, increasing national revenue by 5% from 2010 to 2015.

Keskin et al. (2010) asserted that SMEs are vital actors in promoting innovation, entrepreneurship and competition in developing countries. Rotar et al. (2019) further highlights the significance of SMEs, in the context of Europe, by which more than 60% of its SMEs have contributed to the continent's 2020 strategy in achieving a smart and sustainable regional economy by providing and increasing employment opportunities within the region.

Success factors of digital transformation

As mentioned previously, the scholarship on the success factors of digital transformation is seriously limited, despite increasing interest and ongoing research by scholars seeking to contribute to the body of knowledge of digital transformation. The majority of such studies were conducted to conceptualise the phenomenon (Osmundsen et al., 2018; Morakanyane et al., 2017; Henriette et al., 2015; Reis et al., 2018; Vial, 2019); understand its strategies (Fitzgerald, 2013; Chanias, 2017; Chanias et al., 2019; Kane et al., 2015; Hess et al., 2016; Ismail et al., 2017, Leischnig et al., 2017), leadership in the context of digital transformation (Kohli & Johnson, 2011; Hansen et al., 2011; Haffke et al., 2016; Singh & Hess, 2017; Heavin & Power, 2018) and the future of digital transformation (Berman & Marshall, 2014; Kane et al., 2015, 2016; Lucas et al., 2013). Most were also aimed to explore and investigate how digital transformation has revolutionised different industries (Chanias, 2017; Schweer & Sahl, 2017; Piccinini et al., 2015; Chanias & Hess, 2016; Schmidt et al., 2017; Liere-Netheler et al., 2018).

Moreover, some research been done to study digital transformation at an organisational level, for instance to share the impacts, experiences, challenges and lessons acquired during organisations' digital transformation journeys (Bonnet, 2012; Hansen & Sia, 2015; Fitzgerald, 2013; Tamm et al., 2015; Sia et al., 2016; Dremel et al., 2017; Mocker & Fonstad, 2017; Kohli & Johnson, 2011). Further, studies conducted by Goworek et al. (2016), Liu et al. (2011) and Mueller and Renken (2017) were aimed to share the transformation experiences at operational and functional levels of organisations.

Despite this somewhat impressive body of literature, the research on understanding digital transformation as a phenomenon is incredibly lacking, particularly in terms of what makes for a successful digital transformation. Several studies that explore and identify factors that enhance the success of digital transformation include Hess et al.'s (2016) study, in which they formulated a framework for digital transformation that includes changes in value creation, technology, finances and structure as the four dimensions for the leading formulation of digital transformation strategy.

Moreover, Osmundsen et al. (2018) examined the objectives, drivers, implications and success factors of digital transformation. They identified agile organisational culture, well-managed transformation activities, knowledge leveraged, staff engagement, growth capabilities of information systems (IS), development of dynamic capabilities and formulation of digital business strategy that features the alignment of both business and IS as conducive factors to successful digital transformation.

Vogelsang et al. (2019), on the other hand, through empirical validation, identified three major dimensions in which digital transformation occurs – organisation, technology and environment – as well as discovered 26 characteristics of a digital transformation success framework. The researchers had also emphasised that digital transformation can only be achieved by collaborating with suppliers, customers and other firms from the branch. In addition, Vogelsang et al. (2019) highlighted that cultural change is essential to establish an agile work environment and encourage more interdisciplinary activities.

Morakanyane et al. (2020) conducted a cross-study analysis aimed at identifying and determining the success factors of digital transformation using 16 single-case articles. A total of seven success factors were identified: determining digital triggers, cultivating digital culture, developing digital vision, ascertaining digital drivers, establishing digital organisation, determining transformed areas and assessing impacts. The researchers also discovered 23 subfactors that correspond to the aforementioned seven factors. These factors represent one of the many initial steps in formulating a digital transformation framework that many organisations seek to adopt to achieve successful digital transformations.

The following section will delineate the success factors that have been deliberately selected from the limited extant literature exploring the contributive factors to digital transformation and its strategies. Some of these factors were commonly identified in Hess et al.'s (2016), Osmundsen et al.'s (2018), Vogelsang et al.'s (2019) and Morakanyane et al.'s (2020) research findings and are as follows: organisational culture, efficiently managed transformation activities, leveraged knowledge, engagement of employees and managers, development of IS capabilities, development of dynamic capabilities, and formulation of digital business strategy that incorporates an alignment of business and IS.

2.3.1 Organisational culture

Mueller and Renken (2017) argue that organisational culture is an important aspect in the initial process and the outcome of digital transformation. Haffke et al. (2016) assert that to achieve digital transformation, the whole organisation must adopt and embrace a supportive culture that IT initiatives and joint businesses can thrive in. In a 2017 Delphi study to investigate cultural values that are crucial to the success of digital transformation, Hartl and Hess (2017) identify customer centricity, which pertains to creating activities to fulfil customers' needs, and openness to change, which refers to the willingness and readiness to accept new ideas and embrace change, as the most prominent values. They emphasised other organisational values that are not as salient yet were as conducive to achieving digital transformation are trust, communication, risk affinity, willingness to learn, participation, entrepreneurial mindset, tolerance of failure and innovativeness. Hartl and Hess's (2017) findings suggest that organisational culture that stresses agility, as opposed to control, is ideal in supporting digital transformation, and this includes both externally and internally driven values.

2.3.2 Efficiently managed transformation activities

Although agility is crucial for organisations undertaking digital transformation, empirical research has shown that there is no universal approach to digital transformation; rather, as contended by Berghaus and Back (2017), an appropriate approach is often determined by looking at the organisation's situational context. Transformation activities, according to Berghaus and Back (2017), are activities that organisations carry out before and during their digital transformation. Their study revealed that an activity that seemed significant and prominent across several case studies was improving the firm's digital channels, that is, establishing, operating and developing such channels and shifting towards a multichannel strategy to reach end users. The researchers further commented on the significance of managing the set-up and induction of updated infrastructures and simplified processes (Berghaus & Back, 2017).

In addition, Berghaus and Back (2017) claim that organisations that were successful in their digital transformation were found to participate in innovation activities as well as developing digital strategies. These activities are typically executed by designated teams within the organisation, who often work jointly with external entities or parties. Finally, Berghaus and Back (2017) claim that for every organisation, there are different paths towards achieving digital transformation, and that not all activities they identified in their study were relevant to every digital transformation journey of every organisation. They assert that each company creates its path towards digital transformation via different combinations and variants of transformation activities.

2.3.3 Leveraged knowledge

Leveraging external and internal knowledge has been identified by several researchers, such as Hildebrandt et al. (2015), as highly significant in the process of digital transformation. In their research, Hildebrandt et al. (2015) studied and examined organisations that merged and acquired digital tech businesses and companies and found that these organisations had become comparatively better in their preparation for mastering the digital transformation of their business. Piccinini et al.'s (2015) research found that leveraging end users' and customers' knowledge to offer and deliver up-to-date and customised digital products and services was also important in digital transformation. In addition, their study also revealed that collaborating and jointly working with start-up businesses as a means of developing more agile project methodologies as well as employing start-up mindsets lessen resistance towards innovation (Piccinini et al., 2015; Bilgeri et al., 2017).

According to Piccinini et al. (2015), in the context of the automotive industry, several key issues have been identified that support the process of designing and creating new digital values and business models as well as providing seamless customer experience. These issues include ameliorating information exchange with different business units and players, minimising gaps and establishing partnerships. Bilgeri et al. (2017) also emphasised these issues in their study, in which they ascertained that external partnerships and business unit collaboration are crucial for big manufacturing firms that are undergoing digital transformation. Nevertheless, according to Bilgeri et al. (2017), in the digital context, most of these firms faced difficulties in encouraging their business units to work jointly due to conflicts in internal pricing and insufficient capabilities in identifying and establishing potential partnerships.

In addition to external knowledge, internal knowledge is also argued to be crucial in achieving successful digital transformation. Mueller and Renken (2017) argue that internally oriented digital transformation depends not only on identifying and applying innovative digital technologies but also on assisting employees in leveraging such technologies to encourage them to be more innovative and become digital transformers. In their research, Mueller and Renken (2017) denote several recommendations for organisations to ascertain that digital technologies are leveraged in employees' work and promote digital transformation. These recommendations include, first, launching a hybrid project structure that stresses the roles of both IS and non-IS functions to make sure that digital technology reaches employees, and second, developing collectives for transformation success to provide localised and specific input for requirements and customised communication. The third recommendation is to focus on communicating with employees so that they easily understand how digital technologies work as well as how they can effectively leverage them. Finally, their final recommendation emphasised the necessity of having an organisational culture that promotes digital transformation.

2.3.4 Engagement of employees and managers

In any organisations' digital transformation journey, human capital plays a significant role in its process as well as in many ways determining the outcome of the transformation. Horlacher et al. (2016) give an example of when a chief data officer (CDO) is initially appointed in a firm, his or her role depends on attaining and building adequate influence in the firm to pursue and engage the intended transformation activities and attain responses. Further, Mihailescu and Mihailescu (2017), and in a separate study with Mihailescu et al. (2015), emphasise the importance for employees who are working on processes impacted by digital transformation to be consistently and continually engaged in the changes so that the digital shift is fully realised. In their study, in the context of employing e-healthcare record (EHR) systems in a hospital, Mihailescu, Mihailescu and Schultze (2015) found that personnel that maintained or continued to perform their traditional practices in their work post EHR employment had restricted the process of organisational transformation. Moreover, Mueller and Renken (2017) and Petrikina et al. (2017) found that it is of the utmost importance for managers to consider their employees' concerns and actively include them in the digital transformation journey to ensure that they fully embrace the transformation and engage in espousing new technologies in their fields. This can be done by collaborating, consulting, informing and involving internal stakeholders. Petrikina et al. (2017) further pointed out that taking part in change processes can assist in minimising employee resistance to such processes and successively improve the organisation's goal attainment and organisational commitment. Finally, Piccinini et al.'s (2015) research revealed and emphasised the significance of attracting, employing and retaining workers that possess the new talent and the capability to incorporate business expertise with digital technological know-how.

2.3.5 Development of IS capabilities

Nwankpa and Roumani (2016) claim that IS capability also contributes to digital transformation and pertains to the organisation's ability in assembling and distributing IS-based resources and combining them with other resources. In addition, in their research, the authors measured IS capability as a multidimensional variable that consisted of IS proactive stance, IS infrastructure capability and IS business spanning capability. Nwankpa and Roumani (2016) further asserted that organisations that possess superior IS capabilities have a better chance to achieve digital transformation by rethinking and redesigning their current business processes as well as by changing conventional offerings into digital ones.

2.3.6 Development of dynamic capabilities

The rapid pace of technological advancements and innovations has proven to cause disruptions to not just organisations, but also entire industries. Berghaus and Back (2017) describe digital disruption as the groundbreaking effect of digital innovations which accentuates the pressing need to act responsively. Based on Karimi and Walter's (2015) research on digital disruption in the context of the newspaper industry, they found that to counteract such disruptions, the development of dynamic capabilities is an absolute necessity. According to Leischnig et al. (2017), dynamic capabilities offer organisations the chance to identify and act on opportunities by transforming the firm, reassembling its resources, as well as building and developing digital platform capabilities, and therefore aptly respond and adapt to any changes or digital disruptions to the industry. Karimi and Walter's study revealed and highlighted the importance of having digital platform capabilities to respond to any disruptive changes, in their case, in the newspaper industry. Conversely, Leischnig et al. (2017) assert that capability in market intelligence is also essential in sensing changes to the organisational environment as well as to identify threats and opportunities and act on them consequently.

2.3.7 Formulation of digital business strategy that incorporates an alignment of business and IS

The alignment of changes with organisational strategies is crucial to achieve digital transformation. This fusion of business and IS strategy is known as digital business strategy, and most organisations have become increasingly aware of the need to establish one. According to Bharadwaj et al. (2013), digital business strategy refers to the organisational strategy that is devised and carried out by leveraging digital resources to generate differential value. Leischnig et al. (2017) state that digital business strategies assist businesses in the transformation and attainment of their intended goals and objectives by accenting agile digital operations, digitally enabled customer experiences, digital leadership qualities and emerging digital innovations. Coincidentally, Nwankpa and Roumani (2016) contend that to achieve objectives derived from digital business strategy, the organisation needs to engage in digital transformation.

Even so, studies have shown that as a firm moves towards adopting digital business strategy, misalignments between the organisation's resources and emergent strategy could lead to internal tensions (Yeow et al., 2017). Yeow et al. (2017) further state that it is crucial for organisations, especially those that have begun to take on new strategic directions, to develop their resource configurations and align them well with their new digital business strategy. In Schmidt et al.'s (2017) study on strategic alignment gaps in the banking industry, they found that digital business strategies of banks are often strongly aligned with customer needs; however, customer needs and digital business strategies are poorly aligned with the internal organisation and its IS. Schmidt et al.'s (2017) study shows how the IS systems and internal processes in the banks that were studied were ill-prepared in meeting the demands of the customer and strategic perspectives, and this has been implicated in the impediment of the organisation's digital plans. Yeow et al. (2017) suggested that to lessen alignment gaps and respond to changes and tensions in the organisation's environment, organisations must actively and continuously pursue proper aligning actions to redefine strategy and reconfigure resources.

Research framework and hypotheses

Theoretical framework

As seen in the prior literature review, several studies have highlighted the contributive factors of successful digital transformation: organisational culture, efficiently managed transformation activities, leveraged knowledge, engagement of employees and managers, development of IS capabilities, development of dynamic capabilities, and finally, the formulation of digital business strategy that incorporates an alignment of business and IS. Figure 2.1 depicts our research framework.

Hypotheses development

From the research framework shown in Figure 2.1, Table 2.1 contains hypotheses between the seven independent variables, which are factors that influence the successful implementation of digital transformation for SMEs, and the dependent variable, which is the successful digital transformation in SMEs.

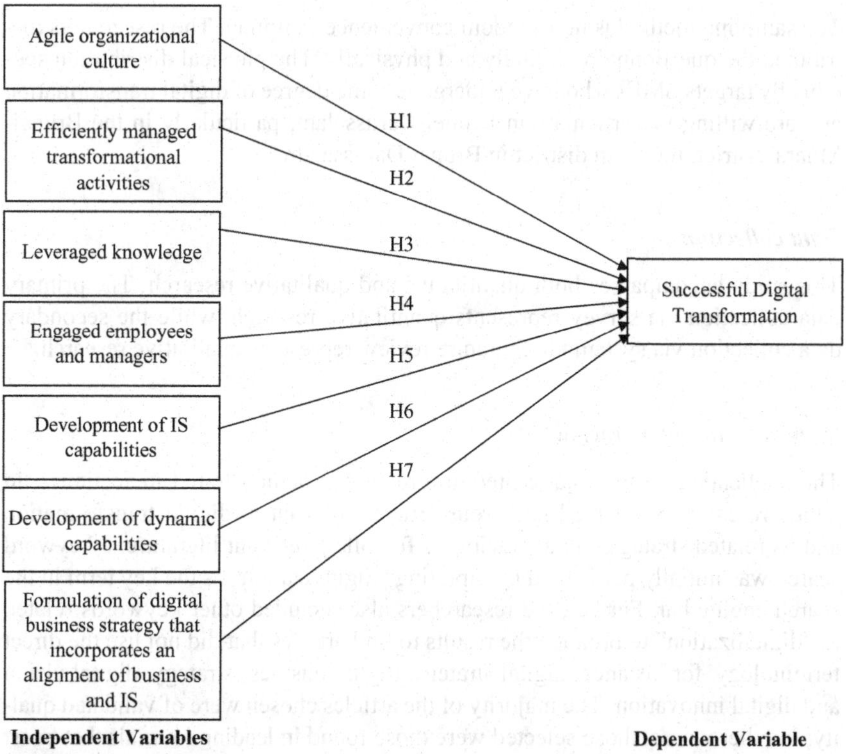

Figure 2.1 The prior theoretical framework illustrates the relationship between the dependent and independent variables

Table 2.1 Hypotheses

H1: Agile organisational culture will contribute to successful digital transformation
H2: Efficiently managed transformational activities will contribute to successful digital transformation
H3: Leveraging knowledge will contribute to successful digital transformation
H4: Engaging employees and managers will contribute to successful digital transformation
H5: Developing IS capabilities will contribute to successful digital transformation
H6: Developing dynamic capabilities will contribute to successful digital transformation
H7: Formulating a digital strategy that incorporates an alignment of business and IS will contribute to successful digital transformation

Methodology

The approach to this study will be in the form of exploratory research in which the researchers aim to identify important contributive factors of digital transformation among Brunei SMEs.

Sampling

The sampling method is non-random convenience sampling. The researchers distributed the questionnaire digitally and physically. The physical distribution specifically targets SMEs who have undergone some degree of digital transformation and are willing to participate in Brunei Darussalam, particularly in the Brunei-Muara district, the main district in Brunei Darussalam.

Data collection

This study encompasses both quantitative and qualitative research. The primary data collection via survey represents quantitative research, while the secondary data collection via systematic literature review represents qualitative research.

Systematic literature review

The application of systematic literature review is demonstrated in section 2, in which researchers selected numerous articles relevant to digital transformation and its related strategies in achieving it. To collect relevant literature, a keyword search was initially performed by inputting "digitalization" as the key term in the search engine bar. Further, the researchers also included other keywords related to "digitalization" to broaden the results to find articles that did not use the direct terminology, for instance, digital strategy, digital business strategy, digital vision and digital innovation. The majority of the articles chosen were of validated quality; in other words, those selected were those found in leading journals that boast a high reputation for quality (Webster & Watson, 2002). The researchers analysed the empirical contributions of the chosen articles to identify the common factors that could potentially lead to successful digital transformation.

Instruments and measurement of items

In order to collect proper primary data, the survey questions were predetermined and constructed in the form of open-ended questions. The researchers used the software application Google Forms in constructing the questionnaire. The researchers intended to approach 25 SMEs who have engaged in digital transformation in different industries: banking, education, food and beverage, hospitality or tourism, sports (gym and fitness) and retail industries. The online survey hyperlink was distributed to local SMEs via Instagram and WhatsApp. Further, a hard copy of the survey was distributed to local SMEs in the commercial area of the Brunei-Muara district.

The first section focuses on the background and nature of the SMEs' business, its activities and its owners' background. The following section features questions that are related to the inferred success factors of digital transformation. Both open-ended questions and a 5-point Likert scale were used to indicate the respondent's acceptance and opinions towards the success factors. The researchers then proceeded to analyse the results and findings obtained from the survey. The analyses were supported by multiple literature reviews and academic articles in accordance with the objectives outlined by the researchers to contribute to the body of knowledge of digital transformation, in the context of Brunei SMEs.

Data analysis

The data analysis was performed using statistical software, SPSS Statistic. In order to meet the objectives of this research, the research questions were addressed using a descriptive analysis and correlation analysis, specifically Pearson correlation analysis, which is performed to test whether there exists a statistically significant relationship between the seven success factors and digital transformation.

Concerning the correlation analysis, a dependent variable (DV) and independent variables (IV) needed to be identified. The DV consists of grouping variables, which are later created as a new variable and determined as "Digital Transformation" (see Table 2.2). Meanwhile, to determine the IVs, every subfactor from each

Table 2.2 Pearson correlation table between variables

Correlations		*1*	*2*	*3*	*4*	*5*	*6*	*7*	*8*
1 Organisational culture	Pearson Correlation	1	.371	.296	.579**	.674**	.463*	.511*	.588**
	Sig. (2-tailed)		.117	.218	.009	.002	.046	.025	.008
	N	19	19	19	19	19	19	19	19
2 Managing transformation activities	Pearson Correlation	.371	1	.765**	.270	.656**	.659**	.743**	.607**
	Sig. (2-tailed)	.117		.000	.264	.002	.002	.000	.006
	N	19	19	19	19	19	19	19	19
3 Leverage knowledge	Pearson Correlation	.296	.765**	1	.215	.642**	.705**	.865**	.607**
	Sig. (2-tailed)	.218	.000		.378	.003	.001	.000	.006
	N	19	19	19	19	19	19	19	19
4 Engaging employees and managers	Pearson Correlation	.579**	.270	.215	1	.411	.214	.206	.317
	Sig. (2-tailed)	.009	.264	.378		.081	.379	.397	.185
	N	19	19	19	19	19	19	19	19
5 Develop IS capabilities	Pearson Correlation	.674**	.656**	.642**	.411	1	.738**	.811**	.810**
	Sig. (2-tailed)	.002	.002	.003	.081		.000	.000	.000
	N	19	19	19	19	19	19	19	19
6 Develop dynamic capabilities	Pearson Correlation	.463*	.659**	.705**	.214	.738**	1	.706**	.593**
	Sig. (2-tailed)	.046	.002	.001	.379	.000		.001	.007
	N	19	19	19	19	19	19	19	19
7 Formulate business strategy	Pearson Correlation	.511*	.743**	.865**	.206	.811**	.706**	1	.717**
	Sig. (2-tailed)	.025	.000	.000	.397	.000	.001		.001
	N	19	19	19	19	19	19	19	19
8 Digital transformation	Pearson Correlation	.588**	.607**	.607**	.317	.810**	.593**	.717**	1
	Sig. (2-tailed)	.008	.006	.006	.185	.000	.007	.001	
	N	19	19	19	19	19	19	19	19

* Correlation is significant at the 0.05 level (2-tailed).
** Correlation is significant at the 0.01 level (2-tailed).

of the seven success factors is grouped together to form new variables. Altogether, there are a total of seven IVs which were later determined as "Organisational culture," "Managing transformation activities," "Leverage knowledge," "Engaging employees and managers," "Develop IS capabilities," "Develop dynamic capabilities," and "Formulate business strategy" (see Table 2.2).

Results and discussion

Demographics of respondents

Researchers distributed 25 survey questionnaires. However, only 19 valid survey questionnaires were returned and compiled. Out of 19 respondents, 42.1% were from retail, 21.1% were from the food and beverage industry, 5.3% were from the education sector and the remaining were from hotel accommodation, service, hospitals and medical centres and sports (gym and fitness). Additionally, the majority of the respondents were from the Brunei-Muara district. In relation to the business operation, 52.6% of the SMEs have been operating for at least five years, 26.3% for less than three years and other respondents stated that they have been operating their business for less than one year and less than five years. Moreover, the majority of the respondents (52.6%) were from small (10–99), 31.6% were from micro (1–9) and 15.8% were from medium (100–199) sized enterprises.

Digital technologies, tools and methods currently used in the business

This section of the survey concerns the digital technologies, tools and methods currently used in the business. Researchers found that some of the SMEs are using social media (Instagram, Facebook, SnapFeed, WhatsApp and WeChat), a point of sales (POS) system, a learning management system (LMS), internet banking, a branch opening system (online and counter banking), a business website, cloud computing, digital communications, digital marketing, computers, laptops, and mobile phones.

Hypotheses testing

Table 2.2 shows Pearson correlation among variables. This table indicates that all hypotheses (H1 to H7) are accepted. H1 indicates *agile organisational culture* has a moderate positive and statistically significant relationship with *digital transformation* (r=.588, p<.01). H2 indicates that there is a moderate positive and statistically significant relationship between *efficiently managed transformational activities* and *digital transformation* (r=.607, p<.01). H3 reveals that there is a moderate and positive relationship between *leveraging knowledge* and *digital transformation* (r=.607, p<.01). H4 shows that *engaging employees and managers* has a weak positive but statistically insignificant relationship with *digital transformation* as the p-value is greater than 0.05 (r=.317, p=.185). H5 stipulates a strong and positive relationship between *developing IS capabilities* and *digital transformation* (r=.810, p<.01). H6 indicates that there exists a moderate positive relationship between *developing dynamic capabilities* and *digital transformation* (r=.593, p<.01). Finally, H7 indicates that there is a strong positive relationship between *formulating digital strategy that incorporates an alignment of business and IS* and *digital transformation* (r=.717, p<.01).

Factors that contribute to successful digital transformation

Based on the Pearson correlation analysis, it is evident that all seven of the proposed hypotheses were accepted. In other words, all participants agree that the factors such as organisational culture, efficiently managed transformation activities, leveraged knowledge, engagement of employees and managers, development of IS capabilities, development of dynamic capabilities, and formulation of business strategy that incorporates an alignment of business and IS are conducive to successful digital transformation.

Organisational culture

The result indicates that an agile organisational culture is conducive to digital transformation. Specifically, respondents agree that the workplace environment must promote a supportive and agile culture, trust, communication, risk affinity, spirit of willingness to learn, participation, an entrepreneurial mindset, a high tolerance towards failure and innovation to achieve digital transformation. This is in line with findings of Morakanyane et al. (2020) and Osmundsen et al. (2018), as both studies emphasised the significance of having an agile and supportive corporate culture in the pursuit of digital transformation. According to Piccinini et al. (2015), the crucial virtues for successful digital transformation among organisations are agility and flexibility, which are especially important in an increasingly unstable market environment where constant adaptation is required. Such transformation processes or changes can be facilitated by an organisation's agile culture, as it could ease the adoption and restructuring of new management concepts. Nevertheless, business transformations and changes can only be effectively integrated if change is accepted. This involves an organisational culture that values openness toward change and fosters the willingness to implement, accept, promote and implement a mindset that is change oriented, an essential requirement to master digital transformation, an important skill for leaders and digital talents (Kane et al., 2016).

Efficiently managed transformation activities

Efficiency in managing transformation activities is essential for achieving digital transformation. It is important for organisations to participate in innovative activities that help to digitally transform their business; develop new and multiple channels to reach customers; provide a fully integrated shopping and browsing experience for customers; and collaborate with external parties to develop its transformation activities. These findings are in line with those of Berghaus and Back (2017).

Important digital tools include visual and conceptual design to project management and programming as well as tools that enable analytics monitoring and social media channels for feedback. Berghaus and Back (2017) emphasise that strong connection and collaboration are essential for successful digital transformation, which are mainly impelled by top management, the human resource department and the designated digital transformation project team. Moreover, they also explained that organisations that adopt a channel-centred approach to digital transformation are usually those that have low digital readiness, for example do not have online shops and instead have a strong focus on physical or brick-and-mortar shops. These organisations focus on developing and improving their digital channels as their initial key activity in their digital transformation process in hopes of strengthening and reinforcing relationships with customers through various efforts. According to Hansen and Sia (2015), it is a common starting point for organisations to first focus on digital channels in their digital transformation process, one of which requires deep organisational transformations.

Leveraged knowledge

Leveraging knowledge is indeed conducive to the success of digital transformation. Local SMEs find it significant for their organisation to have an information database, especially on their customers, to keep their profile and purchase history, to use the database to find innovative ideas and to collaborate with external parties in developing new projects. This is in line with Piccinini et al.'s (2015) research in which they discovered that leveraging customers' knowledge to offer the latest and personalised digital products is crucial in digital transformation. Furthermore, this finding is also consistent with Piccinini et al.'s (2015) and Bilgeri et al.'s (2017) research showing that working together with external parties to build more agile projects reduces innovation barriers. For a digital transformation to work, it requires a further capable environment for technological innovation to develop. In line with Mueller and Renken (2017), digital transformation relies not just on identifying and implementing innovative digital technology, but also on supporting employees utilising those technologies to enable them to be more innovative and to mature into digital transformers. The findings further support Mueller and Renken (2017), who found that SMEs find it fundamental to assist in leveraging knowledge and using digital technology.

Engagement of employees and managers

Combining both technical and business skills can be an added strength that creates a synergy. Management must both include employees as active agents in their digital transformation journey by means of collaborating, informing, consulting and involving them in the process and believe that consistent engagement between employees and managers can accelerate the digital transformation. It is crucial for management to take into consideration employees' concerns during the transformation process; the success rate of digital transformation depends on how an organisation attracts and employs workers with the ability to combine both technical and business skills – businesses must retain workers with digital expertise. Following McAfee and Welch (2013), digital transformation can achieve its full potential if businesses have the right digital skills, identify the gap and make the right investment such as the correct training for honing employees' digital skills and internal support communication. McAfee and Welsh added building employee engagement and trust with managers takes time and will not happen in an instant. Managers should proactively engage with employees to ensure they are on the same page and share and exchange skills and knowledge, combining individual strengths to achieve business digital innovation. Agushi (2019) stated that employee engagement and participation can reduce resistance to changes, enhancing the workers' commitment to achieving the organisation's goals. Every business must therefore engage with employees in adopting new digital transformation, embracing the new era of digitising business, by involving and informing the stakeholders as an active part of the business transformation.

Development of IS capabilities

The organisation needs to have the ability to assemble and distribute IS-based resources; rethink and redesign its current business processes into digital ones; and invest in digital tools and technologies that facilitate internal business processes. These findings are in accordance with Nwankpa and Roumani's (2016) research. Aral and Weill (2007) argued that the digital posture of an organisation is a function of its IT capabilities; hence, according to Mithas et al. (2013), IT capabilities are essential to pursue an effective digital business strategy. Galante et al. (2013) claimed that many giant companies, such as the likes of P&G, Amazon and Unilever, over the years have developed IT capabilities that allow high digital transformation in their service, product offerings, as well as other activities in their value chains. To successfully attain digital transformation, organisations are required to leverage IT capability, and it is further argued that having IT capabilities will likely produce greater digital transformation since organisations try to capitalise on the digital marketplace (Nwankpa & Roumani, 2016).

Development of dynamic capabilities

Developing dynamic capabilities is considered to be one of the key success factors of digital transformation. Most of the respondents find it necessary for the organisation to acquire technological advancements and innovations in the rise of digital disruptions; assess the opportunities and consumer needs existing outside of the organisation; react to market needs, which involves designing innovative models and securing access to capital resources; renew company processes and maintain their relevance to consumers; reassemble its resources in the rise of digital disruption; and develop digital platform capabilities for its business in the rise of digital disruption or changes in the industry. These findings align with the study conducted by Leischnig et al. (2017). Furthermore, Karimi and Walter (2015) also highlighted that one way to tackle the fast-changing environment in an organisation and to counteract any disruptive changes, particularly digital disruption, is by developing dynamic capabilities.

Formulation of business strategy that incorporates an alignment of business and IS

Most of the participating SMEs agree that it is important for the organisation to adopt a business strategy that aligns both business and IS to achieve digital transformation. Specifically, it is crucial for an organisation to adequately prepare its IS systems and internal processes in meeting demands of the customer and strategic perspectives; to actively and continuously align its actions to reconfigure resources and redefine strategy to meet customer demands and strategic perspectives; and explore other revenue streams and integrate other facets of their business. This is supported by the arguments made by Schmidt et al. (2017) and Yeow et al. (2017).

Tallon (2008) argued that effective alignment between IS and business is critical for an organisation, as it can potentially be a source of competitive advantage for them, for example facilitating its operations in terms of increased security and productivity, improving communications and workflows as well as reducing costs. Besides, this new digital strategy allows the organisation to gain customer loyalty from its users. Schmidt et al.'s study has highlighted the importance of strategic alignment with the business's internal process and IS systems in meeting customer demands and needs. Berman (2012) claimed that organisations are highly encouraged to focus on crucial customer interactions by means of developing user profiles for inventing and creating products that correspond to the respective customer's preference (Koye and Auge-Dickhut, 2014). Bain and Company (2014) emphasised that customer loyalty is essential and can be established through the innovation of outstanding service and innovative products.

Limitations

The sampling method as well as the small sample size means that the results and findings of this study cannot be used to make inferences about the larger population. This means that the applicability of the research is limited, though it may still present utility as a pilot study or as basic research. The difficulty of conducting interviews to collect qualitative data means that the initial framework could not be adapted to be more relevant to local business conditions. The absence of rich qualitative data also means that context is lost in analysing the results of the survey. For example, the majority of the respondents to this survey were from micro enterprises. Interviews could have investigated the potential challenge in having such a small work force to implement digital transformation, which may add context to the factor relating to lack of employee skill, or the factor of management having a low tolerance for failure by employees, among others.

Conclusion

Digital transformation is an important trend for SMEs, as the whole business is influenced by the digitalisation of the value chain. Technology is one of the main factors that helps businesses compete and thrive in the competitive marketplace. The emergence of digital technology helps businesses to grow, innovate and address development challenges to sustain businesses and secure their long-term future. The seven proposed hypotheses were accepted by SMEs in Brunei. This means that the seven factors; *agile organisational culture*, *efficiently managed transformation activities*, *leveraged knowledge*, *engagement of employees and managers*, *development of IS capabilities*, *development of dynamic capabilities*, and *formulation of business strategy that incorporates an alignment of business and IS*, are all conducive to successful digital transformation.

References

Agushi, G. (2019). *Understanding the digital transformation approach-a case of Slovenian enterprises* [master's thesis]. https://repozitorij.uni-lj.si/IzpisGradiva.php?id=113619&lang=eng

Aral, S., & Weill, P. (2007). IT assets, organizational capabilities, and firm performance: How resource allocations and organizational differences explain performance variation. *Organization Science*, *18*(5), 763–780.

Azimah & Kamariah. (2019). *Impact of innovation on SMEs performance in F&B manufacturing and service industry in Brunei*. The 1st International Conference on Business, Management and Information Systems.

Bain & Company. (2014). *Loyalty in retail banking 2013*. http://bain.de-/Images/BAIN_REPORT_Loyalty_in_Retail_Banking_2013.pdf

Barann, B., Hermann, A., Cordes, A. K., Chasin, F., & Becker, J. (2019). *Supporting digital transformation in small and medium-sized enterprises: A procedure model involving publicly funded support units* (pp. 4977–4986). Proceedings of the 52nd Hawaii International Conference on System Sciences.

Berghaus, S., & Back, A. (2017). *Disentangling the fuzzy front end of digital transformation: activities and approaches* (pp. 1–17). ICIS 2017 Proceedings.

Berman, S. J. (2012). Digital transformation: Opportunities to create new business models. *Strategy & Leadership*, *40*.

Berman, S. J., & Marshall, A. (2014). The next digital transformation: From an individual-centered to an everyone-to-everyone economy. *Strategy & Leadership*, *42*.

Bharadwaj, A., El Sawy, O. A., Pavlou, P. A., & Venkatraman, N. (2013). Digital business strategy: Toward a next generation of insights. *MIS Quarterly*, *37*(2), 471–482. https://doi.org/10.1.1.216.1018

Bilgeri, D., Wortmann, F., & Fleisch, E. (2017). *How digital transformation affects large manufacturing companies' organization* (pp. 1–9). ICIS 2017 Proceedings.

Bonnet, D. (2012). *Burberry's digital transformation: An interview with Angela Ahrendts CEO of Burberry*. Capgemini Consulting. Consultado em Março 19, 2017.

Boulton, C. (2016). *"Digital laggards" must harness data or get left behind.* www.cio.com/article/3122806/digital-laggards-must-harness-data-or-get-left-behind.html

Boutetière, H., Alberto, M., & Angelika, R. (2018). *Unlocking success in digital transformations.* McKinsey & Company. www.mckinsey.com/business-functions/organization/our-insights/unlocking-success-in-digital-transformations

Chanias, S. (2017). *Mastering digital transformation: The path of a financial services provider towards a digital transformation strategy.* https://aisel.aisnet.org/ecis2017_rp/2/

Chanias, S., & Hess, T. (2016, June). *Understanding digital transformation strategy formation: Insights from Europe's automotive industry* (p. 296). PACIS.

Chanias, S., Myers, M. D., & Hess, T. (2019). Digital transformation strategy making in pre-digital organizations: The case of a financial services provider. *The Journal of Strategic Information Systems, 28*(1), 17–33.

Dremel, C., Wulf, J., Herterich, M. M., Waizmann, J. C., & Brenner, W. (2017). How AUDI AG established big data analytics in its digital transformation. *MIS Quarterly Executive, 16*(2).

Fitzgerald, M. (2013). How starbucks has gone digital. *MIT Sloan Management Review, 54*(4), 1.

Galante, N., Moret, C., & Said, R. (2013, Winter). Building capabilities in digital marketing and sales: Imperatives for consumer companies. *Perspectives on Retail and Consumer Goods, 10.*

Gölzer, P., & Fritzsche, A. (2017). Data-driven operations management: Organisational implications of the digital transformation in industrial practice. *Production Planning & Control, 28*(16), 1332–1343.

Goworek, H., Perry, P., Kent, A., Straker, K., & Wrigley, C. (2016). Emotionally engaging customers in the digital age: The case study of "burberry love". *Journal of Fashion Marketing and Management, 20*(3), 276–299.

Haffke, I., Kalgovas, B. J., & Benlian, A. (2016). *The role of the CIO and the CDO in an organization's digital transformation.* ICIS.

Hansen, A. M., Kraemmergaard, P., & Mathiassen, L. (2011). Rapid adaptation in digital transformation: A participatory process for engaging IS and business leaders. *MIS Quarterly Executive, 10*(4).

Hansen, R., & Sia, S. K. (2015). Hummel's digital transformation toward omnichannel retailing: Key lessons learned. *MIS Quarterly Executive, 14*(2).

Hartl, E., & Hess, T. (2017). *The role of cultural values for digital transformation: Insights from a Delphi study.* In *AMCIS 2017 proceedings* (pp. 1–10). http://aisel.aisnet.org/cgi/viewcontent.cgi?article=1369&context=amcis2017

Heavin, C., & Power, D. J. (2018). Challenges for digital transformation – towards a conceptual decision support guide for managers. *Journal of Decision Systems, 27*(Sup1), 38–45.

Henriette, E., Feki, M., & Boughzala, I. (2015). *The shape of digital transformation: A systematic literature review* (pp. 431–443). MCIS 2015 Proceedings.

Hess, T., Matt, C., Benlian, A., & Wiesböck, F. (2016). Options for formulating a digital transformation strategy. *MIS Quarterly Executive, 15*(2).

Hildebrandt, B., Hanelt, A., Firk, S., & Kolbe, L. M. (2015). *Entering the digital era – the impact of digital technology – related m & as on business model innovations of automobile OEMs chair of information management* (pp. 1–21). ICIS 2015. http://aisel.aisnet.org/icis2015/proceedings/ISstrategy/13%5Cnhttp://aisel.aisnet.org/icis2015/proceedings/ISstrategy/13/

Horlacher, A., Klarner, P., & Hess, T. (2016). *Crossing boundaries: Organization design parameters surrounding CDOs and their digital transformation activities* (pp. 1–10). AMCIS 2016 Proceedings. http://aisel.aisnet.org/amcis2016/HumanCap/Presentations/7

Ismail, M. H., Khater, M., & Zaki, M. (2017). Digital business transformation and strategy: What do we know so far. *Cambridge Service Alliance,10*.

Kane, G. C., Palmer, D., Phillips, A. N., & Kiron, D. (2015). Is your business ready for a digital future? *MIT Sloan Management Review, 56*(4), 37.

Kane, G. C., D., Palmer, D., Phillips, A. N., & Kiron, D. (2016). Aligning the organization for its digital future. *MIT Sloan Management Review, 58*(1).

Karimi, J., & Walter, Z. (2015). The role of dynamic capabilities in responding to digital disruption: A factor-based study of the newspaper industry. *Journal of Management Information Systems, 32*(1), 39–81. https://doi.org/10.1080/07421222.2015.1029380

Keskin, H., Sentruk, C., Sungur, O., & Kiris, H. M. (2010). *The importance of SMEs in developing economics*. International Symposium on Sustainable Development.

Kohli, R., & Johnson, S. (2011). Digital transformation in latecomer industries: CIO and CEO leadership lessons from encana oil & gas (USA) inc. *MIS Quarterly Executive, 10*(4).

Koye, B., & Auge-Dickhut, S. (2014). Big data als game changer. *Zeitschrift Führung+ Organisation, 83*(6), 386–391.

Leischnig, A., Wölf, S., Ivens, B., & Hein, D. (2017). *From digital business strategy to market performance: Insights into key concepts and processes*. ICIS.

Li, L., Su, F., Zhang, W., & Mao, J. Y. (2018). Digital transformation by SME entrepreneurs: A capability perspective. *Information Systems Journal, 28*(6), 1129–1157.

Liere-Netheler, K., Vogelsang, K., Packmohr, S., & Hoppe, U. A. (2018). *Towards a framework for digital transfor-mation success in manufacturing*. http://muep.mau.se/handle/2043/27176

Liu, D. Y., Chen, S. W., & Chou, T. C. (2011). *Resource fit in digital transformation*. Management Decision.

Lombardi, R. (2019). Knowledge transfer and organizational performance and business process: Past, present and future researches. *Business Process Management Journal, 25*(1), 2–9.

Lu, Y. (2017). Industry 4.0: A survey on technologies, applications and open research issues. *Journal of Industrial Information Integration, 6*, 1–10.

Lucas, H., Agarwal, R., Clemons, E. K., El Sawy, O. A., & Weber, B. (2013). Impactful research on transformational information technology: An opportunity to inform new audiences. *MIS Quarterly*, 371–382.

Matt, C., Hess, T., & Benlian, A. (2015). Digital transformation strategies. *Business Information System, 57*(5), 339–343.

McAfee, A., & Welch, M. (2013). Being digital: Engaging the organization to accelerate digital transformation. *Digital Transformation Review, 4*, 37–47.

Mihailescu, M., & Mihailescu, D. (2017). *Understanding healthcare digitalization: A critical realist approach* (pp. 1–12). ICIS 2017 Proceedings.

Mihailescu, M., Mihailescu, D., & Schultze, U. (2015). *The generative mechanisms of healthcare digitalization* (pp. 1–12). ICIS.

Mithas, S., Tafti, A., & Mitchell, W. (2013). How a firm's competitive environment and digital strategic posture influence digital business strategy. *MIS Quarterly*, 511–536.

Mocker, M., & Fonstad, N. O. (2017). How AUDI AG is driving toward the sharing economy. *MIS Quarterly Executive, 16*(4).

Morakanyane, R., Grace, A., & O'Reilly, P. (2017). *Conceptualizing digital transformation in business organizations: A systematic review of literature*. BLED.

Morakanyane, R., O'Reilly, P., McAvoy, J., & Grace, A. (2020, January). *Determining digital transformation success factors*. Proceedings of the 53rd Hawaii International Conference on System Sciences.

Mueller, B., & Renken, U. (2017). *Helping employees to be digital transformers – the olympus. connect case*. ICIS.

Nwankpa, J. K., & Roumani, Y. (2016). *IT capability and digital transformation: A firm performance perspective* (pp. 1–16). ICIS 2016 Proceedings.

Osmundsen, K., Iden, J., & Bygstad, B. (2018). *Digital transformation: Drivers, success factors, and implications* (p. 37). MCIS.

Petrikina, J., Krieger, M., Schirmer, I., Stoeckler, N., Saxe, S., & Baldauf, U. (2017). *Improving the readiness for change – Addressing information concerns of internal stakeholders in the smartPORT Hamburg* (pp. 1–10). AMCIS 2017 Proceedings.

Piccinini, E., Gregory, R. W., & Kolbe, L. M. (2015). Changes in the producer-consumer relationship-towards digital transformation. *Changes*, *3*(4), 1634–1648.

Polsaram, P., Kulsiri, P., Techasermsukkul, L., Htwe, T. D., & Kwanchainoid, K. (2011). *A survey research project on small and medium enterprises development policies of 4 ASEAN countries: Brunei Darussalam, Cambodia, Lao PDR, Myanmar*. ASEAN.

Reis, J., Amorim, M., Melão, N., & Matos, P. (2018). Digital transformation: A literature review and guidelines for future research. *Trends and Advances in Information Systems and Technologies*, 411–421.

Rotar, L. L., Panic, R. K., & Bojnec, S. (2019). Contribution of small and medium enterprise to employment in the European Union countries. *Economic Research Journal*, *32*(1).

Schmidt, J., Drews, P., & Schirmer, I. (2017). *Digitalization of the banking industry: A multiple stakeholder analysis on strategic alignment*. AMCIS.

Schweer, D., & Sahl, J. C. (2017). The digital transformation of industry – the benefit for Germany. In *The drivers of digital transformation* (pp. 23–31). Springer.

Sebastian, I., Ross, J., Beath, C., Mocker, M., Moloney, K., & Fonstad, N. (2017). *How big old companies navigate digital transformation*. https://core.ac.uk/download/pdf/132606601.pdf

Sia, S. K., Soh, C., & Weill, P. (2016). How DBS bank pursued a digital business strategy. *MIS Quarterly Executive*, *15*(2).

Singh, A., & Hess, T. (2017). How chief digital officers promote the digital transformation of their companies. *MIS Quarterly Executive*, *16*(1).

Tallon, P. P. (2008). Inside the adaptive enterprise: An information technology capabilities perspective on business process agility. *Information Technology and Management*, *9*(1), 21–36.

Tamm, T., Seddon, P. B., Shanks, G., Reynolds, P., & Frampton, K. M. (2015). How an Australian retailer enabled business transformation through enterprise architecture. *MIS Quarterly Executive*, *14*(4).

Verhoef, P. C., Broekhuizen, T., Bart, Y., Bhattacharya, A., Dong, J. Q., Fabian, N., & Haenlein, M. (2019). Digital transformation: A multidisciplinary reflection and research agenda. *Journal of Business Research*. Elsevier Inc. www.sciencedirect.com/science/article/pii/S0148296319305478

Vial, G. (2019). Understanding digital transformation: A review and a research agenda. *Journal of Strategic Information Systems*, *28*(2), 118–144.

Vogelsang, K., Liere-Netheler, K., Packmohr, S., & Hoppe, U. (2019). Success factors for fostering a digital transformation in manufacturing companies. *Journal of Enterprise Transformation*, 1–22. https://doi.org/10.1080/19488289.2019.1578839

Wasil, W. (2018). More than $8 billion of national revenue generated by SMEs. *The Scoop*. https://thescoop.co/2018/11/16/more-than-8-billion-of-national-revenue-generated-by-msmes/#:~:text=BANDAR%20SERI%20BEGAWAN%20%E2%80%93%20Revenue%20from,it%20was%20disclosed%20on%20Thursday

Webster, J., & Watson, R. T. (2002). Analyzing the past to prepare for the future: Writing a literature review – writing_a_literature_review.pdf. *MIS Quarterly*, *26*(2), xiii. https://web.njit.edu/~egan/Writing_A_Literature_Review.pdf

Yeow, A., Soh, C., & Hansen, R. (2017, September). Aligning with new digital strategy: A dynamic capabilities approach. *Journal of Strategic Information Systems*, *1*. https://doi.org/10.1016/j.jsis.2017.09.001

Zott, C., & Amit, R. (2008). The fit between product market strategy and business model: Implications for firm performance. *Strategic Management Journal*, *29*(1), 1–26.

3 How digital transformation connects knowledge exploration and exploitation with business model innovation

A fintech perspective

Rossana Piccolo, Armando Papa, Veronica Scuotto and Manlio Del Giudice

Introduction

Recently, Asia was the first area to be attacked by a massive health crisis known as the Covid-19 pandemic, which has since spread worldwide, causing a general freeze and severe restrictions with social and economic impact. The lack of an adequate pharmacological response has increased the difficulties, which are even more evident in less developed countries (De Guzman & Malik, 2020).

In an advanced digital ecosystem such as China's, Covid-19 fostered, even during the months of lockdown, growth in the use of financial technologies and mobile applications, ensuring more efficient and, most importantly, faster pandemic management. China has long focused on developing the most advanced technologies, investing significant public resources. The development of technologies is rapidly transforming the economy and society in which we live, changing consumer spending habits and production and distribution processes. Technologies have enabled the economy, especially in emerging countries, to continue functioning, being a vital part of the pandemic response (Kenney & Zysman, 2016). In Asia, they have been recognized as essential tools for avoiding contact with potential Covid carriers, helping to tame the spread of the virus (World Health Organization, 2020).

Sudden technological innovation is profoundly changing the structural characteristics of modern economic systems, extending existing ones and radically transforming business models. In particular, the development of new technologies often requires the redefinition of the contents and tools for the business process management and the restructuring of models and strategies through business model innovation, where innovation means not only of products/services, but also of the business model, requiring new and more flexible organizational forms (Evans et al., 2017; Wieland et al., 2017).

Companies will have to adapt quickly to these new challenges through the management of two different but complementary issues, namely the search for

DOI: 10.4324/9781003224532-3

new knowledge (i.e., knowledge exploration) and the use of existing knowledge (i.e., knowledge exploitation), thus drawing benefits through the balance between the exploitation of existing technologies and the exploration of new marketing knowledge (Zhang et al., 2020). By leveraging a combination of dynamic and technological capabilities and a high degree of involvement in the knowledge management process, companies will be able to find an optimal position in the marketplace (Scuotto et al., 2020). Companies can no longer be isolated entities in today's dynamic competitive environment; rather, they should tend to establish alliances and networks with external parties (Santoro et al., 2020).

Specifically, when we talk about knowledge exploration, we refer to organizations with different capabilities and cultures through which creative teams acquire new knowledge, overcoming the limits that current technology imposes and breaking down technological boundaries. Conversely, knowledge exploitation responds to the needs of today's markets by expanding existing products and services and improving the efficiency of processes (Gonzalez & de Melo, 2018).

The power and speed with which digital technologies influence individual behaviors are disruptive, especially in access to financial services, bringing numerous benefits. The technological revolution in emerging markets continued to expand access to financial services during the Covid-19 pandemic, with solid growth in all digital financial services influencing daily life in Chinese cities, changing the *modus operandi* and the thinking of individuals (Del Giudice et al., 2019).

These phenomena have had significant impacts on the economic development of the Asian market for several reasons. The size of the phenomenon, justified by an ever-expanding population and an ever-growing economy, has pushed companies to invest in the digital sphere, offering increasingly advanced and innovative products and services. After the closures and continued need for social distancing resulting from the Covid-19 epidemic, the banking and finance ecosystem throughout fintech (financial technology) has brought technological innovation to monetization services, transforming how customers access financial products and services (Puschmann, 2017).

Fintech represents a disruptive innovation capable of shaking up traditional financial markets, bringing a new paradigm in which technology drives innovation in the financial industry. It differs from traditional models in its high reliance on technology, streamlined procedures, and small but highly skilled workforce (Lee & Shin, 2018).

WeChat is a "super social network" that also serves as an instant, cashless payment method (WeChat Pay) with the support of a digital bank (WeChat Wallet). Its various functionalities positively reflect the company's digital development and structure (Plantin & de Seta, 2019).

This chapter includes different theoretical and practical contributions. First, it contributes to the literature on the relationship of knowledge exploration and exploitation with innovation by showing how, despite organizations being affected by the Covid-19 epidemic, innovations in technology have increased, especially in access to financial services, bringing numerous benefits. In particular, it shows how, through its dynamic capabilities, Asia is continuously transforming towards digital (Kogut & Zander, 1992). Second, the chapter shows how business model innovation, which links the exploration and exploitation of knowledge to digital transformation, generates a disruptive effect in the allocation and use of financial services to citizens (He & Wong, 2004). The originality of the chapter lies in showing, through an overview of fintech, the various benefits associated with the use of digital technologies in the Asian economy, especially in terms of social welfare. This is a system in which commercial relationships have shifted from the traditional "face-to-face" to "human-to-human" networks, giving rise to a new model of digital interconnection (Caputo & Walletzký, 2017; Grigoriou & Rothaermel, 2017).

The chapter provides an answer to the following research questions: (1) *How has Covid-19 accelerated digital transformation, revolutionizing the fintech industry?* and (2) *How does digital transformation impact business model innovation (BMI) by providing new fintech solutions to increase knowledge exploration and exploitation from social networks?*

The chapter is divided as follows: the first section highlights the importance of digital technologies and their centrality for improving social services during hyper-challenging and crisis times. In particular, we demonstrate how the effective use of financial technologies and mobile applications have positive effects, allowing the problem to be solved more efficiently and, most importantly, more quickly.

The second section of the chapter, on the other hand, shows how the combination of exploration and exploitation of knowledge marks the pathway for digital innovation allowing the growth and renewal of companies, emphasizing how disruptive technologies enhance business model innovation and entrepreneurial intensity in the social welfare industry. From this perspective, fintech has facilitated access to financial services with a solid growth of all digital financial services affecting daily life in Chinese cities, where WeChat – discussed in the third section – with its various functionalities, positively reflects on both the daily life of individuals and the structure of society through the support of a digital bank.

The social impact of Covid-19 and the role of innovative technologies

Recently, Asia has been the first to be attacked by a massive health crisis known as Covid-19 that initially appeared to be a localized outbreak in China's Hubei province and then quickly became a potential pandemic. After nearly two months, the World Health Organization declared the status of global pandemic, with more than 4.3 million confirmed cases worldwide through mid-May 2020 (Bhutta et al., 2020). The infection was highly contagious, representing a warning about new health regulations for businesses, citizens, universities, and even public institutions (Health Emergency Dashboard, 2020). Globalization has also helped turn Covid-19 into a pandemic through international travel. The Covid-19 pandemic differs from previous epidemics (i.e., severe acute respiratory syndrome, better known as SARS, and Middle East respiratory syndrome, better known as MERS) because their widespread effects attributable to transmissibility were due to the lack of effective drug intervention, whose management depends primarily on effective public health measures to mitigate the spread (Lim et al., 2020). In order to contain the spread of the disease, stop the spread of the virus, and flatten the pandemic curve, most countries' governments have decided to close schools and public spaces, imposing isolation to various degrees and declaring "lockdown" or mandatory quarantine in the entrances. In this vein, inpatient and outpatient practices have also changed, where the greater emphasis has been placed on containing the spread of the virus, resulting in various positive effects on the natural environment (Kanniah et al., 2020). During a public health emergency, it is critical that collective action is based first on individuals' cooperative behavior and then on their trust in others and the interplay between their decision-making and risk perception (Van Bavel et al., 2020).

While implementing these measures, the pandemic has caused social and economic disruption worldwide and has had a significant impact on global public health. In the Asian context, these considerations are particularly salient, given its diversity among countries in terms of sociocultural heritage, health setting, and resource availability, as well as the fact that Asia has the world's most densely populated cities and its developing countries are facing challenges in their socioeconomic and health systems (De Guzman & Malik, 2020). This scenario, globally, has profoundly changed and revolutionized the *modus operandi* of companies in all sectors – healthcare, education, government, and banking – where enabling technologies seem to dominate (Lu & Zhang, 2020).

With limited resources and an immediate need for medical supplies, the crisis called for innovative solutions. New uses of emerging technologies were proposed in order to meet the growing demands, where collaboration between medical researchers and engineers was key for developing rapid and less expensive ways to address the pandemic. In this scenario, open access to knowledge, tools, and technology is essential for timely response (Vafea et al., 2020).

In a rapidly technology-driven economy, digital innovation has several benefits, allowing one to become more efficient in organizational growth (Scuotto et al., 2017).

Technologies represent the engine for change in the business context because, thanks to them, changes are expected not only in business models, but also in the social context.

With the advent of digital innovation, companies have found themselves operating in a more complex and dynamic environment, where a strategy that companies can use to shed light on this complexity is the reworking of the business model, both by completely changing the business and by identifying critical points in the current model where opportunities could be present (Del Giudice et al., 2020). Accordingly, business model innovation can be considered a tool that helps the company identify, understand, design, analyze, and change its business (Massa et al., 2017).

While the pandemic has shown the failure of many businesses, it is also showing how powerful and resilient technology and platform giants are central to society, despite their differences in social and economic organization. Platforms, being digital, provide services and tools that have made closures tolerable, as well as connected institutions and individuals, enabling the rapid movement of economic and social activities online and making societies more dependent. Technologies have led companies to be more resilient and healthier (Kenney & Zysman, 2020; Papa et al., 2020). The Covid-19 pandemic fostered, especially during these months, growth in the use of financial technologies and mobile applications, ensuring that the pandemic was managed more efficiently and, most importantly, quickly (He & Tian, 2018).

While minimizing physical in-person contact, technologies have allowed the economy to continue to function by facilitating remote work. They represent a vital part of the response to the pandemic, where their systemic importance has grown. While the pandemic has been global, its responses have varied depending on local governance and the socioeconomic and cultural context of reference (Kenney & Zysman, 2016). In Asia, technologies have been recognized as essential tools for avoiding contact with potential Covid carriers, helping to tame the spread of the virus (World Health Organization, 2020). During Covid-19, digital transformation accelerated fintech through new digital banking services that enabled both greater and immediate accessibility and transferability of money value, especially respecting the regulation for health protection and social distancing.

Digital innovation and the fintech perspective

The Covid-19 pandemic has significantly impacted the acceleration of the process toward a cashless society worldwide, where the trend toward financial technology transactions has increased. In the aftermath of the pandemic, consumers have decreased the use of cash in their financial transactions and activities, moving towards contactless payment methods to perform transactions electronically, without any physical intervention. This is because they believe that avoiding physical contact with cash and any payment instrument or method helps reduce the spread of Covid-19 (Daqar et al., 2021).

In particular, the monetization ecosystem has been revolutionized by technology, where fintech has brought technological innovation to financial services, representing an important source of opportunities for new and old players in the financial market. Likewise, the digital revolution is transforming, not only in the financial market, how customers access products and services. Fintech deals with this revolution by sitting in the intersection of the financial and technological services; it is a set of new entrants offering, in innovative ways, a range of services and products that were historically delivered by the traditional bank, with a substantial impact on digital payments affected by the innovations and technologies (Puschmann, 2017). This has disrupted the traditional way of providing financial services, bringing increased competition by a new class of players entering the financial industry and forcing incumbents to reduce prices (Berg et al., 2020).

In emerging markets, fintech fostered access to financial services during the Covid-19 pandemic, with strong growth in all digital financial services influencing daily life in Chinese cities, thus changing the *modus operandi* and the thinking of individuals (Del Giudice et al., 2019).

Several startups are bouncing their business model off technological innovations, increasing their competitiveness and generating more social welfare and well-being. This has been happening thanks to the intervention of new technological operators that increase competition within the whole system.

There are several approaches to funding innovation and value creation for companies due to knowledge management strategies and processes (Rossi et al., 2020).

Fintech is derived from "financial technology," an increasingly used phenomenon given the growing intersection of finance and technology and the rapid growth in recent years, which has become more and more substantial in some economies, including China, the United States, and the United Kingdom.

Specifically, fintech relies on electronic platforms through digital technologies and innovations to fully, or nearly fully, interact with users online and hold large volumes of customer information (Gomber et al., 2017). For investors, the lending platform serves the same function as an agent: It guarantees loan servicing in exchange for ongoing fees; it records transactions, collects borrower repayments, and distributes cash flows to investors (Gai et al., 2018). Notably, lending decisions are made through predictive algorithms and machine-learning techniques, where platforms control a much broader spectrum of data than other lenders do. Also, fintech lending tends to adapt more precisely to investors' risk and maturity preferences (Jagtiani & Lemieux, 2018).

Besides, banks have to digitize their financial services. Fully digital and mobile banks were born to serve large market shares with much lower costs than traditional intermediaries, which is an excellent example of industrial integration and innovation. It represents a collaborative relationship between banks and fintech companies that find themselves setting aside competition to address the market need for contactless payments.

Today, financial institutions, mainly thanks to the development of blockchain technology, are increasingly endorsing the quality of fintech solutions, given the implications of this technology. In this context of innovation, the term blockchain is increasingly recurring, representing a paradigm of innovation that allows giving new answers to businesses and consumers (Davidson et al., 2016). The adoption of this technology by fintech companies is a step towards achieving sustainability, security, and privacy. Blockchain streamlines business process management by reducing activities and tasks in the business system and improves communication and information flow, refining strategic and market intelligence. In fintech, blockchain improves the value proposition by providing customers with a privacy-based relationship, where transactions and contracts are conducted in an automated and legally secure manner. It also enables business model innovation through new business models (Fernandez-Vazquez et al., 2019).

In the battle against Covid-19, Asia has been implementing the advancements made in digital technologies since early on, moving towards the trend of electronic payments through fintech (Abdillah, 2020).

Financial innovations enabled by fintech have begun to play an essential role in the delivery of many financial services (Dermine, 2016), where consumers in advanced and emerging economies are increasingly opting for financial services better suited to their needs (Ernst & Young, 2017).

The Europe, China, and Central Asia regions appear to have excellent potential in fintech, given the high levels of mobile and Internet access and the potential to increase the use of digital payments (Berg et al., 2020).

Asia is a very innovative continent, reflected in the fintech companies that distinguish themselves through constant innovation, know-how, and adaptability. In Asia, the most successful fintech services operate for monetization and payment. Alibaba Group represents an emblematic case, a fintech "giant" with a billion users who use the Alipay platform to buy online and in stores; it is also used by tourists from all over the world to carry out money exchanges between individuals.

Fintech's "Ant Financial" today represents one of the largest financial institutions. This model starts with Alipay, in which all that is necessary to enable cashless payments, without requiring cash or credit cards, is to register the app. The payment is automatic and authorized by PIN. Alipay has the advantage of offering online payments, in which the amount paid is transferred to the merchant's account only when the buyer communicates that the goods have been received. Alipay is revolutionizing financial services, although the WeChat Pay payment app is preferred by the Chinese and Asian population, which is turning out to be the real revolution. It works as both businesses to consumer and consumer to consumer, precisely because of direct exchange between two consumers, through the support of an online platform facilitating the transaction (Lu, 2018).

These technological innovations have little value without adequate business models; to this aim, companies increasingly shift their focus from technological conversion to business model innovation. In times of transformational change, business models thus assume a fundamental role, as they stimulate creativity and help overcome cognitive barriers in the process of business model innovation (Chesbrough, 2010). The business innovation model occurs when a company modifies or improves one or more of its business model elements. Thus, the design and implementation of new business models can be more efficient than technological innovation (Abdelkafi et al., 2013).

With more complex procedures, however, fintech can facilitate the provision of credit, improving the system in terms of efficiency gains as well (Gai et al., 2018).

It also improves financial access and inclusion, where providers can adopt different business processes and models through more customized products. Financial inclusion is a powerful development tool that encourages the use of fintech, on the one hand, in order to improve the access to digital banking services, and on the other hand to support vulnerable individuals and households during the Covid-19 crisis, and is considered a disruptive well-being tool (Ozili, 2020). Some scholars argue that financial inclusion reduces poverty levels (Mader, 2018), while others argue that greater financial inclusion presents an opportunity to improve financial stability (Hannig & Jansen, 2010; Ozili, 2020). To this end, fintech platforms can offer monitoring functions similar to those of traditional credit providers. In addition to having an economic function in emerging countries, fintech platforms also take on a social welfare function. The extent of an economy's fintech is positively correlated with its income level and is negatively correlated with the competitiveness of its banking system and the rigidity of banking regulation. With the advent of fintech, the market will be more competitive and more efficient and will provide more choice to the customer; new products, services, and business models will emerge. Financial institutions will be prompted to intensify their competitive strategies as they seek to reduce costs to a level as close as possible to the latest fintech players. With this in mind, it will be crucial for banks to ensure security, maintain transparency and fairness to consumers, and continue to foster innovation (Claessens et al., 2018).

Exploration and exploitation of knowledge as a driver for business model innovation

The Covid-19 grand challenge is mainly to convert the micro-foundations of business competition factors, explicating the need for the exploration and exploitation knowledge strategies in their business models for the firms worldwide. This drives business model innovation (Fenwick et al., 2020; Scuotto et al., 2019).

The digital revolution also helps, through information technology tools, to identify and capitalize on corporate knowledge in order to organize and disseminate it, representing an intangible source of value that can create a competitive advantage, as well as a strategic resource, because it allows the company to create cultural, intellectual, social, and economic value (Zack et al., 2009). Corporate knowledge also represents a fundamental element for all organizations that must possess a high degree of knowledge to be successful (Del Giudice et al., 2017). In order to grow and be competitive, these organizations must pay more and more attention to knowledge management. As a result, several companies around the world are beginning to dynamically manage their knowledge and innovation (Ferreira et al., 2018).

In an increasingly globalized world, knowledge systems become increasingly complex, dynamic, and adaptive. The survival of business management depends on organizational intelligence, which results from the information and knowledge systems companies have, the skills of their employees, and how they relate to stakeholders (Carayannis & Campbell, 2009).

Knowledge is considered the primary organizational resource that can generate a competitive advantage through innovation. Specifically, when we talk about knowledge exploration, we refer to organizations with different capabilities through which creative teams acquire new knowledge, overcoming the limits that current technology imposes and breaking down technological boundaries. Likewise, knowledge exploitation responds to the needs of today's markets by expanding existing products and services and improving the efficiency of processes (Gonzalez, 2019).

There are several types of contributions to knowledge management, including how knowledge is renewed (knowledge exploration) and transformed (knowledge exploitation). Organizations can explore new knowledge or transform it (i.e., starting with the prior knowledge and then achieving incremental improvements). Knowledge exploration and exploitation are topics of great interest to researchers, because, in addition to generating innovation, they improve processes and products, creating new competitive advantage (Gupta et al., 2006).

Therefore, knowledge exploitation and knowledge exploration represent two fundamentally different modes of learning; knowledge exploitation relates to rapid learning, control, continuous improvement, and short-term efficiency, while knowledge exploration relates to slow learning, flexibility and creativity, risk-taking, and long-term innovation efficiency (Eriksson, 2017).

In this vein, it is not always pursuable to combine the two modes of learning due to their inherent differences. However, especially among slack resource organizational settings, knowledge exploration and exploitation draw inbound and outbound innovative synergies that enhance sustainable performance (De Clercq et al., 2013)

Some studies suggest that an excessive focus on exploitation may hinder innovation, leading to a process of obsolescence (Ganzaroli et al., 2016; Gupta et al., 2006). There is a complementary effect between the two strategies: While knowledge exploitation promotes static optimization, knowledge exploration supports dynamic optimization (Lee et al., 2018). Organizations that invest significant resources to implement technological innovation believe that new knowledge is critical because it ensures a continuous influx of ideas that generate innovation, creating strategic flexibility.

Exploratory knowledge and innovations enhance existing components and build on existing technology, while exploratory innovation tends to move toward a different technological trajectory (Benner et al., 2002). In order to develop innovative ideas through exploratory activities, knowledge other than what is possessed is sought, while exploitation activities seek solutions based on existing knowledge (Al-Dmour et al., 2020).

In order to achieve optimal performance levels, organizations will need to be able to maintain an appropriate balance between exploration and exploitation activities (Brix, 2019).

The combination of exploration and exploitation of knowledge sustains innovation strategies, leading firms ambidextrously towards new technologies and dominant design through the exchange of knowledge being considered as central activities for the survival and growth as well as renewal of their competitive dynamics (Gonzalez & de Melo, 2018).

Recently, the digital transformation has affected various activities, embracing the business models with new forms of cooperation and leading to new product and service offerings, as well as new forms of company relationships with customers and employees. Accordingly, companies need to innovate business models ever stronger, so as to improve both the performance and scope of the business, impacting any type of organization (Rachinger et al., 2019).

As a matter of fact, we are witnessing a radical transformation of the financial system, in which several new actors and new operating business models arose under technology-driven innovations. Likewise, business model innovation (BMI) can serve as an essential strategic tool in market design and formation processes (Evans et al., 2017; Wieland et al., 2017).

On the one hand, BMI is described as a process for developing a business model that may be new to the company or an entire industry. On the other hand, it is described as the result of an innovation initiative that replaces or revises an organization's existing business model or changes the existing business model completely. The business model describes the logic of how an organization creates, delivers, and captures value, where increased investment in technology and knowledge exchange and sharing helps businesses cope with today's dynamic global environment by facilitating the collection of big data and information (Scuotto et al., 2017). It is an "ecosystem" in which employees, customers, and suppliers play an active role in supporting innovation (Soto-Acosta et al., 2018).

BMI can disrupt a company's structure by changing and presenting new unique business models, thus fostering more sales, higher profit margins, and more significant cash flows than their competitors do. It can be defined as a change in the value creation and value appropriation of a company that results in a significant change to its value proposition (Bashir & Verma, 2017).

BMI does not have to be designed around product innovation, nor does it have to be disruptive: It merely generates a change in value creation. These innovations are designed through a collection process to simplify the market research process and increase the likelihood of identifying an unmet consumer need (Sorescu, 2017).

BMI is attracting increasing attention in academia. Despite the strong interest in the phenomenon, a common understanding of the concept's meaning has not been established yet, hindering dialogue and progress in this research field (Spieth & Schneider, 2016).

Fintech fits with this consideration, as it represents a phenomenon through which investments in technology and knowledge allow for the rapid realization of not only the rewriting of operational methods for carrying out traditional financial activities, but also the design of new business models, responding to customer needs with increasingly efficient and intuitive products. The digitization of financial activities, therefore, impacts the structural factor of the new financial industry able to determine beneficial effects on the economic system. In this system, fintech companies do not represent a "new industry" but a new component of the financial industry, which challenges the business models traditionally adopted (Schena et al., 2018).

The Asian fintech market is undoubtedly the most innovative and developed globally; it is profoundly changing how financial resources allocation and risk management processes are defined.

The Asian market is constantly evolving economically and socially, where digital is a further step towards an increasingly "computerized" world and where companies are required to offer immediate but straightforward services to attract more consumers. To date, the Asia-Pacific region is considered the global leader in mobile payments; in China, more than half a billion people use mobile payment services such as WeChat Pay to perform online transactions.

From this perspective, BMI can serve as a competitive advantage (Bashir & Verma, 2017). Among them, proprietary social platforms such as WeChat represent an opportunity to capture new profitability that comes through an extension of the value proposition, representing an advancement in technological capabilities, likewise representing a strategic knowledge management tool to incentivize internal venturing and innovation (Del Giudice & Della Peruta, 2016).

The changing business model of WeChat: from social network to mobile monetization service provider

China seems to possess great potential in technology; several companies such as Alibaba are revolutionizing all financial sectors, including banking services. The Internet social platform WeChat represents a successful product innovation management, demonstrating how a society changes and develops through a social network and how citizens use apps to build a life governed by current standards (Zhang et al., 2019). WeChat can be considered a fintech social network differing from traditional ones, as it serves to facilitate communication through instant messaging. Likewise, it acts as an instant and a cashless payment method (WeChat Pay) with the support of a digital bank (WeChat Wallet). It is considered a "super social network" because of its various features that reflect on society's development and digital structure. Further, through the WeChat Payments function, it is possible to control the payments made, also allowing people to make transfers through the message interface or receive money in the WeChat Wallet (Plantin & de Seta, 2019).

WeChat Wallet supports payment means similar to Alipay, through which users can perform a variety of transactions using WeChat Pay, including engaging in businesses to consumer (B2C) and consumer to consumer (C2C) digital transactions, investing in wealth management funds, and paying bills. The solutions adapted from WeChat are proprietary and incorporate attractive features that help users to conduct financial transactions more conveniently (Zhang et al., 2019).

Figure 3.1 presents the analysis framework showing the business model innovation made by WeChat, confirming how digital transformation enabled a social media to provide fintech solutions by creating a business platform that stimulates knowledge exploration and exploitation.

The use of technology has reduced the risk of spreading the disease. Chinese people's smartphones, for example, have been equipped with apps that can track the spread of the virus. The app Alipay Health Code was issued by Alibaba's Ant Financial for the Chinese government and is active on the Alipay and WeChat platforms. The aim was identifying all likely infected people to increase control,

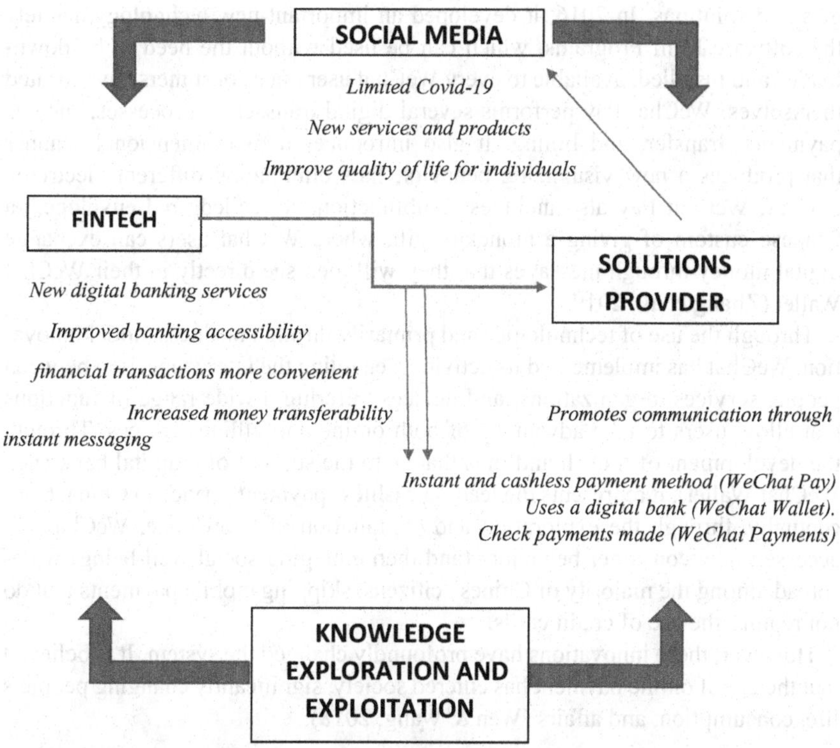

Figure. 3.1 WeChat business model map and value creation

thus improving public health education and communication. Thus, people and public services are digitally connected, facilitating developments in transportation, healthcare, environmental protection, public safety, and other social areas. Specifically, users have been assigned a color based on their health status and travel history using a connected quick response (QR) code, where the red color of the QR code indicates that the person should be quarantined for 14 days, the yellow color indicates the need for a one-week quarantine, and the green color indicates the ability to freely pass through a screening (Marucci, 2020).

In China's daily life, these changes have involved citizens of all ages having to adapt their offline life to their online life. WeChat has emerged as the most used social network, managing to bring about a new consumption behavior for the vast majority of Chinese citizens, skipping mobile payments that do not require the use of credit cards. It is currently the leading instant, cashless payment service in China (Harwit, 2017).

In 2013, WeChat evolved into an integrated medium, rather than just a social network, from a messaging application to a hybrid of application, payment method, and operating system. It is a practical and effective product for combining online and offline communications. WeChat has become a social and economic phenomenon, bringing improvement through innovative technologies and solutions. In 2016, it developed an important new technology, namely the software Mini Programs, which can be used without the need to be downloaded and installed, available to every WeChat user once consumers have located themselves. WeChat Pay performs several digital transaction processes, such as payments, transfer, and billing. It also introduces a two-dimensional scanner that produces a new visualizing behavior, thus eliminating different electronic devices. WeChat Pay also includes a subfunctionality called "red envelope," a Chinese custom of giving a monetary gift, where WeChat users can exchange digital money through messages that they will then see directly in their WeChat Wallet (Zhang et al., 2019).

Through the use of technologies and primarily through business model innovation, WeChat has implemented its activities, enabling the interconnection between people, services, organizations, and devices, offering a wide range of functions that allow users to take advantage of both online and offline services. Through the development of fintech and thus thanks to the support of a digital bank (i.e., WeChat Wallet), it represents the leading cashless payment service in China. Conceptually, through the exploration and exploitation of knowledge, WeChat has accessed new consumer behaviors (and then emerging social well-being) widespread among the majority of Chinese citizens, skipping mobile payments that do not require the use of credit cards.

However, these innovations have profoundly changed the system. It is believed that the era of online payment has entered society, significantly changing people's life, consumption, and affairs (Wen & Wang, 2018).

Concluding remarks: how fintech innovation improves social well-being

Following the various limitations of Covid-19, all traditional cash transactions have evolved into electronic payments in order to limit contagion and money handling. In this vein, fintech encouraged access to digital services, impacting the daily life of Chinese cities, changing not only the *modus operandi*, but also individuals' lives (Del Giudice et al., 2019). In these countries, fintech benefits from several positive stimuli, including the absence of infrastructure, high smartphone penetration, and the approach of governments that see the fintech sector as a tool to foster financial inclusion.

Covid-19 has accelerated digital transformation, revolutionizing the fintech sector through innovative solutions and ecosystems of players capable of guaranteeing value by taking measures to meet new user consumption habits, which are set to consolidate even post-pandemic (Gai et al., 2018).

During the Covid-19 pandemic, Asia showed great potential in technology, providing essential tools to contain the health crisis and reboot the economy. The technology revolution helped immensely in stemming the contagion through the use of the QR-code-based WeChat app, which allows for quick identification of individuals by ranking everyone's contagion risk. Notably, WeChat payment changed the way of life in the Chinese city and facilitated the growth in the use of financial technologies and mobile apps, even during the months of blockade, ensuring that the pandemic was managed more efficiently and, most importantly, quickly (He & Tian, 2018).

WeChat breaks the definition of a social network that only serves users for communication and social interaction, becoming a holistic digital social solution platform that provides an instant, cashless payment method (WeChat Pay) and digital banking account (WeChat Wallet). Its functions and goals far exceed those of other social networks, positively impacting the development of the company's digital structure (Plantin & de Seta, 2019).

The success of WeChat Pay demonstrates how social payments in a digital environment can solve the shortcomings of the business model and reduce the educational barriers that limit the use of financial services.

To this aim, the chapter shows how digital transformation links knowledge exploration and exploitation with business model innovation. Specifically, it highlights how this revolution appears to depend on both macro factors, such as a knowledge-intensive ecosystem that supports technological and digital development, and micro factors, such as the organizational and financial resources that support the exploration and exploitation of knowledge by firms pushing digitization (Fenwick et al., 2020; Scuotto et al., 2019). The best strategy for innovation turns out to be the combination of knowledge exploration and exploitation, so that organizations can improve the dominant technology through the exploitation of prior knowledge and then access new technologies (Gonzalez, 2019). By endorsing a fintech perspective, we show how the business transformation of this social media substantially impacts digital payments affected by innovations and technologies.

Blockchain is a digital ledger in which entries are grouped into concatenated blocks in chronological order that can be distributed publicly or privately to all users, allowing data to be managed and updated without the need for a central controlling entity. The first case is decentralized, and the second distributed (Di Pierro, 2017). Prospectively, WeChat would be considered a tool of big data analytics promising a new age of digital enlightenment that is designed to allow for efficient data mining and information from consumer behaviors.

In this vein, the adaption of the blockchain digital ledger helps WeChat to defend and guard customer data, ensuring protection, reliability, transparency, and integrity, which are guaranteed by the use of encryption (Puschmann, 2017).

Given the concern of consumers towards the use of their personal information, WeChat has always been committed to online privacy and transparency to users. Through WeChat's unique feature design and robust data protection system, privacy and security have been improved, eliminating the risk of data misappropriation (Wang & Gu, 2016). Mombeuil and Uhde (2021) show how perceived privacy and security positively influence the intention to use social media as WeChat Pay among users for monetization services. Through the endorsement of cybersecurity policies, WeChat sustains marketing strategies to target and attack neighboring social markets. WeChat has also achieved TRUSTe certification to provide a high level of user privacy and security protection to safeguard information.

Finally, the chapter demonstrates how the increasing use of digital technology has reshaped the global market, especially for financial services, showing how fintech constitutes a new branch of holistic business model that challenges traditional firms' competitiveness and profoundly alters how resource allocation processes are defined.

It also shows how the financial services fintech offers with WeChat capture both product and process innovations, spreading digital innovation and showing the real impact of technology in the social and business context.

This chapter shows the effects of digital transformation in the Asian context during a specific period, that is, when the pandemic took over. For future research, it would be interesting to understand how the fintech system will evolve when the pandemic ends. At a firm's level, it would also be interesting to perform a comparative analysis of the Asian context with other realities to grasp the main differences from alternative case studies and best practices. This consideration confirms that the main limitation of this study is that it is based on a conceptual single case study (Gustafsson, 2017).

Covid-19 indeed highlighted the ability of people and companies to resist and respond to change. Will the future fintech innovation challenges lead society to an increasingly digital social well-being? This will be the grand question for the near future.

References

Abdelkafi, N., Makhotin, S., & Posselt, T. (2013). Business model innovations for electric mobility: What can be learned from existing business model patterns? *International Journal of Innovation Management, 17*(1), 1–41.

Abdillah, L. A. (2020). *FinTech e-commerce payment application user experience analysis during COVID-19 pandemic*. arXiv preprint arXiv:2012.07750. https://journal.unnes.ac.id/nju/index.php/sji/article/view/26056

Al-Dmour, H. H., Asfour, F., Al-Dmour, R., & Al-Dmour, A. (2020). The effect of marketing knowledge management on bank performance through fintech innovations: A survey study of Jordanian commercial banks. *Interdisciplinary Journal of Information, Knowledge, and Management, 15*, 203–225.

Bashir, M., & Verma, R. (2017). Why business model innovation is the new competitive advantage. *IUP Journal of Business Strategy, 14*(1), 7.

Benner, M. J., & Tushman, M. (2002). Process management and technological innovation: A longitudinal study of the photography and paint industries Michael Tushman. *Administrative Science Quarterly, 47*(4), 676–706.

Berg, G., Guadamillas, M., Natarajan, H., & Sarkar, A. (2020). *Fintech in Europe and Central Asia*. https://openknowledge.worldbank.org/handle/10986/33591

Bhutta, Z. A., Basnyat, B., Saha, S., & Laxminarayan, R. (2020). *Covid-19 risks and response in South Asia*. https://www.bmj.com/content/368/bmj.m1190

Brix, J. (2019). *Innovation capacity building: An approach to maintaining balance between exploration and exploitation in organizational learning*. The Learning Organization.

Caputo, F., & Walletzký, L. (2017). Investigating the users' approach to ICT platforms in the city management. *Systems, 5*(1), 1–15.

Carayannis, E. G., & Campbell, D. (2009). Mode 3 and "quadruple helix": Toward a 21st century fractal innovation ecosystem. *International Journal of Technology Management, 46*(3–4), 201–234.

Chesbrough, H. (2010). Business model innovation: Opportunities and barriers. *Long Range Planning, 43*(2), 354–363.

Claessens, S., Frost, J., Turner, G., & Zhu, F. (2018). *I mercati del credito fintech nel mondo: Dimensioni, determinanti e questioni relative alle politiche.* https://www.bis.org/publ/qtrpdf/r_qt1809e_it.htm

Daqar, M. A., Constantinovits, M., Arqawi, S., & Daragmeh, A. (2021). The role of Fintech in predicting the spread of COVID-19. *Banks and Bank Systems, 16*(1), 1.

Davidson, S., De Filippi, P., & Potts, J. (2016). *Economics of blockchain.* SSRN 2744751. https://papers.ssrn.com/sol3/papers.cfm?abstract_id=2744751

De Clercq, D., Thongpapanl, N., & Dimov, D. (2013). Shedding new light on the relationship between contextual ambidexterity and firm performance: An investigation of internal contingencies. *Technovation, 33*(4–5), 119–132.

De Guzman, R., & Malik, M. (2020). Dual challenge of cancer and COVID-19: Impact on health care and socioeconomic systems in Asia Pacific. *JCO Global Oncology, 6*, 906–912.

Del Giudice, M., Carayannis, E. G., & Maggioni, V. (2017). Global knowledge intensive enterprises and international technology transfer: Emerging perspectives from a quadruple helix environment. *The Journal of Technology Transfer, 42*(2), 229–235.

Del Giudice, M., & Della Peruta, M. R. (2016). The impact of IT-based knowledge management systems on internal venturing and innovation: A structural equation modeling approach to corporate performance. *Journal of Knowledge Management, 20.*

Del Giudice, M., Garcia-Perez, A., Scuotto, V., & Orlando, B. (2019). Are social enterprises technological innovative? A quantitative analysis on social entrepreneurs in emerging countries. *Technological Forecasting and Social Change, 148*, 119704.

Del Giudice, M., Scuotto, V., Papa, A., Tarba, S., Bresciani, S., & Warkentin, M. (2020). A self-tuning model for smart manufacturing SMEs: Effects on digital innovation. *Journal of Product Innovation Management, 38.*

Dermine. (2016). *"Digital banking and market disruption: A sense of déjà vu?", Banque de France, financial stability review*. Dermine.

Di Pierro, M. (2017). What is the blockchain? *Computing in Science & Engineering, 19*(5), 92–95.

Eriksson, P. E. (2017). Procurement strategies for enhancing exploration and exploitation in construction projects. *Journal of Financial Management of Property and Construction, 22.*

Ernst and Young. (2017). *EY FinTech Adoption Index 2017: The rapid emergence of FinTech.* Ernst and Young.

Evans, S., Vladimirova, D., Holgado, M., Van Fossen, K., Yang, M., Silva, E. A., & Barlow, C. Y. (2017). Business model innovation for sustainability: Towards a unified perspective for creation of sustainable business models. *Business Strategy and the Environment, 26*(5), 597–608.

Fenwick, M., Van Uytsel, S., & Ying, B. (2020). Regulating FinTech in Asia: An introduction. In *Regulating FinTech in Asia* (pp. 1–10). Springer.

Fernandez-Vazquez, S., Rosillo, R., De La Fuente, D., & Priore, P. (2019). Blockchain in FinTech: A mapping study. *Sustainability, 11*(22), 6366.

Ferreira, J., Mueller, J., & Papa, A. (2018). Strategic knowledge management: Theory, practice and future challenges. *Journal of Knowledge Management, 24.*

Gai, K., Qiu, M., & Sun, X. (2018). A survey on FinTech. *Journal of Network and Computer Applications, 103*, 262–273.

Ganzaroli, A., Noni, I., Orsi, L., & Belussi, F. (2016). The combined effect of technological relatedness and knowledge utilization on explorative and exploitative invention performance post-M & A. *European Journal of Innovation Management, 19*(2), 167–188.

Gomber, P., Koch, J. A., & Siering, M. (2017). Digital finance and FinTech: Current research and future research directions. *Journal of Business Economics, 87*(5), 537–580.

Gonzalez, R. V. D. (2019). Knowledge exploration and exploitation in team context. *Total Quality Management & Business Excellence, 30*(15–16), 1654–1674.

Gonzalez, R. V. D., & de Melo, T. M. (2018). The effects of organization context on knowledge exploration and exploitation. *Journal of Business Research, 90*, 215–225.

Grigoriou, K., & Rothaermel,F. T. (2017). Organizing for knowledge generation: Internal knowledge networks and the contingent effect of external knowledge sourcing. *Strategic Management Journal, 38*(2), 395–414.

Gupta, A., Smith, K., & Shalley, C. (2006). The interplay between exploration and exploitation. *Academy of Management Journal, 49*(4), 693–706.

Gustafsson, J. (2017). *Single case studies vs. multiple case studies: A comparative study.* https://www.semanticscholar.org/paper/Single-case-studies-vs.-multiple-case-studies%3A-A-Gustafsson/ae1f06652379a8cd56654096815dae801a59cba3

Hannig, A., & Jansen, S. (2010). *Financial inclusion and financial stability: Current policy issues*. Asian Development Bank.

Harwit, E. (2017). WeChat: Social and political development of China's dominant messaging app. *Chinese Journal of Communication, 10*(3), 312–327.

He, J., & Tian, X. (2018). Finance and corporate innovation: A survey. *Asia-Pacific Journal of Financial Studies, 47*(2), 165–212.

He, Z. L., & Wong, P. K. (2004). Exploration vs. exploitation: An empirical test of the ambidexterity hypothesis. *Organization Science, 15*(4), 481–494.

Health Emergency Dashboard. (2020, December). https://extranet.who.int/publicemergency

Jagtiani, J., & Lemieux, C. (2018). *The roles of alternative data and machine learning in fintech lending: Evidence from the LendingClub consumer platform.* Federal Reserve Bank of Philadelphia, Working Papers.

Kanniah, K. D., Zaman, N. A. F. K., Kaskaoutis, D. G., & Latif, M. T. (2020). COVID-19's impact on the atmospheric environment in the Southeast Asia region. *Science of the Total Environment, 736*, 139658.

Kenney, M., & Zysman, J. (2016). The rise of the platform economy. *Issues in Science and Technology, 32*(3), 61–69.

Kenney, M., & Zysman, J. (2020). COVID-19 and the increasing centrality and power of platforms in China, the US, and beyond. *Management and Organization Review, 16*(4), 747–752.

Kogut, B., & Zander, U. (1992). Knowledge of the firm, combinative capabilities and replication of technology. *Organization Science, 3*(3), 383–397.

Lee, I., & Shin, Y. J. (2018). Fintech: Ecosystem, business models, investment decisions, and challenges. *Business Horizons, 61*(1), 35–46.

Lee, S. U., Park, G., & Kang, J. (2018). The double-edged effects of the corporate venture capital unit's structural autonomy on corporate investors' explorative and exploitative innovation. *Journal of Business Research, 88*, 141–149.

Lim, W. S., Liang, C. K., Assantachai, P., Auyeung, T. W., Kang, L., Lee, W. J., . . . Arai, H. (2020). COVID-19 and older people in Asia: Asian working group for sarcopenia calls to action. *Geriatrics & Gerontology International, 20*(6), 547–558.

Lu, L. (2018). Decoding alipay: Mobile payments, a cashless society and regulatory challenges. *Butterworths Journal of International Banking and Financial Law*, 40–43.

Lu, Y., & Zhang, L. (2020). Social media WeChat infers the development trend of COVID-19. *Journal of Infection, 81*(1), e82–e83.

Mader, P. (2018). Contesting financial inclusion. *Development and Change, 49*(2), 461–483.

Marucci, M. (2020). *Tecnologie digitali e controllo sociale ai tempi del Covid-19*. Menabò di Etica ed Economia.

Massa, L., Tucci, C. L., & Afuah A. (2017). A critical assessment of business model research. *Academy of Management Annals, 11*(1), 73–104.

Mombeuil, C., & Uhde, H. (2021). Relative convenience, relative advantage, perceived security, perceived privacy, and continuous use intention of China's WeChat Pay: A mixed-method two-phase design study. *Journal of Retailing and Consumer Services, 59*, 102384.

Ozili, P. K. (2020). *Financial inclusion and Fintech during COVID-19 crisis: Policy solutions*. SSRN 3585662. https://www.researchgate.net/publication/340934186_Financial_Inclusion_and_Fintech_during_COVID-19_Crisis_Policy_Solutions

Papa, A., Chierici, R., Ballestra, L. V., Meissner, D., & Orhan, M. A. (2020). Harvesting reflective knowledge exchange for inbound open innovation in complex collaborative networks: An empirical verification in Europe. *Journal of Knowledge Management, 25*.

Plantin, J. C., & de Seta, G. (2019). WeChat as infrastructure: The techno-nationalist shaping of Chinese digital platforms. *Chinese Journal of Communication, 12*(3), 257–273.

Puschmann, T. (2017). Fintech. *Business & Information Systems Engineering, 59*(1), 69–76.

Rachinger, M., Rauter, R., Müller, C., Vorraber, W., & Schirgi, E. (2019). Digitalization and its influence on business model innovation. *Journal of Manufacturing Technology Management, 25*.

Rossi, M., Festa, G., Papa, A., Kolte, A., & Piccolo, R. (2020). Knowledge management behaviors in venture capital crossroads: A comparison between IVC and CVC ambidexterity. *Journal of Knowledge Management, 24*.

Santoro, G., Bresciani, S., & Papa, A. (2020). Collaborative modes with cultural and creative industries and innovation performance: The moderating role of heterogeneous sources of knowledge and absorptive capacity. *Technovation, 92*, 102040.

Schena, C., Tanda, A., Arlotta, C., & Potenza, G. (2018). *Lo sviluppo del FinTech: Opportunità e rischi per l'industria finanziaria nell'era digitale*. https://www.researchgate.net/publication/323965904_Lo_sviluppo_del_FinTech_Opportunita_e_rischi_per_l%27industria_finanziaria_nell%27era_digitale

Scuotto, V., Arrigo, E., Candelo, E., & Nicotra, M. (2019). Ambidextrous innovation orientation effected by the digital transformation. *Business Process Management Journal*. https://doi.org/10.1108/bpmj-03-2019-0135

Scuotto, V., Garcia-Perez, A., Nespoli, C., & Petruzzelli, A. M. (2020). A repositioning organizational knowledge dynamics by functional upgrading and downgrading strategy in global value chain. *Journal of International Management, 26*(4), 100795.

Scuotto, V., Santoro, G., Bresciani, S., & Del Giudice, M. (2017). Shifting intra-and inter-organizational innovation processes towards digital business: An empirical analysis of SMEs. *Creativity and Innovation Management, 26*(3), 247–255.

Sorescu, A. (2017). Data-driven business model innovation. *Journal of Product Innovation Management, 34*(5), 691–696.

Soto-Acosta, P., Del Giudice, M., & Scuotto, V. (2018). Emerging issues on business innovation ecosystems: The role of information and communication technologies (ICTs)

for knowledge management (KM) and innovation within and among enterprises. *Baltic Journal of Management*. https://www.emerald.com/insight/content/doi/10.1108/BJM-07-2018-398/full/pdf

Spieth, P., & Schneider, S. (2016). Business model innovativeness: Designing a formative measure for business model innovation. *Journal of Business Economics*, *86*(6), 671–696.

Vafea, M. T., Atalla, E., Georgakas, J., Shehadeh, F., Mylona, E. K., Kalligeros, M., & Mylonakis, E. (2020). Emerging technologies for use in the study, diagnosis, and treatment of patients with COVID-19. *Cellular and Molecular Bioengineering*, *13*(4), 249–257.

Van Bavel, J. J., Baicker, K., Boggio, P. S., Capraro, V., Cichocka, A., Cikara, M., Crockett, M. J., Crum, A. J., Douglas, K. M., Druckman, J. N. et al. (2020). Using social and behavioural science to support COVID-19 pandemic response. *Nature Human Behaviour*, 1–12.

Wang, X., & Gu, B. (2016). The communication design of WeChat: Ideological as well as technical aspects of social media. *Communication Design Quarterly Review*, *4*(1), 23–35.

Wen, H., & Wang, C. (2018). *Tencent in-depth research*. TF Securities.

WHO. (2020). *Report of the WHO-China joint mission on coronavirus disease 2019 (COVID-19)*. World Health Organization.

Wieland, H., Hartmann, N. N., & Vargo, S. L. (2017). Business models as service strategy. *Journal of the Academy of Marketing Science*, *45*(6), 925–943.

Zack, M., McKeen, J., & Singh, S. (2009). Knowledge management and organizational performance: An exploratory survey. *Journal of Knowledge Management*, *13*(6), 392–409.

Zhang, X., Liu, Y., Tarba, S. Y., & Del Giudice, M. (2020). The micro-foundations of strategic ambidexterity: Chinese cross-border M&As, mid-view thinking and integration management. *International Business Review*, *29*(6), 101710.

4 Is digital money an alternative to conventional money in the Asian emerging economy context of the pandemic?

Rituparna Das, Harish Chandan and Mononita Kundu Das

Introduction

In the emerging economies, COVID-19 has escalated the incidence of poverty because of job loss. The accumulation of disposable cash coupled with the erosion of purchasing power attributed to both less opportunity to spend and a lower return on investments caused by suspended real production. This means (a) on the one hand blue-collar workers and small-scale entrepreneurs are suffering from a crunch in the inflow of money and (b) on the other hand a relatively sizeable number of gold-collar, white-collar and open-collar workers and middle-scale and large-scale entrepreneurs are finding money less and less useful because of the inflated prices of necessities due to the small production permitted by the governments *pari passu* with shrunken interest earnings. From this arises the issue of people's faith in money.

In a globalised economy, money to the general public normally means fiat money backed by the sovereign. The faith of the public in money is largely because of the sovereign charter and the efficacy of the institutional mechanism governing (i) the creation, use and channels of flow of money, (ii) balance between inflation and unemployment in the domestic economy and (iii) exchange rates and balance of payments in the external sector. Though the monetary literature has grown out of the contributions starting from the field of political economy since Plato's time to a host of other disciplines today that include banking, finance and institutional economics, this growth could not save the First World from hyperinflation and the Third World from hunger and famines.

Chaos and catastrophes in the regulated monetary system as witnessed in the USA and East Asia in the last two decades and the hyperinflation of government money in Germany in 1923, Greece in 1944, Hungary in 1946, Zimbabwe in 2008, and so on. These cast suspicion on the success of government money as an asset. This suspicion combined with various restrictions imposed by central banks on select activities like gambling, money laundering, and tax evasion through mandatory KYC (know your customer) or similar norms for banks worldwide gave rise to the search for an alternative to government money. The result of the search is the birth of digital currency.

DOI: 10.4324/9781003224532-4

Digital currency is an internet-based medium of exchange for goods and services. Such transactions occur on the internet instantaneously and allow borderless transfer of ownership. There is no currency conversion from one nation to another. Digital currency can be defined as entries in a database that can be changed only after certain verified transactions. Money in one's bank account represents a verified entry in a database of accounts, balances and transactions. Through gradual evolution of vocabularies, the terms 'digital', 'virtual' and 'crypto' are used as synonyms. The terms 'money', 'currency' and 'cash' are also used synonymously in this context. Digital currency appeared first in the form of Bitcoin in 2008. It has become so popular as a medium of exchange that there are online platforms for shopping using bitcoin.

The fun of cryptocurrency is that it does not need a supplier like a central bank, and there is an upper cap on the supply of a cryptocurrency imposed by technological constraints. As a result, the interest rate increases as demand increases. There are multiple suppliers of private digital money – Bitcoin, Ethereum and XRP are among the most popular. Secondly, the technological character of cryptocurrency is that a unit of cryptocurrency cannot be spent twice; that is, the transaction velocity of cryptocurrency is unity (one) only. Thirdly, inflation of cryptocurrency cannot be controlled by the conventional monetary policy of targeting interest rate or otherwise in absence of a central bank. Though no government has attached any official status to cryptocurrency, Bitcoin futures are traded in leading international exchange houses like the Chicago Mercantile Exchange.

This chapter provides an overview of the nature and use of cryptocurrency and its compatibility with the smooth functioning of the macroeconomic system of some of the Asian emerging economies such as Cambodia and the plausibility of implementing it as a monetary system in lieu of the traditional fiat money system.

Digital currency vis-à-vis conventional money

Conventional money was born as a medium of exchange endorsed by the sovereign, and then evolved into a common measure of value (numeraire) and finally into a store of value (asset). The public acceptance of conventional or fiat money crops up out of guarantee of the sovereign or the monetary authority with precious metals, such as gold, serving as a base. A currency refers to a nation-specific system of money as a medium of exchange for goods and services within a nation. The money is in the form of banknotes and coins. Different nations have different currencies; for example, the currencies of the permanent members of the UN Security Council are USD, CNY, GBP, Euro and RUB. The US dollar is also used as a world currency similar to gold.

Money is part and parcel of our daily life. Its strength lies in being a universally acceptable medium of exchange/payment, measure of value, store of value and so on. The holder of conventional money has the opportunity to buy and sell in the market as an asset or good. The weakness of fiat money, unlike other goods, lies in the fact that the charter of supplying money is vested with a single agent or a few agents permitted by the monetary authority or government. The purchasing power of fiat money is connected to price level and continuously faces the threat of inflation.

The strength of digital money as an asset in the hands of a few lies in its being outside the regulation of any monetary authority. Its weakness lies in its lack of access to the vast untrained and uneducated population of Asia. It offers an opportunity of lucrative lending. It suffers from the threat of hacking.

The monetary authority is backed by the sovereign, which is so far not the case for private money, born out of some computer programmes. Secondly, the intrinsic value of fiat money is less than the denominated value, so the holder is not very concerned about the cost of acquiring private money, but holding digital money calls for enormous initial cost in terms of having computer literacy, access to software platforms and above all huge operating costs in terms of electricity consumption and the consequent social cost of pollution.

Digital currency

This verified entry can be changed only after certain physical or electronic monetary transactions.

Virtual currency or virtual money was defined in 2012 by the European Central Bank as a type of unregulated, digital money, which is issued and usually controlled by its developers, and used and accepted among the members of a specific virtual community (ECB, 2012). A virtual currency is a digital currency. The original digital currency was also based on trusted third-party-based systems, for example DigiCash. These third-party-based digital currency systems were centralised systems, and they had the double-spending problem that prevented the widespread use of digital currency. This type of digital currency needed a central authority to declare the correct state of balances.

The transition from a central authority to a peer-to-peer network made the central authority unnecessary. In a decentralised currency system, if the peers of the network disagree about only one single, minor balance, everything is broken. They need an absolute consensus.

Digital currency terms

Numeraire

A numeraire is the base good, say one ounce of gold, used to price commodities. Between 1944 and 1971, the US dollar was priced in terms of gold. Naturally, all other currencies were then priced as a multiple or fraction of USD. In short, USD acted as the numeraire because it was fixed to 1/35th of one ounce of gold (Goldstein & Pevehouse, 2014). The numeraire plays an important role in maintaining the stability of the price of conventional money, which is absent in the case of existing digital currencies because there is no concept of a single monetary authority; rather, the monetary system here is decentralised in the way that a P2P network of computers governs the system in which one can enter and exit at any time. In short, Bitcoin does not have any intrinsic value and in time its price can crash to nil.

Mining

Mining means keeping the record of transactions in digital currencies. Miners are the agents keeping the records. The miners need rewards. The rewards come from transaction fees and, as such, there are welfare losses to the benefits of the transaction because of this very nature of transactions (Chiu & Koeppl, 2017). Unlike conventional money or fiat money, cryptocurrency does not have an immediate settlement system. There is welfare loss because of that as well.

The blockchain system

The blockchain system is the system of transaction record keeping, and updating and distributing information. The monetary authorities of Singapore, China, Canada and Germany are very positive about launching digital currency based on blockchain.

Cryptocurrency

In 2008, a new digital cash system was developed using a peer-to-peer decentralised network by an unknown person or group who used the pseudonym Satoshi Nakamoto (Nakamoto, 2008). This digital cash system was called Bitcoin, which is one of the many forms of cryptocurrencies. A Bitcoin white paper was published, and Bitcoin was implemented using the first blockchain database. Using a peer-to-peer network, they solved the double-spending problem of digital currency.

A cryptocurrency represents a decentralised, digital cash system with no central authority, which is like a peer-to-peer file sharing network. The word 'crypto' means hidden or secret. Cryptocurrencies are built on cryptography. Both virtual currencies and cryptocurrencies are types of digital currencies, but the converse is not correct. The cryptocurrency represents the entries about tokens in decentralised consensus databases. The consensus-keeping process for cryptocurrencies is secured by strong cryptography. They are not secured by a third party, people or trust, but by mathematics. Examples of cryptocurrency include Bitcoin, Ethereum, Ripple, Litecoin, Monero, Etherium Classic, Dash and Augur. Bitcoin was the first cryptocurrency and had the largest market share until recently.

Distributed ledger technology (DLT)

The term 'distributed' refers to the decentralised nature as opposed to a centralised silo of a database. The term 'ledger' is a traditional connotation for a database of records. The term 'technology' refers to the protocol of working of the database in a decentralised way eliminating the need for a central authority to check against manipulation.

Many organisations maintain their confidential data at different locations, which are connected to a central system. This central system updates each of the subsystems periodically. However, this makes the central database vulnerable to cybercrime and prone to delays, since a central body has to update each distantly located note. The distributed ledger technology (DLT) allows for storage of all information in a secure and accurate manner using cryptography. Once the information is stored, it becomes an immutable database and is governed by the rules of the network. The same can be accessed using 'keys' and cryptographic signatures.

DLT refers to the technological infrastructure and protocols that allow simultaneous access, validation and record updating in an immutable manner across a network spread across multiple entities or locations. To realise digital cash, one needs a payment network with accounts, balances and transactions, but one major problem every payment network has to solve is to prevent so-called double spending: to prevent any entity from spending the same unit of currency twice. Usually, this is done by a central server that keeps a record of the balances.

The DLT was introduced by Bitcoin and is based on an idea of a decentralised network, in contrast to the conventional centralised mechanism. This DLT technology is expected to have a big influence on sectors and entities that have traditionally relied upon a 'trusted third party.' The decentralised nature of a distributed ledger makes it immune to cybercrime, as all the copies stored across the network need to be attacked at the same time for the attack to be successful. In addition, the simultaneous (peer-to-peer) sharing and updating of records make the whole process much faster, more effective, and cheaper.

Cryptocurrency is very secure. For example, the chances of compromising a Bitcoin asset or a Bitcoin account are smaller than an asteroid falling on a house. The bitcoin represents a new currency that is based on a decentralised blockchain-powered design where real-time updates to a single decentralised ledger ensure a tamper-proof medium of exchange. A cryptocurrency like Bitcoin deals with the issue of the separation of money and state.

The traditional asset classes like property, stocks, bonds and fine arts have a physical backing, whereas cryptocurrency digital assets have value only because other people believe it to have value. Investors and traders view cryptocurrency as a profit-making opportunity and, quite possibly, a long-term store of value. A 'bubble' or price inflation can occur based on lack of supply, increased demand or the perception of a future change.

DLT has the potential to change the way governments, institutions and corporations work. DLT is having a big impact on many sectors like finance, music and entertainment, diamond and precious assets, art and supply chains of various commodities. IBM, Microsoft and many start-ups are using blockchain technology. Some of the most popular distributed ledger protocols include Ethereum,

Hyperledger Fabric, R3 Corda and Quorum. DLT can help governments carry out their functions securely and efficiently. Examples include tax collection, issuance of passports, record land registries, licenses and outlay of social security benefits as well as voting procedures.

Blockchain technology

DLT is based on the blockchain technology. DLT forms a chain of blocks. Each block includes information and data that are bundled together and verified. These blocks are then validated and strung onto the chain of transactions and information in previous blocks. These blocks of transactions are permanently recorded in the distributed ledger that is called the blockchain. In a decentralised network, there is no server. So there is need for every single entity of the network to do this job. Every peer in the network needs to have a list with all transactions to check if future transactions are valid or are attempts to double spend.

Biais (2018) lucidly described blockchains. They are decentralised protocols for recording transactions and asset ownership. In contrast with centralised protocols in which one authority is in charge of maintaining a unique common ledger, a blockchain operates within a network, each of whose participants possesses and updates her/his own version of the ledger, which is therefore distributed. The blockchain design was the main innovation underlying the digital currency network Bitcoin. The trustworthiness of the decentralised monetary system arose out of utilising proof of work and timestamps in a decentralised network of nodes as a solution to the double-spending problem. In brief, this new method eliminates the need for a trusted third party to clear transactions between two parties (Huhtinen, 2014). This is the incident of double spending a unit of cryptocurrency, say, bitcoin. Double spending to defraud the cryptocurrency depends on individual incentives to reverse a particular transaction. Suddenly the interest in bitcoin skyrocketed because of erratic fluctuations in its price (Livemint, 2017). The bitcoin standard is even expected to resemble to the gold standard (White, 2018). There is no commodity like gold or any intrinsic value underlying bitcoin. Till very recently, it was not known to monetary authorities or government and hence on principle its value may be zero, but a bitcoin appears to derive its value from the number of the people who accept it as a means of payment and store of value, that is, the size of acceptance of the alternative monetary system. The value of bitcoin soared up to $21,000 in December 2017. Bitcoin is used for transacting as well hoarding similar to how conventional money is used. The valuation of bitcoin is explained lucidly by Bloomenthal (2021).

Literature review

This literature review centres on descriptive research in the form of a fact-finding enquiry. The major purpose of such research is to describe the state of affairs as it exists or has been existing. We are using here *ex post facto research*, which is popular for descriptive research studies in social science and business research.

We have no control over the variables, so we shall report only what has happened or what is happening to discover new meaning and to describe what exists and has some impact on the lives of the subjects connected to it across space and time. As usual, we plan to neither identify causes behind the reported phenomena nor make any conclusion.

The literature review here portrays the feasibility of digital money as an operating institution in place of a conventional monetary system in the emerging economies, where lack of literacy in banking, finance and computers is a socio-economic deficiency.

Nitsure (2003) discussed some of the problems of developing countries, which have a low penetration of information and telecommunication technology and face difficulties in realising the advantages of e-banking initiatives. Major concerns such as the 'digital divide' between the rich and poor, the different operational environments for public and private sector banks, problems of security and authentication, management and regulation, and inadequate financing of small and medium-sized enterprises (SMEs) are highlighted.

Böhme (2015) presents Bitcoin's design principles and properties for a non-technical audience; reviews its past, present, and future uses; and points out risks and regulatory issues as the platform interacts with the conventional financial system and the real economy, given that Bitcoin's rules were designed by engineers, with no apparent influence from lawyers or regulators, in a way that each individual bitcoin can readily be traced back through all transactions in which it was used, and thus to the start of its circulation. This work brought to notice the major issues of irreversibility of unintentional transactions and absence of any governance or legal structure underlying the platform.

Chiu and Koeppl (2017) threw light on e-money technologies including Bitcoin, PayPal and M-Pesa, platform-specific digital currencies like Facebook Credits, adoption of digital currencies to facilitate the implementation of a negative interest rate policy and subsidise the provision of digital money to the unbanked in order to phase out paper currency that facilitates undesirable tax evasion and criminal activities, the problem of double spending in which following a transaction, the buyer attempts to convince the entire network to accept an alternative history in which the payment was not conducted; when the attack succeeds, the buyer keeps both the balances and the product while the seller will be left empty-handed. Differences in the working of three payment systems in (i) the conventional frame with physical tokens (cash), (ii) digital tokens with a trusted third party like PayPal and (iii) digital tokens in a decentralised network are diagrammatically explained.

Huhtinen (2014) studied the past development of monetary systems to see how Bitcoin is positioned as the forerunner of a new category. This work also examined bitcoins as an investment instrument by studying price drivers and the degree of predictability of future returns. This work reported that because bitcoin is freely priced by the market without any tangible underlying fundamentals, its valuation process is made extremely challenging and very different compared to other financial instruments. Bitcoin appears risky to the general public because its innovations combine finance, economics and advanced computer science.

Why cryptocurrency is not getting the status of fiat money

Cryptocurrency is not getting public trust because of the following reasons described by Carstens (2018).

1 As discussed in the existing literature, the supply of a cryptocurrency like bitcoin is limited. But there can be several cryptocurrencies. There could be as many cryptocurrencies as there are peer-to-peer networks. A process called forking can give birth to several bitcoins out of a single bitcoin, such as bitcoin diamond and bitcoin gold. Forking needs new programmes. This is how the supply of cryptocurrencies could be unlimited and hence unregulated. A community accepting one cryptocurrency may not accept another cryptocurrency used by another community.
2 Money is an institution. It is a set of rules followed by the collective and has sovereign backing. So far, none of the cryptocurrencies have a sovereign stamp. Even Canada, where the central bank is positive about the future of cryptocurrency, is not looking upon cryptocurrency as an alternative to the Canadian dollar.
3 Historical volatility in the price of bitcoin has made it unreliable as a payment system.
4 Cryptocurrency creates externality. The huge use of electricity for computers is a pressure on the environment. In the emerging economy of India, where a sizeable portion of the population is out of financial inclusion, such a digital means of payment is not acceptable.
5 Hacking and cyberattacks may destabilise the network and lead to a loss of customers' money.
6 From the conventional literature of money, we know that if money is an asset of someone, side by side it must be the liability of someone else. In the case of cryptocurrency, it is an asset of the customer but a liability for no one. Secondly, all money in circulation is backed by some reserve of foreign exchange or gold. Cryptocurrencies are virtual assets and not backed by any reserve.

The next section represents the regulators' comparative mindsets in the developed economies of Canada, Japan, USA, Singapore, Switzerland, South Korea and UK and the fast-growing emerging economies of China and India.

Cybercrimes against cryptocurrency

There have been a series of cybercrimes on cryptocurrency. Some of them lead to huge losses of the investors and stakeholders and are mentioned as follows.

i Hackers withdrew (stole) $400,000 worth of Stellar Lumen (XLM) coins from wallets hosted by Blackwallet.co without users' permission (Suberg, 2018).

ii CoffeeMiner hacked public Wi-Fi to mine for cryptocurrency. A script was used to perform an autonomous MITM (a man in the middle) attack to inject some malicious JavaScript code into the HTML pages. The attack has been tested in a real-world scenario to turn smartphones and PCs into crypto mining bots. To perform an MITM attack, the ARP (Address Resolution Protocol) spoofing technique is used. The researcher used the dsniff library to perform the ARP spoofing attack. Using another tool named mitmproxy, the traffic going to the host is analysed and JavaScript code is injected. To make the process cleaner, a single line of HTML code is injected; this line calls the miner. The miner being used in the concept is from CoinHive. It's a Monero miner that uses CPU power to calculate hashes with Cryptonight PoW hash algorithm for mining (Verma, 2018).

iii Again on 26 January, Coincheck, a large digital currency exchange in Japan, suspended all deposits in NEM on their exchange. NEM is an Argentinean blockchain platform. NEM Foundation president Lon Wong confirmed that Coincheck was hacked, calling the stolen funds "the biggest theft in the history of the world." The hack resulted in a loss of 523 million NEM coins, worth approximately $534 million (Pollock, 2018).

iv A sudden regulatory ban of lending bitcoin led to huge losses to bitcoin investors. Benebit stole the stakeholders' USD 4 million after suddenly announcing the run (The Coin Bureau, 2018).

v In the month of May, Bitcoin Gold (BTG) hard fork, originating from the Bitcoin (BTC) blockchain, suffered an attack and suffered a loss worth $17.5 million (Osborne, 2018).

Regulated currency

Conventional currency is safeguarded by the monetary policy of the central bank. The banking system creates money through lending. The central bank controls the credit volume using monetary policy rates like repo, reverse repo and bank rate; monetary policy ratios like statutory liquidity ratio and cash reserve ratio; and some activities like open market operations. If the central bank wants to control inflation using monetary policy, it tightens the aforementioned rates or ratios and vice versa. The conventional money is created via lending. The base of lending is bank deposits. These deposits are the embodiment of purchasing power. Apart from being a medium of exchange, store of value and asset, the regulated money plays the role of stable and regulated purchasing power (Clayes et al., 2018). But the wild fluctuations of the price of bitcoin (Rajadhyanksha, 2017) failed in this role as money.

Canada is a developed economy. As much as 98% of the entire population has access to the banking and financial system. The problem of financial exclusion does not exist there. Further, a concern for the Bank of Canada, as it reported, arising from declining values of bank notes is a threat to their core revenue stream – seigniorage, which is a function of the value of bank notes outstanding multiplied by the prevailing interest rate, less costs of production and distribution of notes.

Therefore, the regulator is afraid that the seigniorage would decline as the value of bank notes falls, and seigniorage would be especially affected if higher-denomination notes declined since they generate more revenue than do smaller-value notes. The issue here is that if seigniorage declines significantly, a central bank might need to rely on government funding, and this could ultimately undermine its autonomy. Hence, the Bank of Canada thinks that (i) because of recent technological developments, they could consider providing digital currency to the public through centralised accounts on its books, (ii) on principle there should be provision of reserves, which so far is accessible only to certain financial institutions, not to the general public. In this case, the Bank of Canada believes that the central bank should play the role of a 'narrow bank' providing accounts to the general public and allowing account holders to use the balances in these accounts to make payments over the central bank's ledger, or alternatively, the Bank of Canada can issue a digital currency in a decentralised manner, similar to how physical cash is distributed. Thus, the Canadian regulator is very positive on digital currency.

Japan has 50% volume of daily trading of bitcoins, whereas in the USA it is 26%. Regulators in both countries are aware of increasing trading volume and public participation in digital currency but have not yet taken any step to legalise it. The UK is very protective of its own currency sterling against cryptocurrency. Switzerland legalised cryptocurrency and is very positive in allowing new initial coin offering (ICO) ventures. Singapore and South Korea also allow digital currency, subject to registration with their financial market authorities. India and China would like to ban it. The European Union suspects that digital currency is used in illegal activities like money laundering.

Discussion

Since there could be several peer-to-peer networks, each of which can give birth to new digital currencies and out of a digital currency further new ones can be created through forking, it seems that the digital money supply can increase at any time in an unpredictable manner and can shrink following hacking and theft. A digital monetary system, if not centrally controlled, will lead to random fluctuations in price level. Essentially, digital money is private money that defies the government's monopoly on fiat money. As per the famous quantity theory of velocity that assumes that the velocity of money is constant, output growth depends on exogenous factors and money supply directly influences inflation. Villevarde and Sanches (2018) rightly observed that if inflation happens with private money, not only will the value of private money diminish, but also no private money producer can deliver an optimum quantity of money. If centrally controlled and only one entrepreneur is allowed to produce digital currency, there can be price stability because of the cap on production. However, the quantity of money will depend on available technology only. If both government money and private money exist *pari passu* and the return on holding government money as an asset is very low, private money will attract more buyers of digital currency and threaten the government's endeavours towards efficient allocation. So the government must drive out private money. Qian (2017), however, argues next that digital money can coexist with government money.

Digital currency is categorised as M0, a measure of money supply in a central bank. It is the liability of the currency-issuing bank or the issuing bank. It is not on the balance sheet of the bank providing the account, that is, the account bank. Qian (2017) proposed incorporating digital currency wallet attributes into the existing commercial bank account system so that electronic currency and digital currency are managed under the same account in order to offset the shock to the current banking system imposed by an independent digital currency system and to protect the investment made by commercial banks on infrastructure. Digital currency here needs to be managed in compliance with the standards on wallet design specified by the central bank. It is suggested that digital currency wallet ID fields could be added to the bank account to enable the account-based and non-account-based models to co-exist and operate at different layers. The aforementioned wallets could be useful in controlling the siphoning off of government money in the emerging economies like India (The Indian Express, 2017) meant for expenditure on welfare-enhancing projects, where the wallets of the beneficiaries could be filled up with digital currency in lieu of hard cash.

The determination of the volume of three concepts are referred to in Figure 4.1 – liquidity preference (Panel 1), loanable fund market (Panel 2) and liquidity trap (Panel 3). The concept of liquidity preference is that the supply of money is an exogenous variable determined by the central bank of the country. The concept of loanable fund is that the supply of the fund by the savers is a positive function of interest rate, but aggregate savings is a function of national income which is again a positive function of supply of money, qualitatively the same exogenous variable mentioned in the concept of liquidity preference. The situation in which it is no longer possible to reduce the interest rate for pushing up real investments is called liquidity trap. Here, the liquidity preference of the public is the downside of inelastic interest, that is, despite increasing the exogenous money supply the central bank cannot help any rise in investment. The concept when applied to a crypto fund means that savers will choose the cryptocurrency market as an avenue of parking their savings in lieu of the banks

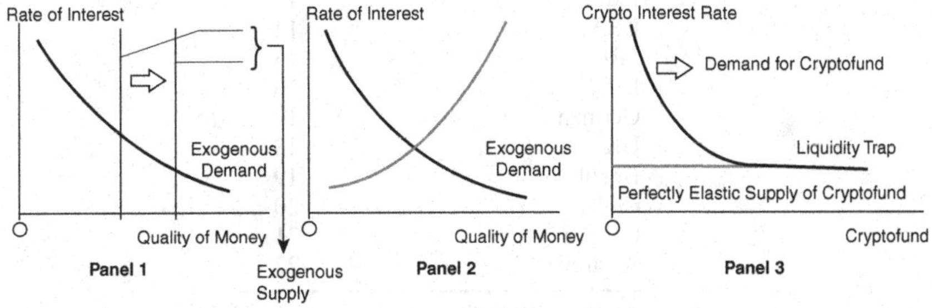

Figure 4.1 Interest rates in fiat money market and crypto fund market

or financial markets. As a result of infinite supply, the crypto rate of interest will fall to a minimum and real investments will plummet to the nadir, pushing the economy into the liquidity trap.

As a result, it is difficult for a central bank to award the status of fiat money to a cryptocurrency.

Except for Canada and Switzerland, until September 2020 hardly any country in the world viewed cryptocurrency positively. In October 2020, Cambodia launched an official cryptocurrency. The year 2018 witnessed a series of attacks on cryptocurrency. The Bank for International Settlement seems to be aware of it (Auer & Claessens, 2018). So there is a need for some global forum or body to regulate cryptocurrency.

Recently, the COVID-19 pandemic caused a formidable swell in the volume of digital transaction in an infrastructure characterised by peer-to-peer transactions and real-time interbank settlements (Dalal, 2020), leading to an eightfold growth over a span of six years, poising India seventh in terms of digital payment use by countries and having the third out of 250 leading fintech companies of the world. The current digital banking and payment artefacts are more developed compared to what was depicted by Nitsure (2003).

Table 4.1 Share of ICT sector in GDP

ICT Sector as % of GDP	*2015*
Country	**Rank**
China	1
Republic of Korea	2
Ireland	3
Malaysia	4
Singapore	5
Philippines	6
Thailand	7
Indonesia	8
Sweden	9
Japan	10
Luxemburg	11
Estonia	12
India	13
USA	14
PRC	15
EU	16
Germany	17
UK	18
Brazil	19
Chile	20
Canada	21
Australia	22

Source: ADB Institute (2019)

Table 4.2 Export of ICT

Export of ICT	*2015*
Continent	**Rank**
Asia and the Pacific	1
Europe	2
Western Hemisphere	3
Middle East and Central Asia	4
Africa	5

According to the database Statista:

- Total transaction value in the digital payments segment is projected to reach US$3,717,507 million in 2021.
- Total transaction value is expected to show an annual growth rate (CAGR 2021–2025) of 10.47%, resulting in a projected total amount of US$5,537,038 million by 2025.
- The market's largest segment is digital commerce with a projected total transaction value of US$2,237,110 million in 2021.
- From a global comparison perspective, it is shown that the highest cumulated transaction value is reached in China (US$2,915,347 million in 2021).

Tables 4.1 and 4.2 describe the growth of the world's ICT (internet, communication and technology) sector, according to figures from the ADB Institute (2019).

One thing is very clear – as more and more people embrace the culture of digital transactions in banking and payments, the quest for higher and higher gains keeps on escalating and drawing attention to the crypto world.

Conway (2021) gives an account of the cryptocurrency exchanges in the world that have any legal reference. Except for the UK, there is no legal framework in the world that allows an entity to disclose investments in cryptocurrencies in the balance sheet or incomes from trading thereof in the income statements, though many companies like MicroStrategy Inc. are investing in bitcoin.

Policy recommendation

The pandemic has made the digital monetary system popular among those very few who can afford access to digital money because of the fear of handling corona-infected cash. Unfortunately, in the Asian emerging economies, a large portion of the population is outside the banking and financial system. They do not own a computer or have literacy in computers, banking and finance. Rent seeking, illegal payments and siphoning away public funds impact their lives.

According to the GSMA Intelligence Report 2015, more than half of the Asian population are not users of mobile internet. According to Pew Research Center 2015, only 22% of the adults in India use the internet (Business Today, 2018).

In this study, the digital divide is wider for those countries with a lower per capita income and a population with a lower level of education. There is also a skewed gender ratio – men have more access to social media than do women.

A digital monetary system can prevent such corruption because a digital currency cannot be spent more than once. So, we recommend that a monetary authority should launch a digital currency in the form of medium of exchange and payments only, without dismantling outright the existing conventional monetary system at the initial stage, not as an asset for trading and investment. In order to prevent the ill effects of this measure in terms of widening the gap between the privileged and underprivileged in terms of access to technologically advanced payment systems, the government and monetary authority should conduct programmes for inculcating the required literacy and training among the people.

Conclusion

This chapter gives an overview of digital currency as a system vis-à-vis the conventional monetary system, the technical details of the digital currency system, the vulnerability of the digital currency system, the attacks on it, the thinking of the monetary authorities of the G-20 countries, bold initiatives taken by a few emerging economies like Cambodia and the plausibility of implementing a digital monetary system in the Asian emerging economies.

The chapter reveals the disastrous macroeconomic consequence of liquidity trap as a result of prospective replacement of a conventional monetary system with a digital currency system, and it sharply distinguishes between the good effects of a digital payment system and the ill effects of digital currency system on public life. The chapter also provides a SWOT-based comparison between a conventional monetary system and a digital currency system.

The authors recommend that digital currency as private money is still not in a position to compete with or substitute for government money in Asian emerging economies. However, if allowed to coexist with government money, digital money can be a solution for corruption and gradually, with increasing literacy and training of people in using digital currency, the departure from a conventional monetary system toward a digital currency system can take place.

References

ADB Institute. (2019). *Central Bank Digital Currency and Fintech in Asia*. https://www.adb.org/publications/central-bank-digital-currency-and-fintech-asia

Auer, R., & Claessens, S. (2018). *Regulating cryptocurrencies: Assessing market reactions*. www.bis.org/publ/qtrpdf/r_qt1809f.htm

Biais, B., Biserie, C., Bouvard, M., & Casamotta, C. (2018). *The blockchain folk theorem*. www.tse-fr.eu/publications/blockchain-folk-theorem

Bloomenthal, A. (2021). *What determines the price of 1 bitcoin*. https://www.investopedia.com/tech/what-determines-value-1-bitcoin/

Böhme, R., Christin, N., Edelman, B., & Moore, T. (2015). Bitcoin: Economics, technology, and governance. *Journal of Economic Perspectives*, *29*, 213–238.

Business Today. (2018). *Only 25% of Indian adults use internet, 80% do not social media: Pew Research Centre*. https://www.businesstoday.in/latest/economy-politics/story/only-25-percent-indian-adults-use-internet-80-percent-dont-use-social-media-pew-research-148537-2018-06-20

Carstens, A. (2018). *Money in the digital age: What role for central banks?* www.bis.org/speeches/sp180206.htm

Chiu, J., & Koeppl, T. (2017). *The economics of crypto currencies, bitcoin and beyond*. www.chapman.edu/research/institutes . . . /economic . . . /koeppel-april2017.pdf

Claeys, G., Demertzis, M., & Efstathiou, K. (2018). *Cryptocurrencies and monetary policy*. www.europarl.europa.eu/cmsdata/150000/BRUEGEL_FINAL%20publication.pdf

The Coin Bureau. (2018). *Benebit – The biggest ICO exit scam in history nets up to $4 million*. www.coinbureau.com/ico/benebit-biggest-ico-exit-scam-history-nets-4-million/

Conway, L. (2021). *Best crypto exchanges*. www.investopedia.com/best-crypto-exchanges-5071855

Dalal, V. (2020). *Where India leads in digital payments, and where it lags?* www.livemint.com/news/india/where-india-leads-in-digital-payments-and-where-it-lags-11603181605154.html

ECB. (2012). *Virtual currency schemes*. https://www.ecb.europa.eu/pub/pdf/other/virtualcurrencyschemes201210en.pdf

Goldstein, J. S., & Pevehouse, J. (2014). *International relations*. Pearson.

GSMA. (2015). *Mobile internet usage challenges in Asia*. www.gsma.com/mobilefordevelopment/wp-content/uploads/2015/07/150709-asia-local-content-final.pdf

Huhtinen, T. (2014). *Bitcoin as a monetary system: Examining attention and attendance*. http://epub.lib.aalto.fi/en/ethesis/pdf/13626/hse_ethesis_13626.pdf

The Indian Express. (2017). *Welfare project in Nandurbar: Crores meant for poor tribals siphoned off*. https://indianexpress.com/article/india/india-news-india/welfare-project-in-nandurbar-crores-meant-for-poor-tribals-siphoned-off-2849578/

Livemint. (2017). *Bitcoins, gold standard, monetary stability*. www.livemint.com/Opinion/YRS1fpxZ3J49T9XwlS5j2K/Bitcoins-gold-standard-monetary-stability.html

Nakamoto, S. (2008). *Bitcoin: A peer-to-peer electronic cash system*. https://bitcoin.org/bitcoin.pdf

Nitsure, R. (2003). E-banking: Challenges and opportunities. *Economic and Political Weekly*, *38*, 5377–5381.

Osborne, C. (2018). *2018's most high-profile cryptocurrency catastrophes and cyberattacks*. www.zdnet.com/article/2018s-most-high-profile-cryptocurrency-catastrophes-ico-failures-and-cyberattacks/

Pollock, D. (2018). *Story of coincheck: How to rebound after the biggest theft in the history of the world*. https://cointelegraph.com/news/story-of-coincheck-how-to-rebound-after-the-biggest-theft-in-the-history-of-the-world

Poushter, J. (2016). *Internet access growing wordwide bu remains higher in advanced economies*. www.pewresearch.org/global/2016/02/22/internet-access-growing-worldwide-but-remains-higher-in-advanced-economies/

Qian, Y. (2017). *Can crypto currency and central bank coexist?* www.coindesk.com/peoples-bank-china-can-cryptocurrency-central-banks-coexist

Rajadhyanksha, N. (2017). *Bitcoins, gold standards, monetary stability*. www.livemint.com/Opinion/YRS1fpxZ3J49T9XwlS5j2K/Bitcoins-gold-standard-monetary-stability.html

Sidon, F. (2020). *How to put bitcoin on your balance sheet*. www.taxtrends.org/2020/10/how-to-put-bitcoin-on-your-balance-sheet.html

Statista. (2021). *Digital payments India*. https://www.statista.com/outlook/dmo/fintech/digital-payments/india

Suberg, W. (2018). *BlackWallet hack: $400K in stellar stolen, hosting provider possibly at fault*. https://cointelegraph.com/news/blackwallet-hack-400k-in-stellar-stolen-hosting-provider-possibly-at-fault

Verma, A. (2018). *How CoffeeMiner attack hacks public wi-fi and uses your pc for mining cryptocurrency*. https://fossbytes.com/coffeeminer-attack-wifi-attack-cryptomining/

Villevarde, J., & Sanches, D. (2018). *On the economics of digital currencies*. www.philadelphiafed.org/-/media/frbp/assets/working-papers/2018/wp18-07.pdf

White, L. (2018). *How a bitcoin system is like and unlike a gold standard*. www.alt-m.org/2018/01/11/how-a-bitcoin-system-is-like-and-unlike-a-gold-standard/

Further Reading

For regulatory and legal provisions relating to virtual or digital currency, we suggest that the reader peruse the 'Regulation of Cryptocurrency around the World' of the Law Library of Congress, Washington, DC, available at its blog: https://blogs.loc.gov/law/2018/07/our-new-reports-on-regulation-of-cryptocurrency-around-the-world/

5 Impact of digital connectivity on ease of doing business

The Asian experience

Subhanil Banerjee and Shilpi Gupta

Introduction

A change in business regime always precedes a change in the mode of production. The Fordist mode of production that introduced the world tothe assembly line mode of production dominated the world for more than seventy years. However, it was augmented by cheaper availability of information at the end of the eighties of the last millennium, following the microelectronic revolution and a deregulatory regime that was paved by the Uruguay Roundand GATT negotiations (Goddard & Gillespie, 2017; Garnham, 1990; Hepworth, 1989). David (1989, 1990) illustrated it as time-space convergence, an electronic revolution that changed both what to know and how we know that (Poster, 1990). Even fifty years ago economists considered technological change as the single most important parameter for growth and labour productivity (Abramovitz, 1986; Kendrick, 1956; Solow, 1957). This sudden emergence of and shift to an informational mode of production succeeded a series of crises that started with the fall of the Bretton-Wood system and Japanese automobile companies' discovery of the US market, whichmarked the end of worldwide industrial hegemony of the USA (United States of America) (Castells, 1992).

Further to this, the worldwide transition from fixed to floating exchange rates and the Organization of Petroleum Exporting Countries' (OPEC) crisis from 1973 to 1980, which released $375 billion petrodollars and threw the West into the cocoon of a recession and stagflation, may be considered as some of those evil necessities. Debt dependence of the Third World went to an all-time high, and depending upon debt instead of equity became a usual trend (McGill, 1984; Corbridge, 1984). On the other side of the Pacific, a war-devastated Japan restructured itself and became the new financial pivot of the world (Vogel, 1985), and the Euro market flourished more than ever before (Pecchioli, 1983; Walter, 1988). All these are further moulded by the weakening of the historically industrialized nations such as the USA and UK (United Kingdom) and the concurrent rise of Japan from Asia, and Germany from Europe, to fill that gap. The role of the Thatcherite and Reaganite administrations towards these transformations deserves special attention. The computerization of commerce and production brought parity in their operation, and that reduced the inventory cost to a great extent through the

DOI: 10.4324/9781003224532-5

'just-in-time inventory system.' The agents of modern production, commerce, and trade, the multinational corporations, showed great flexibility in exploring and operating beyond the existing boundaries of time and space. Their success ushered in the change from state monopolies to globalization (Graham et al., 1988). Finally, the titan of state monopoly, Soviet Russia inclusive of the Soviet bloc, faltered and put the final nail inthe coffin of the static world to embrace dynamism. All these would have been fruitless without the integration of the global financial system, but the aforementioned revolutionary changes in the global telecommunication system facilitated such integration (Einhorn, 1987). The stage was ready for the redefining of the Ricardian comparative advantage (Gillespie & Williams, 1988), and the precondition of such a significant change was to implement the contemporary shift in data regime together with amplified telecommunication capability (Howard, 1988). By this time, the changes of data from analogue to digital made computer service and telecommunication complementary to each other. Innovations in these technologies were recognized as a key feature of the prime period of economic growth in the 1990s, and the economic changes brought by these technologies have received several names over the years, including the new economy and the knowledge economy (Cohen et al., 2000; Pohjola, 2002).

Further, the private players assumed the role of a viral force in global telecommunication. The United Nations (UN) realized the importance of this new viral force and announced the formation of the Integrated Service Digital Network (ISDN) to bring parity among its member nations regarding the technological changes associated with telecommunications. ISDN was facilitated by the US-placed fibre-optic cable network that was spreading quickly around the world, primarily to bring aboutparity and more symmetry tothe global information system (Warf, 1995).

Telephonic communication through fixed lines was a popular form of business and personal communication; however, it was subject to a spatial barrier. It was a useful communication tool that was static in terms of space but dynamic in terms of time (Brewster, 1994). The introduction of mobile phones broke this spatial barrier that turned telephonic or mobile communication dynamic in terms of both time and space. This transformation from landline to mobile is known as the digital divide. The first prototype mobile came into origin long back in 1973, and ten years later, it became available in the market. However, it took another seventeenyears and the commencement of the new millennium to take its current shape, in terms of both accessibility and usefulness (Tan et al., 2012). The conjunction of mobile with broadband in this new millennium turned it into a millennium of mobiles (Regazzi, 2018). The first time the Internet became mobile, in terms of both time and space, so did information as a corollary. It was suggested that broadband speed substitutes for the agglomerative benefits of urban locations and enables firms to carry out operations in rural areas (Mack, 2014).

The coupling of mobile and broadband or the Internet has transformed business, resulting in savings in accounting and opportunity costs in international trade (Meijers, 2014), among others. Lund and Manyika (2016) pointed out that using digital platforms like eBay has led to a reduction of transaction costs by as much as 64% (eBay, 2015). The use of radio frequency identification technology is another innovation that leads to substantial cost savings and reduces the transit cost for Bayerische Motoren Werke GmbHi by 11%–14% (Manyika et al., 2015). According to them, such advances not only elevate the level of competition but also simplify the process of the business itself. The coming together of these elements ushered in a new breed of 'digital' entrepreneurs, who helped generate employment for an ever-expanding population. Ford and Koutsky (2005) used an unrelated regressions framework to estimate the effect of broadband on economic development for Lake County with broadband and other counties in Florida without broadband. They did not address the employment effects but concluded that Lake County had a 100% greater growth in economic activity. Since monetary transactions are a fundamental element of cross-border trade, this is also the area most positively impacted by the twin aspects of digitization discussed earlier. The issues related to monetary exchanges with remote nations before such digitization were challenging to resolve, apart from suffering from the drawback of extended cycle times. The result was rust-related concerns anddelayed profit realization, apart from causing deferred reinvestment of capital for expansion. Digitization, coupled with the convergence of technology, created a disruptive change, making the mobile phone synonymous with the Internet. Thus, the cycle time for business transactions collapsed, and concerns relating to physical distance with the business partner are no longer a vexing issue. With cheaper and more convenient communications, even small organizations feel emboldened to enter the area of international business. Broadband is often recognized as an essential component of regional infrastructure that contributes to the growth and development of regional economies (Mack, 2014). Withthis background, the present chapter-delves into the impact of the digital duo on ease of doing business. A brief prelude might be helpful to understand the necessity of the aforementioned impact. The ease of doing business (EoDB)[1] index has been introduced by the World Bank that provides a ranking based on the level of safety of the countries to start new business ventures. It also reflects the sustainability of already established businesses. The combination of smart phone, high-speed broadband, and innovative pricing policies of the mobile service providers have indeed transformed the one technological invention complementary to the other. Not only that, it relaxed the benefit of this digital duo from the domain of the elites to the reach of the common people and this eventually guided the business from the physical market into the palm of common people. In this era of start-ups and digital marketing, such development will definitely affect the ease of doing business ranking. The time is apt that an effort should be made to quantify such impact. However, before that, it undertakes a detailed literature review to find similar articles that already exist.

Literature review

The literature review section has been divided into three subsections as follows:

The emergence of the Asian economies

The emergence of the Asian economies is not a Cinderella story. Traditionally improved economies such as the USA and UK and countries like France and

Germany still have a stronghold over the global economy. However, the emergence of Asian economies like Japan and China has proven that they are no longer interested to sit as the audience. China and Japan have left the UK behind as far as GDP and trade is considered. Singapore has also shown considerable promise in terms of global competitiveness. In terms of ease of doing business, Singapore, South Korea, and Hong Kong are ahead of their European and American neighbours. Such an upsurge is no doubt a gift of digitalization and positive political will. As global financial capitals, Hong Kong, Singapore, Tokyo, and Beijing are closely following New York and London (Lea, 2019). Rao (2001) and Thomas and Carvalho (2012) have commented that the ability of an individual or a country is directly proportional to digitalization as far as positive economic transformation is concerned. Anuraadha (2014) commented,

> Increase in broadband connectivity is being seen as an integral driver of improved socio-economic performance. Broadband services empower the masses and allow individuals to access new career and educational opportunities, help businesses to reach new markets and improve efficiency and enhance the Government's capacity to deliver critical services like health, banking and commerce to all citizens.
>
> (Anuraadha, 2014)

Chen et al. (2011) mentioned that broadband can be useful for senior citizens in terms of placing orders and getting home delivery. Kabaklarli and Atasoy (2019) saidthat broadband connection positively contributes to economic growth and that countries should channelize resources to provide improved broadband to their people. Schwertner (2017) statedthat digitalization might help business, but it also raises problems associated with the cloud, mobile, social, and big data initiatives with the present level of technology. Giventhis background, improvement of IT can significantly help in adopting the technology concerned more broadly. LaRose et al. (2012) opined that broadband incorporates a sense of self-efficacy, and prior exposure to broadband can lead to better business. Yadav et al. (2020) mentioned that broadband-based e-governance is helping India to increase the ease of doing business. Mbogo (2010) illustrated how e-payments are facilitating small and micro business and, obviously, they will help to improve the ease of doing business. Anderson et al. (2016) mentioned that broadband is capable of introducing change in business practices in rural areas. However, concerning complex applications, rural people are without the necessary know-how to adjust to that change. It implies that if proper training should be delivered, then broadband couldbring a lot of change in innovation and application of business ideas that will eventually improve the ease of doing business ranking. Bartelsman et al. (2019) commented that broadband uses leads to better business and improvement in the EoDB index.

Digitalization and the knowledge-based economy: a new hierarchy

The knowledge-based economy owes its origins to the forces of global deregulation arising out of the post-Fordist production systems, making its presence felt through a series of treaties, coupled with the digital revolution in the ICT space (Warf, 1995). Spearheaded by the easy availability of information at low costs, it expressed itself through the platform of the World Wide Web, also known as the 'Internet.' It spread like wildfire through areas primed for such success –countries like Singapore, Hungary, and the Dominican Republic, to name a few –through rapid growth in telecom infrastructure.

However, Warf (1995) points out that rather than the borderless world visualized by the pioneers of the digital revolution, it created a new hierarchy. The Third Worldended up with the low technology end of the business, whereas the high-tech functions were limited to a few centres such as London, New York, Tokyo, and Singapore. It was suggested by Shideler et al. (2007) that broadband access encourages small and medium business growth, which confirms the adoption of technology. Karakaya and Karakaya (1998) opined that many business entities are using the Internetfor the promotion of their business and eventually that will give them an edge over their competitors, creating an inter-firm hierarchy.

Such cosmetic changes in the world power structure will merely reshape the existing order without overhauling it, as promised by proponents of these new technologies. It is the authors' opinion that such changes will bring forth new and hitherto unforeseen challenges, which will be more challenging to resolve than the existing ones.

A further concern has been expressed by Dunning and Wymbs (2001) that although conventional theory can explain the basic parameters of the impending change, the applications related to e-commerce will operate in an environment that is explainable only by employing the tenets of Internet transports that might be well beyond the capacity of some countries. Needless to say, these countries will suffer, and their gap with the others will widen.

In a study on the effect of digitization on tax revenue in the Caribbean, Bristol (2001) found that, given the existing growth trend of e-commerce on the Caribean Community island, the traditional imports of goods and services will expand. He also expressed concern that the process may lead to the replacement of traditional products with digitized products, and organizations that fail to adapt may cease to survive. Petersen et al. (2002) suggested that firms need to learn improved methods of adopting the Internet to traditional production structure to optimize utility and the process of internationalization. They felt that the failure of firms to internationalize reflected the impact of the Internet on multiple facets of a firm's functioning, and firms which develop an integrated mesh of strategy, structure, technology, human, and financial resources through the use of the Internet are likely to benefit significantly in their efforts at internationalization. Cohill (2002) in a critical note expressed his concern that unless a community marketplace is built and supported by a community network, the entire system of online marketing will collapse. To avoid that, the government needs to make a huge expenditure towards digitalization. Skerratt and Warren (2004) and LaRose et al. (2007) opined that unless the governmenttakes necessary actions, soon there will be a rural-urban hierarchy that will find rural people at the receiver's end.

Gansler et al. (2003) expressedthat broadband can facilitate e-procurement, e-finance, and e-logistics and help the ease of doing business, thus improving the rank. Crandall et al. (2001) mentioned that the indirect effects of broadband, the so-called network externalities or spill-over effect will have the most significant economic impact, but that we will not see these for a while yet as they may take time to disperse through an economy.

Thompson and Garbacz (2007) found that telecommunication services and theirpenetration rates are an important measure of economic institutional freedom, using the Heritage Foundation's Economic Freedom Index (EFI), and the complementarity of both factors improve the productive efficiency of the world as a whole.

Peronard and Just (2011) notedthat broadband might widen the rural-urban difference and that the tech-savvy urban area might have an edge over a technologically backward rural area. This might end up in a hierarchical relation. Forman et al. (2012) used the cost of Internet deployment, local connections to ARPANET, and a proxy of the demand for advance Internet investment outside the county, to identify a positive causal effect of investments in advanced Internet technologies on wages and employment in US counties from 1995 to 2000. Chakravorti et al. (2019) mentioned that e-commerce is changing our purchasing habitsfrom offline to online. Such transformation and quick adoption of this change will improve the ease of doing business ranking. However, to attain this ranking, countries need to concentrate on the balanced growth of the digital platform. Otherwise, places having good digital connectivity will move forward at the cost of places with bad digital connectivity.

Digitalization, factor productivity, and supply chain management: the interlinkage

Madden et al. (2003) focused on the increase in total factor productivity in the telecommunication sector and the factors impacting it. They point out,

> between 1992 and 1994, international telephone circuits increased 64% in China, 69% in Thailand, and 52% in Singapore. Further, outgoing Australia–Asia-Pacific telephone traffic increased from 39.6 million minutes in 1987 to 274.4 million minutes in 1992 (an average increase of 16% p.a.), and Thailand–Asia-Pacific traffic increased from 22.8 to 104.2 million minutes (an average increase of 36% p.a.).
>
> (Madden et al., 2003)

According to them, this growth incapacity and traffic indicates that telecommunications are important to regional business expansion and trade links. Gillett et al. (2004) emphasized creating a broadband environment to promote better business and governance. Wu (2004) said that symmetric information through broadband would eventually help to improve the business and thereby ease of doing business ranking. As per Sife et al. (2010),

> mobile phones contribute to reduce poverty and improve rural livelihoods by expanding and strengthening social networks; increase people's ability to

> deal with emergencies; cut down travel costs; maximize the outcomes of necessary journeys; increase temporal accessibility, and amplify the efficiency of activities. The use of mobile phones also reduces costs of doing business and increases productivity by helping rural traders and farmers to secure better markets and prices; and promptly communicate business-related information.
> (Sife et al., 2010)

Isenberg (2010) emphasized the role of broadband regarding the exceptional jump of Rwanda in ease of doing business ranking. Troulos and Maglaris (2011) emphasized high-speed broadband for better business-led economic growth. Study has also been conducted on the diversity of channels through which ICT can contribute to enhance productivity and promote economic growth (Cardona et al., 2013). Out of the three types of Internet marketing models: the representative model, the online community model, and the virtual business model, the last two models are most relevant for today's business and trade. Cardona and colleagueshave suggested that the online community model provides the customer with real-life experiences without really being a part of real life, often resulting in a 'bandwagon effect.' The virtual business model, on the other hand, literally runs the online business today, Amazon being a prominent example.

Internet usage is likely to lead to an increase in productivity, and Internet-related data analysis may reveal leakages in the supply chain and subsequently address those. It follows that if access and use of the Internet augment productivity, boosting of trade is expected to follow (Bernard et al., 2007), strengthening the supply chain by improving distribution and transport schedules, whichis supported by the findings of Grossman and Helpman (1991).

Dharma et al. (2010) opined that businesses with online communication facilities are subject to perform better than are those without it. Chou et al. (2014) cite USITC reports (2014) stating that Internet-led labour productivity growth has increased the real GDP of the USA by almost 3.5%, although such rise through an increase in total factor productivity (TFP) is hard to capture, as TFP does not take into account IT-led externalities (Chou et al., 2014). Similarly, a recent study on the European Union has found that the use of e-commerce has augmented labour productivity by 17% from 2003 to 2010 (Falk &Hagsten, 2015). Lessons have been learned from studying the role of supply chain management in the evolution of places, such as Hong Kong, from a conventional business model to a digitized one. Pun et al. (2008) studied this phenomenon by collecting views of industry practitioners and determined the key drivers, impediments, and expected gains from digitization for the country as well as the businesses operating there. The authors suggested a collaborative approach for supply chain management in response to the globalization and digitization of business for the enterprises involved. Alrawabdeh et al. (2012) positively correlated ICT and the ease of doing business ranking and highlighted the fact that the Arab world is lagging behind American and European countries regarding ICT. Dobson et al. (2013) emphasized building community-level demand for smooth adoption of digitalization and opined that it wouldeventually improve the ease of doing business ranking. Alderete (2017) emphasized mobile technology in conjunctionwith the Internetfor the betterment of the business environment that will lead to better ease of doing business. Gaur and Padiya (2017) highlighted the efforts of the Indian government towards digitalization that will eventually improve the rank of India in ease of doing business. Nwakanma et al. (2018) have empirically proven that broadband improves the ease of doing business in a country. Banga et al. (2020) have mentioned that introducing digitalization in a low-cost set-up will improve the ease of doing business in agriculture, thus will have a positive impact on the EoDB index.

As the priorexhaustive literature review reveals, only a few papers deal with the issue under consideration. Again, their approach is country-specific and indirect. Giventhis background, we have started our analysis more directly as depicted in the methodology section. However, before that, we provide a theoretical underpinning.

Theoretical underpinning

The ease of doing business ranking is gaining popularity all over the world. It is becoming an index determining the level of domestic investment and foreign investment inflow in a country. To theoretically associate itself with the digital duo of mobile and broadband, the present chapterhas considered tenof its subcomponents individually and illustrated their improvement following the digital duo. Considering starting of business if the process is digitalized, the endeavour will take much less time and hence will have less opportunity cost, and if all remains in soft copy, it will save paper costs and the cost of preserving the documents. If construction permits and registration of property can be applied and approved online, it will result in much less time and costs. If the application and bill payment for electricity connection can be digitized, again it will save much time. Getting an easy hassle-free loan or credit is a pivotal factor in any business, and if the applicant can check their eligibility online and apply for the loan online, that will save themfrom running door to door. If the authenticity of the client can be checked online, then loan approval will also be fast, saving much valuable time for the applicant and the approver. Similarly, if tax filing and payment of tax can be done online, it will save time by avoiding much paperwork and opportunity cost. Trade across borders involves huge paperwork considering documentary compliances (such as certificate of origin, customs clearance etc.); if such compliances can be done through online means, then the ease of doing trade across borders will improve. If contracts can be made online among parties and later disputes if any can be solved through an audiovisual online exchange, that will improve contract enforcement and eventually improve the ease of doing business. The minority investors' rights are protected through transparency in the utilization of corporate assets by the directors for their gains. The Internet acts as a boon in managing the corporate governance norms by transparent disclosures as per the International Financial Reporting Standards (IFRS) rules. Resolving insolvency involves recovery rates that are calculated by creditors through reorganization and liquidation. The lending rates from central banks and external agencies are disclosed to the common person through the Internet, which in turn creates awareness ofthe outcome of resolvency proceedings. The insolvency literacy awareness discourages high-risk loans and warnsthe managers abouttaking faulty financial decisions (World Bank Group, 2013). Considering the aforementioned discussion, the digital duo at least theoretically should have a positive impact on the EoDB index. However, this theoretical proposition needs to be empirically validated.

Methodology

The present econometric analysis considers data of forty-twocountries throughoutAsia on ease of doing business ranking (edb_{it}), per 100 broadband penetration (pcb_{it}), per 100 mobile subscriptions ($pmss_{it}$) and air transport freight (million ton-km, atf_{it}) for the year 2019. The number of countries has been determined based on the simultaneous availability of the aforementioned data. Data on per 100 mobile and broadband subscriptions, as well as air transport freight, has been collected from the World Development Indicator (https://databank.worldbank.org/source/world-development-indicators) interactive database; data on the ease of doing business has been collected from doingbusiness.com. Trans-continental countries like the Russian Federation and Turkey have been kept in the considered countries. Per 100 mobile and broadband subscriptions have been chosen as they depict the level of digitalization. Air transport freight might look like a variable that has been taken to avoid omitted variable bias, but it has serious implications to the regression equation. In a digital world where there are no space or time boundaries, products often travel from one destination to another throughthe air; that has been the sole reason to keep it as an independent variable. There are indeed many variables that deserve to be included in the regression equation, but considering the small sample size, such temptation has been avoided. The analysis intends to estimate one regression equation as specified laterthrough cross-sectional data analysis. If any statistically significant association is there between the dependent and the independent variables as specified, then it might be concluded that 100 broadband subscriptions, per 100 mobile subscriptions, impact the ease of doing business. The robust standard errors have opted irrespective of the homo/heteroskedastic nature of the error terms (Angrist &Pischke, 2009; Imbens &Kolesar, 2016; Banerjee et al., 2020). However, first the multicollinearity has been tested using the vector inflation factor

Data analysis

The regression equation to be estimated is

$$\mathbf{edb_{it} = a + b.\ pcb_{it} + c.\ pmss_{it} + d.\ atf_{it} + u_{it},\ where;\ i = 1, 2, 3 \ldots 42\ and\ t = 2019}$$

In the above equation, ‘a’ is the constant term, b, c, and d are the coefficients of pcb_{it}, $pmss_{it}$, and atf_{it} respectively; u_{it} is the stochastic error term. Considering the

Table 5.1 Econometric test results

Econometric test results		
edb_{it} (Dependent variable)	$lpcb_{it}$, $lpmss_{it}$, atf_{it} (Independent variables)	
Econometric tests	**Results**	
	Stat	Prob
Multicollinearity: Variance inflation factors (vif)	1.62<2	NA

Source: Computed

Table 5.2 Regression results

Regression Results (Dependent Variable edbit)							
List of independent variables	*Coefficient*	*t statistics*	*Probability*	*R2*	*Adjusted R2*	*F statistics (3, 39)*	*Probability*
$pmss_{it}$	−0.28	−1.78	0.082				
pbc_{it}	−2.29	−4.21	0.000	0.4733	0.4317	20.55	0.000
atf_{it}	−0.0006	−0.72	0.477				
Constant	143.21	6.98	0.000				

Source: Computed

cross-sectional structure of the data, the presence of multicollinearity hasbeen tested in Table 5.1.

As illustrated in Table 5.1, there is no multicollinearity.

As depicted in Table 5.2, the coefficients per 100 fixed broadband subscriptions and 100 mobile subscriptions are negative, as is the transport freight (million ton-km); however, only per 100 fixed broadband subscriptions is statistically insignificant. Furthermore, the model as a whole is highly significant, as reflected through the F statistics in Table 5.2. It implies that better digital connectivity might have facilitated business (González & Jouanjean, 2017). As with the increase per 100 fixed broadband connections, the rank in ease of doing business declines, whichis good, as lesser rank (in numerical terms) is better. Nowadays, business through the Internet is a common phenomenon. Apps like Amazon and Flipkart are growing popular day by day, and both are dedicated to online business, whether domestic or international. Existing refund policy in case the customer is unsatisfied has boosted customer confidence to opt for digital markets. Busy schedulesand a fast-paced life has also encouraged customersto consider shopping virtuallyinstead of physically. The bandwagon effect must be considered as well, and there might be a significant level of peer influence on the consumer.

Conclusion

The focus of the present article is on digitalization and its dynamics with business as might be experienced by forty-twocountries of Asia. The cross-sectional analysis that comprised the relevant data on forty-twocountries for 2019 depicts that per 100 broadband penetrations has a negative and statistically significant impact on the ease of doing business ranking. Since the lower the rank the better, it might be concluded that digitalization leads to improvement in ease of doing business.

Further, over time, the enactment of strict refund policies has established consumer faith in digital merchants. Innovative policies like free offers, discounts, and festival bonanzas have attracted consumers from every corner. There is no separate advertising cost as the visual impact of the digital market serves that purpose, unlike the real-life marketplace. We are living in a corporate world, and time is scarce; on the other hand, consumers are better informed than before, so they are prone to compare their products in a quick time. The digital marketplace is complementary to both purposes, and that is propelling digital business like never before. Amidst globalization, consumers are also geared towards internationalization; this explains the dynamism between digitalization and international business as experienced by the selected forty-twocountries of Asia. Similar to the budget line, time itself is another constraint to consumption. In the present era, life has become a deadline, and all those deadlines should be met to remain relevant to society. In this background, people have little luxury to spend time in shops and malls. The footfall of malls is mainly from young people and elites who have the luxury of time. On the other hand, ordinary people who have similar needs in the market are blessed with fixed broadband. A click of a finger on mobile (which might be connected tofixed broadband through Wi-Fi) opens up a virtual marketplace that makes life easy both in terms of time and variety of items placed before us. Repeated amendments ofthe refund policiesfavouring consumers has turned the online market into a reliable source. The popularity is such that nowadays, established businesses of the real world aremaking their virtual presence felt online. Most obviously, such a market is neither geographically restricted nor bound by time, and that stretches the market hour to twenty-fourhours a day.

From the producer side, people do not have to own a shop to sell their productsbut can easily display their itemsonline and sell directly to customers. From the customer's point of view, home delivery is always welcome, and advancement in e-payment has made an online payment to the seller quite easy. There can always be payment on receipt. Digitalization has touched all the shores of the world. An increase in sales following digitalization, consumer satisfaction considering timesavingsand more varied product options, and competition have led to a price decline. This win-win situation for both producer and consumer might be considered the biggest gift of digitalization. Hence, we may conclude that digitalization as discussed in this chapter will surely improve the ease of doing business.

Note

1 The Ease of Doing Business (EoDB) index is a ranking system established by the World Bank Group.

References

Abramovitz, M. (1986). Catching up, forging ahead, and falling behind. *Journal of Economic History, 46*(2), 385–406.

Alderete, M. V. (2017). Mobile broadband: A key enabling technology for entrepreneurship. *Journal of Small Business Management, 55*(2), 254–269.

Alrawabdeh, W., Salloum, A., &Mingers, J. (2012). Key Factors influencing the diffusion of information and communication technology (ICT) in the Arab world: A comparative study. *Europe, 6*, 28.

Anderson, A. R., Wallace, C., & Townsend, L. (2016). Great expectations or small country living? Enabling small rural creative businesses with ICT. *Sociologiaruralis, 56*(3), 450–468.

Angrist, J. D., &Pischke, J. S. (2009). Instrumental variables in action: Sometimes you get what you need. *Mostly Harmless Econometrics: An Empiricist's Companion*, 113–220.

Anuraadha, M. V. (2014). A cram on customer satisfaction on broadband &wireless services. *International Journal of Managerial Studies and Research, 2*(9), 23–31.

Banerjee, S., Sar, A. K., & Pandey, S. (2020). Improved yet unsafe: An aquatic perspective of Indian infant mortality. *Journal of Health Management, 22*(1), 57–66.

Banga, K., Rodriguez, A. R., & te Velde, D. W. (2020). *Digitally enabled economic transformation and poverty reduction.* https://set.odi.org/wp-content/uploads/2020/09/DEET-and-poverty-reduction_final-2.pdf

Bartelsman, E. J., Falk, M., Hagsten, E., & Polder, M. (2019). Productivity, technological innovations and broadband connectivity: Firm-level evidence for ten European countries. *Eurasian Business Review, 9*(1), 25–48.

Bernard, A. B., Jensen, J. B., Redding, S. J., & Schott, P. K. (2007). Firms in international trade. *Journal of Economic Perspectives, 21*(3), 105–130.

Brewster, R. L. (Ed.). (1994). *Data communications and networks 3* (Vol. 3). IET.

Bristol, M. A. (2001). *The impact of electronic commerce on tax revenues in the Caribbean community.* https://caricom.org/documents/9782-e-commerce_tax_revenues_bristol.pdf

Cardona, M., Kretschmer, T., & Strobel, T. (2013). ICT and productivity: Conclusions from the empirical literature. *Information Economics and Policy, 25*(3), 109–125.

Castells, M. (1992). *The informational city: Economic restructuring and urban development* (reprint ed.). https://www.wiley.com/en-us/The+Informational+City%3A+Economic+Restructuring+and+Urban+Development-p-9780631179375

Chakravorti, B., Fillpovic, C., & Chaturvedi, R. S. (2019). Ease of doing digital business 2019. *Which Countries Help Expedite Entry, Growth, and Exit of Technology-Based Businesses*. https://sites.tufts.edu/digitalplanet/files/2020/03/Ease-of-Doing-Digital-Business-2019_2020.pdf

Chen, M. L., Lu, T. E., Chen, K. J., & Liu, C. E. (2011). A TAM-based study on senior citizens digital learning and user behavioral intention toward use of broadband network technology services provided via television. *African Journal of Business Management, 5*(16), 7099–7110.

Chou, Y. C., Chuang, H. H. C., & Shao, B. B. (2014). The impacts of information technology on total factor productivity: A look at externalities and innovations. *International Journal of Production Economics, 158*, 290–299.

Cohen, S. S., Zysman, J., & DeLong, B. J. (2000). *Tools for thought: What is new and important about the economy.* Working Paper No. 138. Berkeley Round Table on International Economics.

Cohill, A. M. (2002). *Why broadband? A community perspective.* www.designnine.com/sites/default/files/resources/whybroadband.pdf

Corbridge, S. (1984). Political geography of contemporary events V: Crisis, what crisis? Monetarism, brandt II and the geopolitics of debt. *Political Geography Quarterly*, *3*(4), 331–345.

Crandall, R. W., & Jackson, C. L. (2001). *The $500 billion opportunity: The potential economic benefit of widespread diffusion of broadband Internet access*. Criterion Economics, LLC.

David, P. A. (1989). *Computer and dynamo: The modern productivity paradox in a not-too distant mirror*. No. 2068-2018-760.https://ideas.repec.org/p/ags/uwarer/268373.html

David, P. A. (1990). The dynamo and the computer: An historical perspective on the modern productivity paradox. *The American Economic Review, 80*(2), 355–361.

Dharma, D., Amelia, B., Powell, A., Joe, K., & Jaewon, C. (2010). *Broadband adoption in low-income communities*. http://eprints.lse.ac.uk/29459/1/Powell_etal_Broadband-adoption-in-low-income-countries_2010.pdf

Dobson, P., Jackson, P., & Gengatharen, D. (2013). Explaining broadband adoption in rural Australia: Modes of reflexivity and the morphogenetic approach. *MIS Quarterly*, *37*(10), 965–991.

Dunning, J. H., & Wymbs, C. (2001). The challenge of electronic markets for international business theory. *International Journal of the Economics of Business*, *8*(2), 273–301.

eBay. (2015). *USsmall business global growth report*. https//www.ebaymainstreet.com/sites/default/files/2015-us-small-biz-global-growth-report_0.pdf

Einhorn, M. A. (1987). Optimality and sustainability: Regulation and intermodal competition in telecommunications. *The RAND Journal of Economics*, *18*(4), 550–563.

Falk, M., & Hagsten, E. (2015). E-commerce trends and impacts across Europe. *International Journal of Production Economics*, *170*, 357–369.

Ford, G. S., & Koutsky, T. M. (2005, November). Broadband and economic development: A municipal case study from Florida. In *Review of Urban & Regional Development Studies: Journal of the Applied Regional Science Conference* (Vol. 17, No. 3, pp. 216–229). Blackwell Publishing Asia.

Forman, C., Goldfarb, A., & Greenstein, S. (2012). The Internet and local wages: A puzzle. *American Economic Review*, *102*(1), 556–575.

Gansler, J., Lucyshyn, W., & Ross, K. (2003). *Digitally integrating the government supply chain: E-procurement, e-finance, and e-logistics*. https://drum.lib.umd.edu/bitstream/handle/1903/7041/Digitally+Integrating+the+Government+Supply+Chain.pdf?sequence=1

Garnham, N. (1990). *Capitalism and communication: Global culture and the economics of information*. Sage.

Gaur, A. D., & Padiya, J. (2017). *International conference on technology and business management* (pp. 77–84). www.researchgate.net/profile/Ashutosh-Gaur/publication/316062485_Ease_of_Doing_Business_in_India_Challenges_Road_Ahead/links/58ee876aaca2724f0a28adab/Ease-of-Doing-Business-in-India-Challenges-Road-Ahead.pdf

Gillespie, A., & Williams, H. (1988). Telecommunications and the reconstruction of regional comparative advantage. *Environment and Planning A*, *20*(10), 1311–1321.

Gillett, S. E., Lehr, W. H., & Osorio, C. (2004). Local government broadband initiatives. *Telecommunications Policy*, *28*(7–8), 537–558.

Goddard, J. B., & Gillespie, A. E. (2017). Advanced telecommunications and regional economic development. In *Managing the city* (pp. 84–109). Routledge.

González, J. L., & Jouanjean, M. A. (2017). *Digital trade: Developing a framework for analysis*. OECD Trade Policy Papers, No. 205, OECD Publishing.www.iccia.com/sites/default/files/library/files/OECD%20Trade%20Policy%20Papers.pdf

Graham, J., Gibsón, K., Horvath, R., & Shakow, D. M. (1988). Restructuring in US manufacturing: The decline of monopoly capitalism. *Annals of the Association of American Geographers*, *78*(3), 473–490.

Grossman, G. M., & Helpman, E. (1991). Trade, knowledge spillovers, and growth. *European Economic Review, 35*(2–3), 517–526.

Hepworth, M. E. (1989). *Geography of the information economy*. St. Martin's Press.

Howard, J. H. (1988). *An overview of the andrew file system* (Vol. 17). Carnegie Mellon University, Information Technology Center. http://ra.adm.cs.cmu.edu/anon/anon/usr0/ftp/itc/CMU-ITC-062.pdf

Imbens, G. W., & Kolesar, M. (2016). Robust standard errors in small samples: Some practical advice. *Review of Economics and Statistics*, *98*(4), 701–712.

Isenberg, D. J. (2010). How to start an entrepreneurial revolution. *Harvard Business Review*, *88*(6), 40–50.

Kabaklarli, E., & Atasoy, B. S. (2019). Broadband infrastructure and economic growth: A panel data approach for selected countries. *DIEM: Dubrovnik International Economic Meeting*, *4*(1), 105–114. Sveučilište u Dubrovniku.

Karakaya, F., & Karakaya, F. (1998). Doing business on the internet. *SAM Advanced Management Journal*, *63*, 10–14.

Kendrick, J. (1956). Productivity trends: Capital and labor. In *Productivity trends: Capital and labor* (pp. 3–23). NBER. www.nber.org/system/files/chapters/c5596/c5596.pdf

LaRose, R., DeMaagd, K., Chew, H. E., Tsai, H. Y. S., Steinfield, C., Wildman, S. S., & Bauer, J. M. (2012). Broadband adoption| measuring sustainable broadband adoption: An innovative approach to understanding broadband adoption and use. *International Journal of Communication*, *6*(25), 2576–2600.

LaRose, R., Gregg, J. L., Strover, S., Straubhaar, J., & Carpenter, S. (2007). Closing the rural broadband gap: Promoting adoption of the Internet in rural America. *Telecommunications Policy*, *31*(6–7), 359–373.

Lea, R. (2019). The UK economy in a global context: An important second tier economy. *Arbuthnot Banking Group*, *8*. www.arbuthnotgroup.com/upload/marketmatter/documents/8_july_2019.pdf

Lund, S., & Manyika, J. (2016). *How digital trade is transforming globalisation*. By International Centre for Trade and Sustainable Development (ICTSD.http://e15initiative.org/wp-content/uploads/2015/09/E15-Digital-Lund-and-Manyika.pdf

Mack, E. A. (2014). Businesses and the need for speed: The impact of broadband speed on business presence. *Telematics and Informatics*, *31*(4), 617–627.

Madden, G., Savage, S. J., & Ng, J. (2003). Asia – Pacific telecommunications liberalisation and productivity performance. *Australian Economic Papers*, *42*(1), 91–102.

Manyika, J., Bughin, J., Lund, S., Nottebohm, O., Poulter, D., Jauch, S., & Ramaswamy, S. (2015). *Global flows in a digital age: How trade, finance, people, and data connect the world economy*. McKinsey Global Institute.

Mbogo, M. (2010). The impact of mobile payments on the success and growth of micro-business: The case of M-Pesa in Kenya. *Journal of Language, Technology & Entrepreneurship in Africa*, *2*(1), 182–203.

McGill, S. (1984). The political economy of third world debt. *Journal of Australian Political Economy*.www.ppesydney.net/content/uploads/2020/04/The-political-economy-of-Third-World-debt-review-article.pdf

Meijers, H. (2014). Does the internet generate economic growth, international trade, or both? *International Economics and Economic Policy, 11*(1), 137–163.

Nwakanma, I. C., Ogbonna, A. C., Asiegbu, B. C., Udunwa, I. A., & Nwokonkwo, O. C. (2018, July 2–4). *Broadband telecommunication deployment: A supply side analysis of penetration drivers in a developing country case*. The Tenth International Conference on Construction in the 21st Century (CITC-10).

Pecchioli, R. M. (1983). *The internationalisation of banking: The policy issues*. Organisation for Economic Co-operation and Development, OECD Publications and Information Center, Sales Agents.

Peronard, J. P., & Just, F. (2011). User motivation for broadband: A rural Danish study. *Telecommunications Policy*, *35*(8), 691–701.

Petersen, B., Welch, L. S., & Liesch, P. W. (2002). The Internet and foreign market expansion by firms. *MIR: Management International Review*, *42*(2), 207–221.

Pohjola, M. (2002). The new economy: Facts, impacts and policies. *Information Economics and Policy*, *14*(2), 133–144.

Poster, M. (1990). *The mode of information: Poststructuralism and social context*. University of Chicago Press.

Pun, K. F., Chin, K. S., & Lau, H. C. (2008). Towards e-business and supply chain operations: An empirical study of Hong Kong's trading industry. *International Journal of Value Chain Management*, *2*(4), 450–467.

Rao, B. (2001). Broadband innovation and the customer experience imperative. *International Journal on Media Management*, *3*(2), 56–65.

Regazzi, J. J. (2018). The shifting sands of the information industry. In *Information retrieval and management: Concepts, methodologies, tools, and applications* (pp. 1–23). IGI Global.

Schwertner, K. (2017). Digital transformation of business. *Trakia Journal of Sciences*, *15*(1), 388–393.

Shideler, D., Badasyan, N., & Taylor, L. (2007). *The economic impact of broadband deployment in Kentucky*. TPRC. https://d1wqtxts1xzle7.cloudfront.net/43192159/Shideler.pdf?1456743535=&response-content-disposition=inline%3B+filename%3DThe_economic_impact_of_broadband_deploym.pdf&Expires=1618697342&Signature=DfvHNtPqW-Cuo09C-M7YBIiIyZi~PFovxdlkEbnQvh5QcnWaI5~5zh5vqxZ29c-gG2RrDZXll6D1kRIEO5MA~-CCJBM-tKRdo1qjqHqSRiFUvyHS-J6qwp-xmmu4j6pFGPnA~NOseCmmISgWLXWiYqiWYHExtweOo6uhDBMqpjcn3~EoRqAdo09r-RvSZNJ3A3Bw8nTSQDEQ23B5OOR9zUaeoO0GkPW4NBTbilzqZKGS3b04-cRyrZf9oet4YkrbUUhcIRYC6z0BDmjhsUArMXxzJuvnCJYslNAe6CnNCGegUzka7bKj8r1H08~pFAkit5hHQ5svfk7cyvguTXh1u8A__&Key-Pair-Id=APKAJLOHF5GGSLRBV4ZA

Sife, A. S., Kiondo, E., & Lyimo-Macha, J. G. (2010). Contribution of mobile phones to rural livelihoods and poverty reduction in Morogoro region, Tanzania. *The Electronic Journal of Information Systems in Developing Countries*, *42*(1), 1–15.

Skerratt, S., & Warren, M. (2004). Broadband in the countryside: The new digital divide. *Farm Management-Institute of Agricultural Management*, *11*, 727–736.

Solow, R. M. (1957). Technical change and the aggregate production function. *The Review of Economics and Statistics*, *39*(3), 312–320.

Tan, G. W. H., Ooi, K. B., Sim, J. J., & Phusavat, K. (2012). Determinants of mobile learning adoption: An empirical analysis. *Journal of Computer Information Systems*, *52*(3), 82–91.

Thomas, C. S., & Carvalho, F. (2012). Reaching the third billion: Arriving at affordable broadband to stimulate economic transformation in emerging markets. *The Global*

Information technology report Journal, 12. https://citeseerx.ist.psu.edu/viewdoc/download?doi=10.1.1.455.2017&rep=rep1&type=pdf

Thompson, H. G., & Garbacz, C. (2007). Mobile, fixed line and Internet service effects on global productive efficiency. *Information Economics and Policy, 19*(2), 189–214.

Troulos, C., & Maglaris, V. (2011). Factors determining municipal broadband strategies across Europe. *Telecommunications Policy, 35*(9–10), 842–856.

Vogel, E. F. (1985). Pax Nipponica. *Foreign Affairs, 64*, 752.

Walter, I. (1988). *Global competition in financial services: Market structure, protection, and trade liberalization.* Ballinger Publishing Company.

Warf, B. (1995). Telecommunications and the changing geographies of knowledge transmission in the late 20th century. *Urban Studies, 32*(2), 361–378.

World Bank Group. (2013). *Crowdfunding's potential for the developing world.* World Bank. https,//www.infodev.org/infodevfiles/wb_crowdfundingreport-v12.pdf

Wu, T. (2004). The broadband debate, a user's guide. *Journal of Telecommunication and High Technology Law, 3*, 69. https://scholarship.law.columbia.edu/cgi/viewcontent.cgi?article=2329&context=faculty_scholarship

Yadav, R. K., Bagga, T., & Johar, S. (2020). E – governance impact on ease of doing business in India. *PalArch's Journal of Archaeology of Egypt/Egyptology, 17*(7), 6188–6203.

6 Application of knowledge management and digitalization in an Islamic view

Ahmad Rafiki

Introduction

Globalization and knowledge advancements pose business challenges. Technological innovation escalates creativities and productivities as well as contributes to the increase of competitiveness, in which many organizations are looking for uniqueness and new opportunities to satisfy customer needs and enhance organizational performance (Akbari & Ghaffari, 2017; Raudeliuniene et al., 2018a; Raudeliuniene & Szarucki, 2019). By adopting knowledge management and digitalization, an organization could manage and anticipate these unpredicted changes.

Numerous studies have been conducted on different dimensions of knowledge management, including knowledge creation, knowledge storage, knowledge sharing, knowledge accessibility, and knowledge application, as well as the application of knowledge management practices to business processes and information technologies (Rechberg & Syed, 2014). Other research on knowledge management focuses on creativity, innovation, and performance (Inkinen, 2016), top management's commitment (Keramati & Azadeh, 2007), the role of foreign domestic investment (FDI) in developing countries (Yıldırım & Arun, 2019), and interactions between human resources, technologies, and techniques (Bhatt, 2001). However, the relationship between knowledge management (KM) and Islamic principles or teaching is not explored by researchers. In fact, Islamic teaching emphasizes the importance of seeking knowledge from birth until death.

Moreover, Islam sees digitalization as part of the process of efficiently delivering messages, news, or any data which is important to be accessed by many people. When any element or process (in this case relating to a kind of technology) gives more benefit to many people (referred to as *mashlahah*), it should be encouraged in Islam. This could help the process of *mu'amalah*[1] that enhances the exchanges, transactions, or interactions of information to achieve a better life. Islam does not prohibit or discourage any advancement in science and technology, particularly when those are aligned with the *maqasid sharia*.[2]

Muslims are encouraged to explore the sciences that have been explained in the Al-Qur'an. All predictions, assumptions, clues, and signs have been highlighted in the Al-Qur'an and are available for Muslims to search for and study. Islam's

DOI: 10.4324/9781003224532-6

high civilization has made 'ilm (knowledge) a priority in life, where it can guide human beings in following the right path as well as bring happiness in the world and the hereafter. Allah Subhana Wa Ta'ala (SWT) will see the efforts and initiatives of every Muslim in pursuing 'ilm and always give easiness to it because these actions are considered *fisabililah* (in the way of God – Allah SWT; in the cause of Allah SWT; for the sake of Allah SWT).

Moreover, Imam Syafi'i[3] said that if a Muslim wants to achieve a victory in this world and the hereafter, it must be with knowledge. This could emphasize that prosperity can only be obtained by having knowledge. The verse in the Al-Qur'an states that a person with knowledge and without knowledge couldn't be the same. As stated in verse al-Mujâdilah 58:11, Allah SWT will raise the amount of people who believe and are knowledgeable in various degrees. In certain cases, even when Muslims are facing a war, the Prophet Muhammad (PBUH) suggested not to ignore pursuing knowledge or conducting any studies. This means that pursuing knowledge is more important than being involved in a war. Technology also receives high attention in the holy book of the Koran. In fact, around 750 verses of the Qur'an discuss nature and its phenomena, which include technology and science matters. Thus, Muslims must be able to adopt technology and science to bring prosperity, security, and comfort to all human beings. This chapter adopts a content descriptive analysis which elaborates on and discusses knowledge management and digitalization in Islam, as well as the issues that arise.

Literature review

Knowledge management and Islam

Knowledge management has been adopted by various organizations across industries and countries. However, the implementation of KM may differ depending on the operational adaptability in those organizations. A successful implementation of KM relies on the coordination and integration among the units or departments in an organization. Meanwhile, Kamara et al. (2002, p. 205) defined KM as a "developing body of methods, tools, techniques and values through which organizations can acquire, develop, measure, distribute and provide a return on their intellectual assets". Halkias et al. (2013) added that KM is a complex, multifaceted, and multidimensional system that may be best understood through example.

Knowledge management confirms the close relationship between the topics investigated, in particular the impact of innovation in knowledge management processes and the effects on business models (Gil-Gomez et al., 2020; Hock-Doepgen et al., 2020; Del Giudice et al., 2019a, 2019b; Gupta & Bose, 2019; Huesig & Endres, 2019; Kamble et al., 2020; Raut et al., 2019; Santoro et al., 2019; Lokshina & Lanting, 2019; Scuotto et al., 2019 Bogers et al., 2018; Nielsen, 2018; Bresciani et al., 2018; Lin et al., 2018; Pappas et al., 2018; Carayannis et al., 2017; Seele, 2017; Xia et al., 2017; Del Giudice & Della Peruta, 2016; Parmentier & Mangematin, 2014).

As depicted in Figure 6.1, the three components of knowledge of management – people, technology, and process – are interrelated. Knowledge cannot be processed without people who will act to adjust or manage the dissemination of knowledge, while technology will be used to ease the process and make it effective and efficient.

Islam has another reason for using knowledge, which is to please (*ridha*) Allah (Almighty God). Whatever the practices and processes, all must be done for seeking Allah's blessing. This is a unique point of Islamic teachings.

In the Islamic perspective, education encompasses the three concepts of knowledge, maturity, and good manners (Halstead, 2004), while knowledge is a source of excellence and achievement. The pursuit of knowledge in Islam is a religious core duty. One Hadith reminds believers, "seeking knowledge is obligatory for every Muslim man and woman".[4] The Al-Qur'an is full of exhortations to pursue knowledge (Al-Qur'an. Taha 20:114). It proclaims the superiority in God's eyes of those who have knowledge (Al-Qur'an. Al-mujadalah 58:11; Az-zumar 39:9), but also emphasizes wisdom and guidance rather than the blind acceptance of

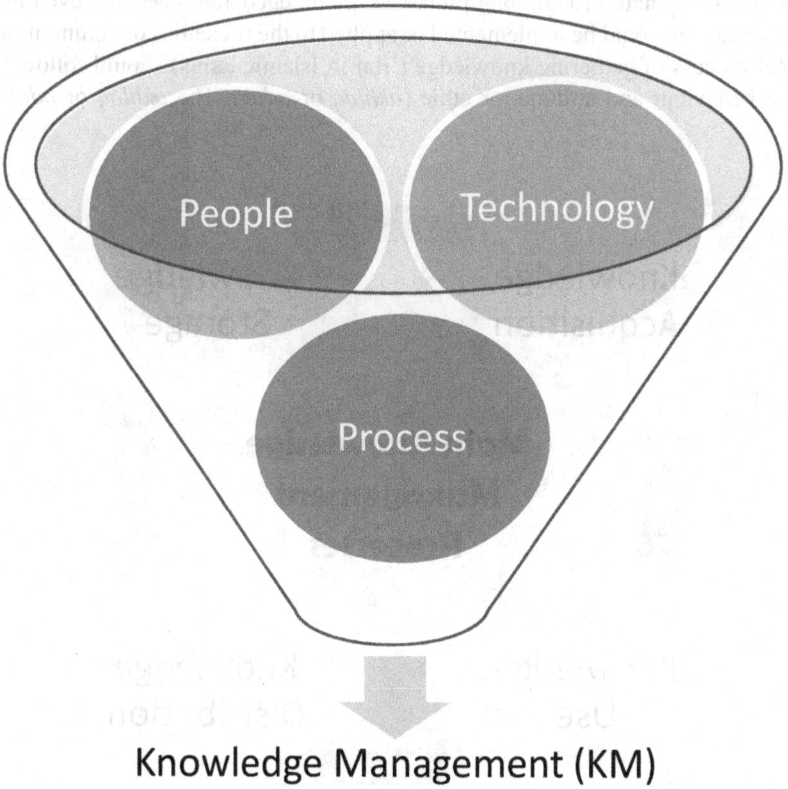

Figure 6.1 Element of knowledge management (*Source*: www.apqc.org)

tradition (Al-Qur'an. Al-baqarah 2:170; Al-isra' 17:36; Al-an'am 6:148). Wisdom comprises three elements, namely logic, knowledge, and emotional control, that have an important place in the Islamic view (Bagheri & Khoisravi, 2006). Besides that, numerous passeges can be cited in Al-Qur'an and Hadith on gaining knowledge to be successful; all Muslims are reminded frequently to go and achieve beyond the boundaries (the zones of heavens and the earth) only with knowledge and skills (Al-Qur'an. Ar-Rahman 55:33).

Figure 6.2 shows the main knowledge management process, which consists of knowledge use, knowledge acquisition, knowledge distribution, and knowledge storage. All of these are interrelated and cannot stand alone. If one component fails to function, the knowledge management process cannot give any positive effect to the individual or an organization, or in other words, it cannot contribute as expected.

Islam admitted the importance of knowledge, which has been discussed in numerous literatures. Knowledge in Islam comprehensively explains its existence, boundaries, categories, and types. Every Muslim must obtain knowledge, because it is part and parcel of all life activities. Importantly, knowledge must be gathered genuinely and through long processes. Islam encourages seeking even little knowledge but could be implemented or applied to the socienties or communities.

All process of gathering knowledge ('ilm in Islamic terms) should follow the good behaviour and attitude, or ethic (*akhlaq* or *adab*). The *akhlaq* or *adab* is

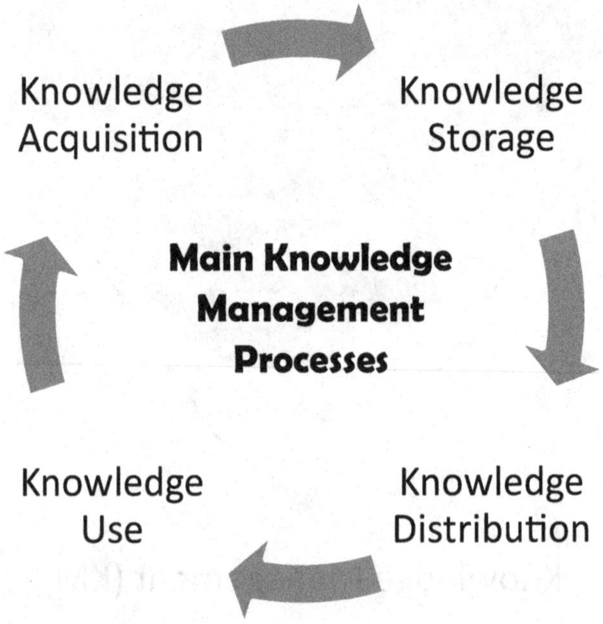

Figure 6.2 Main knowledge management process (*Source*: https://todayfounder.com)

more important than the 'ilm itself, which will direct the scholars adopting their knowledge ('ilm) in either the right or wrong directions. In fact, mathematically, it suggested that the period or length of gathering knowledge should be half of that of acquiring *adab*; for example, if a student takes 3–4 years to complete their degree, they should take 6–8 years to learn about *akhlaq* or *adab*. *Adab* is considered a higher degree than having knowledge in Islam. Al-Qur'an emphasizes the use of knowledge for the good of helping people. Al-Qur'an mentions the importance of knowledge in a staged process to ensure that Muslims able to implement gradually and not be overburdened.

Moreover, Islamic knowledge management (IKM) focuses on the delivery of benefits for long term, which brings sustainability. However, evaluation and extensive assessment on the methods of seeking knowledge are needed. The methodology should be updated to precisely able to gain knowledge comprehensively. Muslims must refer to two main sources of the Holy Quran and the Hadith of the Prophet Muhammad (PBUH).

As depicted in Table 6.1, the concept of the three-dimensional foundation of Islamic knowledge management is derived from the verses of Qur'an in (Al-Qur'an. At-Takathur 102:5; 7 and Al-Haaqqa 69:51). The nature of IKM practices is based on the continuous involvement with understanding, developing, and seeking knowledge, which is considered as a complete process and expectedly has impacts on the individual or an organization. These three elements of IKM practices enhance efficiency, promote stability, and produce excellent outcomes, productivity, and creativity (Yaakub & Othman, 2017).

Table 6.1 The description of three-dimensional foundation of IKM

No	*Dimension*	*Description*
1	Knowledge Diffusion (KD)	KD is the fundamental basis of IKM practices, especially in establishing knowledge. Unlimited access to knowledge will help the organizational productivities.
2	Knowledge Concentration (KC)	KC is a dimension that relates to the flow of the specific knowledge involved actively in the creation process, the dissemination and distribution of knowledge, and the initiation of core competencies, as well as understanding strategy.
3	Knowledge Purification (KPL)	KPL is a dimension in which Muslims are suggested to evaluate and ensure all processes of knowledge gathering through permissible actions. As highlighted by the Prophet (PBUH), Muslims are responsible for all knowledge gathered and will be questioned about it in the hereafter (the Day of Judgment). Therefore, Muslims have to purify their knowledge as a precondition to the purification of their soul.

Source: Yaakub & Othman (2017)

Islam considers knowledge as a root in human life. Knowledge relates to individual thinking and actions and follows with the creation of organizational socio-cultural productivities and performance. Therefore, every Muslims must be a worker that possesses sufficient and well-equipped knowledge. Through knowledge, Muslims will be able to obtain virtue and to attain power over nature in fulfilment towards their duty as a servant of God (Allah SWT). This concludes that IKM used as a basis in an organizational operation will enhance innovation and effectiveness.

Islamic knowledge management introduces a systematic process or reliable methodology that produces an excellent outcome. The knowledge gathered should be based on its needs and functions, thus Muslims who are as *khalifah* on earth are able to resolve various issues with that knowledge. Indeed, knowledge used to be a solution in life. Many verses in Al-Qur'an reminds one of the importance of knowledge, which even could be used to change the life of every Muslim economically and socially. The personality of a person could be shaped by knowledge, or knowledge could be an indicator in any assessment of a person which has explicitly and obviously shown up. Through its construction, IKM is very crucial to any progress and advancements in life.

A worker who has both Islamic knowledge and other specific knowledge expectedly will contribute to the performance of an organization. IKM has certain characteristics which are adaptable in any places or circumstances of the employees..One of the characteristics of IKM is to continuously contribute to the positive impacts of all humankind.

There are 35 articles relating to knowledge management and Islam, however none of the researches specifically explain the Islamic approach in implementing knowledge management, which should become a concern of Muslim researchers.

Meanwhile, knowledge relates to the concept of data and information, which recently must be filtered and assessed before using it to make any decisions. Managing knowledge involves processing data and information which are disseminated easily through social media and other new sophisticated tools. Credible sources who supply the data and information could be tested and justified, in Islamic terms '*tabayyun*', meaning cross-checking and verifying the data and information before processing it to the next actions. Although data and information are quite complex, a very thorough analysis is required for creating excellent knowledge.

Finally, some characteristics of the IKM system are superior to common knowledge management. Any organization relies nowadays more on knowledge management, which will be needed in the future for helping organizations' structures, systems, and employees to accomplish daily responsibilities. IKM helps employees in measuring the degree of precision and accuracy of their works as well as for their personal and capacity development. All of these are rooted in the principles of Islam, which are written clearly and explicitly in the Al-Qur'an. Therefore, a Muslim must become a knowledge worker by practice. A person's religious identity will not be recognized in Islam until he or she has succeeded in effectively building up knowledge in him- or herself.

Table 6.2 Articles on knowledge management and Islam in five years (2016–2020) in Scopus

Title of Articles	*Year*	*Total Citations*
From sacrilege to sustainability: the role of indigenous knowledge	2020	**1**
Youths and credit: An analysis of debt perspective and management	2020	0
TAM integration in thematic learning; preliminary study of . . .	2020	**1**
New Public Management (NPM) in the Iranian higher education; . . .	2020	**1**
The Effects of Spirituality and Religiosity on the Ethical J . . .	2020	0
Importance-performance matrix analysis of Kota Bharu in Islam . . .	2020	0
Towards development and validation of scale for ethical deci . . .	2020	0
Towards the Development of an Empirical Model for Islamic Co . . .	2020	0
Reviewing past and present values of Islamic leadership	2019	0
India – an untapped market for halal products	2019	**10**
Towards conceptualizing ethical decision-making model in mar . . .	2019	**2**
Integration of education: The case study of Islamic elementa . . .	2019	0
Knowing what you know about your faith an interactive applic . . .	2018	0
Ontology matching: A case of English translation of Al-Quran . . .	2018	0
A citation analysis of corporate social responsibility (1970 . . .	2018	**4**
Development and Assessment of an Interprofessional Curriculum . . .	2018	**1**
The influence of knowledge and religiosity on intention to r . . .	2018	0
Muslim ethics and the spirit of capitalism: The characteristic . . .	2018	0
The teaching policy of imperial Russia directed to "Foreign" . . .	2018	**1**
Ethical conflicts in the treatment of fasting Muslim patient . . .	2017	**6**
Is our well poisoned?: A historical/economic analysis of Chr . . .	2017	0
Lifting the veil on allowing headscarves in football: A co-c . . .	2017	**3**
Does it Pay to be Socially Responsible? Comparative Evidence . . .	2017	**2**
Effect of knowledge management on service innovation in acad . . .	2017	**24**
Muslim Scholars' Knowledge, Attitudes and Perceived Barriers . . .	2017	**2**
Impacts of organizational culture, support and IT infrastructure . . .	2017	**1**
Assessment formats and student learning performance: What is . . .	2017	0
Organizational commitment: Does religiosity matter?	2016	**13**
Who are the French jihadists? Analysis of 12 cases to help . . .	2016	**13**
Equitable education for Bangladeshi indigenous children: Per . . .	2016	0
The foundation of Islamic knowledge management practices	2016	0
How can professional associations continue to stay relevant? . . .	2016	**4**
Calm Vessels: Cultural expectations of pregnant women in Qat . . .	2016	**4**
Islamic values and negotiator behavior	2016	**1**
Managing CSR initiatives from the Islamic perspective: The c . . .	2016	**1**

Figure 6.3 indicates that knowledge is rooted or owned by Allah SWT and then disseminated to all human beings in various ways, including by intuition, revelation, perception, and reason. Knowledge is an existing phenomenon that humankind has to explore and investigate. Once the knowledge acquired by a person, it becomes information to him and becomes a science after it is applied by him and taught to others. This is explained in Al-Qur'an in Al-Baqarah 2: 30–33. As the servant of God, every Muslim has responsibility in seeking knowledge. They have to find ways on how to apply the knowledge in daily activities. Knowledge must be applied, otherwise it is meaningless.

Moreover, the output of an Islamic educational process is a learner that has adequate information aligning with the principles of the religion. It is important to note that the process of how knowledge is delivered is to be through or with credible capacity and analysis. The competency of human resources in terms of

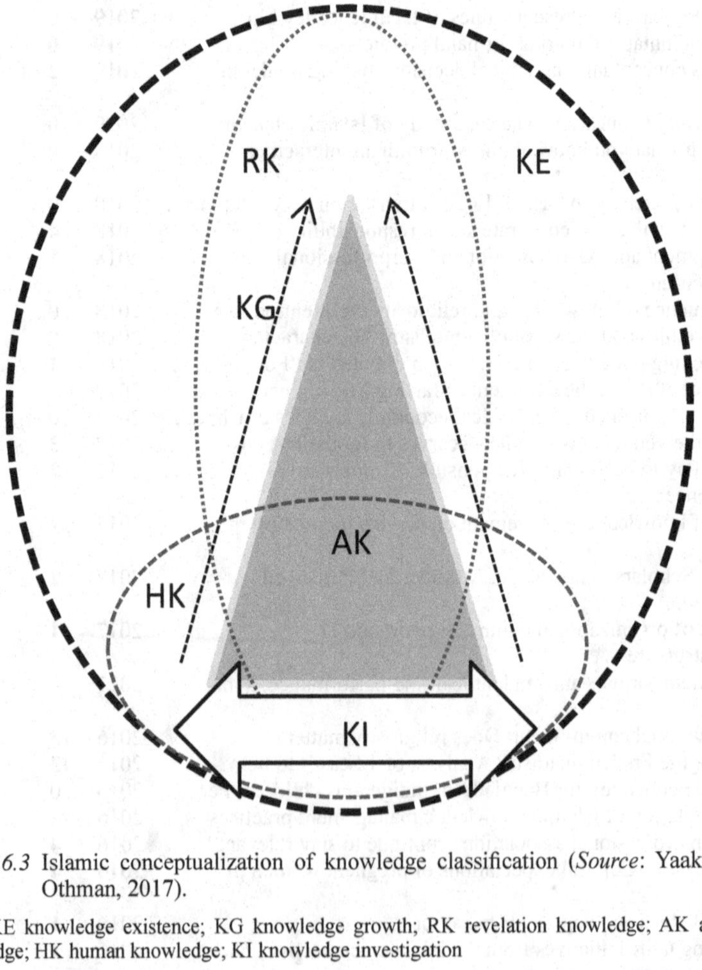

Figure 6.3 Islamic conceptualization of knowledge classification (*Source*: Yaakub and Othman, 2017).

Note: KE knowledge existence; KG knowledge growth; RK revelation knowledge; AK acquired knowledge; HK human knowledge; KI knowledge investigation

qualification and experiences is required to disseminate knowledge effectively. When managing knowledge, all must refer to the principles and values, including ethics, that are highlighted in the Al-Qur'an and hadith.

In fact, the sense of knowledge from the Islamic perspective is based on proofs, justifications, and evidence which are in accordance with the verses in Al-Qur'an. Muslim scholars agree that the highest source of knowledge in Islam is rooted in the Al-Qur'an. Islam considers knowledge as a means of attaining virtue in this world and eternal life (Al-Quran, Fussilat 41:53) and as absolute truth. This means that every Muslim must seek knowledge through sincere process, thus results the truth. Inversely, if Muslims are not obeying the given ways, the knowledge may lead to meaningless outcomes. It is crucial to ensure that the process, formation, and structure of obtaining knowledge is permissible in order to get the blessing from Allah SWT as the Owner of the knowledge.

Furthermore, the impact of having knowledge can be capitalized on by individuals or organizations in many ways (Usai et al., 2018), internally and externally, which then develop the capability and capacity of an organization (Bogers et al., 2018; Huesig & Endres, 2019; Pappas et al., 2018; Raut et al., 2019; Seele, 2017; Xia et al., 2017).

Digitalization and Islam

Digitization is the process of converting information into a digital format. The result is the representation of an object, image, sound, document, or signal by generating a series of numbers that describe a discrete set of points or samples.

A Muslim digital group is expected to be formed to upgrade and enhance digital literacy and understanding. Internet access is one of the issues that is still relevant to explore. In fact, it has been found that the Muslim world is one of the slowest segments of global civil society to transition to the information age. Three quarters of the world's poor live in the developing world, and a significant portion of the developing world is Muslim. Like in Egypt, those with access to the Internet are less than half a million out of a population of 68 million. Even in some of Gulf countries, the number of Internet users is less than 5% of the population (including expatriates). These figures are thus a motivation for every Muslim to learn, explore, and be involved in cyber practices.

In 2019, over 150 million Indonesians were users of social media, an increase of 15%–20% compared to 2018, and the majority of these users are Muslims. Table 6.3 presents the figures related to social media users.

As depicted in Table 6.3, Indonesia as the most populous Muslim country has potential in terms of number of users in Instagram, Facebook, YouTube, and Twitter as among the highest ranked in the world. Additionally, Figure 6.4 indicates the digital users in Indonesia. Knowledge dissemination might occur effectively through these social media platforms as well as the development of digital literacy among Muslim users.

According to Arifin (2017), his study found that a majority of respondents received religious teachings from TV (68.4%), home-based study (54%),

Table 6.3 Figures related to social media users

Social Media Platform	*User Monthly Worldwide (Million Users) – April 2019*			*Penetration of Leading Social Networks in Indonesia (%)*
	Worldwide Users (Million Users)	*Indonesia Users (Million Users)/Share Percentage (%)*	*Indonesia Rank in the World*	
Instagram	1,000*	56 / 12.3%	4th	80
Facebook	2,375	120 / 40.88%	4th	81
YouTube	1,900**	50***/ 19.3%	–	88
Twitter	330	22.8 /17.23%	3rd	52

*June 2018; **Sept 2018; *** Dec 2017
Source: Statista Internet (2018)

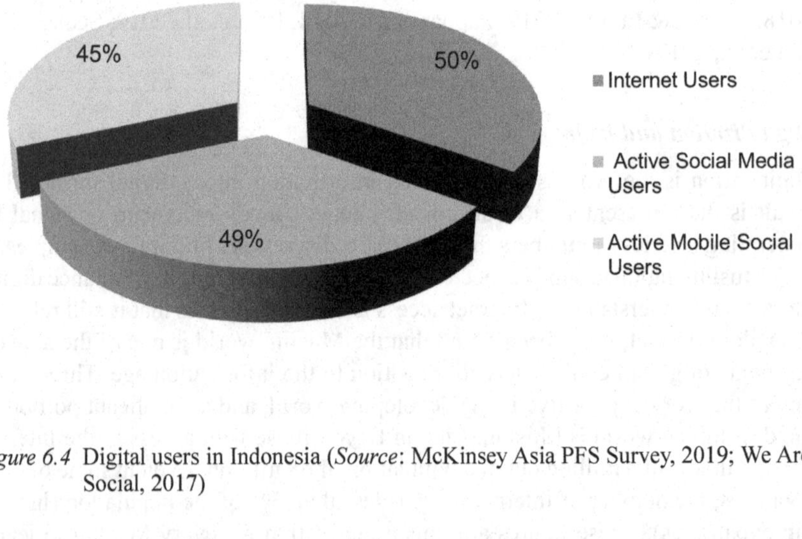

Figure 6.4 Digital users in Indonesia (*Source*: McKinsey Asia PFS Survey, 2019; We Are Social, 2017)

messenger account broadcast (17%), articles in social media (14.1%), and articles on the Internet (13.9%). These percentages are encouraging, and expectedly more Muslims could engage with religious teachings on TV and other sources. Moreover, in this IT era, media literacy evolves into digital literacy. Indeed, it relates to capability and competence. In the digital world, the capability to access, understand, and create communication in various contexts and by using available technology and related software is required. In Indonesia, media literacy and digital literacy are relatively low. Media literacy is more related to literacy skills – the literacy rate reached 97.93% while illiteracy rate is approximately 2.07% or 3.4 million people.[5]

The Muslim millennial should be engaged with various programs of digital literacy through educational institutions. With this digital platform, every Muslim could interact openly to discuss important topics instantly via sharing of knowledge, data, and information. By engaging in a very fast-changing technology and knowledge transfers, Muslims are able to understand the issues or problems that arise and the solutions needed for Muslim communities. It is important to absorb and know all Muslims' expressions and ideas and thus develop human capital and improve Muslims' behaviours.

It is important for Muslims to be concerned with morality of when they engage with cyber practices or social media because the Prophet Muhammad (PBUH) put moral or ethics, or *akhlaq*, as a priority for every Muslim in their life. Sophistication, modernism, and high technology are meaningless without good morals. In fact, the moral level of Muslims in urban and rural areas is different. Some Muslims living in cosmopolitan cities are denied ethical behaviour compared to those who are in rural areas or villages that more obedient to Islamic teaching. This could be due to the influence of digitalization and the openness of information, which sometimes results in an individual forgetting his/her obligation to religious instructions. Islam emphasizes understanding values that are to be shared among Muslims. Continuous advice and reminders are important to the groups that are actively involved in cyber practices or the digital sector.

As depicted in Figure 6.5, the three of goals of digitalization are beneficial to the individual as well as the organization and bring effectiveness and efficiency.

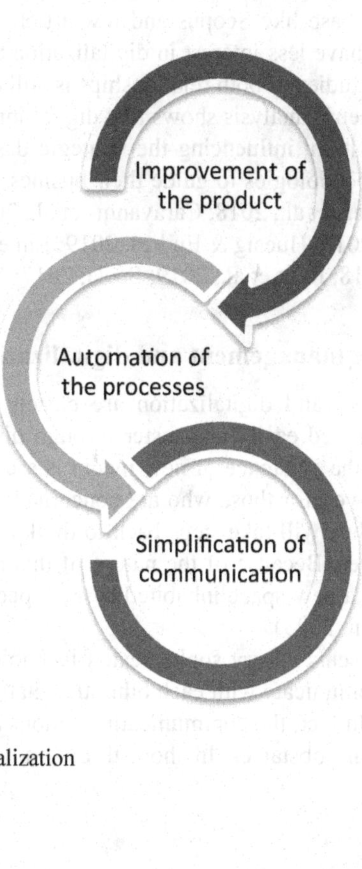

Figure 6.5 Goals of digitalization

Table 6.4 Articles on digitalization and Islam since 2013 in Scopus

Title of Articles	*Year*	*Total Citations*
The main reasons for the revival of Islam in independent Kaz . . .	2020	0
Religion in the age of digitalization: From new media to spi . . .	2020	0
(De-)differentiation and religion in digital news	2020	0
Studying religion in Nordic newspapers: An introduction	2019	**4**
Redesign of User Interface Zakat Mobile Smartphone Applicati . . .	2019	**1**
Taking selfies in Mecca: Haram or still the venerable Hajj? . . .	2019	0
Muslims and the new information and communication technologi . . .	2013	**2**

Source: McKinsey Asia PFS Survey (2019), We Are Social (2017)

These three goals also are aligned with the unpredictable business environment that needs to be anticipated to be proactive. In order to compete openly and internationally, either an individual or an organization must look into simplifying communication and automation processes and improving products and services.

There are only seven articles related to digitalization and Islam since 2013 in a highly reputable database like Scopus and few articles have been cited. This means the researchers have less interest in digitalization and Islam, and thus the potential of exploring studies of both relationships is still open.

Moreover, a bibliometric analysis shows that digital innovation involves business processes from within, influencing the strategic design of companies that use new information technologies to guide their business model, especially in a sustainable sense (Bogers et al., 2018; Carayannis et al., 2017; Ghezzi & Cavallo, 2020; Gupta & Bose, 2019; Huesig & Endres, 2019; Lin et al., 2018; Nagy et al., 2018; Pappas et al., 2018; Raut et al., 2019; Seele, 2017; Xia et al., 2017).

Issues on knowledge management and digitalization

Knowledge management and digitalization are closely related. For example, knowledge could be shared easily and faster through digital platforms such as social media. Perhaps the existence of new media is a common thing for Indonesian Muslims. However, for those who are concerned about the impact of the new media critically, they will take steps back to think and compare from other sources and perspectives. Because of the nature of this new media, it becomes a new public entity, as a new space inhabited by new people with new thoughts (Eickelman & Anderson, 2003).

This new media presents a very sophisticated technology that helps modern educated Muslims communicate with each other transnationally or globally, promoting social agency. In fact, the communicative actions are often taken without having to face significant obstacles. In short, through this new media, everyone has various freedoms, be it freedom of thought, freedom of religion and belief, or freedom of expression.

For Muslims, with this freedom, they have the opportunity to challenge any structural and cultural actors who dominate their social and political life. Because they are able to think independently, they can also interpret all meanings regarding general benefit or virtue. Consequently, they can also serve to rebut various opinions of the authorities and even religious leaders. This is where liberal contestation has its place. This also provides a good opportunity to answer socio-political problems in the Islamic world itself (authoritarianism, corruption, and Islamism). In fact, for example, social media (Twitter, Facebook, blogs, and various websites) played a significant role in the process of socio-political revolution that occurred in Arab countries. It appears that the data, information, and knowledge could be misunderstood. Some groups of people rely on information or short news pieces without clarifying it.

Meanwhile, in Indonesia people have also used social media to organize certain political actions, for example the 212 or 411 actions. Although, of the various actions that exist, some social agencies use religion as an instrument to achieve political goals. Millions of people involved may not be aware of this. Making religion an instrument to gain power or accumulate capital will degrade the value of religion itself. It cannot be denied that this has led to further decline, hindered a substantial democratization process, and prevented Muslims from realizing the ideals of the birth of a modern *ummah*. Moreover, in this digital and global era, Muslims as much as possible must participate in voicing all progressive and civilized ideas (Mandaville, 2001, p. 176). On the other hand, fighting for social justice, equality, and humanity is the main thing.

Moreover, Yuswohady (2015) mentioned changes in consumer behaviour during the Covid-19 outbreak. Four changes to digital processes resulted in Muslims actively engaging in various activities.

Digital Da'wah

Da'wah,[6] as one of the missions of Islam, develops rapidly through conventional and digital media. Da'wah, which has been carried out using lectures, sermons, and *tabligh*, approach or one-way communication, is no longer applicable in the view of millennial Muslims. Nowadays, all religious messages are shared and delivered instantly, for example through WhatsApp groups, YouTube, podcasts, and even live streaming with Zoom, which offers unlimited access. This successfully enlarges the range of audiences. Some attractive images and audios are made to make the content more impressive. This way of da'wah is continuously recommended which may save more times and costs.

Muslim commerce

In recent years, many e-commerce services or online marketplaces have started to appear specifically targeting the Muslim market. Various products are offered from food, fashion, and cosmetics to financial and tourism services. As the most Muslim population in the world, the potential of consuming and making transactions is huge. It can be seen in various reports in the increasing spending of Muslims, particularly of halal products. It is also could contribute to the taxes in each country that help in developing the economy in general. E-commerce enhances creativity and triggers better competition, because it is openly accessed by all businesspersons.

Muslim-friendly digital content

The growth of the Muslim market in Indonesia is directly proportional to the emergence of Islamic media and content, especially in the digital realm. Online media grows like mushrooms in the rainy season, and Muslim-themed content creators are scattered throughout various social media channels such as Twitter, Instagram, and YouTube.

Activities of daily life have also begun to switch to digital, including looking for information through digital media, shopping through e-commerce, engaging in financial activities with fintech, and traveling to *ta'aruf* online.[7] This has led to the emergence of many digital start-ups that specifically target millennial Muslims. The development of technology and the digital world have helped change the behaviour and lifestyle of Muslims today. Moreover, the Covid-19 outbreak has accelerated digital literacy among Muslim consumers. As a digital-savvy segment, Muslims today cannot easily be separated from the digital lifestyle, especially social media. They seek information, get news, share knowledge, and show off what they have through social media.

Sharia blockchain

Along with Muslim consumers who are increasingly tech savvy and digitally literate, the massive use of technology increasingly provides solutions for the Muslim market. Among them are the use of blockchain for halal certification and *waqf*.[8] WhatsHalal, a start-up from Singapore, is a platform that simplifies the halal certification process from upstream to downstream through blockchain technology.

With blockchain, a product can be tracked and recorded for its halal content from farmers' crops, manufacturing processes, restaurants, and retailers to the hands of consumers. In other words, the effort, cost, and time to test the halal content of a product can be cut because everything has been aggregated in the blockchain. The use of blockchain for halal certification is based on the amount of data that is collected, stored, and processed in the certification process. In addition, the use of blockchain aims to encourage transparency and security aspects of their services.

Conclusion

This chapter explains knowledge management and digitalization from an Islamic point of view, which needs to be explored and exposed. The uniqueness of

Islamic teaching on knowledge management and digitalization could be learned and applied in any organization. Islam emphasizes that data and information are shared to reach wisdom. The misuses or manipulations of data cause fraud and do not result in wisdom.

Both knowledge management and digitalization play important roles in shaping new Muslims' behaviours and actions, particularly during the Covid-19 pandemic, in which everyone has to do things from a distance. All Muslims are able to gather knowledge easily and efficiently via online learning and teaching. A variety of sources is available to be accessed, and everyone can respond to any interactions related to knowledge management effectively. Digitalization, meanwhile, is crucial for expediting processes, including business and social activities. Muslims should take advantage of this digitalization, which may be used for changes in life. Every justification on the encouragement of knowledge management and digitalization can be found in the verses of Al-Qur'an as well as the hadith of Prophet Muhammad (PBUH), which then proves the advancements in Islamic thoughts.

Notes

1 *Mu'amalah* is a part of Islamic jurisprudence, or fiqh includes Islamic "rulings governing commercial transactions".

2 *Maqasid al shariah* (objectives of shariah) explain the objectives and wisdom (hikmah) of Allah SWT and Prophet (PBUH) in all its direction to maintain the people's wealth.

3 Abū ʿAbdillāh Muhammad ibn Idrīs al-Shāfiʿī was an Arab Muslim theologian, writer, and scholar, who was the first contributor of the principles of Islamic jurisprudence.

4 Hadith. Ibn Majah. Muhammad Ibn Yazid Abu Abdullah. Sunan Ibn Majah. Juz. 1:#224. p. 81.

5 www.kemdikbud.go.id/main/blog/2017/09/indonesia-peringati-hari-aksara-internasional-tahun-2017

6 Da'wah is the act of inviting or calling people to embrace Islam.

7 *Ta'aruf* refers to formally making a person known to another or to the public.

8 *Waqf* known as hubous or mortmain property is an inalienable charitable endowment under Islamic law.

References

Akbari, N., & Ghaffari, A. (2017). Verifying relationship of knowledge management initiatives and the empowerment of human resources. *Journal of Knowledge Management*, *21*(5), 1120–1141.

Arifin, S. (2017). Digital literacy of middle class Muslims. *Journal of Islamic Educational Thoughts and Practices*, *1*(1), 152–173.

Bagheri, K., & Khoisravi, Z. (2006). The Islamic concept of education reconsidered. *The American Journal of Islamic Social Science*, *23*(4), 88–103.

Bhatt, G. D. (2001). Knowledge management in organisations: Examining the interaction between technologies, techniques, and people. *Journal of Knowledge Management*, *5*(1), 68–75.

Bogers, M., Chesbrough, H., & Moedas, C. (2018). Open innovation: Research, practices, and policies. *California Management Review*, *60*(2), 5–16.

Bresciani, S., Ferraris, A., & Del Giudice, M. (2018). The management of organizational ambidexterity through alliances in a new context of analysis: Internet of things (IoT) smart city projects. *Technological Forecasting and Social Change*, *136*, 331–338.

Carayannis, E. G., Grigoroudis, E., Del Giudice, M., Della Peruta, M. R., & Sindakis, S. (2017). An exploration of contemporary organizational artifacts and routines in a sustainable excellence context. *Journal of Knowledge Management*, *21*(1), 35–56.

Del Giudice, M., & Della Peruta, M. R. (2016). The impact of IT-based knowledge management systems on internal venturing and innovation: A structural equation modeling approach to corporate performance. *Journal of Knowledge Management, 20*(3), 484–498.

Del Giudice, M., Garcia-Perez, A., Scuotto, V., & Orlando, B. (2019a). Are social enterprises technological innovative? A quantitative analysis on social entrepreneurs in emerging countries. *Technological Forecasting and Social Change*, *148*, 119704.

Del Giudice, M., Scuotto, V., Garcia-Perez, A., & Petruzzelli, A. M. (2019b). Shifting wealth II in Chinese economy: The effect of the horizontal technology spillover for SMEs for international growth. *Technological Forecasting and Social Change*, *145*, 307–316.

Eickelman, D. F., & Anderson, J. W. (2003). *New media in the Muslim world: The emerging public sphere*. Indiana University Press.

Ghezzi, A., & Cavallo, A. (2020). Agile business model innovation in digital entrepreneurship: Lean startup approaches. *Journal of Business Research*, 519–537.

Gil-Gomez, H., Guerola-Navarro, V., Oltra-Badenes, R., & Lozano-Quilis, J. A. (2020). Customer relationship management: Digital transformation and sustainable business model innovation. *Economic Research-Ekonomska Istra˘zivanja*, 1–18.

Gupta, G., & Bose, I. (2019). Strategic learning for digital market pioneering: Examining the transformation of Wishberry's crowdfunding model. *Technological Forecasting and Social Change*, *146*, 865–876. https://doi.org/10.1016/j.techfore.2018.06.020

Halkias, D., Cader, Y., O'Neill, K. K., Blooshi, A. A., Al Shouq, A. A. B., Fadaaq, B. H. M., & Ali, F. G. (2013). Knowledge management in Islamic and conventional banks in the United Arab Emirates. *Management Research Review*, *222*.

Halstead, M. (2004). An Islamic concept of education. *Comparative Education*, *40*(4), 517–529.

Hock-Doepgen, M., Clauss, T., Kraus, S., & Cheng, C. F. (2020). Knowledge management capabilities and organizational risk-taking for business model innovation in SMEs. *Journal of Business Research*. https://doi.org/10.1016/j.jbusres.2019.12.001

Huesig, S., & Endres, H. (2019). Exploring the digital innovation process. *European Journal of Innovation Management*, *22*(2), 302–314. https://doi.org/10.1108/EJIM-02-2018-0051

Inkinen, H. (2016). Review of empirical research on knowledge management practices and firm performance. *Journal of Knowledge Management*, *20*(2), 230–257.

Kamara, J. M., Augenbroe, G., Anumba, C. J., & Carrillo, P. M. (2002). Knowledge management in the architecture, engineering and construction industry. *Construction Innovation, 2*(1), 53–67.

Kamble, S. S., Gunasekaran, A., & Gawankar, S. A. (2020). Achieving sustainable performance in a data-driven agriculture supply chain: A review for research and applications. *International Journal of Production Economics*, *219*, 179–194. https://doi.org/10.1016/j.ijpe.2019.05.022

Keramati, A., & Azadeh, M. (2007). Exploring the effects of top management commitment on knowledge management success in academia: A case study. *World Academy of Science, Engineering and Technology*, *27*, 292–297.

Lin, F., Lin, S. W., & Lu, W. M. (2018). Sustainability assessment of Taiwan's semiconductor industry: A new hybrid model using combined analytic hierarchy process and two-stage additive network data envelopment analysis. *Sustainability*, *10*(11), 4070. https://doi.org/10.3390/su10114070

Lokshina, I., & Lanting, C. (2019). A qualitative evaluation of IoT-driven eHealth: Knowledge management, business models and opportunities, deployment and evolution. In *Data-centric business and applications* (pp. 23–52). Springer. https://doi.org/10.1007/978-3-319-94117-2_2

Mandaville, P. (2001). Reimagining Islam in diaspora: The politics of mediated community. *Gazette (Leiden, Netherlands)*, *63*(2–3), 169–186.

McKinsey Asia PFS Survey. (2019, February). *Digital banking in Indonesia: Building loyalty and generating growth.* https://www.mckinsey.com/~/media/McKinsey/Industries/Financial%20Services/Our%20Insights/Digital%20banking%20in%20Indonesia%20Building%20loyalty%20and%20generating%20growth/Digital-banking-in-Indonesia-final.pdf

Nagy, J., Ol'ah, J., Erdei, E., M'at'e, D., & Popp, J. (2018). The role and impact of industry 4.0 and the internet of things on the business strategy of the value chain – the case of Hungary. *Sustainability*, *10*(10), 3491.

Nielsen, C. (2018). Relating successful business models to intellectual capital and knowledge management practices. *Electronic Journal of Knowledge Management*, *16*(1), 48–55.

Pappas, I. O., Mikalef, P., Giannakos, Krogstie, J., & Lekakos, G. (2018). Big data and business analytics ecosystems: Paving the way towards digital transformation and sustainable societies. *Information Systems and e-Business Management*, *16*, 479–491. https://doi.org/10.1007/s10257-018-0377-z

Parmentier, G., & Mangematin, V. (2014). Orchestrating innovation with user communities in the creative industries. *Technological Forecasting and Social Change*, *83*, 40–53.

Raudeliuniene, J., Davidaviciene, V., & Jakubavicius, A. (2018a). Knowledge management process model. *Entrepreneurship and Sustainability Issues*, *5*(3), 542–554.

Raudeliuniene, J., & Szarucki, M. (2019). An integrated approach to assessing an organization's knowledge potential. *Engineering Economics*, *30*(1), 69–80.

Raut, R. D., Mangla, S. K., Narwane, V. S., Gardas, B. B., Priyadarshinee, P., & Narkhede, B. E. (2019). Linking big data analytics and operational sustainability practices for sustainable business management. *Journal of Cleaner Production*, *224*, 10–24.

Rechberg, I., & Syed, J. (2014). Knowledge management practices and the focus on the individual. *International Journal of Knowledge Management*, *10*(1), 25–41.

Santoro, G., Ferraris, A., & Bresciani, S. (2019). Assessing the breadth of open innovation practices: The impact on innovation performance. Sinergie. *Italian Journal of Management*, *37*(1), 63–84.

Scuotto, V., Arrigo, E., Candelo, E., & Nicotra, M. (2019). Ambidextrous innovation orientation effected by the digital transformation: A quantitative research on fashion SMEs. *Business Process Management Journal*, *26*(5), 1121–1140.

Seele, P. (2017). Predictive sustainability control: A review assessing the potential to transfer big data driven "predictive policing" to corporate sustainability management. *Journal of Cleaner Production*, *153*, 673–686. https://doi.org/10.1016/j.jclepro.2016.10.175

Statista Internet. (2018). *Mobile Internet & Apps*. https://www.statista.com/markets/424/topic/538/mobile-internet-apps/

Usai, A., Scuotto, V., Murray, A., Fiano, F., & Dezi, L. (2018). Do entrepreneurial knowledge and innovative attitude overcome "imperfections" in the innovation process?

Insights from SMEs in the UK and Italy. *Journal of Knowledge Management*, *22*(8), 1637–1654. https://doi.org/10.1108/JKM-01-2018-0035

We are Social. (2017). *Digital in 2017*. https:// www.juancmejia.com/wp-content/uploads/2017/03/Digital-2017-WeAreSocial-y-HootSuite.pdf

Xia, D., Yu, Q., Gao, Q., & Cheng, G. (2017). Sustainable technology selection decision making model for enterprise in supply chain: Based on a modified strategic balanced scorecard. *Journal of Cleaner Production*, *141*, 1337–1348. https://doi.org/10.1016/j.jclepro.2016.09.083

Yaakub, M. B. H., & Othman, K. (2017). The foundation of islamic knowledge management practices. In *Entrepreneurship and management in an Islamic context* (pp. 91–117). Springer.

Yıldırım, D. C., & Arun, K. (2019). Effects of economic clusters, FDI and R & D on innovation: Developing countries in the European monetary union example. *International Journal of Innovation*, *7*(2), 236–251.

Yuswohady. (2015). *Marketing to the middle-class Muslim*. https://www.yuswohady.com/2014/07/06/marketing-to-the-middle-class-moslem/

7 Designing a simple house of knowledge management

Muhammad Mahreza Maulana and Arif Imam Suroso

Introduction

Managing data, information and knowledge is still a challenge for every company or organization. The biggest challenge is how to make data, information and knowledge provide the maximum benefit for the organization. For some companies, knowledge management (KM) makes it more competitive in today's digital era.

The challenge starts from how organizations and companies understand the definition of data and information. What are the differences in the quality of data and information, and how does one achieve knowledge so that wisdom can be obtained to make the right decision (Baškarada & Koronios, 2013)? Then, how can technology be used to process data, information and knowledge into a competitive advantage? It is believed that the rapidly developing internet technology today can prepare a person to achieve the desired competence (Benito-Osorio et al., 2013). Other technologies, such as artificial intelligence, including neural networks, machine learning, or deep learning, are used especially to increase economic competition, namely by carrying out digital business transformation (Ruiz-Real et al., 2021). Organizations or companies are required to always innovate in creating both knowledge and the resulting products (Anggraeni et al., 2017).

Besides technology, another thing that needs attention is how the organization or company processes the data and information. Some studies hope that the knowledge management process will generate innovation in it (Leber et al., 2015). It is also important to have a strategic knowledge management plan, because knowledge is a resource of the organization (Newell, 2005).

Every organization or company has different targets, capabilities and resources, so that the assets owned can adjust the process of managing data, information and knowledge. In this case, a process of improving knowledge management and continuous learning can be achieved. Therefore, we need a knowledge management design that includes all the aspects that have been mentioned.

This paper is conceptually based and aimed at developing a model of knowledge management. Using the methods of literature review and modelling like a house, it attempts to provide guidance to help organizations and companies in managing information and knowledge. So they can create and enhance their knowledge in

DOI: 10.4324/9781003224532-7

achieving the visions and missions to compete in the digital economic environment, a simple knowledge management design is proposed.

In order to achieve aforementioned aim, the following structure is needed. First is a literature review of information definition, knowledge and learning, and design methodology. The next section discusses the foundation of knowledge management, such as organization, leadership, basic technology and a management model. The following section concentrates on the latest technologies in managing data and information as a knowledge pillar. The subsequent section discusses knowledge management process and creation, sharing, transfer and innovation and then the knowledge stages in achieving competitive advantages. The last section provides final conclusions and suggestions for further research.

Literature review

The objective is for every organization or company to better recognize its assets and its current stage of knowledge management.

Information

The explanation of information will start from information 1.0 (one-to-one of format, owner, publisher and delivery) to information 4.0 (many-to-many of format, owner, publisher and delivery). This application will be explained in more detail. Information 1.0 is information in one format (one paper form, one publisher, one owner and one delivery). An example of this information is a publication in the form of a printed book (Frederiksen, 2017).

Information 2.0 is information that has developed in various formats. A book is not available only physically but also online (in a pdf file or on a web page). Although they have different forms, the information provided covers the same topic. Information 3.0 also developed in many formats, with many owners and channels for delivery. Information at this stage has been already in the form of components, such as supporting information on portals, help functions, CRM (customer relationship management) applications, feedback forms, and so on.

Meanwhile, information 4.0, which already distinguishes many publishers, has the characteristics that information is molecular (not in the form of documents), dynamic (updated continuously), ubiquitous (can be found and searched online) and contextual driven (offered but not provided automatically and spontaneously) based on a profile.

Knowledge

Beginning with knowledge creation from natural events (knowledge 1.0), knowledge developed from life events, industry and value creation to digitizing public knowledge (knowledge 4.0) (North, 2018). Knowledge 1.0 began in the 16th–17th centuries with the inception of natural science from several experts such as Galilei, Newton, Rousseau and others. In this phase, there was scientific development.

New knowledge and the interaction between scientists and practitioners used systematic methods. Hence, it birthed a knowledge institution (university).

Knowledge 2.0 then appeared in the 18th–19th centuries with the presence of the industrial era, in which the production of knowledge appeared in all aspects of life. The knowledge planning and designing process had separated from knowledge implementation in the form of a machine. Pieces of knowledge generated professionals such as doctors and technicians.

Knowledge 3.0 emerged in the 20th century with the existence of an information society. Knowledge 3.0 was the dominant factor in the production process. Computer technology, the internet, AI and algorithms are applied to support production routines. The active population of knowledge workers increased rapidly, including technicians, scientists, teachers, consultants, bankers, managers and journalists and practitioners of medicine, law and the arts.

Meanwhile, knowledge 4.0 emerged in the 21st century with the existence of the digitalization era of knowledge. Knowledge digitalization has been used in daily life and provides value. Knowledge capabilities have been achieved in cognitive, social, knowledge collaboration, network systems and augmented intelligence. Digital penetration has entered all professions and education.

Learning

Organizational learning has developed from learning 1.0 using e-learning to learning 4.0, called digital learning. Learning 4.0 as a future learning target has the following characteristics (North & Maier, 2018):

- *Digital form.* There will be more learning through digital media than through traditional learning using printed books.
- *Network oriented.* A personal knowledge network will form with connectivity. The individual with the same knowledge interest classifies using a social network, digital databases and connected knowledge archives of various types and sources.
- *Diverse.* The informal learning environment, especially about social learning, will mix with the formal learning environment by determining a good learning path.
- *Constructive.* The learning environment requires centralized control media. Computer knowledge in the national curriculum to achieve algorithm recognition competencies can be a significant skill.
- Based on *semantically enhanced material.* This understanding allows for different views of semantic data items, reuse and basis for sharing. This characteristic needs to understand the meaning of the data and learn quickly about the brief knowledge to get a conclusion on whether this knowledge fits into the existing ontology.
- *Individual and adaptive.* Learning is carried out independently of time and space. For example, workers can prepare themselves to carry out their routine work either in front of a computer or by using a cellphone while traveling

using train transportation. However, the learning process will differ between the two activities.

Society

Information, knowledge and learning are going to play a significant role in the formation of society 5.0. It will be an era where all technology is a part of humanity itself. The internet is not only for sharing information but also for daily life. Society 5.0 is a society formed by digital transformation by means of the use of technologies such as AI, IoT and blockchain.

History shown that society 1.0 is a group of people who hunt for their food. Then continue to society 2.0, where it changed from hunting to an agrarian society, or farming. With the emergence of the industrial revolution, society 3.0, or industrial society, was formed starting from early industries such as steam engines and textiles to heavy industries such as electricity, oil and motorcycles. The era of the emergence of computers formed a society 4.0, called the third-generation industrial revolution with the using of the internet and automation; it is also called the information society.

There is a slight difference between society 4.0 and society 5.0. Society 4.0 focuses more on cyber-physical systems (CPS), the Internet of Things (IoT) and mass customization (Deguchi et al., 2020), whereas society 5.0 encompasses:

- High-level cyber-physical space convergence. Combining the virtual world with the physical space where data flows from the physical space to the virtual world, then flows back from the virtual world to the physical space.
- Balance of economic development with the resolution of social issues. By providing goods and services that specifically meet various needs based on age, gender or language, it ensures that all citizens lead high-quality lives full of comfort and vitality.
- Human-centered society. Society 5.0 regulates the relationship between people and technology. It also organizes the relationship between individuals and society. It is a society that converts data and information into knowledge, making a society that moves from an information society to a data-driven society.

Methodology

In conducting a knowledge management design, a house component analogy was used (Vela & Koong, 2017), incorporating at least three components, namely the foundation, pillars and roof. The components of the knowledge management house are defined as follows:

- Knowledge foundation: the basis of knowledge management. It is hoped that the components on the foundation will always exist, such as the organization, leadership and management models that will be implemented.

- Knowledge pillar: development of information and knowledge infrastructure for knowledge discovery and management. It begins with a discussion of information systems and information science as a knowledge infrastructure. Each organization has the right to determine the knowledge infrastructure to be built, whether in the form of a stand-alone or integrated information system and whether to build independently or to use existing KM tools. Here are the missions to achieve the knowledge management vision.
- Knowledge roof: discussion of the knowledge management cycle. Starting from creating knowledge, sharing knowledge, transferring knowledge and making innovative knowledge, this process determines how data becomes information and knowledge and therefore provides a competitive advantage for the organization or company. This is the where the vision of the organization must be set.

The choice to use "simple" in the title was intended to show that this knowledge-management house can be applied by new organizations or companies or those that have been managing knowledge for a long time. To ensure the knowledge management that has been carried out can achieve the desired target and optimize all the knowledge assets that are already owned.

Result and discussion

The main foundation of knowledge

Organization

Knowledge organization discusses roles and activities starting from describing, indexing and classifying knowledge in the era of VUCA (volatility, uncertainty, complexity and ambiguity). Knowledge organization is the activities of the classification, indexing and description of documents. It is carried out in libraries, bibliographic databases, archives and other types of "memory institutions" by librarians, archivists, information specialists, subject specialists and computer algorithms (Hjørland, 2008). There are six approaches to classifying knowledge:

1. In the *traditional approach*, the knowledge classification system used libraries and databases.

   a. Dewey Decimal Classification (DDC). Dewey classification modified and developed. The classification was based on subject. The code is three digits followed by a period.
   b. Library of Congress Classification (LCC), this classification system is used by the American congressional library by using letter codes to denote objects. Then it is further divided into more specific subclasses, identified by two or sometimes three letters.

c Universal Decimal Classification (UDC), developed from the DDC by arranging bibliographic cards, including books, articles, abstracts and so forth. It consists of two numbers. Symbols and signs represent the main and auxiliary numbers.

2 In an *aspect-based analytical approach*, developed by Ranganathan, relevant units and concepts are combined to explain the subject. Subjects are grouped into several general categories. Ranganathan proposed the PMEST formula (personality, matter, energy, space and time). Then the British Classification Research Group (CRG) developed the list. Colon classification (CC) and Bliss 2 (BC2) are the most critical systems developed based on this theory.
3 The *information retrieval* (IR) method tries to give solution that allows the user to find relevant information. IR is a process of obtaining relevant information sources from a collection of knowledge. The searching process is done by full text or content-based indexing. The searching process for information in documents can be in text, images and sound.
4 A *user-oriented approach* determines how the system is designed on user-empirical studies. For this reason, algorithms are running to evaluate the average user. From the preliminary research, it has been found that users prefer a verbal search system based on notation classification.
5 The *bibliometric approach* is based on the use of bibliographic references to organize a network of papers. The second point is that the indexing depth level is partially determined by the number of terms assigned to each document and reference, which serve as access points. The names of authors in leading journals provide the second access point.
6 The *domain-based analytical approach* is based on a sociological-epistemological point of view. The indexing of certain documents must reflect the needs of dedicated user groups or some ideal goals. In other words, any description or representation of a given document is more or less suitable for the fulfillment of a particular task. This description is never objective or neutral. The goal is not to standardize or create one description for all documents of different target groups.

Leadership

Leadership requires knowledge development with characteristics such as agile, participatory, open and trusting (North & Maier, 2018).

- *Agile leadership.* A leader must direct and think of several possible scenarios, consider several options, try new ideas and learn quickly from failure and success.
- *Participative leadership.* Using the company's intelligence, a leader must create conditions of knowledge and self-motivation from workers. They need experience and competence to complete specific jobs. Leaders are considered more as community leaders and trainers.

- *Networking leadership.* Each knowledge worker must link with another individual's knowledge. The leader must be a liaison between these individuals, both inward and outward relationships.
- *Open leadership.* A leader must be open, willing to accept input and corrections.
- *Trust-based leadership.* Leader must have confidence in colleagues and partners.

Technology

The basic technology that supports knowledge is inseparable from web development. It started with Web 1.0 and developed into Web 5.0 (Benito-Osorio et al., 2013).

1 Web 1.0 is a basic internet-based web. It is used by companies to publish company information, develop marketing and sales plans and transact with customers.
2 Web 2.0 is the social web. In term of technology, it does not change much. It was designed only to facilitate information sharing, interoperability and collaboration and user-oriented design. Examples include web services, web applications, social network services, video hosting services, wikis, blogs, and so on.
3 Web 3.0 is a combination of human intelligence and artificial intelligence to provide access to relevant information. Web 3.0 has already used neural networks and genetic algorithms. Some efforts are required to analyze processing capacity and generate new ideas based on user-generated information. Web 3.0 also needs to support artificial intelligence (AI) technology, the semantic web, the 3D web, the geospatial web and so on.
4 Web 4.0 arose because of cellular technology that connects humans and objects anywhere and anytime, physically or virtually in real time. For example, the GPS (global positioning service) provides recommendations for cars to take the fastest route using the least fuel.
5 Web 5.0 is the sensory and emotive web designed to develop interactions between computers and humans. This interaction is used to get personalization from the user and to create a pleasant experience for users in obtaining information and knowledge.

Management model

This section discusses the management model and analysis of knowledge based on the value chain. It consists of input, activity (process, feedback, learning), output (sharing and transfer) and the impact of these values (Toszewska, 2015).

- *Input* contains tangible inputs such as budget allocation, management and effectiveness of the HR function.

- *Activity* contains specific actions from the organization. Some practices include implementing and creating intangible capabilities. It is impacting peoples' management to produce the value of the organization's business.
- *Output* contains tangible or intangible results or deliverables. Tangible deliverables are the number of individuals, observable behavior and assessable skills and knowledge. Meanwhile, intangible results are the creation of people, social and organizational capital, capabilities and attachments, and opportunities for people to contribute.
- *Impact* contains the business/organization's impact.

Concerning the creation and development of knowledge, the Kirkpatrick model divides it into the following four categories:

1 *Reaction*: this evaluation measures how participants respond to actions of knowledge creation and sharing.
2 *Learning*: this process evaluates whether each individual knows and remembers the implementation of specific learning activities. These include testing the behavior and knowledge of participants before and after the actions and reactions.
3 *Behavior*: this category measures whether the individual/participant exhibits new skills and behaviors.
4 *Result*: this category requires an evaluation because the desired action has been successfully implemented and has had an impact on the business/organization.

Value chain mapping and the Kirkpatrick model are shown in Table 7.1. as

Table 7.1 Knowledge management model (Author's elaboration based on Toszewska, 2015)

Value Chain	*Description*	*Kirkpatrick Model*
Input	What are service key elements?	
	Who are our key customers?	
	What are our strategic objectives?	
Activity	Key performing indicators in human capital process.	
	What are the effects of actions?	Reaction
	What is the reaction of the recipients of services?	
	What are the relationship results from the employee's actions?	
	How do we develop knowledge of individual employees?	Learning
Output	Have skills and knowledge improved?	Behavior
	Has there been observable performance improvement?	
Impact	What is the knowledge influence on services?	Result
	What is the change to organizational culture?	

The pillar of knowledge

Information science

Here are some of the latest technologies in managing data and information:

- *Cloud computing*. This is a technology that provides applications and hardware and software systems in the data center by using internet-based services. This data center is known as the cloud. There are two types of cloud, public cloud and private cloud. Cloud-based applications offer the organization the opportunity to deliver products that are economical and inexpensive. This service also makes it easy to access data from anywhere for employees and customers.
- *Internet of Things*. IoT consists of devices that communicate and interact with each other to obtain, process and store data and information intelligently with adequate bandwidth, computing and storage capabilities.
- *Big data*. This is the study of the acquisition, storage, processing and display of complex data. An example of big data technology is Apache Hadoop.
- *Business intelligence and analytics* (BIA). Big data analytics (BDA) is a process to manage large amounts of data that have potential value to support decision-making. Most predictive analysis uses business intelligence (BI). BI provides information on trends in the past or on current events. Predictive analysis also uses business analytics (BA), commonly for predicting future results and utilizing data values. BA is used to plan, optimize service operations, estimate results, increase efficiency, make better decisions, offer new services and capture new opportunities (Bayrak, 2015). When developing BDA, it is necessary to define the five Vs: data volume (amount of data), velocity (speed of data moving), variety (many types of data), veracity (chaos or data trust) and value (the importance of the data) (Iqbal et al., 2020).

Information system

The desire to share information impacts the creation of an information system that supports this process. These information systems include:

1 *Enterprise resource planning* (ERP). ERP functions as a business application that provides a knowledge-sharing platform between various processes. The objective is increasing the company's internal capabilities effectively and efficiently.
2 *M-learning*. This is a form of distance learning using a mobile device for learning anytime and anywhere. The mobile phone offers several features such as telephone calls, text messages, access to social media and the internet, taking pictures and recording sound and video.
3 *Weblog*. Blogs are web-based writing tools that allow users to use the media to store writing online. The personal desire of the author to share knowledge influences weblog creation.

4 *Social media.* People use social media such as Facebook, Twitter, YouTube and LinkedIn for gathering people when there is an incident or when a disaster occurs. Social media can also improve the company's internal communication processes. It can become a medium for workers to share knowledge.

Data-to-information-to-knowledge-to-wisdom (DIKW) structures can be applied to knowledge management. The following provides a definition of each component (Baškarada & Koronios, 2013):

- *Data* are physical signs that have no meaning because they are still outside the human mind, such as characters in books, road signs, bits in computer memory and so on. Meanwhile, data quality is determined by the difference between physical characteristics and specifications.
- *Information* arises from processing data as the results of human (cognitive) thinking, for example, when reading books and watching TV. Meanwhile, the quality of information is determined by whether the information is suitable for its purpose. Using recipe A, food will taste better than that made from using recipe B, so recipe A has better information quality.
- *Knowledge* is a person's belief that is considered socially correct. For example, the sun is the center of the solar system. Cognitive behavioral therapy (CBT) is more effective in reducing fear (phobia), which is considered more effective than psychoanalytic therapy. Therefore, CBT has a better quality of knowledge than the psychotherapeutic method does.
- *Wisdom* is a normative assessment of a person's social desire. For example, we have to reduce carbon emissions. The wisdom quality is the wisdom that is appropriate for its purpose.

Knowledge information systems are built from the ground up. These start from the database and information tools and services. These are followed by the information integration layer, the knowledge processing layer and the presentation layer. One example is ITIL (IT infrastructure library) in the knowledge management domain that has created a service knowledge management system (SKMS).

KM tools

At the end of this chapter, we will explain how to use knowledge management tools, which are still relevant in using the following (Dilnutt, 2006):

- *Content management.* Content management is a knowledge management tool used to maintain information on web pages related to an organization's products or services so all employees and customers can find the information easily. Web content on XML should be made more attractive. The customers/employees can get the information in other formats such as pdf, Excel, Word, or PowerPoint. Content management provides access control and the use of appropriate information.

- *Document management*. This uses KM tools to manage information of unstructured documents through the management communication cycle, starting from the process of creating, storing and providing access to document usage. Documents are not structured because they can be text, images, sound, video, reports or graphics. Therefore, standard document settings are needed. These can be managed either by desktop or document management applications or by using the Open Document Management API by the Association for Information and Image Management.
- *Record management*. This is a derivative of document management. The objective is managing and protecting organizational information. Each document is given a classification based on its risk to the continuity of the organization's business. It has a retention period. Thus, a regular evaluation process is required. When the storage is no longer needed, it must be destroyed.
- *Collaboration tools*. These are tools that can facilitate communication between one individual and a group in a different place to share information or knowledge. Collaboration tools can include email, discussion forums, chat rooms, video conferencing and workflow applications.
- *Portal*. This technology provides easy access to information or knowledge in a structured or unstructured form. Portals can integrate data from various sources. Users do not need to log into every application and can get information from one portal.
- *Workflow*. This is a series of business process activities. A workflow is typically a stream of paper documents (usually automated) that collects data and consent.
- *Search and retrieval*. This tool or system is needed to help users find the necessary information or knowledge.
- *Imaging*. This is a method for entering data and information into databases or applications, whether by online entry or EDI (electronic data interchange). Physical documents are almost no longer needed and are turned into digital documents using barcode reading and optical character recognition.

Knowledge management process

Knowledge creation

The knowledge-creation process starts with business ideas coming from opportunities and concepts, designing models and establishing projects. Knowledge comes from an individual, then acknowledge by group level and become an organizational knowledge (Brix, 2017). Individual knowledge creation is an intuitive process from a person using their sensemaking approach to interpret new information (Figure 7.1).

Knowledge is formed from each individual when he or she finds an opportunity to solve a problem. Ideas that generate opportunities in the form of new information from each individual will be integrated and interpreted. Knowledge is also created through interaction process in a team/group by using sensemaking and

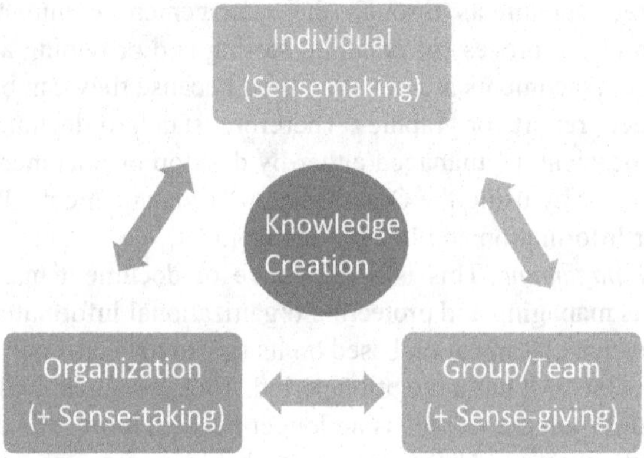

Figure 7.1 Knowledge creation

sense-giving approaches. Based on the collective knowledge and culture of the team/group, decisions are taken.

There will be new knowledge for all organization members with an approach to decision-making or sense-taking. The following are some definitions that support the references (Rom & Eyal, 2019):

- *Sensemaking* is how humans record, select and interpret ideas in their environment. They use their ideas to make it more meaningful. Sometimes each individual has different perceptions and ways of identifying and using them.
- *Sense-giving* is how humans try to influence other people's narratives with existing ideas.
- *Sense-taking* is how humans interpret and evaluate the narrative results of other people's ideas.

The organization knowledge is formed by the more acceptance ideas from individual to group idea and decision takingin the organization level.

The creation of knowledge cannot be freed from the basic understanding of knowledge, tacit and explicit knowledge. Knowledge tacit is thought and intuition that is very subjective and valuable but difficult to be caught and shared because it is in one's own mind. In contrast, explicit knowledge means official and systematic knowledge that is easy to get and share to every individual. There are four types of knowledge creation in an organization (Nonaka, 2007):

- *From tacit to tacit.* This means the process of sharing knowledge from one individual to another. It is also called socialization. For example, someone imitates others' work by observation and practice. This process is not able yet to increase the whole organization's knowledge.

- *From explicit to explicit*. This means that combination form several explicit knowledge into one knowledge bound; for example, reports from different several units combined into one reports. This process is not able yet to increase the organization's knowledge.
- *From tacit to explicit*. This means transformation from tacit knowledge to explicit knowledge. For example, there is a new approach or innovation that is different from the usual methods of the organization. This is called externalization. This process is able to increase and develop the organization's knowledge.
- *From explicit to tacit*. This means sharing explicit knowledge to all the individuals in one company so that there will be an internalization of knowledge. With that knowledge, employees are able to innovate or develop new methods to solve daily work faster or with higher quality. This process is also able to increase the organization's knowledge.

Knowledge sharing

The knowledge-sharing process will be considered the intention to share knowledge (intrinsic and extrinsic motivation), knowledge-sharing behavior (social interaction), the quantity of knowledge sharing and the quality of knowledge sharing (trust) (Uden & Hadzima, 2018). These considerations arise especially in virtual communities that want to share knowledge with others through media such as blogs, social networks, community aggregators, forums and content. The following is a detailed explanation of this understanding:

- *Intention to share knowledge*:
  - *Intrinsic motivation* is motivation to share knowledge in virtual communities. These motivations are usually not intended to get rewards but to acquire comfort, satisfaction and happiness in helping others.
  - *Extrinsic motivation* is motivation from outside to share knowledge because there is a specific goal to be achieved. It can result in appreciation and an improved reputation.
- *Knowledge-sharing behavior*, the habitual factor for sharing, is known by social capital factors. This social capital will influence every individual and group to share information. Characteristics of social capital such as network relationships, trust and social norms affect how a person relates to others to achieve goals.
- *Quantity of knowledge sharing* is how often (frequency) the virtual community shares knowledge.
- *Quality of knowledge sharing* is how much benefit or value is given from sharing knowledge to a virtual community.

Knowledge transfer

Knowledge transfer can be accomplished by mentoring, simulation, guide experience, work shadowing, paired work, the community of practice and e-learning (instructor-led learning). Some characteristics of knowledge are difficult to transfer because of the following (Newell, 2005):

- *Knowledge distribution.* The lack of knowledge distribution is a problem for recipients who may need that knowledge. Therefore, the recipient may wear a blindfold (knowledge blinder). They do not know whether it is helpful for them or others.
- *Ambiguous knowledge.* This causes problems for accepting knowledge that does not match one's view. Sometimes the recipient does not believe in knowledge transfer. It is not suitable for their mental perspective.
- *Disruptive knowledge.* This causes problems in receiving knowledge. It changes things that regularly happen when it threatens the basic views of the recipient. The recipient usually uses a strait jacket to protect themselves from the knowledge that threatens their fundamental strengths.

Knowledge innovation

Innovation is the successful creation, development and implementation of new and unprecedented ideas. This activity has the objective to upgrade the quality of a product, process or strategy. These result in commercial success and have the potential to lead the market and create value for stakeholders. Innovation drives economic growth and increases the standard of quality of life (Leber et al., 2015).

Innovation arises because of knowledge novelty, commercial aspects or value. Knowledge innovation is the process of the newness of existing knowledge. The knowledge is valuable. The knowledge affects the commercial aspects visible at the time of knowledge implementation. Innovation is a knowledge management process that releases new value from the knowledge assets of an organization.

Finally, we will discuss a study related to measuring knowledge creation and knowledge innovation. The aim is to understand the knowledge creation system in one department in a higher education organization (Anggraeni et al., 2017). A knowledge-making system was already in place. The learning environment was very conducive. The learning process was concrete and there was leadership. An average of three patents each year were created in this department. This means that the formation of knowledge and innovation of each individual was achievable. However, the distribution and commercialization of their agro-industrial innovation products were still limited. The openness of each individual to new ideas and exploring new approaches and thinking was very low. They felt safe in being different, so they were reluctant to explore new areas. Their knowledge only focused on individuals, while at the group level or with the external community it was still limited. The management took the initiative to increase effectiveness. They facilitated the knowledge-making process with external organizations, socialization forums (conferences, seminars, factory visits) and access to various external information.

Knowledge-driven competitive advantage

This realizes the importance of remaining competitive to succeed in achieving goals by extracting all potential knowledge from an organization's members (see Figure 7.2).

DATA TO INFORMATION

This section will discuss the ladder from the need for data to processing that data into a competitive advantage, which refers to the earlier discussion that information and knowledge come from data. What is the challenge of having a large amount of data? Data management is then performed by interpreting data, for example, by finding data patterns and grouping and classifying large amounts of data with neural networks or deep learning. With big data analytics technology, every organization seeks to exploit large amounts of data from the organization and turn it into information for insights. To recognize data, see patterns and classify large amounts of data, machine-learning algorithms such as neural networks are applied.

The system can extract data. Human knowledge can take action based on the information provided by the data (example: biometric recognition). Information obtained from data processing can also be monetized by looking at the preferences of customers. Optimizing products or services follow customer needs. The

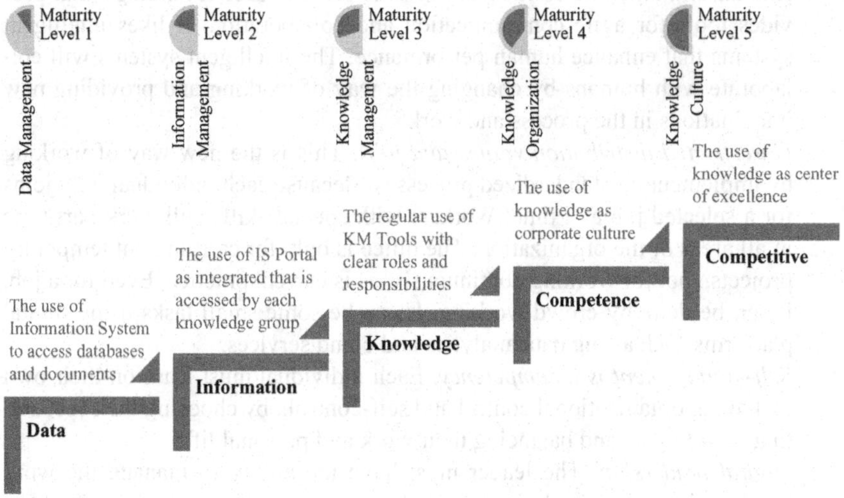

Figure 7.2 Knowledge ladder (Author's elaboration based on North & Maier, 2018)

company will survive if data and information continue generating income for an organization (North & Maier, 2018).

This stage is the first stage of the knowledge management maturity level. The focus is on managing information when implementing information and communication technology infrastructure to access databases and documents. It is similar to intranet creation and community platform development (North, 2018).

INFORMATION TO KNOWLEDGE

After converting data into information, how does one change this information into knowledge? In every process of extracting knowledge from information systems, it is necessary to add context, experience and expectations. Generally, the context begins with the systems that manage business processes. Then a content analysis is carried out to extract the context from the existing content. An example of grouping content is using semantic meanings such as a minute of meeting document, project proposal or product data sheet.

At this stage of the second maturity level, the use of information systems is deemed insufficient. Organizations create groups for the development of specific knowledge. It can be knowledge about services, customers and employees. An example of implementation at this stage is the establishment of a CRM system in a single portal. It can be accessed partially by each knowledge group. Especially for technical knowledge, the technical team will contribute a lot.

KNOWLEDGE TO COMPETENCE

This section discusses how to change knowledge into competence.

- *Human and machine collaboration*. This process uses technology that provides tools for agile communication and collaboration. It likes intelligent systems that enhance human performance. The intelligent systems will collaborate with humans by changing the way of working and providing new imaginations in the process and work.
- *Unrestricted distribution values and jobs*. This is the new way of working by implementing standardized processes. Because each individual only joins for a selected job at a time. Workers with special skills will work part-time in all areas of the organization. The office is only for carrying out temporary projects,. not for working continuously, as is current practice. Even for a job, it can be done by crowd working. It can be some small tasks using digital platforms such as big data analytics and cloud services.
- *Self-management is a competency*. Each individual must learn on their own by having organizational control and self-control,. by choosing their job, setting their targets and balancing their work and personal life.
- *Digital leadership*. The leader must have the ability to manage the work by changing from a culture of attendance to a culture of results, managing

capabilities to achieve organizational goals. This is helped by communication and information technology (North, 2018).

At this third maturity level, managers need to appoint processional knowledge organizations' cross-departmental and business units. One of the criteria is easy access to relevant information. Employees are awarded for sharing knowledge. They can integrate knowledge management into organizational goals, processes and projects. And they can exchange knowledge through competency centers and the benefits of measurable pieces of knowledge. An example, at this level, is the formation of KM tools with the division of roles and responsibilities, either centralized or distributed. Employees routinely attend the training to use KM tools.

COMPETENCE TO COMPETITIVE ADVANTAGE

Every organization develops dynamic capabilities by creating a digital business strategy (North & Maier, 2018). Capabilities consist of the following:

- *Sensing capabilities*: how to receive and process information and match the knowledge held or change it to get conclusions. It requires synchronizing with customer needs, technology and market trends and the business environment. The next challenge is how to inform changes in knowledge from organizations that share the same understanding.
- *Learning capabilities*: with the digitalization trends, there will be many changing opportunities and threats. That requires new learning and expertise to change products, services and business models. The challenge is how to integrate the fast-learning process in operational and organizational development.
- *Integration capabilities* how organizations build an understanding of knowledge, how to share knowledge and turn individual knowledge into team/ organization knowledge, and how knowledge contributes to the digital business of the organization and has economic value.
- *Coordination capabilities*: how to organize such that each worker accepts changes, systems are monitored and financial and human resources are supported. The challenge is how to manage the knowledge and training needs of each individual in facing the digital environment.

At the fourth maturity level, the exchange of knowledge has pulled out actively. It is no longer only between business units or internal organizations, but now includes the outside, such as customers, competitors, suppliers, technology, markets and others and the search for innovations within an open and trusted culture. The corporate culture supports mature information and communication systems and media, including many centers of competence. A center of excellence is the symbol of the fifth level of knowledge maturity, but only if the organization is successful at all levels of collaboration, knowledge sharing and continuous innovation.

One study shows that strategic knowledge management (SKM) can increase competitive advantage by high-level management support. The other things are company performance and the knowledge management process cycle (Shih et al., 2018). SKM was measured in an agribusiness industrial area in Vietnam. Top management support, knowledge management process cycle, knowledge management performance and firm performance were the four main aspects measured using 22 industry criteria and evaluated assessment from experienced experts. There was a gap between the SKM process and positive knowledge managed by top management. This knowledge was used to carry out the operations of the agribusiness industry. Company performance was supported competency development through learning and interaction, thereby increasing the ability to create product or service innovations. The knowledge management cycle process generated benefits from the use of information in company activities. In conclusion, it was recommended to improve the closed-loop knowledge management cycle process.

Conclusion

Information and knowledge are significant resources for competitive advantage in the digital economy. Organizations need to invest in managing information and knowledge. These create and enhance value and help organizations achieve their visions and missions. Without proper information and knowledge management, organizations are unable to compete in the digital economic environment. First, organizations or companies should understand the definition of data, information, knowledge and learning organization as their assets, so they can understand their current position and can take steps to get to the desired position. Knowledge foundation is namely organization, leadership, management models assisted by technology. Then they have to set their knowledge management process, which starts from the creation, sharing, transfer and innovation of knowledge. An understanding of data and information, information system support and documentation tools are required. This part will include methods of managing knowledge. It also includes information and knowledge sharing, organizational learning, knowledge organization and knowledge discovery. The ultimate goal is achieving competitive advantage by making a transition process from data, information, pieces of knowledge and competence knowledge. Specifically, the goal is to migrate from an information society to a data-driven society (see Figure 7.3).

For the future, the foundation of knowledge can be added to other components according to the differing needs of each organization or company. The pillar of knowledge can also be adjusted to current technological developments to technology that may develop in the future, for example with the increasing internet speed and cloud-based storage capacity. Meanwhile, the knowledge management process starts from data to become a catalyst for a competitive advantage that is unique to each organization. For this reason, it is necessary to carry out continuous studies so that the design of this knowledge management house develops and helps increase the number of organizations that can process data, information and knowledge maximally.

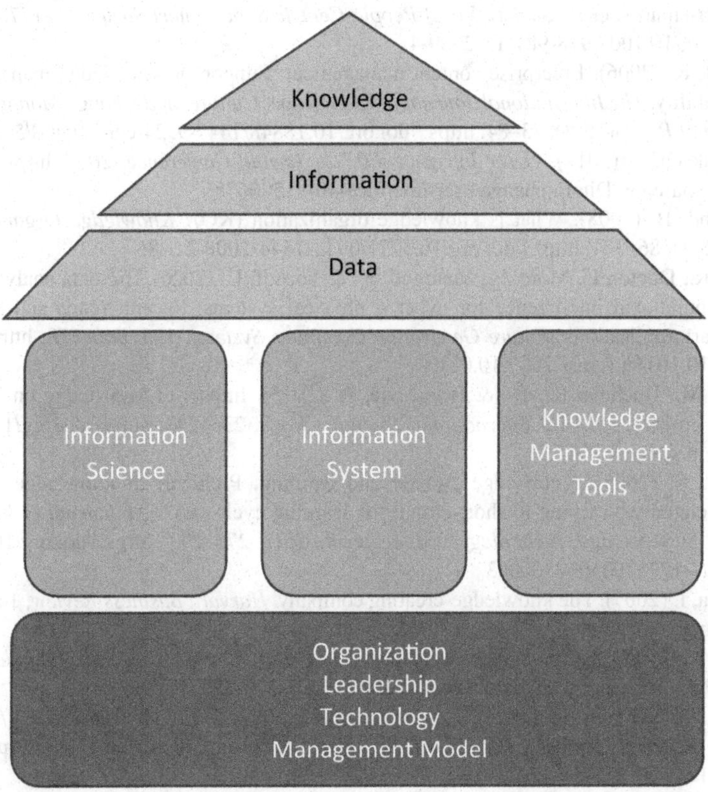

Figure 7.3 House of knowledge management

References

Anggraeni, E., Machfud, Maarif, M. S., & Hartrisari. (2017). Contextual-based knowledge creation for agroindustrial innovation. *Gadjah Mada International Journal of Business*, *19*(2), 97–122. https://doi.org/10.22146/gamaijb.23287

Baškarada, S., & Koronios, A. (2013). Data, information, knowledge, wisdom (DIKW): A semiotic theoretical and empirical exploration of the hierarchy and its quality dimension. *Australasian Journal of Information Systems*, *18*(1), 5–24. https://doi.org/10.3127/ajis.v18i1.748

Bayrak, T. (2015). A review of business analytics: A business enabler or another passing fad. *Procedia – Social and Behavioral Sciences*, *195*, 230–239. https://doi.org/10.1016/j.sbspro.2015.06.354

Benito-Osorio, D., Peris-Ortiz, M., Armengot, C. R., & Colino, A. (2013). Web 5.0: The future of emotional competences in higher education. *Global Business Perspectives*, *1*(3), 274–287. https://doi.org/10.1007/s40196-013-0016-5

Brix, J. (2017). Exploring knowledge creation processes as a source of organizational learning: A longitudinal case study of a public innovation project. *Scandinavian Journal of Management*, *33*(2), 113–127. https://doi.org/10.1016/j.scaman.2017.05.001

Deguchi, A., Hirai, C., Matsuoka, H., & Nakano, T. (2020). Society 5.0: A people-centric super-smart society. *Society 5.0: A People-Centric Super-Smart Society*, 1–177. https://doi.org/10.1007/978-981-15-2989-4

Dilnutt, R. (2006). Enterprise content management: Supporting knowledge management capability. *The International Journal of Knowledge, Culture, and Change Management: Annual Review*, *5*(8), 73–84. https://doi.org/10.18848/1447-9524/cgp/v05i08/50146

Frederiksen, S. (2017). "*User Interface 4.0,*" *at Tcwold Conference, 2017*. https://www.slideshare.net/DitaExchange/user-interface-40-81500678.

Hjørland, B. (2008). What is knowledge organization (KO)? *Knowledge Organization, 35*(2–3), 86–101. https://doi.org/10.5771/0943-7444-2008-2-3-86

Iqbal, R., Doctor, F., More, B., Mahmud, S., & Yousuf, U. (2020). Big data analytics and computational intelligence for cyber – physical systems: Recent trends and state of the art applications. *Future Generation Computer Systems*, *105*, 766–778. https://doi.org/10.1016/j.future.2017.10.021

Leber, M., Buchmeister, B., & Ivanisevic, A. (2015). Impact of knowledge on innovation process. *DAAAM International Scientific Book*, 235–248. https://doi.org/10.2507/daaam.scibook.2015.21

Newell, S. (2005). Knowledge transfer and learning: Problems of knowledge transfer associated with trying to short-circuit the learning cycle. *JISTEM Journal of Information Systems and Technology Management*, *2*(3), 275–290. https://doi.org/10.4301/s1807-17752005000300003

Nonaka, I. (2007). The knowledge-creating company. *Harvard Business Review*, 162–171. hbr.org

North, K. (2018). *Knowledge management value creation through organizational learning* (2nd ed.). Springer. https://doi.org/10.1007/978-3-319-59978-6

North, K., & Maier, R. (2018). *Knowledge management in digital change new findings and practical cases* (O. Haas, Ed.). Springer International Publishing AG. https://doi.org/10.1007/978-3-642-01665-3_71

Rom, N., & Eyal, O. (2019). Sensemaking, sense-breaking, sense-giving, and sense-taking: How educators construct meaning in complex policy environments. *Teaching and Teacher Education*, *78*, 62–74. https://doi.org/10.1016/j.tate.2018.11.008

Ruiz-Real, J. L., Uribe-Toril, J., Torres, J. A., & Pablo, J. D. E. (2021). Artificial intelligence in business and economics research: Trends and future. *Journal of Business Economics and Management*, *22*(1), 98–117. https://doi.org/10.3846/jbem.2020.13641

Shih, D. H., Lu, C. M., Lee, C. H., Parng, Y. J. M., Wu, K. J., & Tseng, M. L. (2018). A strategic knowledge management approach to circular agribusiness. *Sustainability (Switzerland)*, *10*(7), 1–21. https://doi.org/10.3390/su10072389Toszewska, W. (2015, May). Knowledge management model. *Polish Journal of Management Studies*, *12*. www.researchgate.net/publication/290455619

Uden, L., & Hadzima, B. (2018). Knowledge management in organizations. In I. Ting (Ed.), *Communications in computer and information science* (Vol. 877). KMO.

Vela, M. E. P., & Koong, S. N. (2017). Designing a fitted house of dynamic knowledge management strategy to strengthen competitive advantage: Qualitative research among UN agencies and their . . . www.diva-portal.org/smash/record.jsf?pid=diva2:1069880

8 Enterprise social media as knowledge management system in higher education institutions (HEIs)

Fahmi Ibrahim, Muhamad Sanusi Hussin, Heru Susanto and Norazillah Abdullah

Introduction

Higher education institutions (HEIs) or universities are in knowledge intensive environments and play a central role in knowledge creation and production through research, learning and teaching. As learning organisations, they will be able to extend knowledge skills, produce top-quality graduates and enhance innovation and creativity. Knowledge management (KM) has been typically discussed in relation to for-profit organisations, but it is important to consider that knowledge plays a vital role in HEIs, and thus they could benefit from established KM practices (Prahalad et al., 1990). In comparison, universities are in the business of generating and disseminating knowledge (Cheng et al., 2009). With this in mind, it has become evident to such institutions that KM is a valuable tool to meet organisational goals (Kidwell et al., 2000; Loh et al., 2010). In fact, KM has gained acceptance in the academic sector once it became clear that universities have a major role to play in the knowledge economy, bringing new challenges for HEIs (Abdullah et al., 2005; Sedziuviene & Vveinhardt, 2009). Accordingly, it might be reasonable to expect that universities would adopt a proactive approach to the development of KM strategies and that they would have a well-honed understanding how to manage and optimise the value of their knowledge assets.

HEIs are recognised to be in the knowledge business (Goddard, 1998), and increasingly they are exposed to marketplace pressures in a similar way to other businesses. It might be reasonable that KM has something to offer in HEIs, as Rowley (2000) posed the with question, "Is higher education ready for knowledge management?" There are challenges from HEIs, however, due to the individualistic nature of research (Tippins, 2003), the "idiosyncratic and complex" nature of academic departments (Lee, 2007), and loyalty to discipline rather than organisation (Cronin, 2000). Much of the research that has been conducted on KM and universities reflects on the ways in which universities differ from other working environments and the consequences for how knowledge might be managed and shared (Fullwood et al., 2013; Fullwood & Rowley, 2017). For instance, the educational landscape has evolved from a traditional teaching environment to a highly open and dynamic knowledge-based environment (Arntzen et al., 2009). This is

DOI: 10.4324/9781003224532-8

mainly due to the large adoption of computers, internet, intranet and instructional software applications, including social media on campus.

There are many enterprise social network channels developed by different companies like 'Yammer' by Microsoft, 'Connections' by IBM and the most recent one called 'Workplace' by Facebook, Inc., but they mainly cater to profit-making organisations. However, it is still unclear whether the use of this enterprise social media (ESM) can be applied to non-profit organisations such universities for the purpose of knowledge sharing. Hence, the aim of this chapter is to extend the knowledge within the literature and to explore KM practices through ESM while identifying the contributing factors that may facilitate and hinder the implementation, specifically in Brunei Darussalam.

Defining enterprise social media

Social media has revolutionised the way people communicate – a new virtual social world has been created in the cyberspace. There are many social media tools available for various type of user-generated contents that people can upload on the internet. Social media allows the users to do many things like blog (Blogger, WordPress), micro-blog (Twitter) and photo-blog (Instagram, Flickr) and engage in 'informal' social networking (Facebook, WhatsApp, Telegram), 'professional' social networking (Wikis, LinkedIn, Research Gate), content communities video (YouTube, TikTok) and various online board forums. Indeed, the availability of such powerful platforms allow individuals to create content, uniquely identifiable profiles, status updates, publicly articulated online sites, chat spaces and related discussions (Eid and Al-Jabri, 2016; Ellison et al., 2015; Everson et al., 2013). In sum, social media has transformed into a platform that facilitates information exchange between its users externally. From an organisational perspective, most organisations that use social media to communicate with external parties have a multipronged strategy that crosses various platforms (Piskorski, 2011). For this reason, ESM is described as follows:

> Web-based platforms that allow workers to (1) communicate messages with specific coworkers or broadcast messages to everyone in the organization; (2) explicitly indicate or implicitly reveal particular coworkers as communication partners; (3) post, edit, and sort text and files linked to themselves or others; and (4) view the messages, connections, text, and files communicated, posted, edited and sorted by anyone else in the organization at any time of their choosing.
>
> (Leonardi et al., 2013, p. 2)

In essence, ESM can be defined as internet-based platforms that allow employees to communicate messages with co-workers or broadcast messages to everyone in the organisation, post, edit and store text and files shared by themselves or others, and view the posts and communication by others online.

Social media and knowledge management

The fundamental idea of KM, as originally proposed, is dealing with the management of knowledge in related activities (Wiig, 1997). This includes creating, sharing and using knowledge in order to create value and achieve competitive advantage for an organisation. In the same line, social media refers to the activities through which people share their knowledge within a collaborative online environment (Papadopoulos et al., 2013), internet-based media that allows individuals to share information and knowledge (Chang & Chuang, 2011), and "the means of interactions between people in which they create, share, and exchange knowledge and ideas within virtual communities and networks" (Zeng & Gerritsen, 2014). Against this backdrop, KM successfully implemented through information technology (IT), particularly social media within an organisation, has a great role to play.

Based on the view that social media is a technology which has and will transform the means of communication, collaboration and networking, this chapter presupposes that social media challenges an organisation's KM processes too. It shows the important role of IT in KM through social media. It is important to note that IT consists of a combination of hardware and software technologies (Ruikar et al., 2007), including social media. However, the role of IT (both hardware and software) in KM rests predominantly on the key assumptions of the *objectivist perspective* or *practice-based perspective* (Ibrahim et al., 2009; Ibrahim & Reid, 2010; Ibrahim & Sallleh, 2019; Ibrahim & Ali, 2021). This refers to the codification and personalisation KM strategy coined by Hansen et al. (1999).

Building on the assumptions of the objectivist perspective, organisations believe that IT can play a direct role in the knowledge-sharing process. In other words, IT is a 'driver' of KM practices. Yet, IT simply acts as a medium to search, codify, categorise, store and share explicit knowledge (Hislop, 2005, p. 108). So, in principle, IT seems to offer people – and the organisations for which they work faster, cheaper and broader sources of data and to enable them to generate and share knowledge. Although great claims have been made about the use of IT for KM, there are limitations for such initiatives which rely heavily on IT. There is much more to KM than the technology alone (Sarvary, 1999, p. 95). This confirms arguments that there has been far too much reliance on the idea that KM has to do with IT. The problem of over-reliance on IT-driven KM is supported by evidence that there is no direct correlation between IT investment and business performance or KM (Malhotra, 1998; Strassman, 1997).

The criticisms of the role of IT in KM from an objectivist perspective have not led to a position where the role of IT is questioned. For example, IT supports knowledge sharing through video conferencing, social media within or between community of practices, without losing tacitness of knowledge. According to Newell et al. (2002), organisations using a personalisation strategy encourage knowledge and experience sharing. The application of information technology in a personalisation strategy is a means to locate knowledgeable people and enable efficient communication (Hansen et al., 1999). Therefore, those who emphasise the 'people side' of KM still believe that IT can play a role as an 'enabler' in relation to facilitating and supporting the social relationships, collaborations and communication processes which underpin the KM process. Hansen et al. (1999) concluded that organisations must decide which of the two KM strategies to follow. Organisations that try to exploit both strategies risk the failure of both. As an approximate division, Hansen et al. (1999) suggest an 80–20 split: 80 per cent of the organisation's knowledge practices follows one strategy, 20 per cent the other.

Nevertheless, Ibrahim et al. (2009) proposed a hybrid towards a comprehensive framework that provides a balanced view of both KM strategies. In particular, a framework called KMPro was developed as a guideline which is applicable in higher education institutions (HEIs) for the understanding of the role of KM through its practical manifestations (Ibrahim & Ali, 2021). HEIs have embraced information technology, which has resulted in the development of techno-centric institutional infrastructures and wired classrooms in colleges and universities (Metcalfe, 2006). The use of information and communication technologies (ICT) provides a mean to fulfil numerous requirements and challenges that need to be overcome, such as providing lectures anytime, anywhere or increasing and to improving the communication between faculty, staff and students.

Methodology

There is a lack of research on the use of social media tools for KM and knowledge sharing specifically in the university context, indicating that this topic is still in its infancy. Hence, a qualitative research method is adopted to get in-depth data that is specific for Brunei's context. Eleven semi-structured interviews were conducted with university academics from the three universities in Brunei: Universiti Brunei Darussalam (UBD), Universiti Teknologi Brunei (UTB) and Universiti Islam Sultan Sharif Ali (UNISSA). Thematic analysis was used to analyse the interview data, which involved creating a framework as a method to manage the themes and data. It is "a method for identifying, analysing, and reporting patterns" (themes) within data. This study followed the six processes of thematic analysis suggested by Clarke and Braun (2013).

Findings and discussions

Perceived practice and concept of ESM

Enterprise social media is a social web application similar to social media but run on a private network within a specific organisation. One of the benefits of ESM is that it creates a network or community of people that share a common goal or objective. Thus, any activities or knowledge transfer using ESM will be within a specific organisational context.

The interview analysis, when the concept of ESM was introduced, showed various positive and negative responses. The positive responses indicated that participants were keen on inter-university collaboration and expanding their research database as well as to facilitating communication for sharing content and experiences.

> It's good because we can share our interests . . . we can share the new issues with other academics, we can share the challenges we are facing . . . because I am still junior, so there are other Professors who I can ask them online easily without boundaries and without having to meet them.
>
> (Interviewee 2)

> I think ESM should be encouraged to be implemented because from my experience doing research in overseas, various of databases with different of information to share.
>
> (Interviewee 3)

> It's a good thing because it allows integration within university.
>
> (Interviewee 5)

> We'd love to learn from others' success stories and mistakes.
>
> (Interviewee 6)

Nevertheless, the negative responses reasoned on a preference for physical collaboration than for virtual communication.

> I prefer physical collaborationeven communication can be done via Email and WhatsApp.
>
> (Interviewee 7)

In comparison to common social media, ESM gives an opportunity for the users to benefit without revealing their private life because the accounts are usually created within the company's network or intranet, so they do not have to mix it with their private social media accounts. However, there could be an issue of privacy and ownership leading to budget and staff planning that implied scepticism towards ESM;

> So there's other things that need to be looked at, if you say that one university is going to be in charge of hosting the data, there will be budget issues, and also are they going to have enough manpower to look after the servers, applications and so on.
>
> (Interviewee 4)

> We are given a certain amount of money to do research . . . but the amount itself is quite limited to some extent.
>
> (Interviewee 8)

> One thing is that the university is not subscribing to everything we need . . . because they can be very costly. The resources are limited; we can't get everything online for free.
>
> (Interviewee 9)

Another confidentiality issue is with regard to sharing teaching materials that may be a source of competitive advantage.

> But for . . . materials that are specifically for new modules, this could be a slight issue, because universities have to be competitive, they have to be at the forefront in their area. So this means if you are giving up something new, within a very short time, other universities will also be providing the same material.
>
> (Interviewee 4)

In a similar view on research context, for instance, if someone posted the initial raw research idea on a public space, anyone can just replicate the idea, make some adjustments and publish it.

> Not everything online can be trusted and not all knowledge can be disclosed to the public.
>
> (Interviewee 9)

> Misuse of knowledge, trusted resources and accuracy of information.
>
> (Interviewee 10)

These arguments derived from the objectivist perspective assume that all or most relevant knowledge can be made explicit or codifiable whilst the practice-based perspective argues that much tacit knowledge can never be made explicit, as argued by Hislop (2005). This will not endanger the 'knowledge' sharing, as it suggests that tacit knowledge can be accessed through the use of metaphor and direct storytelling, and ESM has the capability to personalise the sharing without losing a high degree of tacitness.

Usability is one of the determining factors that may encourage the usage of ESM. It was stated that the platform needs to be intuitive or otherwise it will be rendered useless and redundant with other technology. When people are not familiar with a new technology, they tend to abandon it and revert to their old methods.

> If it is not user friendly, I tend not to use it. Physical collaboration needs to happen first.
>
> (Interviewee 8)

> People must be well-versed in this platform because every time we implement new technology, people will give up on using, not knowing how to use it.
>
> (Interviewee 7)

It is suggested to have a training and development program within the organisation that can ensure that employees are comfortable with the platform, encouraging them to use it more often as it more convenient.

> There needs to be a facilitator to ensure people will use it and actually participate in knowledge-sharing activities.
>
> (Interviewee 3)

> Training is needed to convince them the [ESM] platform is actually beneficial.
>
> (Interviewee 7)

> So before this concept ESM can even happen, the physical collaboration needs to happen first.
>
> (Interviewee 8)

While training and development is important for staff, reasonable technology infrastructure should be developed to have effective ESM implementation. The findings highlighted the reliability of the university internet connection when using ESM. They have encountered lagging and disconnected signal issues at their workplace.

> There were technical issues such internet lagging and weak signal.
>
> (Interviewee 1)

> The server tends to go down and takes time to get fixed so I'd rather use traditional method.
>
> (Interviewee 8)

> Technical is always an issue . . . usefulness and easiness is very important.
>
> (Interviewee 9)

It was mentioned that issues were managed inefficiently by the maintenance team of their university, indicating the lack of staff organisation and technology infrastructure. In summary, the responses demonstrate the perceived usefulness of ESM implementation, although few of contradicts views perhaps more towards lacks of conceptual understanding of knowledge type can be utilised for benefit of organisation.

Significance of knowledge sharing

This section addresses the respondents' understanding of 'knowledge sharing' as a term. Addressing this understanding was not a core objective of the study but emerged as an important theme during the interviews. Given the extensive use of the term knowledge sharing in the literature, but not in the HEIs' context of ESM, some consideration of how the term is understood from the interviewee's point of view was merited. In general, the participants defined knowledge sharing in the context of their own practices and implementation. This can be seen through the recognition of the importance of knowledge sharing held by key and experienced people categorised as teaching-related, research related and admin-related as demonstrated by the following extract taken from the interview with the Interviewee 2.

> But there are three different things, one, teaching-related knowledge sharing, another one is admin-related knowledge sharing . . . for example Facebook we only have a private group on Facebook where they can share information and sometimes and to someone if you want to share research-related information it goes out.
>
> (Interviewee 2)

This categorisation has helped in analysing what social media functions are frequently used the most when handling matters related to knowledge sharing.

> Yes, I can help others by sharing knowledge through social media and expand our knowledge outside the box.
>
> (Interviewee 7)

> I learnt a lot from the knowledge that my colleague shared regarding their experiences.
>
> (Interview 5)

It has been highlighted in the literature that knowledge is claimed as the main distinguishing factor of business success and competitive advantage (Carlucci & Schiuma, 2006; Pan & Scarborough, 1999) and adds value to organisations (Ibrahim & Reid, 2010). The findings demonstrated how knowledge sharing is beneficial to their work practices.

> So, sharing actually reduces your work and I can use the time for something else, which is more creative.
>
> (Interviewee 1)

> We do knowledge sharing practices all the time . . . sometimes when it is not formally required, we still do share our knowledge via social media because when we think that this particular knowledge can help with our common goals . . . then that's when we automatically share.
>
> (Interviewee 4)

> It reduces amount of work, can learn from mistakes of others so they don't have to reinvent the wheel.
>
> (Interview 2)

This is aligned with what has been highlighted by Christensen (2007) to "discover new knowledge by combining a variety of existing knowledge or develop an expertise to manipulate the existing knowledge."

Another determining factor of successful knowledge-sharing activities in an organisation is its culture and environment. From the findings, all of the interviewees believe that their universities do not enforce a knowledge-sharing culture but that it is strongly encouraged by the university academics because it is considered part of their jobs facilitated by ESM.

> It is an encouraging environment for knowledge sharing and we use technology [ESM] to enhance it.
>
> (Interviewee 1)

> It is normal culture for us to share knowledge and even more with the social media technology.
>
> (Interviewee 3)

> . . . not mandatory but it is encouraged in a way.
>
> (Interviewee 10)

From the data analysis, it was revealed that all of the researchers believe that their universities promote a healthy environment for knowledge-sharing activities. However, two interviewees revealed some underlying issue of knowledge sharing in universities in terms of research activities;

> . . . there's lack of research culture in the faculty, in our university or in Brunei as well . . . people don't value research, I'm not saying that people don't value but the recognition, in terms of recognizing that the research will contribute positively to society and to the faculty . . . it's still not there.
>
> (Interviewee 8)

The issue highlighted here is the research culture in local universities. The interviewee then elaborated more on the issue.

> We are given a certain amount of money to do research. Research in terms of going to conferences and so forth . . . but the amount itself is quite limited to some extent.
>
> (Interviewee 8)

The response indicated that the reward and recognition should make the importance of appropriate knowledge sharing visible. Davenport (cited in Wah, 1999) suggested that sharing knowledge is usually considered a sideline activity, and employees will only take it seriously when rewards are built into compensation and benefits packages. Further, he noted, "the best kind of knowledge transfer is informal, but the best way to get knowledge transferred is to reward people for transferring it" (Davenport, quoted in Wah, 1999, p. 27). Rewards could range from monetary (extrinsic) incentives, such as bonuses, and research funds to non-monetary (intrinsic) incentives, such as such as praise and public recognition that do not have a monetary value (Bartol & Srivastava, 2002). Accordingly, people need incentives to participate in the knowledge-sharing process (Hansen et al., 1999, p. 113).

> I don't know if it is because of the hierarchical structure or the power-distance balance in the context of our region . . . so it's, people are scrutinising you when you share your knowledge, they judge you, they question you, and they expect you to be the expert in your field.
>
> (Interviewee 8)

> But in other countries, the case is quite different . . . for example if there are any research loopholes in your research so they are there to provide guidance and to give advice, so it's more like a platform, a friendly discussion compared to the context of Brunei. Here they expect you to know everything, but you know everyone is still learning . . . so yeah, the culture is quite different. So I think that is one of the hindrances, why the faculty members might be reluctant to share knowledge even with social media technology.
>
> (Interviewee 8)

Basically, the responses refer to knowledge-sharing motivations, and social behaviour depends on individuals' personal values (Ibrahim & Barr, 2009). According to Schein (2004), culture can be defined as shared values, beliefs and practices of the people in organisations that refer to the 'ways things are done in the organisation.' It is described further that culture is tightly connected to certain groups of people in organisations who have been working together for a considerable length of time; throughout this period they have developed certain behaviours to deal with and solve problems as well as a collective identity and know-how to work together effectively (Ribiere & Sitar, 2003, p. 40). Based on the aforementioned, the primary determinant of knowledge sharing is a culture that emphasises and encourages active participation in knowledge sharing. In an organisation with a knowledge-sharing culture, people would share ideas and insights because they see it as natural, rather than something they are forced to do (McDermott & O'Dell, 2001).

Hofstede's cultural taxonomy has been extensively validated and can be applied to explain the national knowledge-sharing culture of Brunei. Hofstede (2001) defined culture as "the collective mental programming of the human mind" which distinguishes the members of one human group from another. Based on the findings, there are two work-related cultural dimensions – *power distance* and *individualism* – that are related to Hofstede's (2001) national cultural taxonomy explanations. Power distance is the extent that people within a society accept that power is distributed unequally.

In view of Brunei's socio-political tradition of monarchy rule, it shapes knowledge-sharing culture with high power distance. The way the distribution of power is perceived and how power is defined are subject to each culture's biases. Some cultures are able to perceive positive 'inequality,' such as Brunei, and some aren't. High-power-distance cultures tend to value things like tradition, which keeps society stable and prevents massive changes to power relations. They also tend to be very hierarchical, which means that people are ranked within society. This also means, in theory, that these cultures tend to place little emphasis (low) on individualism (opposite to *collectivism*), where people are discouraged to solve problem by themselves. Therefore, Brunei societies are very collectivistic societies, in which people from birth onwards are integrated into strong, cohesive in-groups, often extended families, which continue protecting them in exchange for unquestioning loyalty (Blunt, 1989). Collectivistic societies prefer being in a close group, whether it's a business group, working group, religious group or family. Anything that could harm or endanger the group could mean a loss in pride or shame or even worse a loss of face – loss of face is a big deal to this society, as face is a reference to reputation. However, the theory is contradicted in this study as the findings show a high emphasis on individualism, where academic staff has little collaborative support from colleagues and it is expected he/she knows everything. This implies the uniqueness of the knowledge-sharing culture in the Brunei context.

However, IT utilisation in knowledge sharing has led to criticisms that IT alone would not be adequate for knowledge sharing. This suggests that people are capable of successful knowledge sharing. For knowledge to be shared there has to be voluntary action on behalf of the individual. This is because to share knowledge is a human characteristic, before engaging technology social media. Moreover, technology alone would not result in an individual who is uninterested in seeking knowledge to use a computer and start searching and browsing. This means IT is, arguably, not able to facilitate knowledge sharing if people do not use it.

It is often perceived that the value of knowledge depends on how tacit it is; more tacit tends to hold higher values (Dalkir, 2005). From the analysis, it was implied that it is not possible that tacit knowledge can be shared and transferred through online platform such as ESM. From the study, FAQs are classified as 'technical tacit knowledge' which has been codified, and this is evidence of the possibility of tacit knowledge transfer through an IT medium. This is a codification process where tacit knowledge is codified to explicit knowledge in the form of FAQs. In return, FAQ knowledge can be internalised into tacit knowledge from the interactive process of the receiver.

FAQ is an abbreviation for frequently asked question. It entails a list of questions that are commonly asked in some context and concerning with a specific topic and the answers to the questions. FAQs are commonly found in online forums, and they are usually generated based on people's experiences when encountering problems and their solutions.

> I would like to see actually is like more on like blogs . . . or FAQs, topic-wise, descriptions – things like that. This is the one that would be critical for knowledge sharing.
>
> (Interviewee 3)

> I learnt a lot from others' mistakes and problem solving – FAQs.
>
> (Interviewee 2)

> So if there are issues, ok, so many people have already faced the issue, so we won't have to reinvent the wheel, spending lots of hours debugging the problem right? So the issue is already solved so you just go online, go to the blog, FAQs, and look for the particular problem and just solve the problem. So I have used many of these for my projects.
>
> (Interviewee 4)

The criticisms of the role played by IT highlights the significant implications of the findings into the way that knowledge particularly is conceptualised. It is worth briefly restating that, on the one hand, knowledge is explicit in the form of an entity/object than can be codified and stored by using IT in the form of FAQs. On the other hand, knowledge is tacit and only exists because of people. Therefore, despite the extensive utilisation, IT has its limitations in capturing tacit knowledge. In reference to the literature, FAQs can be considered the end-product of the tacit knowledge conversion process, thus proving that tacit knowledge sharing through IT is actually possible. Having analysed the findings with regard to the role of technology social media, the most substantial issue is that knowledge sharing is not IT but rather IT is an enabler for knowledge-sharing practices. Nevertheless, the findings did not lead to a position where IT was regarded as having no useful role at all.

Perceived usefulness of ESM

Interviews with the participants have disclosed several themes related to the perceived usefulness resulting from ESM usage. It is important to note that the findings are based on interviewee's perceptions and their own context. The findings have indicated that the advantages of using ESM platforms are their stability, low cost, effective and efficient way of delivering messages and responsiveness.

> Because it's a very low-cost technology.
>
> (Interviewee 1)

> It is easiest way to upload resources, very useful and faster communication.
>
> (Interviewee 3)

> When using chats in LMS, WhatsApp to me it's very convenient and efficient . . . it is very important, for instance to inform meetings, make announcements and so on because not everyone checks their email all the time so WhatsApp is faster.
>
> (Interviewee 5)

> Social media is a good platform to get latest updates on new knowledge.
>
> (Interview 7)

> So for me WhatsApp is the most efficient way to communicate and to get the fastest response.
>
> (Interviewee 6)

However, the high response rate may also cause inconvenience and be disruptive to the users.

> they have too high expectations when waiting for responses . . . this means that when we ask for a piece of information or some data. It means that usually people are expecting fast responses . . . and this can lead to problems with regards to work-life balance . . . if social media usage is not controlled then requests can happen in the evenings, after work hours . . . So the downside would be if it is not properly controlled with regards to timing of the access, then it can disrupt personal time.
>
> (Interviewee 4)

> Privacy issues especially when using WhatsApp [which] oversteps the boundaries and disrupts work life balance.
>
> (Interview 6)

> I don't like the idea of public network.
>
> (Interviewee 2)

In the findings, the issue was between the privacy and the hassle of maintaining separate accounts when using the normal social media. Using ESM may solve that problem because it can provide a professional working environment within a social network. Nevertheless, the 'professional look' has the disadvantages with its absence of social cues in online platform; such ESM can be problematic.

> Sometimes you write something and other people look at it, it's not actually what you mean.
>
> (Interviewee 10)

> To some extent misinterpretation of messages can happen.
>
> (Interviewee 10)

In face-to-face communication, we can read social cues like body language, eye contact, presence, emotions and gestures. This, however, will be difficult to portray or detect when using IT as the medium. However, these social cues may only be needed when the knowledge to be shared is of a high degree of tacitness. For knowledge with a low to medium degree of tacitness, people prefer to use existing technologies to overcome geographical distance, time and cost barriers. However, with the advent of high-speed broadband internet, video conferencing quality will improve and the issues regarding reading social cues will disappear (Panahi et al.,

2013). In contrast, it was discovered that not necessarily all respondents are really concerned with the lack of social cues.

> As for the absence of social cues in social media, I don't really think it is a problem. It is up to the person actually, but in email it seems more 'gentle' because it is more 'official' because it uses the university email, whereas in Chat/WhatsApp it is a bit informal.
>
> (Interviewee 3)

This suggests that a social media platform has some sort of context, where any message conveyed will be personalised accordingly. This indicates good understanding of the virtual space of social media. ESM offers more social media functions; communication and collaboration that do not require social cues. For instance, the findings show that the communication function includes the sharing and storing of files such as journal articles in Dropbox or Google Drive and then connecting the links to their colleagues, and further discussions and announcements regarding meetings, conferences via chats or WhatsApp. On the other hand, learning management systems (LMS) provide tools and applications for educators to share learning materials and enable the students to share study materials, projects and research materials. It also enables educators to post assessment grades, create forums and chat online. Comparatively, LMS features the same characteristics that other social media provides. However, it was claimed that LMS has limited social cues, lacks stability, and has user interfaces that are not user friendly and responsive in comparison to WhatsApp. This has led users to have a high preference for other informal social media mechanisms. Correspondingly, Google Docs was used for collaboration purposes, although it was only for a short period of time for a specific project. This shows that apart from communication and collaboration, ESM provides a connecting function which can revolutionise the way people do networking or socialise into a specific community (Jalonen, 2014).

Conceptual ESkM model development and recommendation

Given a growing awareness amongst practitioners and researchers concerning the implementation of social media in organisations, this study has provided a new impetus to KM. In examining how ESM tools can enable staff and student knowledge sharing in an HEI, this research has produced a number of findings which informs both theory and practice and which can be used as a basis for guidelines. This study has investigated ESM potential for KM practices and highlighted issues involving conceptual understanding, knowledge-sharing culture and perceived usefulness. Based on this review, we propose a model – ESkM (E–enterprise, S–social, k–knowledge, M–management) for the adoption and effective implementation of enterprise social media as a KM system in HEIs (see Figure 8.1). Lower-case 'k' in ESkM indicates that the 'knowledge' component is vital significantly and *implicitly* in the nexus of social media and KM discussion. The model adopts a holistic view of ESM adoption that incorporates four key

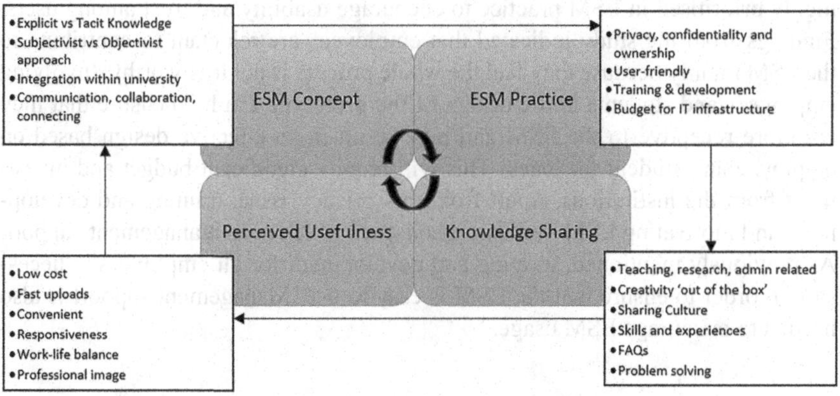

Figure 8.1 Enterprise social media knowledge management (ESkM) model

activities: establishing a concept for the ESM, ESM practice strategy, knowledge sharing and perceived usefulness. In the next section, we discuss each of these elements in greater detail.

ESM concept

It was necessary at the start of this study to identify a suitable definition and understanding of the concept of ESM which is embedded in KM practices. However, in order to identify the definition and understand the concept of ESM, the nature and characteristics of social media should be defined and clearly understood. Significantly, this is important because it not only provides an insight into how the nature of knowledge has been conceptualised, but also provides the roots of ESM practices. In the literature review, it was discovered that many definitions can be perceived as knowledge. Knowledge relates to epistemological differences which can be categorised into two perspectives: objectivist perspective (i.e. explicit knowledge) and practice-based perspective (i.e. tacit knowledge). On the other hand, social media is considered a tool for facilitating communication, collaboration and connecting mechanisms and bringing people together through sharing content, which is known as user-generated communication for the purpose of integration within an organisation. Understanding the concepts is crucial as a characteristic of ESM, as it differentiates to other common social media practices.

ESM practice

Organisations also need to adopt a strategy for the design and implementation of the ESM. This includes selecting the appropriate ESM based on the information-knowledge needs of the institutions. Whichever ESM platform is selected, it should have a friendly and familiar interface, as it is the communication mode

ESM is built upon. In addition, privacy, confidentiality and ownership should be highly prioritised in ESM practice to encourage usability and trust among users. Findings from the study indicated that employees are reluctant to contribute to the ESM mainly because they feel the whole process is not trustworthy. Involving employees and students in the design of the prototype can help ensure that they are more receptive to the ESM and may result in an effective design based on employee and student feedback. This will require significant budget and investment from the institutions. Apart from this privacy issue, training and development and motivating ESM users are also issues which need management support. As previously mentioned, training and development for all employees is necessary in order to ensure that the ESM is easy to use. Management support is also needed to encourage ESM usage.

Knowledge sharing

Knowledge sharing is a central issue in social media literature with researchers mainly focusing on why employees are reluctant to share knowledge. It is suggested that an organisation's culture affects how employees collaborate and share knowledge. For instance, McAfee (2009, p. 26) refers to the culture as "receptive" and "fertile to cultivate new collaborative practices." Similarly, Buffa (2006) argues that there is a strong sharing culture at Google where "employees are pushed to share freely and to learn from each other." Davenport et al. (1998) argue that a knowledge-friendly culture is one of the most difficult to create if it does not exist already. However, according to Gurteen (1999), any organisation can create a knowledge-sharing culture by encouraging employees to work together more collaboratively and share. Although the findings discussed the uniqueness of the knowledge-sharing culture in the Brunei context with *high power distance* and *high individualism* in reference Hofstede's cultural theory, it is suggested that an organisational culture that supports collaboration and knowledge sharing is enabled by an organisational structure that is non-hierarchical and where there is democratisation of knowledge. In HEIs, knowledge sharing is significant as they will be able to extend knowledge skills and experiences, produce top-quality graduates and enhance innovation and creativity. The practice is beneficial in a wide range of HEIs activities, including teaching and research admin works.

Perceived usefulness

The findings reported that perceived usefulness is gained in the practice of ESM. Basically, perceived usefulness is determined and described through the implication and benefits of the ESM. Given that education service is the organisations' nature of business, there is a link between ESM and operational benefits, which suggests that the main reason is because the role of ESM is aimed at improving communication and collaboration processes, which are embedded in the organisation's strategy. In terms of operational benefits, ESM is low cost, faster and convenient to users. Teaching, research and admin processes were improved through conversations and discussions that can generate invaluable knowledge. Employees may not know how to share knowledge via ESM, but they can be taught especially if the benefits of knowledge sharing and ESM are made explicit. These benefits include working more effectively with responsive feedback, work-life balance with privacy restriction on communications, along with a professional outlook.

Conclusions

ESM is likely to remain an important tool for KM systems. ESM will have a positive impact on organisational communication, knowledge sharing and perceived usefulness. However, adopting a social platform such as ESM in HEIs will not be a straightforward exercise. One of the critical success factors in ESM adoption is the state of readiness of the organisation, that is, the extent to which an organisation has a conceptual understanding of ESM practice and is able and prepared to realise the benefits from the use of ESM. In the same line, successful KM practices through IT, particularly ESM, within an organisation plays a significant role. ESM is a technology which has transformed the means of communication, collaboration and networking. It shows the important role of IT in KM through social media. The social media phenomenon has gathered substantial support within KM practices. It has its foundations in a grassroots approach, and much of its appeal is related to its knowledge philosophy. We argue that the successful adoption of ESM requires a formal and structured approach that addresses four key areas as shown in Figure 8.1: understanding the ESM concept, having the right characteristics of ESM practice, driving knowledge sharing and realising suitable perceived usefulness. The model developed in this study has the potential to provide a guideline for HEIs practitioners to succeed in ESM practices. In addition, it can serve as a useful guideline for drawing attention to the theoretical underpinnings of the concept of knowledge as well as KM, understanding the interplay between these two and the knowledge-sharing process.

References

Abdullah, R., Selamat, M. H., Sahibudin, S., & Alias, R. A. (2005, March). A framework for knowledge management system implementation in collaborative environment for higher learning institution. *Journal of Knowledge Management Practice*, *110*.

Arntzen, A. A. B., Worasinchai, L., & Ribière, V. M. (2009). An insight into knowledge management practices at Bangkok university. *Journal of Knowledge Management*, *13*(2), 127–144.

Bartol, K. M., & Srivastava, A. (2002). Encouraging knowledge sharing: The role of organizational reward systems. *Journal of Leadership and Organization Studies*, *9*(1), 64–76.

Blunt, P. (1989). Cultural consequences for organization change in a Southeast Asian state: Brunei. *The Academy of Management Executive*, *2*(3), 235–240.

Buffa, M. (2006). *Intranet wikis*. Paper presented at the Intraweb Workshop, WWW2006. http://www-sop.inria.fr/acacia/WORKSHOPS/IntraWebs2006/Buffa_Intrawebs2006.pdf

Carlucci, D., & Schiuma, G. (2006). Knowledge value spiral: Linking knowledge assets to company performance. *Knowledge and Process Management*, *13*(1), 35–46.

Chang, H. H., & Chuang, S. S. (2011). Social capital and individual motivations on knowledge sharing: Participant involvement as a moderator. *Information Management*, *48*(1), 9–18.

Cheng, M. Y., Ho, J. S. Y., & Lau, P. M. (2009). Knowledge sharing in academic institutions: A study of multimedia university Malaysia. *Electronic Journal of Knowledge Management*, *7*(3), 313–324.

Christensen, P. H. (2007). Knowledge sharing: Moving away from the obsession with best practices. *Journal of Knowledge Management*, *11*(1), 36–47.

Clarke, V., & Braun, V. (2013). *Successful qualitative research: A practical guide for beginners*. Sage.

Cronin, B. (2000). Knowledge management, organisational culture and Anglo-American higher education. *Journal of Information Science*, *27*(3), 129–137.

Dalkir, K. (2005). *Knowledge management in theory and practice*. Elsevier, Butterworth Heineman.

Davenport, T. H., De Long, D. W., & Beers, M. C. (1998). Successful knowledge management projects, *Sloan Management Review*, *39*(2).

Eid, M. I., & Al-Jabri, I. M. (2016). Social networking, knowledge sharing, and student learning: The case of university students. *Computers & Education*, *99*, 14–27.

Ellison, N. B., Gibbs, J. L., Weber, M. S. (2015). The use of enterprise social network sites for knowledge sharing in distributed organizations: The role of organizational affordances. *American Behavior Science*, *59*(1), 103–123.

Everson, M., Gundlach, E., & Miller, J. (2013). Social media and the introductory statistics course. *Computers in Human Behavior*, *29*(5), A69–A81.

Fullwood, R., & Rowley, J. (2017). An investigation of factors affecting knowledge sharing amongst UK academics. *Journal of Knowledge Management*, *21*(5), 1254–1271.

Fullwood, R., Rowley, J., & Delbridge, R. (2013). Knowledge sharing amongst academics in UK universities. *Journal of Knowledge Management*, *17*(1), 123–136. https://doi.org/10.1108/13673271311300831

Goddard, A. (1998, November). Facing up to market forces. *Times Higher Educational Supplement*, *13*, 6–7.

Gurteen, D. (1999). Creating a knowledge-sharing culture. *Knowledge Management*, *2*(5).

Hansen, M. T., Nohria, N., & Tierney, T. (1999, March–April). What's your strategy for managing knowledge. *Harvard Business Review*, 106–116.

Hislop, D. (2005). *Knowledge management in organisations*. Oxford University Press.

Hofstede, G. (2001). *Culture's consequences: Comparing values, behaviors, institutions, and organizations across nations* (2nd Ed.). Sage.

Ibrahim, F., & Ali, D. N. (2021). Evaluating knowledge management practices in higher education institutions (HEIs): Towards KMPro framework guidelines. In S. Zyngier (Ed.), *Handbook of research on knowledge management tools in higher education* (pp. 221–245). IGI Global.

Ibrahim, F., & Barr, S. (2009). Reconfiguring IT and the cultural dimension in knowledge management practices. *The International Journal of Knowledge, Culture and Change Management*, *9*(11), 27–43.

Ibrahim, F., Edgar, D., & Reid, V. (2009). Assessing the role of knowledge management in adding value: Moving towards a comprehensive framework. *Journal of Information & Knowledge Management*, *8*(4), 275–286.

Ibrahim, F., & Reid, V. (2010). Integrated use of information technology and people involvement for knowledge management. *International Journal of Technology, Knowledge and Society*, *6*(2), 163–180.

Ibrahim, F., & Salleh, N. M. (2019). Embedding knowledge management theory in learning and teaching approach. *International Journal of Learning and Development*, *9*(1), 20–40.

Jalonen, H. (2014). *Social media and emotions in organisational knowledge creation* (pp. 1371–1379). Proceedings of the 2014 Federated Conference on Computer Science and Information Systems.

Kidwell, J. J., Vander Linde, K. M., & Johnson, S. L. (2000). Applying corporate knowledge management practices in higher education. *Educause Quarterly*, *3*(4), 28–33.

Lee, J. (2007). The shaping of departmental culture: Measuring the relative influence of the institution and discipline. *Journal of Higher Education Policy and Management*, *29*(1), 41–55.

Leonardi, P. M., Huysman, M., & Steinfield, C. (2013). Enterprise social media: Definition, history, and prospects for the study of social technologies in organizations. *Journal of Computer Mediated Communication*, *19*(1), 1–19.

Loh, B., Tang, A. C., Menkhoff, T., Chay, Y. W., & Evers, H. D. (2010). Applying knowledge management in university research. In T. Menkhoff, H. D. Evers, & Y. W. Chay (Eds.), *Governing and managing knowledge in Asia* (pp. 221–248). World Scientific Publishing.

Malhotra, Y. (1998, July/August). Deciphering the knowledge management hype. *Journal for Quality & Participation*, 58–60.

McAfee, A. (2009). *Enterprise 2.0: New collaborative tools for your organization's toughest challenges*. Harvard Business School Press.

McDermott, R., & O'Dell, C. (2001). Overcoming cultural barriers to sharing knowledge. *Journal of Knowledge Management*, *5*(1), 76–85.

Metcalfe, A. S. (2006). *Knowledge management and higher education: A critical analysis*. Information Science Publishing. https://doi.org/10.4018/978-1-59140-509-2

Newell, S., Robertson, M., Scarbrough, H., & Swan, J. (2002). *Managing knowledge work*. Palgrave Macmillan.

Pan, S. L., & Scarborough, H. (1999). Knowledge management in practice: An explanatory case study. *Technology Analysis & Strategic Management*, *11*(3), 359–374.

Panahi, S., Watson, J., & Partidge, H. (2013). Towards tacit knowledge sharing over social web tools. *Journal of Knowledge Management*, *17*(3), 379–397.

Papadopoulos, T., Stamati, T., & Nopparuch, P. (2013). Exploring the determinants of knowledge sharing via employee weblogs. *International Journal Information Management*, *33*(1), 133–146.

Piskorski, M. J. (2011). Social strategies that work. *Harvard Business Review*, *89*(11), 116–122.

Prahalad, C. K., Krishnarao, C., & Hamel, G. (1990). The core competition of the corporation, *Harvard Business Review*, *68*(3), 79–91.

Ribiere, V., & Sitar, A. (2003). Critical role of leadership in nurturing a knowledge supporting culture. *Knowledge Management Research & Practice*, *1*(1), 39–48.

Rowley, J. (2000). Is higher education ready for knowledge management? *International Journal of Education Management*, *14*(7), 25–33.

Ruikar, K., Anumba, C., & Egbu, C. (2007). Integrated use of technologies and techniques for construction knowledge management. *Knowledge Management Research & Practice*, *5*(4), 297–311.

Sarvary, M. (1999). Knowledge management and competition in the consulting industry. *California Management Review*, *41*(2), 95–107.

Schein, E. H. (2004). *Organisational culture and leadership* (3rd ed.). Jossey Bass.

Sedziuviene, N., & Vveinhardt, J. (2009). The paradigm of knowledge management in higher educational institutions. *Engineering Economics*, *5*, 79–90.

Strassman, P. A. (1997). *The squandered computer: Evaluating the business alignment of information technologies*. Information Economic Press.

Tippins, M. J. (2003). Implementing knowledge management in academia: Teaching the teachers. *International Journal of Education Management*, *17*(7), 339–345.

Wah, L. (1999). Behind the buzz. *Management Review*, *88*(4), 16–26.

Wiig, K. M. (1997). Knowledge management: An introduction and perspective. *Journal of Knowledge Management*, *1*(1), 6–14.

Zeng, B., & Gerritsen, R. (2014). What do we know about social media in tourism? A review. *Tourism Management Perspective*, *10*, 27–36.

9 The risk management of cryptocurrencies based on the prediction of VaR and ES under the quantum wave

Outlook for ASEAN countries

Anuphak Saosaovaphak, Chukiat Chaiboonsri and Satawat Wannapan

Introduction

Economists are apprehensive of economic depressions, while econometricians are anxious about uncertainties. Residuals are the major issue that quantitative researchers struggle to address. The root of uncontrollable error terms is a simple word called "distribution". The distribution is traditionally assumed to be "normal" when researchers need some safety estimated results. Unfortunately, this traditional supposition potentially leads to suspicious predictions. The recent fact is the Covid-19 pandemic is frantic with an enormous number of causes needed to be urgently solved. How can econometricians sensibly deal with such a mass of unobservable information? Can the well-known normal distribution really deal with this kind of chaotic event? Is the logic perspective, "1" or "0", workable for the edge of big data analyses? These queries inspired the authors to search for a novel distributional aspect. Consequently, they discovered "quantum distribution". Quantum distribution (QD) is a kind of novel primitive concept for searching a quantum supremacy between two parties (Bedington et al., 2017).

Figure 9.1 displays two particles simultaneously generated from one beam. Informative particle appearances are seeable as wave densities. In terms of an econometric application, unobservable (latent) and observable samples can be substantially found at once. This seems that quantum distribution is the bridge that reasonably merges physics with econometrics. How can one apply the quantum distribution substantially? To study financial econometrics is to face uncontrollable uncertainties, alternatively referred to as "extremes". Most of the time financial studies are intentionally set to only deal with observable information. Indexes such as equities, inflations, or currencies are famous. In the current moment, cryptocurrencies – a new kind of illustrated money – are highlighted with predominant conditions for a way to live through the pandemic. They are additionally promoted to be a crucial component of free competitive markets in cyber spaces. Even though digital currencies are free from authority controls, they are still forced by a power called "invisible hands". This power exists, but a

DOI: 10.4324/9781003224532-9

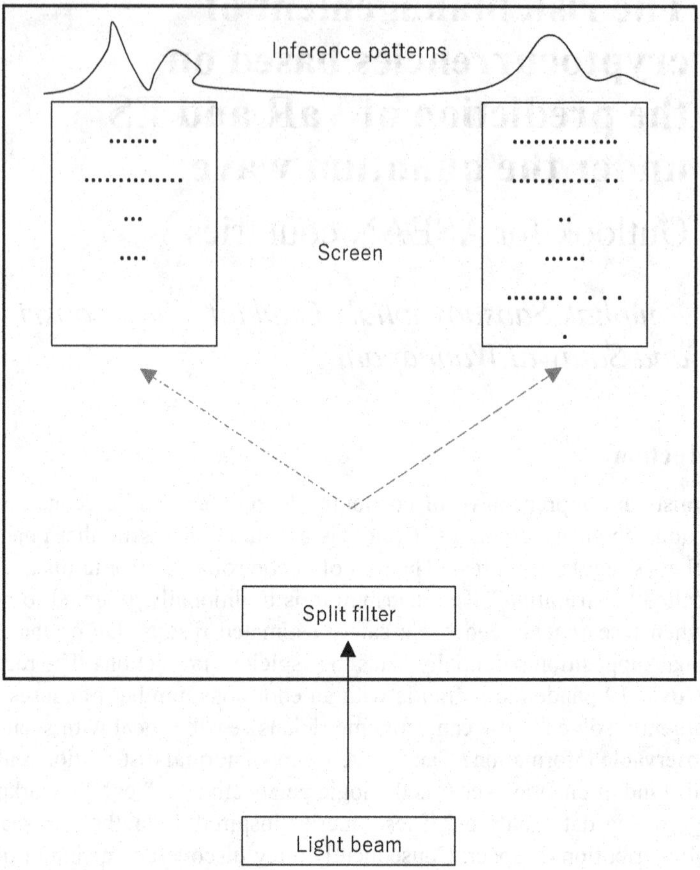

Figure 9.1 The schematic display of quantum supremacy

random-walk distribution cannot reach this reality. Thus, the quantum-walk distribution is a novel econometric connection between visible information and unobservable data, especially financial complexities. Back in 2016, the capacities of ASEAN economies driven by real currencies ranked fifth rank compared to major countries around the world, because digital assets stepped in to play as a fancy tool for financial networks. Southeast Asia was slightly absorbing this revolution. Real money was still a main tool for commercials. However, the multiple speed to generate value chains underneath invisible hands (free market-driven) is the advantage of cryptocurrencies. Numerically, digital money markets have ruled the wealth of world capitalization between US$174 and $246 billion compared with the historical data from 2014 to 2016, between US$1.84 and $3.97 billion. However, although ASEAN economies positively gain benefits from digital currencies, this is not sustainable because of their hybrid condition – real money for payments but cryptocurrencies for speculations. The evolution is a huge challenge and is needed more when digital currencies are becoming an investing marketplace for surviving economic systems under the Covid-19 pandemic. Hence, the main objective of this chapter is to address with the data of major cryptocurrencies during the pandemic outbreak by formalism and provide risk management guides for investing in the market.

Literature review

The argument for traditional economic theory

The issue stated by Vukotić (2011) is that economic crises – especially the current depression caused by the pandemic in 2019 – require the changing the dominant economic paradigm. In terms of traditional economic theory (mainstream), macroeconomic stability is the goal of economic policy. However, the change is highlighted by an individual-wealth-increase paradigm. "Quantum economics", which rely on "economic quantum", is currently popular. This novel way to understand modern economics contains two important words, "quantum" and "economics". The former is defined in physics as a discrete natural unit, or packet, of energy, charge, angular momentum, or other physical property. The latter word in social science is concerned with human behaviors and needs. Merging these two words, quantum economics is broadly described as an emerging research field that applies methods and conceptual ideas from quantum physics to the branch of economics. It is inspired by prior dynamically economic processes – especially financial transactions – which likely have been quantum processes and can be appropriately modelled using quantum formalism.

Financial economics with quantum formalism

It is undeniable that remarkable quantum innovations for modern technologies are usable on a daily basis. However, in social science, quantum formalism explaining human thoughts seems to be far from a simple interpretation. In addition, the quantum representation of economics is a natural outcome of the process of inference using the conceptual of Fisher information (Hawkins & Frieden, 2017). The theory is the center of asymmetrical information (Hawkins & Frieden, 2012), which lies at the heart of financial data. Quantum mechanics (QM) for mathematical models of price dynamics at capital markets was applied by Choustova (2007). The wave motion (Bohmian model) of quantum mechanics was used to describe behavioral financial factors at the "pure state" in the von Neumann equation modified by the Schrödinger equation (Holland, 1993; Choustova, 2007). The endeavor for using QM to understand behavioral economics is unstoppable.

Choustova (2007) proposed the method "quantum-like model" to deal with financial randomness. In 2019, the quantum perspective was raised to be the new direction for economic science by Patra (2019). Choice behaviors of agents under uncertainty are described by the quantum-like model. This is very useful for addressing volatilities in financial markets. Recently, Khrennikov and Haven (2020) point out that the quantum-like approach is the novel crucial role of the revolution elevating dimensions of information theory. This alternative aspect is the new direction in understanding the reasons for human agents' behaviors.

The bridge to connect risk management to cryptocurrencies

Historically, the story of digital money concerned the origin of "Bitcoin" (BTC), which was invented and proposed by a person or group using the pseudonym "Satoshi Nakamoto" in 2008 (Berentsen & Schär, 2018). The motivation behind this invention was the development of cash-like payment systems that permitted electronic transactions but that also included many of the advantageous characteristics of physical cash. The main characteristic of bitcoins was to avoid financial centralization and to free a financial sector from monetary policies and legal tenders. This consequence inspired it to be valuable as an "asset", which can be speculated (mining) and invested (selling). Values of bitcoins have grown dramatically. This phenomenon challenges the limit of real cash by containing no transaction costs along cryptocurrencies which are continuously developed and considerably employed. Ripple (XRP) was the name of a payment network and payment protocol developed and released in 2012. Ethereum (ETH) – an open-source blockchain with a smart contract – was proposed in 2013 by Vitalik Buterin. In 2014, Tether (USDT) was one of most popular of a group of stable coins used to smooth out price fluctuations in order to attract users who may otherwise be cautious. With this review, it is sensible to conclude that cryptocurrencies are replacing real money by their unstoppable modernization.

In financial markets, uncertainties are referred to as "risks". Traditional econometrics concerns these volatilities and generalizes them to be random. The original process of a random walk based on the scaling limit which generalizes the so-called iterated Brownian motion is useable and acceptable. Figure 9.2 displays a generalized form of the random-walk process based on the work of Polish physicist Marjan Smoluchowsk (Kac, 1947). However, the disadvantage of the random-walk distribution is stated by Saghiri et al. (2019). Non-intelligent models like random-walk processes may not be capable as a problem-solving method in real situations because some complex systems such as biological networks or social networks work as a "learning mechanism". They are not static, but thermodynamic. It is sensible to state that the performance of random-walk processes is low when it is used to explain mechanical information about the nature of practical problems.

On the other side of distribution analyzing, an invisible hand is not exactly observed but is the force behind the appearance of uncertainties. On the other side of distribution analyzing, an invisible hand is not exactly observed but is the force behind the appearance of uncertainties. This undetectable power is deliberately linked to quantum behaviors, which are similar to human thinking in driving human decision-making, especially for investment under uncertainty (Wendt, 2015). To efficiently address volatilities is the main aim of risk management. In 2019, Woerner and Egger (2019) used the quantum computer (IBM Q Experience)

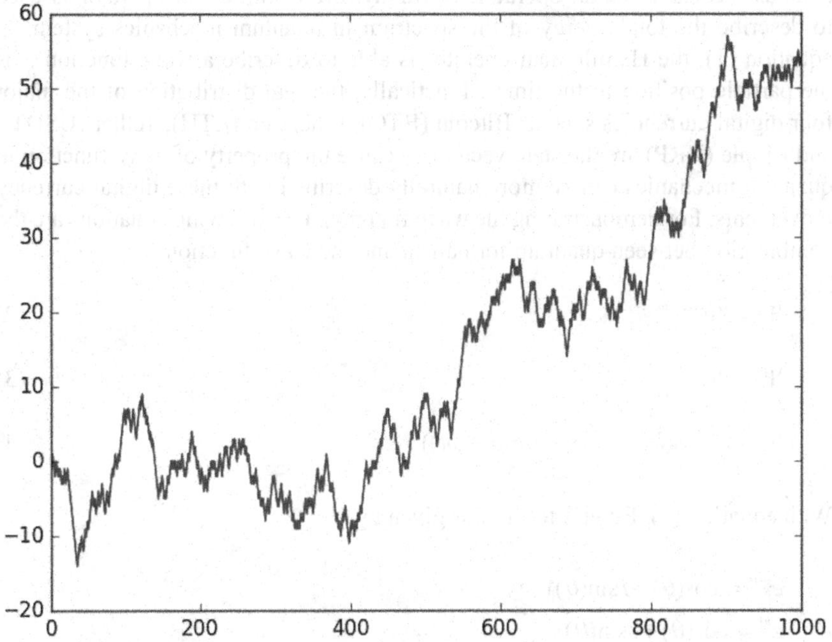

Figure 9.2 The example of random-walk patterns based on Brownian motion

to predictively price a Treasury bill (T-bill) faced with a possible interest rate increase. The empirical result confirmed quantum computations clearly improved the convergence rate over Monte Carlo methods. Tani (2020) employs a quantum computer to deal with a super-speed calculation for providing compact representations of sparse sets in terms of discrete-decision optimization and enumeration.

Recently, Chaiboonsri and Wannapan (2021) applied the quantum mechanism concept combined with a Bayesian perspective to provide a remarkable result of "real distribution" and project risk optimization for financial indexes. Thus, it is interesting that quantum distribution is providing a truly evolutional data analysis for post-modern econometrics, especially financial economics.

Methodology

The function of the quantum-wave distribution

This research still considers the wave function based on the core concept of the Schrödinger equation to describe the quantum mechanics system. In this case, the explanation of the time-dependent quantum wave[1] is demonstrated as equation (1),

$$i\hbar\frac{d}{dt}|\Psi(t)\rangle = \hat{\mathrm{H}}|\Psi(t)\rangle . \tag{1}$$

represents the state vector of the quantum mechanics system depending on time and as the Hamiltonian operator. Normally, the Hamiltonian operator is used to describe the total energy of the spectrum in quantum mechanics system. In equation (1), the Hamiltonian operator is able to describe a wave function . is the particle position at the time . Practically, the real distribution of the major four digital currencies such as Bitcoin (BTC), Ethereum (ETH), Tether (USDT), and Ripple (XRP) are the state vectors, because the property of wave function in quantum mechanics can be more naturally described with these digital currency movements. For demonstrating the wave function, the following equations are the combination between quantum formalism and the wave function.

$$\Psi = Ae^{i(kx-\omega t)} \tag{2}$$

$$\Psi = Ae^{-i(\omega t-kx)} \tag{3}$$

$$\Psi = A(\cos(kx-\omega t)+i\sin(kx-\omega t)) \,. \tag{4}$$

With equation (4), Euler's formula is given by

$$e^{-i\theta} = \cos(\theta)-i\sin(\theta))$$
$$e^{i\theta} = \cos(\theta)+i\sin(\theta))$$

Defined that:

$$k=\frac{2\pi}{\lambda},\ \omega=2\pi f,\ \lambda={}^{h}\!/_{mv},\ \omega = \text{Angular speed},\ i = \text{imaginary unit}$$

$$h = \text{plank's constant},\ m = \text{mass},\ v = \text{velocity},\ \lambda = \text{wavelength}$$

Euler's formula expresses the core concept of transforming equation (2) or equation (3) into the construction of the empirical model for estimating selected digital currencies. Consequently, equation (4) is the summarized equation that implies the process of transforming data into a wave distributional shape.

Extreme value analysis for financial indexes

Volatilities are defined as "heavy tails". However, in the traditional way, many distributions have been mentioned to model share returns as a whole observation (normal tail distributions). The consequence is the weakness of the whole distribution, which is the absence of extreme tail losses. The concept of extreme value theory (EVT) was proposed by Pickands (1975), who intentionally focused on the threshold of the extreme losses by taking the negative of the log returns and then choosing a positive threshold in a generalized Pareto distribution (GPD). The model assumes observations under the threshold, μ, is from a certain distribution with parameters η. $H(\cdot|\eta)$ is from a GPD. Thus, the distribution function f of any sample x can be expressed following Behrens et al. (2004) as equation (5).

$$f(x|\eta,\xi,\sigma,\mu)=\begin{cases} H(x|\eta), & x<\mu \\ H(x|\eta)+(1-H(\mu|\eta))G(x|\xi,\sigma,\mu), & x\geq\mu. \end{cases} \tag{5}$$

For a sample of size η, $x=(x_1,\ldots,x_n)$ from f, parameter vector $\theta=(\eta,\sigma,\xi,\mu)$, $N=[i:x_i<\mu]$, and $P=[i:x_i\geq\mu]$, the likelihood equation is expressed as follows the equation (6).

$$L(\theta;x)=\prod_N h(x|\eta)\prod_P(1-h(x|\eta))\left[\frac{1}{\sigma}\left(1+\frac{\xi(x_i-\mu)}{\sigma}\right)_+^{-(1+\xi)/\xi}\right], \tag{6}$$

for $\xi\neq 0$, and for $\xi=0$,

$$L(\theta;x)=\prod_N h(x|\eta)\prod_P(1-h(x|\eta))\left[(1/\sigma)\exp\{(x_i-\mu)/\sigma\}\right].$$

In other words, Figure 9.3 graphically shows the graphical model of setting a heavy-tail threshold. The threshold μ is the point where the density has a disruption. Depending on the parameters, the density jump can be fluctuated positively

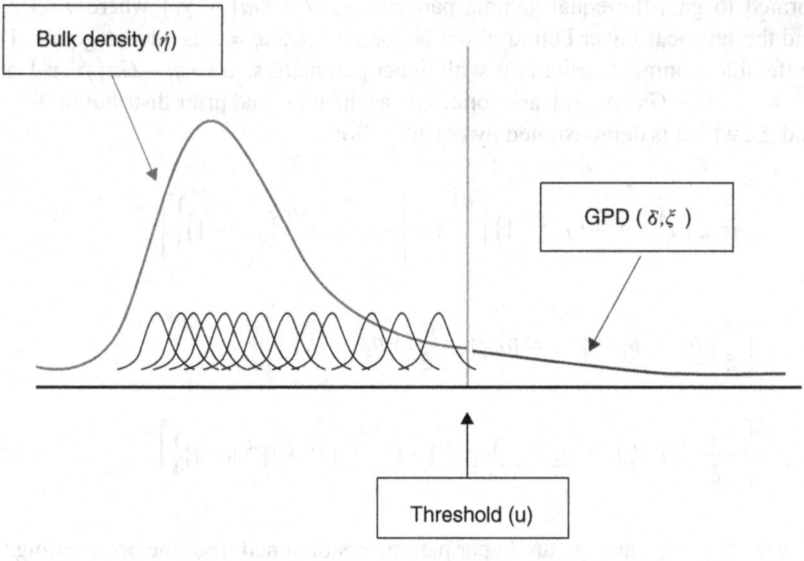

Figure 9.3 Schematic presentation of the GPD extreme value model

or negatively, and in each case the choice of which observations will be defined as exceedances can be more obvious.

Bayesian inference and simulations for extreme value analysis

Recall that the parameters in the extreme value model are $\theta = (\eta, \sigma, \xi, \mu)$. The prior and posterior densities are respectively described as follows.

The setting of the prior

The prior for GPD parameters were implemented to predict the extreme value of four major digital currencies, following the Behrens et al. (2004) study. Equation (7) represents the prior setting of the bayesian inference process for extreme value predition of digital currencies such as Bitcoin (BTC), Ethereum (ETH), Tether (USDT), and Ripple (XRP). Consequently, we obtain the 1-*p* quantile of the heavy-tail distribution as the following equation:

$$q = \mu + \frac{\sigma}{\xi}\left(P^{-\xi} - 1\right). \tag{7}$$

The heavy-tail density, *q*, is defined as the level of returns associated with a return period of 1/*p* time units. The elicitation of the prior information is a definition in terms of (q_1, q_2, q_3), referring to the location scale parameter of GPD. For specific values of $p_1 > p_2 > p_3$, parameters are ordered and $q_1 < q_2 < q_3$. Consequently, the prior information is initialized by setting the median and 90% quantile estimations for specific values of *p*. The elicited parameters for the prior are transformed to gain the equal gamma parameters, $d_i \sim Ga(\rho_i, \gamma_i)$ where $i = 1,2,3$ and the physical lower bound of the factor $e_1 = q_0$. $e_1 = 0$ is advantageous. The preferable gamma distributions with hyper parameters: $d_1 = q_1 \sim Ga(\rho_1, \gamma_1)$ and $d_2 = q_2 - q_1 \sim Ga(\rho_2, \gamma_2)$ are noticeable as the marginal prior distribution for σ and ξ, which is demonstrated by equation (8):

$$\pi(\sigma,\xi) \alpha \left[\mu + \frac{\sigma}{\xi}\left(p_1^{-\xi} - 1\right)\right]^{p_1 - 1} \exp\left[-\gamma_1\left\{\mu + \frac{\sigma}{\xi}\left(p_1^{-\xi} - 1\right)\right\}\right]$$

$$\times \left[\frac{\sigma}{\xi}\left(p_2^{-\xi} - p_1^{-\xi}\right)\right]^{p_2 - 1} \exp\left[-\gamma_2\left\{\frac{\sigma}{\xi}\right\}\left(p_2^{-\xi} - p_1^{-\xi}\right)\right]$$

$$\times \left[-\frac{\sigma}{\xi^2}\left\{\left(P_1 P_2\right)^{-\xi}\left(\log P_2 - \log P_2\right) - P_2^{-\xi}\log P_2 + P_1^{-\xi}\log P_1\right\}\right], \tag{8}$$

where $\rho_1, \rho_2, \gamma_1,$ and γ_2 are hyper parameters obtained from the prior setting. In the form of the median and percentiles, the correspondences are the return periods of $1/p_1$ and $1/p_2$. The prior for q_1 is in the principle relied on in threshold μ. This dependence is substituted by the dependence on the initial mean of μ. Interestingly, in some cases the situation where $\xi = 0$ (conjugated prior) is considered. For instance, a positive probability is set and the prior distribution evaluates a probability as q if $\xi = 0$, and $1-q$ if $\xi \neq 0$. We can define this setting as "prior at threshold". The threshold u is assigned to follow a truncated normal distribution with parameters (u_μ, σ_μ^2), curtailed from below at e_1 with density as in equation (9);

$$\pi\left(\mu \mid u_\mu, \sigma_\mu^2, e_1\right) = \frac{1}{\sqrt{2\pi\sigma_\mu^2}} \times \left\{ \frac{\exp\left[-0.5\left(\mu - u_\mu\right)^2 / \sigma_\mu^2\right]}{\Omega\left[-\left(e_1 - u_\mu\right)/\sigma_\mu\right]} \right\}, \tag{9}$$

with u_μ included in some high percentile and σ_μ^2 sufficient to present a reasonably non-informative prior. In other words, suggested by Bermudez et al. (2001), Chaiboonsri and Wannapan (2021), the higher level to set the prior distribution for μ requires a numerical position for a prior distribution for the hyper thresholds.

Simulation and posterior density

From the expression of the likelihood in the extreme analysis (equation 10) and the prior setting, the posterior distribution is given using the Bayes theorem applied from Ferre (2020), which is combined with the simulation well-known as MCMC methods via Metropolis–Hastings algorithms (Metropolis et al., 1953). To get hold of a gamma distribution for data below the threshold, the functional form on the logarithm scale is derived as the following details (see equation 10);

$$\log p(\theta \mid x) = K + \sum_{i=1}^{n} I(x_i < \mu)\left[\alpha \log \beta - \log \tau(\alpha) + (\alpha - 1)\log x_i - \beta x_i\right]$$

$$+ \sum_{i=1}^{n} I(x_i \geq \mu) \log\left(1 - \int_0^{\mu} \frac{\beta^\alpha}{\tau(\alpha)} t^{\alpha-1} e^{-\beta t} dt\right) - \sum_{i=1}^{n} I(x_i \geq \mu) \log \sigma$$

$$- \frac{1+\xi}{\xi} \sum_{i=1}^{n} I(x_i \geq \mu) \log\left[1 + \frac{\xi(x_i - \mu)}{\sigma}\right]$$

$$+ (a-1)\log\alpha - b\alpha + (c-1)\log\frac{\alpha}{\beta} - d\left(\frac{\alpha}{\beta}\right) + \log\left(\frac{\alpha}{\beta^2}\right)$$

$$- \frac{1}{2}\left(\frac{\mu - u_\mu}{\sigma_\mu}\right) - b_1\left[\mu + \frac{\sigma}{\xi}\left(p_1^{-\xi} - 1\right)\right]$$

$$+(a_2-1)\log\left[\mu+\frac{\sigma}{\xi}\left(p_2^{-\xi}-p_1^{-\xi}\right)\right]-b_2\left[u+\frac{\sigma}{\xi}\left(p_2^{-\xi}-p_1^{-\xi}\right)\right]$$

$$+\log\left\{-\frac{\sigma}{\xi}\left[\left(p_1p_2\right)^{-\xi}\left(\log p_2-\log p_1\right)-p_2^{-\xi}\log p_2+p_1^{-\xi}\log p_1\right]\right\}, \tag{10}$$

where k is the normalizing constant. For the computation, to generate analytical posterior distributions relies on the convergence rate in each iteration of MCMC simulations.

Value at risk (VaR) and expected shortfall (ES)

Uncertainties are not totally erased, but they have to be wisely managed. For risk management, financial researchers and market practitioners have paid more attention to value at risk (VaR) in analyzing the market risk. Cryptocurrencies are being targeted by quantitative econometricians. To contribute a sensible risk control, the highlighted objective of this article is to address with the samples of selected digital currencies by synthesizing quantum distributions and filtering extreme values and to provide them for risk computations by the value-at-risk model. The final aim of this chapter is to provide the risk projection for digital currency contexts. The famous method, VaR, has the performance to summarize the worst loss over a target horizon with a given level of confidence and outline the overall market risk faced by an institution (Assaf, 2009; Chaiboonsri & Wannapan, 2021). For extreme data analyses, the GPD continues to boundlessness. The problem is that extreme distributions are not known with an accuracy that is practical, but the Bayesian framework allows us to quantify and marginalize volatilities by simulations of random hyper-parameters. Expressly, the posterior predictive distribution follows equation (11):

$$p\left(x^f \mid x\right)=\int_\theta p\left(x^f \mid \theta\right)p\left(\theta \mid x\right)d\theta. \tag{11}$$

If uncertainty regarding an unknown parameter is captured in a posterior distribution, a predictive distribution for any quantity μ that depends on the unknown parameter, through a sampling distribution, can be achieved by equation (11). In this case, $p\left(x^f \mid x\right)$ points to an updated GPD observation obtained by a set of parameters. The updated data is generated by the following transformation (see equation (12)):

$$U\sim Uniform(0,1)\gg \log p\left(\theta \mid x\right)=\left[\left(U^{-e}-1\right)+\frac{\sigma}{e}+\mu\right]\sim GPD\left(\mu,\sigma,e\right). \tag{12}$$

By MCMC simulations, a large number of updating iteration samples can be covered. In terms of the GPD, the VaR and ES can be determined using the following expressions:

$$VaR\left(1-\alpha\right)=\left(\alpha^{-e}-1\right)\frac{\sigma}{e}+\mu, \tag{13}$$

$$ES(1-\alpha)=VaR(1-\alpha)+\frac{\sigma\alpha^{-e}}{1-e}. \tag{14}$$

These measures are ordered to obtain quantiles for the purpose of creating intervals. Note that since negative log share returns are included, which are the GPD above a suitable threshold, it is crucial to rescale α by multiplying by the divide between the number of observations and number of exceedances. To further clarify the methodological section, Figure 9.4 displays processes to reach

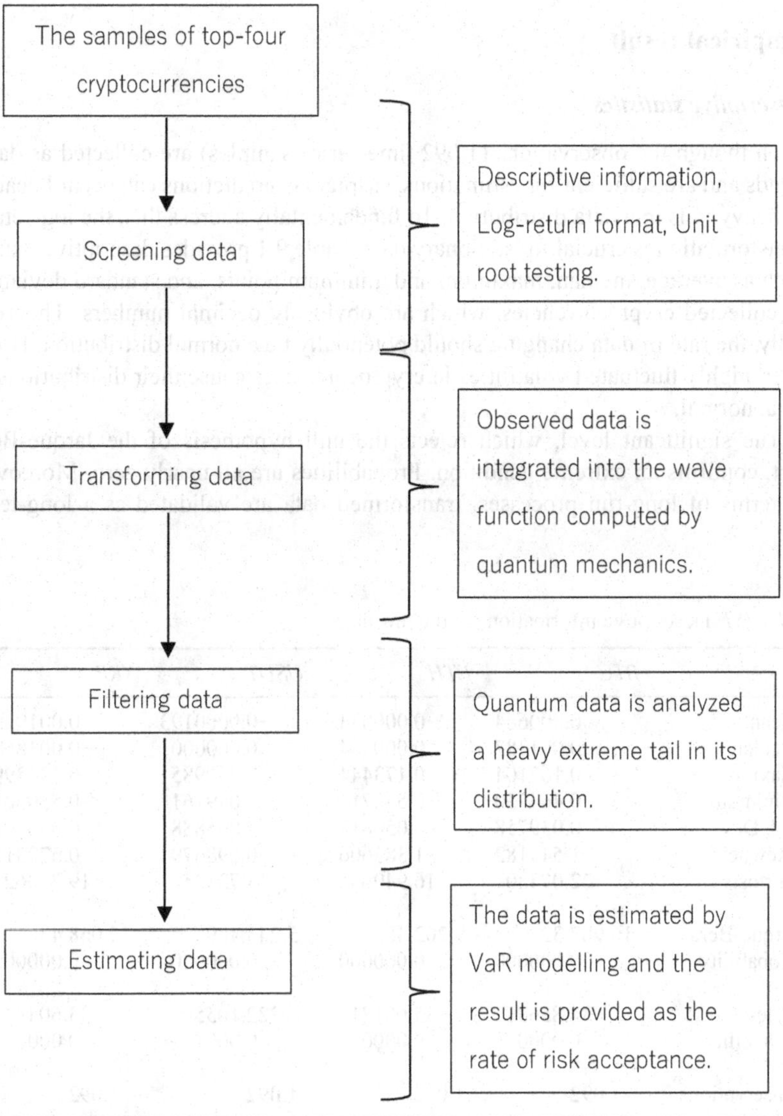

Figure 9.4 The methodological scope of the research

an ultimate risk management that addresses the aim of the chapter. Descriptive details and the result of stationary testing are achieved from the "screening" process. Next, the part of data transformation is the gate to open a new horizon of data science. Quantum computations are employed for the wave equation by Schrödinger's wave function (Jung, 2009). Quantum modified data is filtered as an extreme event by fitting the generalized Pareto distribution in the third process. The filtered data is analyzed by value-at-risk and expected shortfall to provide wise options for evaluating cryptocurrencies as a blue-ocean financial market.

Empirical result

Descriptive statistics

Even though the observations (1,092 time-series samples) are collected as daily trends and are sufficient for estimations, suspicious predictions can occur because of heavy tails in a data distribution. To fundamentally address this, the log-return transformation is crucial for stationary data. Table 9.1 provides descriptive values such as average, median, maximum and minimum points, and standard deviation of collected cryptocurrencies, which are obviously decimal numbers. Theoretically, the rate of data changing should potentially be a normal distribution. However, highly fluctuated volatilities in cryptocurrencies cause their distributions to be abnormal.

The significant level, which rejects the null hypothesis of the Jarque-Bera test, confirms an extreme condition. Probabilities are all nearly zero. Moreover, in terms of long-run processes, transformed data are validated as a long-term

Table 9.1 Descriptive information for the raw data

	BTC	*ETH*	*USDT*	*XRP*
Mean	0.000684	0.000034	−0.0000193	−-0.001920
Median	0.001387	0.000464	0.000000	−0.001868
Maximum	0.167104	0.173444	0.049985	0.334399
Minimum	−0.464730	−0.550714	−0.049161	−0.550503
Std. Dev.	0.039758	0.050817	0.005888	0.056804
Skewness	−1.544182	−1.383606	0.098679	−0.672311
Kurtosis	22.07380	16.94968	13.73325	19.23062
Jarque-Bera	16,987.32	9,202.428	5,243.489	12,068.47
Probability	0.000000	0.000000	0.000000	0.000000
PP-test	−34.85631	−35.00181	−222.1055	−33.60440
Probability	0.0000	0.0000	0.0001	0.0000
Observations	1,092	1,092	1,092	1,092

stationary state by the Phillips-Perron test for data unit roots. Significant probabilities indicate the rejection of the null hypothesis, which is set to stand for non-stationary processes in the data. To conclude this section, the data are readily prepared for the next applied method.

Data visualization

Extreme events can obviously be detected by visualizing data trends. Displayed in Figure 9.5, highly variable rates are seen from 2019 to 2020. The rates are shocked negatively. They significantly lower to −5%, mainly caused by the coronavirus pandemic in the third quarter of 2019. Although cryptocurrencies are continuously promoted to be a less-interfering currency, the data visualization implies that all digital money still relies on a variety of active factors and situations. In other words, it is not totally independent. To make a conclusion from this visual result, collected data must deeply explore invisibly influential factors by applying quantum formalism.

Figure 9.6 graphically details the crucial result of the research. Four major digital currencies are retransformed by modelling in quantum-wave computations. Unlike random-walk processing, quantum distributions are generated from observed data, and this provides novel informative densities, which simultaneously hold visible samples and extreme influences. The shapes of changing rates are transformed. New data distributions are ready to be illuminated for risk management.

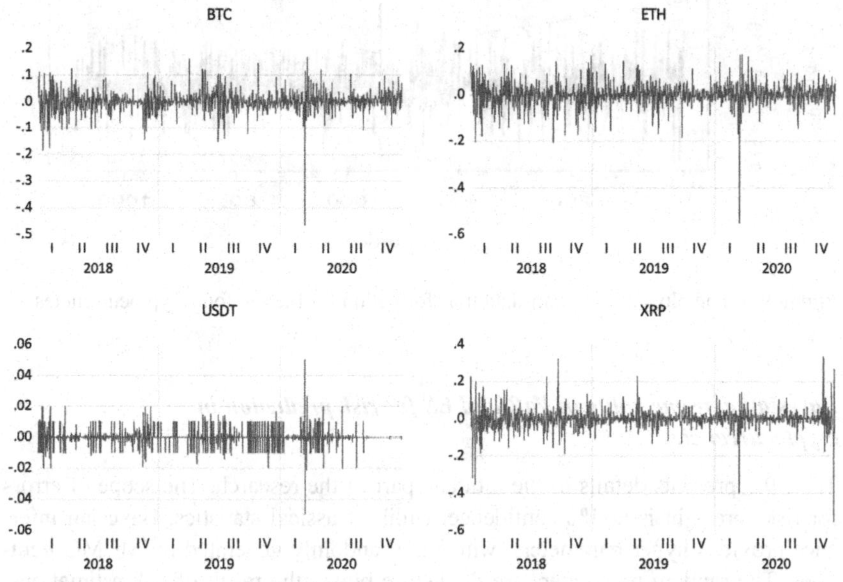

Figure 9.5 The plots of changing rates for the top four digital currencies

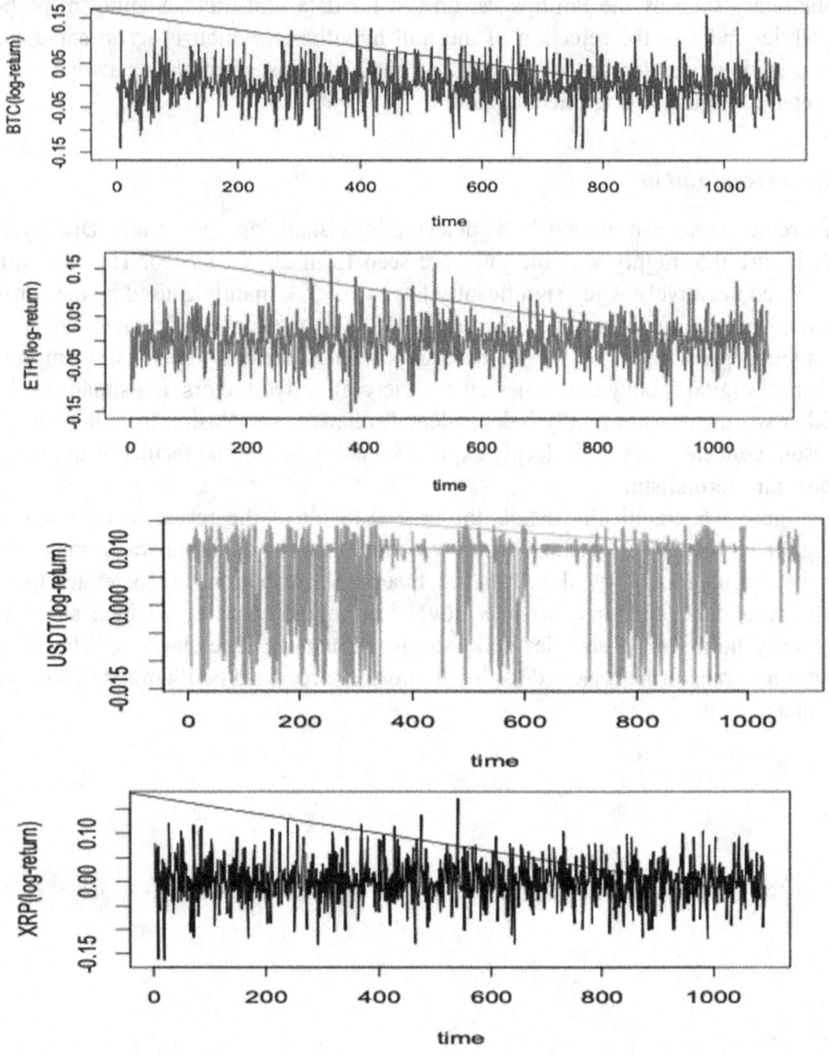

Figure 9.6 The plots of quantum-data transformation for the top four cryptocurrencies

Bayesian extreme value in VaR and ES for risk prediction in cryptocurrencies

Table 9.2 presents details of the ultimate part of the research. The scope of errors for risk foresight is at 1% confidence. Unlike classical statistics, Bayesian inference provides hyper parameters, which are randomly generated by MCMC iterations. The random parameters are the key to power the result of risk estimations. Expressly, the 2.5% interval represents the heavy tail of extreme values, which can be accepted by investors who are risk averse. At the middle interval, the mean point

Table 9.2 The Bayesian extreme value prediction for VaR and ES

Items	*VaR and ES*	*2.5%*	*Mean*	*97.5%*
BTC	VaR(0.01)	0.1637	0.1731	0.1823
(Bitcoin)	**ES**	**0.1960**	**0.2096**	**0.2235**
ETH	VaR(0.01)	0.1650	0.1738	0.1827
(Ethereum)	**ES**	**0.1944**	**0.2069**	**0.2200**
USDT	VaR(0.01)	0.0814	0.0836	0.0860
(Tether)	**ES**	**0.0820**	**0.0844**	**0.0869**
XRP	VaR(0.01)	0.1676	0.1775	0.1882
(Ripple)	**ES**	**0.1968**	**0.2109**	**0.2263**

is the level of extreme situations at which investors who are risk neutral can hold their limits. Lastly, the 95.7% interval of random parameters represents the maximum risk acceptance for risk-lover investors. The expression of VaR calculations indicates two groups of investment plans. For the risk-averse style, the result shows Tether (USDT) contains the minimum risk values between 0.0814% and 0.086%. On other hand, the Ripple, Bitcoin, and Ethereum digital currencies provide more speculative return with high risks. Their risk rates are between 16% and 18%.

In terms of conditional value-at-risk (expected shortfall), the result presents an alternative consideration for investment in digital money markets. For a 99% confidence level, the expected shortfall indicates Ripple, Bitcoin, and Ethereum as the currencies containing efficient information. Their worst cases between 19% and 22.6% of cases for taking the average of returns are sensible. In other words, high values of expected shortfall are not only telling the maximum level of taking risks, but they are implying that invisible factors (hands) are explored and accounted for into the data distribution. Hence, every single investment inevitably has risks, but to expand the ceiling of losses can be an interesting option for planning an efficient portfolio.

Discussion

Decentralization is one of important issues that ASEAN countries are focusing on. Cryptocurrency is the crucial component of this attempt to apply for reducing authorities' interferences in financial markets (Ramdhani et al., 2020). Because of culture and economic diversities, especially real currency transactions, it is not currently possible to implement digital currencies for entire economic systems. However, in terms of investments, digital money is the predominant example to explain that latent information needs to be explored. The conclusion by Chaiboonsri and Wannapan (2021) states a strong result that quantum distributions better capture both observable and hidden information inside data samples of financial indexes by the comparison of deviance information criterion (DIC). This implies that the quantum distribution can be assured to work well with the information of cryptocurrencies and Bayesian inference – referred to as a modern statistical tool for modern econometric researches (Saosaovaphak et al., 2020). As seen in the detailed risk predictions in Table 9.2, values of risks already integrate both observable information and latent factors which can be defined as "invisible hands". Additionally, the interval of hyper-parameters from Bayesian inference represents random situations, which are more reliable on uncertainties of the Covid-19 outbreak. Consequently, the computational result of this paper is a novel way to monitor and foresee risks for digital money markets in Southeast Asia, which is a leading emerging market for traders of digital assets (Loo, 2019).

Conclusion

The quantum distribution is empirically used for real econometric models. Cryptocurrencies are referred to as the group of financial contexts containing extreme volatilities. Quantum distribution satisfies quantitative and qualitative information that better provides more latent dimensions. The consequence is that an extreme distribution can be better verified. In terms of financial management, quantum distribution is the way to deal with uncertainties, referred to as "risks". In macroeconomics, this tool can be a flashlight to monitor hidden influences in economic systems, especially ASEAN countries which have a variety of accessible data sources and a huge gap of inefficient information. The result is clear that investors interested in digital money markets surely take high returns and risks. The risks (uncertainties) are more increased under the Covid-19 pandemic. By collecting data samples during the pandemic outbreak, accessible information can provide an efficient data distribution, and the distribution is the key to address an efficient foresight for risk management. For further research gaps, real distribution can lead to sensible estimation and prediction. Risk management based on quantum distribution and Bayesian statistics is like a foresight with a masterpiece of raw materials. This is the reason why the conclusion of this chapter strongly points out that Bayesian quantum formalism is not beneficial only in medical science or technological manufacturing. In social science, quantum distribution is the predominant alternative for economic forecasting and policy implementing, especially during the current economic downfalls experienced by ASEAN members.

Note

1 Shankar, R. (1994). *Principles of quantum mechanics* (2nd ed.). Kluwer Academic/Plenum Publishers. ISBN 978-0-306-44790-7.

References

Assaf, A. (2009). Extreme observations and risk assessment in the equity markets of MENA region: Tail measures and value-at- risk. *International Review of Financial Analysis*, *18*, 109–116.

Bedington, R., Arrazola, J. M., & Ling, A. (2017). Progress in satellite quantum key distribution. *NPJ Quantum Information Volume*, *3*(30).

Behrens, C. N., Lopes, H. F., & Gamerman, D. (2004). Bayesian analysis of extreme events with threshold estimation. *Statistical Modelling*, *4*, 227–244.

Berentsen, A., & Schär, F. (2018). A short introduction to the world of cryptocurrencies. *Federal Reserve Bank of St. Louis Review*, *100*(1), 1–16.

Bermudez, P. Z., Turkman, M. A. A., & Turkman, K. F. (2001). A predictive approach to tail probability estimation. *Extremes*, *4*, 295–314.

Chaiboonsri, C., & Wannapan, S. (2021). Applying quantum mechanics for extreme value prediction of VaR and ES in the ASEAN stock exchange. *Economies*, *9*(13). https://doi.org/10.3390/economies9010013

Choustova, O. G. (2007). Quantum Bohmian model for financial market. *Physica A: Statistical Mechanics and Its Applications*, *374*(1), 304–314.

Ferre, T. P. A. (2020). Being Bayesian: Discussions from the perspectives of stakeholders and hydrologists. *Water*, *12*(461). https://doi.org/10.3390/w12020461

Hawkins, R. J., & Frieden, B. R. (2012). Asymmetric information and quantization in financial economics. *International Journal of Mathematics and Mathematical Sciences*, *4*, 1–11.

Hawkins, R. J., & Frieden, B. R. (2017). Quantization in financial economics: An information-theoretic approach. *The Palgrave Handbook of Quantum Models in Social Science*, 19–38. https://doi.org/10.1057/978-1-137-49276-0_2

Holland, P. (1993). *The quantum theory of motion*. Cambridge University Press.

Jung, K. (2009). Can the Schrödinger wave function be associated with a concrete physical wave? *Annales de la Fondation Louis de Broglie*, *34*(2), 143–163.

Kac, M. (1947). Random walk and the theory of Brownian motion. *The American Mathematical Monthly*, *54*(7), 369–391.

Khrennikov, A. Y., & Haven, E. (2020). Quantum-like modeling: From economics to social laser.

Loo, M. K. L. (2019). Enhancing financial inclusion in ASEAN: Identifying the best growth markets for fintech. *Journal of Risk and Financial Management*, *12*(4). https://doi.org/10.3390/jrfm12040181

Metropolis, N., Rosenbluth, A. W., Rosenbluth, M. N., Teller, A. H., & Teller, E. (1953). Equation of state calculations by fast computing machines. *Journal of Chemical Physics*, *21*, 1087–1092.

Patra, S. (2019). *A quantum framework for economic science: New directions*. Discussion Paper No. 2019–20. Kiel Institute for the World Economy (IfW).

Pickands, J. (1975). Statistical inference using extreme order statistics. *The Annals of Statistics*, *3*(1), 119–131.

Ramdhani, B. W., Pawirosumarto, S., & Zainudin, Z. (2020). Influence of cryptocurrency on the economy of 5 ASEAN country. *International Journal of Psychosocial Rehabilitation*, *24*(1), 4633–4641.

Saghiri, A. M., Khomami, M. D., & Meybodi, M. R. (2019). *Random walk algorithms: Definitions, weaknesses, and learning automata-based approach* (pp. 1–7). Springer Briefs in Applied Sciences and Technology.

Saosaovaphak, A., Chaiboonsri, C., & Wannapan, S. (2020). The dependence structure and co-movement of cryptocurrency based Bayesian approach. *Journal of Physics: Conference Series*, *1593*(1), 012010.

Tani, S. (2020). Quantum algorithm for finding the optimal variable ordering for binary decision diagrams. *Proceedings 17th Scandinavian Symposium and Workshops on Algorithm Theory (SWAT 2020), LIPIcs*, *162*, 1–19.

Vukotić, V. (2011). Quantum economics. *Panoeconomicus*, *2*, 267–276. https://doi.org/10.2298/PAN1102267V

Wendt, A. (2015). Quantum cognition and rational choice. In *Quantum mind and social science: Unifying physical and social ontology* (pp. 154–173). Cambridge University Press. doi:10.1017/CBO9781316005163.011

Woerner, S., & Egger, D. J. (2019). Quantum risk analysis. *NPJ Quantum Information*, *5*(15). https://doi.org/10.1038/s41534-019-0130-6

10 Developing a digital business ecosystem in Singapore

Mun Heng Toh

Introduction

The publication of the *Strategic Economic Plan* (SEP) by the Ministry of Trade and Industry in 1991 marks the beginning of a new development philosophy in Singapore. Singapore has adopted a cluster-based approach in economic development and has strived to maintain its relevance and usefulness in the global value chain. This new approach to economic development has provided an improved framework for fostering industrial growth and development based primarily on trade and foreign investments. It has enabled better planning in terms of strategic choice of industries for development and promotion, capitalizing on the interdependence of the industries and investing in appropriate infrastructure, technologies and institutions to achieve better outcome and higher returns. The cluster approach is very often discussed in terms of establishing an ecosystem around a specific industry or sector. For instance, in the cluster of electronics and electronic-related companies, an ecosystem can be established. There is co-dependence and co-existence among these companies. The relationship among the companies is synergistic, giving rise to positive spill-over externalities or agglomeration effects for promoting further growth (Toh, 2015; Enterprise Singapore, 2019). This is the adopted development philosophy that has remained unaltered as the digital era unfolds.

The revision of the development approach is not independent of international events and the economic environment. The buoyant international economy after the fall of the Berlin Wall in 1989 as a consequence of international trade liberalization, and domestic deregulation and structural reform in many countries, had spurred growth and development in Southeast Asia, including Singapore. The willingness of emerging economies like India and China, with large markets and populations to adopt capitalistic market principles in development, had fostered notable growth in their economies by embracing export promotion and foreign investments. This has also challenged the continued growth of the newly industrializing economies (NICs) economies like Singapore, Hong Kong and South Korea and somewhat dampened the rise of a new batch of NICs like Indonesia, Malaysia and Thailand. The international economic environment began to dip into more uncertainty and volatility amidst international terrorism and pandemics

DOI: 10.4324/9781003224532-10

from early 2000s. Just before the decade ended, the world was struck by the Great Recession, which was sparked by the housing loan financial crisis in the United States.

Since the subprime financial crisis in 2008, Singapore's economic growth declined by almost half, from an average 5% per annum to slightly more than 3% per annum. Concurrently, productivity growth had also stuttered despite several public schemes implemented to uplift performance. In recent years, the aim to transform into a smart nation together with the drive towards ubiquitous digitalization of the economy has provided the hope and conduit to launch the economy into a new phase of growth.

In this chapter, we begin with a review of the concept of the digital business ecosystem (DBE) and trace the emanation of the digitalization drive as a continuation of the industrialization momentum started more than two centuries ago. The main features and the benefits that can be derived from digitalization of the economy are discussed. Following that, we investigate how Singapore began its digitalization journey with the objective of using technology, especially information technology, to computerize public services and support economic growth. We review the IT plans put forth by the government at regular intervals that help to digitalize the various economic clusters, so they can become digital business ecosystems powering the economy into a new phase of growth. The next section considers the digitalization of small and medium-sized enterprises (SMEs) in Singapore. In particular, we consider the various schemes, incentives and action plans that are crafted to help the SMEs, which make up 99% of total enterprises in the economy, transform their business models into one that makes the best use of digital technologies. We report on the progress of digitalization based on recent surveys before concluding the chapter with some remarks on the challenges faced in digitalizing the economy.

Review of the digital business ecosystem

What is a digital business ecosystem?

A business ecosystem is an economic community of loosely coupled interacting organizations and individuals who produce valuable goods and services (Moore, 1993). It is the network of organizations – including suppliers, distributors, customers, competitors, government agencies and so on – involved in the delivery of a specific product or service through both competition and cooperation.[1] A DBE is an extension of Moore's business ecosystem for which digital technology plays a dominant role. A digital ecosystem is a group of interconnected information technology resources that can function as a unit that creates, disseminates and connects digital services over the Internet. We can view DBE as an integration of the digital and business ecosystems and thus define DBE as a socio-technical environment of individuals, organizations and digital technologies with collaborative and competitive relationships to co-create value through shared digital platforms (Senyo et al., 2019).

Main features of digitalization

Digitalization can be considered the continuation of the industrialization momentum that first started around 1760. This was epitomized by the harnessing of steam power for production and transportation. This era lasted for about 100 years until 1870, when the second industrial revolution is said to have begun with a collection of innovations related to railroads, telecommunication, electric lighting, internal combustion engines and all types of electro-mechanical machinery, including road vehicles, aircraft, radio and televisions, washing machines and industrial chemicals as in fertilizers and plastics. Manufacturing of such products forms the basis of the industrialization program in many aspiring developing economies. This lasted for another hundred years until 1970, when the era of Industry 3.0 emerged with the use of electronic and IT systems that automated production and other processes and became increasingly pervasive in industries. With the advent of the Internet, advancement in data processing power, machine learning, data analytics, automation and artificial intelligence, another industrial shift, Industry 4.0, is reckoned to have evolved. Businesses of different industries are connected via the Internet, which expanded business outreach and prospects significantly. The availability of automation technologies, communication, artificial intelligence and accessibility to big data now greatly facilitate the adaptation (digitization) and creation of the products that offer disruptive competitive advantage and higher returns (Baldwin, 2019).

It is important to make a distinction between digitization and digitalization (Leinwand & Mani, 2021). The two terms are not synonymous. Digitization is creating a digital copy of an object. For instance, a handwritten tennis-court booking form can be converted into an editable digital document using optical character recognition (OCR) software. The booking form is being digitized, and the digital document forms the basic building blocks for digitalization. With digitalization, online forms are created, filled in and submitted within an electronic document management system (EDMS). EDMS is the digital technology that comes with scripts to check form fields in real time, ensuring that all necessary fields are filled correctly. Once submitted, the system will route the digital form from one approving party to the next based on the preset workflow of the form. The information capture can also allow the tennis organization to improve scheduling and to decide on investing in more tennis courts and sales of ancillary equipment and services.

From the perspective of the business environment, digitalization is connected with the use of technologies, products and data in order to maximize revenue, improve business models and replace/change business processes. It creates an environment for digital business. Digitization is a process of converting information into digital form, which facilitates the ease of the interconnection of digitized units, the Internet of Things (IoT) and the collection and transfer of data that can have beneficial opportunities for individuals and businesses. From a practical point of view, different companies apply various approaches to digitize business:

- digitizing products;
- digitizing processes when implementing diverse business management systems/online platforms/applications;
- combining both approaches (using the products of data science, cognitive technology and processing power to create 'intelligent enterprises').

Digitalization affects entire ecosystems, their business models and the underlying business functions of a company's value chain. By digitalizing business functions, data can be provided to enhance and develop each of these functions – and thereby the entire value chain. The well-known online bookseller, Amazon, digitizes by launching the Kindle e-book reader at the expense of its physical books sales. It basically digitizes the content. Meanwhile, WhatsApp uses a lean operating model approach in digitization of its business processes. Hospitals are collaborating with IT companies to build platforms that will transform and optimize the way healthcare is delivered. It will help to set up a new ecosystem of developers with healthcare applications that will support collaboration between patients, doctors and pharmaceutical companies.

Digital products, digital services and digital solutions are becoming common and penetrating markets and production space associated with many industries. Businesses have to rise up to the challenge and adapt to the change. In the new DBE, the relations between companies (competition/cooperation) increasingly depend on this decision. According to a report by McKinsey Global Institute, in 2017 Europe was a net importer of US digital services, running a digital trade deficit amounting to nearly 5.6% of total services trade between the EU and the US. However, if its laggards double their digital intensity, EU can add €2.5 trillion to the GDP in 2025, boosting GDP growth by 1% a year over a decade.

Many scholars have reported that new digital technologies often facilitate changes in products and processes and thereby reshape business models or even entire industries (Porter & Heppelmann, 2014; Digital Vortex, 2015; Björkdahl, 2009). A software platform is considered as one of the important precursors to intensive adoption of digitalization in business. Using a case-based analytical approach, Evans et al. (2006) investigated the economic role of software platforms. Platform technologies can help to transform industries and to develop the strategies that will create value and drive profits. Digitalization is currently frequently reported as an enabler for various changes in company operations, offerings and the overall competitive landscape, for example (Rymaszewska et al., 2017; Porter & Heppelmann, 2014; World Economic Forum, 2016). Companies can use digital technologies to change a business model and provide new revenue and value-producing opportunities. Digitalization induces transformation rather than supporting and developing traditional ways of working (Treutiger et al., 2017). Matt et al. (2015) share the same view. They noted that digitalization may affect large parts of the organization by impacting "products, business processes, sales channels, and supply chains". Very often, digitalization in manufacturing companies leads to an increased emphasis on services, an aspect worthy of attention by management. A well-known example is the case of Rolls-Royce. Famed for its sale of aero engines, it has turned into a service company that leases engines to airlines. By embedding sensors and other digital assets right across its product lines and manufacturing facilities, Rolls-Royce has become a data-rich company with data capability ranging from predicting equipment issues and maintenance requirements to showing airlines how to optimize their routes to minimize operation cost.

The Internet has promulgated e-commerce, starting with business-to-business (B2B) transactions before the proliferation and popularity of businesses-to-consumer (B2C) transactions in recent years. Dinlersoz and Pereira (2007) discuss the viability of retailers adopting e-commerce. They analyse and identify how consumer loyalty, differences in firms' technology and consumers' preferences can affect the timing and sequence of adoption by firms, as well as the post-adoption evolution of prices. A more recent study by Amornkitvikai and Lee (2020) reports that social media and websites are significant drivers of e-commerce utilization levels, and smartphones are found to be a cost-effective tool for e-commerce transactions. New, scalable, digitally networked business models – for example those of Amazon, Google, Uber and Airbnb – are impacting on growth, scale and profit potential for companies in every industry (Aagaard, 2019; Libert et al., 2016).

Benefits of digitalization

The benefits of digital transformation are many. Firstly, it can help companies to increase profits. In a recent Gartner survey, 56% of CEOs said that digital improvements have already led to increases in profits (Gartner, 2017). In another study of companies that undergo digital transformation, the SAP Center for Business Insights and Oxford Economics reported that 80% of organizations that have completed digital transformation report increased profits. Secondly, efficiency of companies is increased, as the main benefit of digital transformation is the streamlining of business operations and processes. This leads to increased efficiency in many aspects of business.

Digital transformation can help businesses maintain a lead over competitors and stand out from the rest with unique offerings. A digitalized business can reach wider markets and even launch new business models. For businesses facing rising labour costs, pursuing digital solutions and modifications to production functions and processes can increase the productivity and efficiency of employees, which will increase the value and production of the work force and allow businesses to remain competitive and stay one step ahead of the curve. Digitalizing the business may not be costly, especially when the government of the country is investing resources and providing financial grants and loans to businesses for digital transformation.

Singapore digitalization journey

National IT plans

The successful industrialization program that started in the 1960s powered by low-cost labour began to experience a work force shortage and limited scope for further growth by the late 1970s amidst rising competition from larger regional economies. In response, the government leveraged on initial economic gains to deepen the industrial based by attracting more capital and technology-intensive foreign investments that can produce higher value-added commodities for export. At this point, the government also began to focus on technological innovation, that is, the application of technology, especially ICT, to solve problems, increase efficiencies, develop new products and services, and create new knowledge. Thus, began Singapore's infotech journey, which has closely mirrored the international eco-techno trend, domestic economic development and social needs.

National infotech master plans and capabilities over 40 years (1980–2020) not only focused on leveraging ICT as an enabler of economic competition and social development but also on building a globally competitive infotech industry and a knowledge-based economy. Such an economy will thrive with talented workers and creative enterprises in various DBEs. Coordinated efforts arising from these master plans have also emphasized infotech worker development, infotech awareness and literacy of the populace and businesses, domestic and international infotech infrastructure and connectivity, efficiencies in government agencies, as well as business transformation (Figure 10.1).

Between 1980 and 2000, there were three national ICT master plans: National Computerization Plan (NCP), National IT Plan (NITP) and IT2000: The Intelligent Island. The aims of the first master plan, NCP, were (a) to initiate the computerization of major functions in all the government ministries to deliver better and efficient services to the public, (b) to facilitate the development and growth of local ICT industry, and (c) to develop a pool of ICT professionals to meet the needs of the ICT industry (Committee on National Computerisation, 1980). The second master plan, NITP, opened up the computerized government systems to the private sector to enable electronic data interchange across government departments, industry and the public (National IT Plan Working Committee, 1985). One prominent example of the use of IT in business economics to help Singapore maintain its premier port status is TradeNet. Launched in 1989, TradeNet is Singapore's National Single Window for trade declaration. It allows various parties from the public and private sectors to exchange trade information electronically. It integrates import, export and transhipment documentation processing procedures and enables trade and logistic communities to fulfil their trade formalities efficiently. This sort of one-stop services portal has also been extended to the legal and health sectors with LawNet and MedNet. The idea of organizing the manufacturing sector into different clusters of industries was formalized. There were five clusters: electronics, chemicals, precision engineering, marine and offshore engineering, and aerospace. The adoption of the cluster approach is extended to the rest of the economy by the third master plan. The aim of the third master plan, IT2000, was to develop a national information infrastructure to transform Singapore into an "intelligent island" where ICT is available everywhere – in homes, offices, schools and factories (Cordeiro and Al-Hawamdeh, 2001).

For the next 15 years from 2000 to 2015, three plans were launched. They are InfoComm 21, Connected Singapore and iN2015. With the ICT infrastructure generally in place, the fourth master plan, InfoComm 21, was targeted at

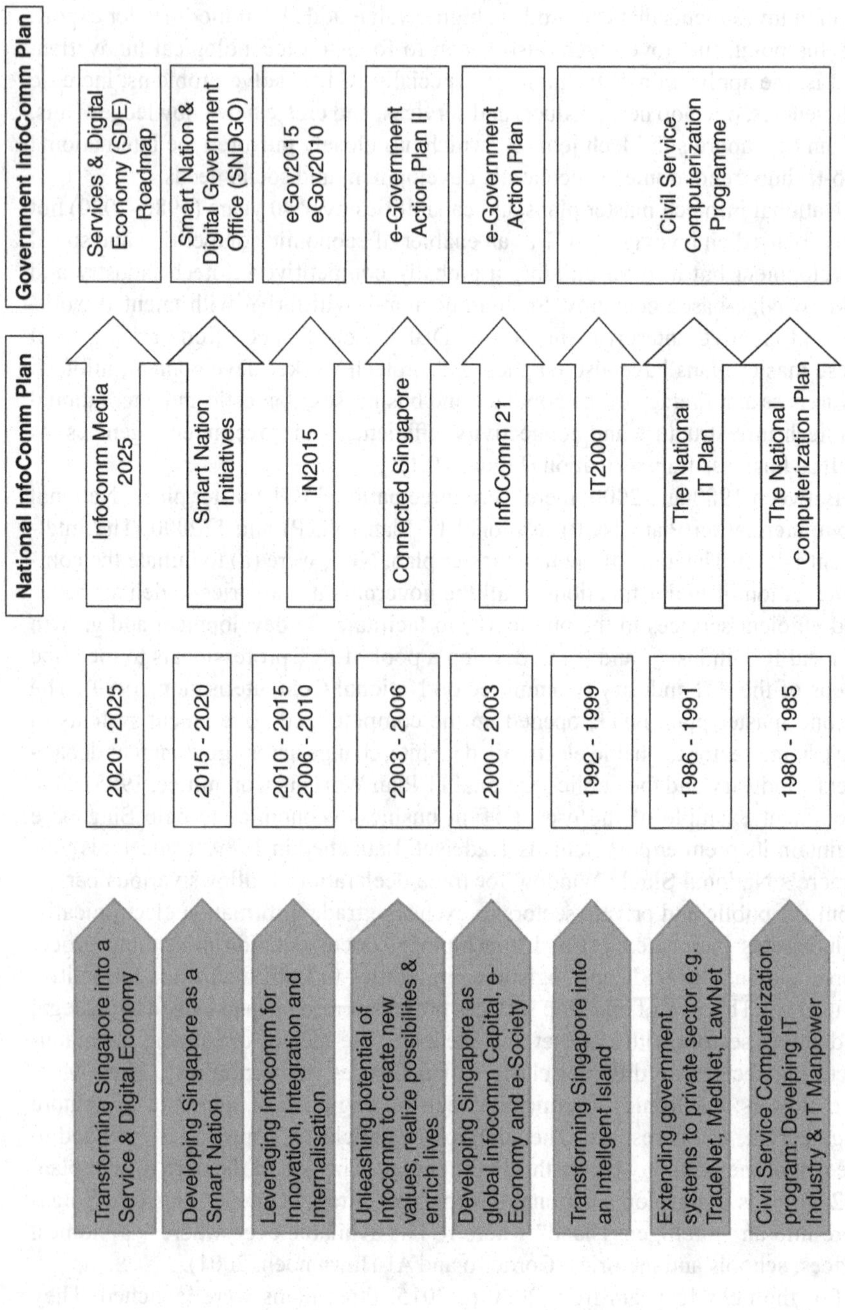

Figure 10.1 Singapore ICT plans (*Source*: IMDA Singapore)

nurturing an environment to develop a sufficient pool of high-calibre ICT workers and Net-savvy users to sustain the growth of the economy as well as to deliver as many integrated public sector services online as possible to increase public access to e-government services (Infocomm Development Authority, 2000). The fifth master plan, Connected Singapore, extended the broadband capabilities to provide an infrastructure that supported wireless and wired networks and value-added mobile services (Infocomm Development Authority, 2003). The sixth plan, iN2015, aims to develop Singapore into a global ICT capital e-economy and e-society. To achieve the latter, an ultra-high-speed network on the order of one gigabit per second was developed to link every home and office. This had included a wireless broadband network throughout the island to further improve the ability of all Singaporeans to stay connected at all times (Koh & Lee, 2008).

Launched in 2014, the Smart Nation initiative aims to "support better living, stronger communities, and create more opportunities, for all". The Smart Nation initiative has the dual goals of improving citizens' lives and allowing them to connect with each other through the use of sensors and smart devices, as well as enhancing economic productivity and exploring new opportunities through such technology (SNDGO, 2018). The Smart Nation initiative built on the Singapore government's earlier efforts to digitize public service delivery through its 'e-government' drive that began with a 'Civil Service Computerisation Programme'. While these earlier e-government initiatives tended to focus on increasing efficiency in public service delivery, the Smart Nation initiative was much more comprehensive, reflecting a broader 'digital transformation' that aimed to digitize all aspects of urban life in Singapore, often through collaborations with non-state actors such as businesses, citizens and NGOs (Woo, 2017).

Infocomm Media 2025 (MCI, 2015; IMDA, 2019) is a ten-year plan released in August 2015 to create a globally competitive infocomm media ecosystem that enables and complements Singapore's Smart Nation vision. This ecosystem supports people and enterprises in tapping into infocomm media to effect economic and social transformation and foster a common identity.

The Services and Digital Economy (SDE) Technology Roadmap (IMDA, 2018) was officially launched in 2019. The Technology Roadmap has identified nine key trends[2] that will move the digital economy significantly over the next three to five years. They may be viewed either as challenges or as opportunities. The biggest impact will be on the services sector as it forms the bulk of the global economy and Singapore's GDP.

Services 4.0 was identified through the SDE Technology Roadmap as a potential growth engine for Singapore's digital economy. Services 4.0 is the vision that will guide Singapore's response to capture opportunities for the economy. In Services 4.0, businesses will need to meet changing customer needs quickly, innovate and create new value in order to differentiate themselves from competitors. Emerging technologies will make it possible for businesses to automate repetitive tasks and achieve higher productivity. However, as customers still demand human interactions, businesses should unlock growth by offering customer-centric services enabled by emerging technologies. Both worker augmentation and automation will ultimately lead to the creation of new and enhanced job opportunities.

Digitalization challenge

Singapore has been through many changes in the past, be it industrialization, automation or internationalization. As a small, open economy, Singapore has nurtured the instincts to be flexible, be adaptable and stay relevant. It is not abandoning the development philosophy based on having Singapore be an important node in the global value chain (GVC). Digital transformation is considered as a means to strengthen the function of the GVC and enable Singapore continue to be a relevant node in the GVC. Nonetheless, digitalization poses fundamental and far-reaching challenges.

The Singapore government has decided to transform the economy by strengthening the digital ecosystem in conjunction with developing the industries, identifying new areas of growth, investing in infrastructure, enhancing regulations, setting up relevant promotional institutions and forging international partnerships. Leading the charge in transformation is the Infocomm Media Development Authority (IMDA), a statutory board under Ministry of Communication and Information, which has laid out plans to anchor global technology leaders, build local champions, spawn start-ups and nurture future-ready talent in the country. Singapore intends to build deep capabilities and stay at the forefront of global technology trends, so that it can tap into growing markets and build new solutions that are globally scalable and exportable.

To facilitate that objective, a new *Digital Industry Singapore*, or *DISG*, office had been established. DISG will work with private companies to address issues on needs for securing talent and market access, building capabilities and internationalizing. An example to illustrate this is DISG's collaboration with SAP, one of the world's largest providers of enterprise application software. Singapore is home to the first SAP Leonardo Centre in Southeast Asia, a digital innovation platform focusing on areas such as AI, analytics, the IOT and blockchain to help their customers innovate and scale their businesses. Through the centre, SAP collaborates with Singapore-based small and medium-sized ICT enterprises to develop solutions based on SAP technology, which they can also scale and sell internationally. DISG is also working with other companies to capture opportunities in areas like ride hailing, e-commerce, fintech, cybersecurity, artificial intelligence (AI) and cloud. A holistic approach is used in engaging the foreign tech companies and bringing them into Singapore to create a vibrant ICT ecosystem and exciting job opportunities for Singaporeans. As many as ten thousand new jobs are expected to be created over the next three years.

Within the tech space, 5G technology is a critical component of a digital transformation strategy. 5G is the fifth-generation of mobile Internet connectivity, making better use of the radio spectrum and enabling far more devices to access the mobile net at the same time. According to the study by Capgemini (2019), 75% of industrial companies' executives mentioned 5G as a key enabler. Singapore is tapping the full potential of 5G technology to spearhead new areas of growth. 5G technology is widely touted to enable the development of new business models and advanced applications, fostering business innovation and spurring economic growth. Communities, businesses and industries are expected to benefit from the transformative impact that 5G enables. It is reckoned that Singapore needs to move decisively, both on the infrastructure supply side and on the industry use-case demand side, to capture opportunities in 5G applications and services.

To catalyse 5G development and adoption in the economy, Singapore has identified six strategic clusters which are believed to have the potential to generate the most value for Singapore.[3] One of the clusters is the maritime sector, which IMDA is working on together with the Maritime and Port of Singapore Authority, and telcos (Singtel and M1) to conduct 5G trials for smart port operations. The trials will allow Singapore's ports to experiment with cutting-edge technology in areas such as remote crane operations, tele-operations of port equipment and automated ground vehicle port navigation.

In the annual budget statement of the government in 2021, digital transformation of the economy is again a key concern. The Singapore government has set aside S$1 billion for a string of new schemes and enhanced support to co-fund mature enterprises' adoption of digital solutions and new technologies. Singapore is allocating more than SG$500 million (US$352.49 million) to support local businesses in their digital transformation efforts. Specifically, the funds will go towards facilitating companies in their adoption of e-payments, e-invoicing, as well as more advanced digital tools. Half of the SG$500 million has also been earmarked to help businesses digitalize alongside with digital platform application providers.

In addition, some SG$285 million will be set aside in venture capitalism to provide financial support for promising start-ups to sustain innovation. This is in addition to an earlier SG$300 million committed to help deep tech start-ups gain access to capital, expertise and industry networks. The Singapore government will also enhance the Productivity Solutions Grant (PSG)–Job Redesign by raising the government co-funding ratio to 80%, from 70% previously, until the end of March 2022. This is to help businesses redesign jobs. PSG is a Singapore government subsidy to encourage SMEs in Singapore to take on IT solution costs and solutions to streamline business operations. A new Emerging Technology Programme will therefore co-fund the costs of trials and the adoption of frontier technologies such as 5G, artificial intelligence and trust technologies.

Overall, the government has set aside $40 million to grow the 5G ecosystem in Singapore. That includes developing open 5G test beds and conducting R&D for 5G in Singapore. Other than enhancing its digital infrastructure and cybersecurity environment,[4] Singapore has also investing significantly in R&D in frontier technologies, targeting areas like AI and cybersecurity. AI Singapore (AISG) is a national AI programme launched by the National Research Foundation (NRF) in 2019. It is public-private partnership to anchor deep national capabilities in AI, grow local talent and build the AI ecosystem in Singapore by looking at actual use cases and application for AI.

There is also an international dimension of digitalization that cannot be ignored. Singapore is a strong proponent of an integrated, global digital economy. Indeed, a strong domestic DBE will help to attract investment from abroad. It can help in elevating an industry's digital standards and practices which can possibly replace legal requirements of physical documentation and increase the velocity and volume of trade. For example, Hong Kong Shanghai Bank (HSBC) has worked on digitalizing the letter of credit process using blockchain technology and has managed to reduce transaction times from five to ten days to under 24 hours. The same technology can be applied to other trade processes heavily reliant on paper and couriers. Across the border, Singapore has teamed up with Indonesia to build the Nongsa Digital Park (NDP) on Batam Island, which is just a 40-minute ferry ride from Singapore (Goh, 2021). In fact, a plan had already been made to expand NDP into a Digital Town that includes a residential village, tech campuses, a town plaza and a commercial centre and is set to house 8,000 tech talents when completed. There are currently about 1,000 tech talents at the existing NDP working for tech companies and start-ups from Singapore and Indonesia.

Singapore has participated in several regional and international initiatives to raise awareness of and build consensus on the rules of responsible state behaviour in cyberspace. The ASEAN Digital Integration Framework Action Plan and the ASEAN Framework for Digital Data Governance are two examples of platforms which, if implemented, could bring about greater ease of business in the region. Singapore has concluded negotiations on two digital economy agreements (DEA): one with Chile and New Zealand, and the other with Australia.[5] A DEA is a treaty that establishes digital trade rules and digital economy collaborations between two or more economies. DEA fosters interoperability of standards and systems and supports businesses, especially SMEs, engaging in digital trade and electronic commerce. It encourages cooperation between Singapore's economic partners in nascent areas such as digital identities, artificial intelligence and data innovation. This gives organizations the scope to trial use cases and technologies across different countries.

Digital transformation of SMEs in Singapore

Digital transformation provides hope for a new path of economic growth and development. More importantly, it will help to create more interesting careers and job possibilities for Singaporeans and exciting opportunities for businesses big or small. Singapore wants the digital transformation to be inclusive and to ensure that all individuals and companies are well equipped to participate in and benefit from Singapore's digital transformation. Singapore's goal is to be a leading digital economy that continually reinvents itself.

Singapore has rolled out a slew of initiatives and programs to quicken the pace of digitalization of companies, especially small and medium-sized enterprises. SMEs account for 99% of enterprises, contribute 50% of GDP and provide jobs for two-thirds of the workforce.

SMEs should strive to be a part of a digital ecosystem, where companies, people, data, processes and things are connected by the shared use of digital platforms. Briefly, such digital ecosystems are created through the business relationships one company has with another. When a company develops a suite of flexible services and resources which can be managed in an agile manner, it is then able to meet its evolving business needs (Noke & Hughes, 2010).

Government grants and initiatives to help digitalization of SMEs

Launched in April 2017, the SMEs Go Digital programme by the IMDA aims to make going digital simple for SMEs. Digitalization initiatives (listed in Table 10.1) in the program help SMEs use digital technologies and build stronger digital capabilities to seize growth opportunities in the digital economy. The digitalization initiatives include Industry Digital Plans, Pre-Approved Solutions and Digital Consultancies.

Table 10.1 Initiatives under the SMEs Go Digital Programme

	Initiatives	*Description*
1	Digital Resilience Bonus *https://enterpryze.com/sg/grants/digital-resilience-bonus/*	Digital Resilience Bonus provides additional support to food services and retail enterprises seeking to uplift their digital capabilities to emerge stronger after the circuit breaker period.
2	InvoiceNow *www.imda.gov.sg/programme-listing/nationwide-e-invoicing-framework/InvoiceNow*	InvoiceNow is a nationwide e-invoicing method that facilitates the direct transmission of invoices in a structured digital format across finance systems.
3	Digital Solutions for Safe Management *https://www.gobusiness.gov.sg/safemanagement/safedigital/*	This directory of digital solutions is specially curated to help businesses use digital solutions to implement safe management measures for safe reopening.
4	Industry Digital Plans *www.imda.gov.sg/programme-listing/smes-go-digital/industry-digital-plans*	IMDA works with industry leaders to develop Industry Digital Plans that make it easier for SMEs to adopt digital technology to boost growth and productivity.
5	Pre-Approved Solutions *https://govassist.gobusiness.gov.sg/productivity-solutions-grant/*	This initiative offers pre-approved solutions that improve productivity and are supported under the Productivity Solutions Grant (PSG).
6	Start Digital Pack *www.imda.gov.sg/programme-listing/smes-go-digital/start-digital-pack*	Start Digital was launched in January 2019 to help newly incorporated SMEs and those who have not adopted any digital solutions before.

(*Continued*)

Table 10.1 (Continued)

	Initiatives	*Description*
7	Grow Digital *www.imda.gov.sg/GrowDigital*	Grow Digital helps business connect to B2B and B2C e-commerce platforms that have regional or global reach to sell overseas without a physical presence there.
8	SME Digital Tech Hub *www.imda.gov.sg/programme-listing/smes-go-digital/sme-digital-tech-hub*	Established by IMDA and operated by the Association of Small and Medium Enterprises (ASME), the SME Digital Tech Hub is a dedicated hub that provides specialist digital technology advisory to SMEs with more advanced digital needs, such as data analytics and cybersecurity.
9	Advanced Digital Solutions *www.imda.gov.sg/programme-listing/smes-go-digital/Advanced-Digital-Solutions*	Connects multiple firms digitally and enables advanced capabilities in the ecosystem.

As of March 2021, more than 63,000 SMEs have adopted digital solutions from the programme, with around 40,000 signing up in 2020. More than 2,000 enterprises have gained access to the overseas market through e-commerce platforms under the Grow Digital initiative.

Of particular relevance to the digitalization push is the sector-specific Industry Digital Plans (IDPs). IDPs provide SMEs with a step-by-step guide on the digital solutions to adopt and provide relevant training for their employees at different stages of their growth. The IDPs serve as a common reference for SMEs and they are aligned with the Industry Transformation Maps (ITMs) for each sector.[6] To date, IMDA has rolled out IDPs for the following 14 sectors – retail, logistics (including air transport), environmental services, security, food services, wholesale trade, media, land transport, sea transport (bunkering, harbour craft and ship agency), accountancy, hotel, construction and facilities management, early childhood, and training and adult education.

To make it easy for SMEs to adopt digital solutions recommended in the IDPs, IMDA provides a list of pre-approved solutions assessed to be market-proven, cost-effective and supported by reliable vendors. SMEs interested in adopting these solutions can start by visiting the website GoBusiness Gov Assist[7] and applying for the Productivity Solutions Grant through the Business Grants Portal.[8] PSG can help to offset up to 80% of the costs of adopting these solutions.

Work force training – digital skills

Emphasis on technology is important for digitalization. However, the best digitalization plan will not succeed if workers are deficient in the skill and knowledge required in the new digital economy. People need to have the requisite skills to take full advantage of the new jobs that are being created. The Singapore government is working with industry partners to enhance training and placement opportunities for ICT jobs across the economy via the SkillsFuture[9] initiative known as TechSkills Accelerator (TeSA),[10] launched in April 2016. The IMDA, which drives TeSA for ICT professional development, takes an integrated approach/framework to ICT skills acquisition and practitioner training – in core ICT skills and in sector-specific ICT skills – and enhances employability outcomes through place and train programmes and career advisory services. The skills identified in the framework can support emerging areas such as cyber security, IoT, immersive media, artificial intelligence and data analytics. More than 80 ICT skillsets and more than 100 job roles have been identified. Interest in TeSA has been very encouraging. Since April 2016, over 74,000 training places have been taken up or committed.

Another programme that can help companies to upgrade and reskill workers on their payroll is the SkillsFuture Funding Support for Employers.[11] Eligible companies can receive up to 90% subsidy on training fees and absentee payroll while attending courses.

In August 2020, AISG launched two new initiatives (AI for Everyone; AI for Industry) in partnership with the IMDA targeted at enabling 12,000 more people to acquire AI know-how, under the TeSA initiative. The latter aims to develop a pipeline of skilled tech professionals to drive Singapore's local tech ecosystem, especially in the AI space. It helps to ensure that businesses and workers can effectively use AI to be more competitive.

Beyond the ICT sector, IMDA is collaborating with the Singapore Computer Society (SCS) to reach out to non-ICT trade associations and chambers (TAC) to equip their businesses with digital skills and prepare them for a digital economy. For a start, IMDA and SCS are working with TACs in the legal, accountancy and manufacturing sectors on an action plan to upskill professionals in these sectors with digital capabilities. Effort is also made to excite young Singaporeans about the new opportunities in the digital economy. All upper primary school students will go through a ten-hour programme to develop an appreciation of the core computational thinking and coding concepts through simple visual programming-based lessons co-developed by Ministry of Education (MOE) and IMDA. They will also be exposed to emerging technologies such as AI as part of the programme.

Progress of digitalization so far

A 2020 *SME Digital Transformation Study*[12] produced jointly by the Association of Small and Medium Enterprises (ASME) and Microsoft Singapore reports that 83% of SMEs in Singapore have digital transformation strategies in place, and more than half (54%) reported delays in their digitalization plans due to COVID-19. Also, despite higher adoption of digital transformation, only two in five SMEs perceive their efforts to be successful. SMEs also faced barriers in their digital transformation journey. The barriers include high cost of implementation (56%), lack of digitally skilled workers (40%), low awareness of government support (30%) and not having the right technology partners (28%).

On a more positive note, the 2020 study also found that more than three-quarters (80%) of Singapore SME leaders are now aware of the term 'digital transformation' – up from 57% since 2018. Overall, the adoption rate of digital technology has also risen, as nearly all companies (99%) surveyed have adopted at least the most basic level of digital technologies such as office productivity tools and web-based email.

In a more recent survey involving 782 SMEs, conducted between November and December 2020 by the United Overseas Bank (UOB),[13] small businesses are lagging behind their larger peers in digital transformation. The survey found that 41% of SMEs that implemented digitalization initiatives last year recorded revenue growth. Among SMEs that had not digitalized, only 24% saw their revenue improve. Those that had digitalized their entire business reported better revenue growth than those that had digitalized only one area.

SMEs in business services, manufacturing and engineering, community and personal services, technology, media and telecommunications as well as consumer goods sectors saw the highest year-on-year percentage increases in productivity and efficiency, ranging from 42% to 49%. The study demonstrates that close to *one in two SMEs* that proactively took steps to adopt digital tools last year are already seeing benefits, such as greater productivity and efficiency gains, improved customer experience and higher revenue, even in a volatile business environment.

In the area of government support, the study revealed that the majority of respondents were unaware of government schemes and initiatives available to SMEs, such as the Productivity Solutions Grant[14] and Start Digital Pack.[15] However, it found that despite low levels of awareness of such initiatives, more than three in five SMEs would be keen to leverage these grants and schemes to support digital transformation in the next year. Existing government support also tends to benefit larger firms, with medium and medium-large companies stating that they are more likely to find government support useful (60% and 73% respectively).

As at March 2021, more than 63,000 SMEs have adopted digital solutions from the programme, with around 40,000 signing up in 2020. More than 2,000 enterprises have gained access to overseas market through e-commerce platforms under the Grow Digital initiative.

Conclusion

Singapore has successfully ridden consecutive waves of digital transformation, starting from the national computerization efforts of the 1980s. This latest digital transformation will open up opportunities on three fronts: new industries, new markets and new jobs. New industries will be formed even as older ones start to evolve and transform. Technologies such as AI have the potential to completely rewire whole industries, from finance to shipping and manufacturing. Singapore's scarce land resources and limited population have been the main constraints to growth. Digitalization provides new options to overcome these constraints.

SMEs surveyed in the ASME-Microsoft study in 2020, referred to in a previous section, also indicated that high implementation cost was the biggest barrier they faced when it comes to digital transformation – a similar observation from the 2018 iteration of the study. Other significant factors include the lack of a digitally skilled workforce, uncertain economic environment, low awareness of government support as well as the lack of appropriate technology partners.

The Singapore government is always very good in pushing out schemes, grants and programs, but the take-up rate is not spectacular. Even with 63,000 signing up for a government program by the end of March 2021, that is only about 23% of all SMEs, though it is reckoned that some SMEs proceeded to digitalize without utilizing government schemes or grants. The take-up rate is still low for an urgent nationwide campaign. Some would blame it on application procedures that involve too-complicated instructions and qualification criteria, or simply ignorance or the low level of awareness of SMEs bosses. Nonetheless, suggestions can be made to help the SMEs on their digitalization journeys. Easier access to funding or grants can be made available so that financial constraint is less binding and budgeting for digitalization can be facilitated via deferred principal payments, bridging loans and tax rebates on investment in digital equipment and software. A directory of accredited technology and solution providers can be compiled by a leading government agency such as IMDA, and this is made available to SMEs planning their technological solutions and digitalization journey. It would be very useful if a digital 'shepherd' could be assigned to companies to help them to navigate the plethora of government initiatives, schemes and grants to achieve the desired outcome faster.

Singapore aspires to be a global-Asia node for digital technology and innovation. It aims to be a choice destination where entrepreneurs consider their start-up projects and where innovators will experiment with their latest ideas. The congregation of start-ups and interaction of innovation endeavours will help to establish an ecosystem for digital business. An enterprise is strengthened by having a vibrant and conducive start-up ecosystem in the country. Start-ups play an increasing role in driving innovation, especially as growing markets demand new solutions. The OECD predicts that emerging Asia (i.e. ASEAN, China and India) will grow by an average of 6% over the next five years. With Asia poised to account for more than half of global GDP by 2050, Singapore can be the gateway for start-ups to develop, test-bed solutions and expand into the region. Enterprise Singapore, a government agency, helms the Startup SG program that helps start-ups build a track record and provides access to mentors, funding and workspaces. With close to 100 partners, Startup SG programmes supported the growth of over 3,690 start-ups across key sectors such as health, urban solutions, fintech and digital services in March 2020.

Digital transformation is not necessarily an easy experience. Some companies may encounter difficulties in the transformation process. One commonly cited difficulty is how to get employees digitally ready. Companies will need to pay attention to hiring the right people and making sure existing employees are trained for using new digital tools. It is important to have patience in identifying who needs more help in the transition and to set aside time for training. While government can make available the grants and training schemes for training, the success of reskilling and upgrading workers still depends very much on the willingness of employers allowing their employees time off to attend courses and training.

Going digital can open gaps in cyber security. Getting the advice of security consultants when implementing wide-ranging digital solutions can help businesses understand risks and adopt appropriate mitigating measures. It can be very expensive in terms of tools and training to get everyone in the company up to speed. Hence, government grants will help to offset some of the costs. The long-term benefits can more than outweigh the short-term costs.

While the pandemic has accelerated the adoption of digital technology, it has also highlighted the gap in skill and literacy across people and countries. The risk is that individuals who lack the necessary financial or digital literacy may fall behind. From the perspective of society, there is a risk that digitalization is a blocker rather than an enabler of prosperity. Government, the education sector and companies must work together to address the challenges and prevent a growing skills gap which creates greater inequality that is inimical to social stability. To get digital transformation right, the focus should not be solely on technology; attention has also to be paid to inculcating a progressive mindset – an attitude of unlearning, relearning and adapting to the changes.

Notes

1 For a more extant discussion on the genesis of the DBE and its use as a framework for research in business and economic transformation, see the report by the European Commission (2007).

2 The nine key trends are pervasive adoption of AI; more empathic, cognitive and affective AI; greater human-machine collaborations; more natural technological interfaces; greater use of codeless development tools; more seamless services enabled by everything-as-a-service (XaaS); the maturing of cloud deployment with hybrid and multi-cloud; trust in decentralized blockchain; and economic growth through application programming interfaces (API).

3 These are maritime operations, urban mobility, smart estates, Industry 4.0, government applications and consumer applications.

4 The Cybersecurity Act was passed in 2018 in tandem with the Cybersecurity Code-of-Practice governing protection of critical information infrastructure (CII). CII owners are also required to submit their cybersecurity risk assessment reports and perform detailed cybersecurity audits once every two years.

5 Ministry of Trade and Industry (2020) *Digital Economy Agreements* www.mti.gov.sg/Improving-Trade/Digital-Economy-Agreements

6 See Annex A for a list of ITMs assigned to six clusters consisting of 23 industries.

7 For more details, please refer to https://govassist.gobusiness.gov.sg/productivity-solutions-grant/

8 For more details, please refer to www.businessgrants.gov.sg

9 SkillsFuture is a national movement to provide Singaporeans with the opportunities to develop their fullest potential throughout life, regardless of their starting points. Through this movement, the skills, passion and contributions of every individual will drive Singapore's next phase of development towards an advanced economy and inclusive society.

10 For more details, please refer to https://www.imda.gov.sg/imtalent/about-us/national-talent-development-initiatives/techskills-accelerator--tesa
11 For more details, please refer to www.ssg.gov.sg/programmes-and-initiatives/funding/funding-for-employer-based-training.html
12 The study can be accessed at https://news.microsoft.com/en-sg/2020/10/22/over-80-of-singapore-smes-embrace-digital-transformation-more-than-half-report-slowdowns-due-to-covid-19-asme-microsoft-study-2020/
13 *Digitalisation efforts pay off for Singapore SMEs with rise in revenue*. Accessible at www.uobgroup.com/web-resources/uobgroup/pdf/newsroom/2021/Digitalisation-efforts-SMEs-revenue-rise.pdf
14 This is one of the initiatives in the SMEs Go Digital program. See Table 10.1.
15 This is one of the initiatives in the SMEs Go Digital program. See Table 10.1.

References

Aagaard, A. (Ed.). (2019). *Digital business models: Driving transformation and innovation*. Palgrave Macmillan, Springer Nature.

Amornkitvikai, Y., & Lee, C. (2020). *Determinants of e-commerce adoption and utilisation by SMEs in Thailand*. Economics Working Paper, No. 2020-01. Institute of Southeast Asian Studies.

ASME-Microsoft. (2020). *Singapore SME digital transformation study*. https://news.microsoft.com/en-sg/2020/10/22/over-80-of-singapore-smes-embrace-digital-transformation-more-than-half-report-slowdowns-due-to-covid-19-asme-microsoft-study-2020/

Baldwin, R. (2019). *The globotics upheaval: Globalization, robotics and the future of work*. Jointly published by Oxford University Press, Weidenfeld & Nicolson.

Björkdahl, J. (2009). Technology cross-fertilization and the business model: The case of integrating ICTs in mechanical engineering products. *Research Policy*, *38*(9), 1468–1477. https://doi.org/10.1016/j.respol.2009.07.006

Capgemini. (2019). *5G in industrial operations: How telcos and industrial companies stand to benefit*. Capgemini Research Institute, Head Office – Capgemini Service – Place de l'Étoile – 11 rue de Tilsitt – 75017. www.capgemini.com/wp-content/uploads/2019/06/5G-in-industrial-operations.pdf

Cordeiro, C. M., & Al-Hawamdeh, S. (2001). National information infrastructure and the realization of Singapore IT2000 initiative. *Information Research*, *6*(2). http://InformationR.net/ir/6-2/paper96.htm

Committee on National Computerisation. (1980). *Report on the committee on national computerisation 1980*. Government Printing Office.

Digital Vortex. (2015). *How digital disruption is redefining industries*. Global Center for Digital Business Transformation. www.cisco.com/c/dam/en/us/solutions/collateral/industry-solutions/digital-vortex-report.pdf

Dinlersoz, E. M., & Pereira, P. (2007). On the diffusion of electronic commerce. *International Journal of Industrial Organization*, *25*(3), 541–574.

Enterprise Singapore. (2019). *Singapore strengthens its startup ecosystem*. www.enterprisesg.gov.sg/media-centre/media-releases/2019/april/singapore-strengthens-its-startup-ecosystem-to-enhance-position-as-a-global-asia-node-for-technology-innovation-and-enterprise

European Commission. (2007). *Digital business ecosystems*. European Commission Directorate General Information Society and Media. www.digital-ecosystems.org/dbe-book-2007

Evans, D. S., Hagiu, A., & Schmalensee, R. (2006). *Invisible engines: How software platforms drive innovation and transform industries*. MIT Press.

Gartner. (2017). *2017 CEO survey: CIOs must scale up digital business*. www.gartner.com/smarterwithgartner/2017-ceo-survey-infographic/.

Goh, G. (2021, March 2). "Nongsa D-town" launched in Singapore-Indonesia tech park. *Business Times, Government and Economy*. www.businesstimes.com.sg/government-economy

IDA. (2000). *Annual report*. Infocomm Development Authority.

IDA. (2003). *Connected Singapore: A new blueprint for Infocomm development*. Infocomm Development Authority.

IMDA. (2018). *The future of services: Services & digital economy technology roadmap (SDE-TRM) main report*. Infocomm Media Development Authority. www.imda.gov.sg/-/media/Imda/Files/Industry-Development/Infrastructure/Technology/Technology-Roadmap/SDE-TRM-Main-Report.pdf

IMDA. (2019). *Infocomm media 2025 plan*. www.imda.gov.sg/Who-We-Are/corporate-publications/infocomm-media-2025-plan

Koh, T. S., & Lee, S. C. (2008). Digital skills and education: Singapore's ICT master planning for the school sector. In S. K. Lee, C. B. Goh, B. Fredriksen, & J. P. Tan (Eds.), *Toward a better future: Education and training for economic development in Singapore since 1965* (pp. 167–190). The World Bank.

Leinwand, P., & Mani, M. M. (2021). Digitizing isn't the same as digital transformation. *Harvard Business Review*. https://hbr.org/2021/03/digitizing-isnt-the-same-as-digital-transformation

Libert, B., Beck, M., & Wind, J. (2016, June 22). How to navigate a digital transformation. *Harvard Business Review*. https://www.coursehero.com/file/43491756/Digital-business-models-driving-innovationpdf/

Matt, C., Hess, T., and Benlian, A. (2015). Digital transformation strategies. *Business and Information Systems Engineering*. https://doi.org/10.1007/s12599-015-0401-5

MCI. (2015). *Infocomm media 2025, report of the infocomm media masterplan steering committee*. Ministry of Communication & Information. https://issuu.com/singaporemci/docs/infocomm_media_2025_full_report

McKinsey Global Institute. (2017). *Digital Europe: Pushing the frontier, capturing the benefits*. www.mckinsey.com/~/media/McKinsey/Business%20Functions/McKinsey%20Digital/Our%20Insights/Digital%20Europe%20Pushing%20the%20frontier%20capturing%20the%20benefits/Digital-Europe-Full-report-June-2016.ashx

Ministry of Trade and Industry. (1991). *The strategic economic plan: Towards a developed nation*. Economic Planning Committee. Ministry of Trade and Industry.

Moore, J. F. (1993). *The death of competition: Leadership and strategy in the age of business ecosystems*. HarperCollins Publishers.

National IT Plan Working Committee. (1985). *National IT plan: A strategic framework*. National Computer Board.

Noke, H., & Hughes, M. (2010). Climbing the value chain: Strategies to create a new product development capability in mature SMEs. *International Journal of Operations & Production Management*, *30*(2), 132–154. https://doi.org/10.1108/01443571011018680

Porter, M. E., & Heppelmann, J. E. (2014). How smart, connected products are transforming competition. *Harvard Business Review*. https://hbr.org/2014/11/how-smart-connected-products-are-transforming-competition

Senyo, P. K., Liu, K., & Effah, J. (2019). Digital business ecosystem: Literature review and a framework for future research. *International Journal of Information Management*, *47*, 52–64.

Rymaszewska, A., Helo, P., & Gunasekaran, A. (2017). IoT powered servitization of manufacturing – an exploratory case study. *International Journal of Production Economics*, *192*, 92–105. https://doi.org/10.1016/j. ijpe.2017.02.016

SNDGO. (2018). *Smart nation: The way forward.* Smart Nation and Digital Government Office. www.smartnation.gov.sg/docs/default-source/default-document-library/smart-nation-strategy_nov2018.pdf?sfvrsn=3f5c2af8_2

Toh, M. H. (2015). Singapore's economic development in the light of modern development concepts. Chapter 7 in M. Yülek (Ed.), *Economic planning and industrial policy in the globalizing economy*. Springer International Publishing.

Treutiger, J., Andrén, J., Dadhich, L., & Kjellén, T. (2017). *Four key questions to consider for successful digital transformation.* http://www.adlittle.com/en/insights/prism/four-key-questions-consider-successfuldigital-transformation

Woo, J. J. (2017). *Singapore's smart nation initiative – a policy and organisational perspective*. Discussion Paper, Lee Kuan Yew School of Public Policy (LKY School), National University of Singapore.

World Economic Forum. (2016). *Digital transformation of industries: Digital enterprise.* http://reports.weforum.org/digital-transformation/wp-content/blogs.dir/94/mp/files/pages/files/digital-enterprise-narrative-final-january-2016.pdf

Annex A

The Singapore government announced the S$4.5b Industry Transformation Programme at Budget 2016. The programme will integrate different restructuring efforts, taking a targeted and industry-focused approach to address issues and deepen partnerships between government, firms, industries, trade associations and chambers.

Under the programme, there will be Industry Transformation Maps (ITMs) developed for 23 industries under six clusters. The Future Economy Council (FEC) established in 2017 takes overall responsibility for the implementation of the ITMs.

Table 10.2 List of ITM clusters and industries

S/No	*Clusters*	*Sectors*	*Lead Agency*
1	Manufacturing	Energy & Chemicals	EDB
2		Precision Engineering	EDB
3		Marine & Offshore	EDB
4		Aerospace	EDB
5		Electronics	EDB
6	Built Environment	Construction (incl. Archi & Engineering services)	BCA
7		Real Estate	CEA
8		Cleaning	NEA
9		Security	MHA
10	Trade & Connectivity	Logistics	EDB
11		Air Transport	CAAS
12		Sea Transport	MPA

(*Continued*)

Table 1.2 (Continued)

S/No	*Clusters*	*Sectors*	*Lead Agency*
13		Land Transport (incl. Public Transport)	LTA
14		Wholesale Trade	IES
15	Essential Domestic	Healthcare	MOH
16	Services	Education (Early Childhood & Private Education)	MOE
17	Professional	Professional Services	EDB
18	Services	ICT and Media	MCI
19		Financial Services	MAS
20	Lifestyle	Food Services	SPRING
21		Retail	SPRING
22		Hotels	STB
23		Food Manufacturing	SPRING

Source: Media Factsheet – Industry Transformation Maps, Annex A

https://www.mti.gov.sg/-/media/MTI/ITM/General/Fact-sheet-on-Industry-Transformation-Maps---revised-as-of-31-Mar-17.pdf

11 P2P lending and philanthropy platform

A new face of Asian digital financial inclusion (evidence from Indonesia)

Khairunnisa Musari

Introduction

Financial inclusion today is presently a global agenda in order to reach sustainable development goals (SDGs). In Asia, Bhowmik and Saha (2013), Asian Development Bank Institute (ADBI) (2014), Ayyagari and Beck (2015), Gopalan and Kikuchi (2016), and Oliver Wyman et al. (2017) confirmed that several emerging market economies in the region are employing financial inclusion as an integral component of financial sector development to achieve inclusive growth. Regional discussions of the issue have also escalated. The Asia Pacific Economic Cooperation (APEC) and the Association of Southeast Asian Nations (ASEAN) have a special forum to examine financial inclusion issues. They address a plethora of initiatives to expand the provision of financial services to households and firms by allowing greater access to the formal credit market.

Unhesitatingly, as a target in eight of the 17 goals in the SDGs, financial inclusion works explicitly as an enabler of other developmental goals, especially at this time when the world is experiencing a digital revolution. McKinsey Global Institute (MGI) (2016), Osafo-Kwaako et al. (2018), United Nations Secretary-General's Special Advocate for Inclusive Finance for Development (UNSGSA), the Better Than Cash Alliance, the United Nations Capital Development (UNCDF), and the World Bank (2018) mentioned that digitalization rapidly may expand and scale up access to financial services. Digital financial inclusion will help in achieving the SDGs.

Indonesia can be a reflection and motor of Asian digital financial inclusion, at least regarding the peer-to-peer (P2P) lending and philanthropy platforms. As Southeast Asia's (SEA) biggest economy and the third-largest population in Asia with more than 260 million people, Soejachmoen (2016) stated that the access to financial services in Indonesia is considered low compared to other Asian countries. However, Mulyani (2020) argued that Indonesia has an enormous productive age population and rapidly increasing cellular phone and internet penetration. The country has a remarkable range of untapped financial technology (fintech) prospects, including P2P lending platforms. Around 40% of Indonesia's huge population of young adults is unbanked, presenting a broad chance for the industry

DOI: 10.4324/9781003224532-11

to grow. Study by Athoillah (2020) also exhibited the development of fintech in Indonesia, brings a positive contribution to gross domestic product (GDP), and stimulates growth in the financial sector and employment.

Then, referring to the report of the Charities Aid Foundation (CAF) (2019), Indonesia has become the most generous country in the world. Since the World Giving Index was first introduced in 2010, five of the top ten countries are found in Asia, with Indonesia as the leading the way. The existence of *zakat* as one of Islamic philanthropy has boosted Indonesia's rank. Referring to Hartnell (2020), philanthropy in Indonesia has always been driven primarily by religion. Islamic philanthropy is based on *zakat*, with most giving going to religious causes or social welfare. Afterward, technology becomes one of the drivers of the growth of philanthropy in Indonesia.

Therefore, this chapter describes the fundamental change in the provision of financial services to the excluded and underserved, underbanked and unbanked, the base of the pyramid (BoP), and micro, small, and midsize enterprise (MSME) segments through digital financial inclusion, namely P2P lending and philanthropy platform. Through literature review, observation, and following discourses/discussions/interviews with informants as representatives of stakeholders, this chapter addresses the P2P lending and philanthropy platform as a new face of Asian digital financial inclusion by focusing on three issues: (1) entry barriers, (2) development of digital financial inclusion ecosystems, and (3) social and economic impacts.

Observation and following discourses/discussions/interviews with informants is intended to complement and confirm some focus of the issues in this chapter, that is, the entry barriers for digital financial inclusion through demand/supply-side constraints, Indonesia's fintech ecosystem, and the social and economic impacts of P2P lending and philanthropy platforms. Observation and following discourses/discussions/interviews with informants cover three P2P lending platforms, three philanthropy platforms, representatives of Indonesia Financial Services Authority (OJK) at central and regional levels, five recipients and five activists of P2P lending and philanthropy platforms.

Overall, this chapter has a mission to invite the public to be more involved in implementing financial inclusion as a form of shared social responsibility. The financial inclusion agenda should not be borne by the government solely because it can create an impetus to seek financing sources that contain high interest, which can actually bring the emerging countries into a debt trap. Indonesia may not represent the best practice in increasing financial inclusion. However, the Indonesian case study is expected at least to inspire the Asian and global community to get involved in funding the financial inclusion agenda through a digital financial inclusion platform. The aim is not oriented to commercial businesses to profit from people who are the target of financial inclusion, but as social finance, which is a source of low-cost funds for helping them to become empowered and able to reach a better living standard.

To clarify the flow of this chapter, the remaining part of the chapter is organized as follows. A background study is described in the second section. The third section provides a discussion by referring to the secondary and primary data with an emphasis the three points concerning barriers to entry, developing a digital financial inclusion ecosystem, and social and economic impacts. The last section concludes the chapter.

Background study

The SEA region can become a strong representation for Asia regarding the financial inclusion agenda. With a population of 570 million and a GDP predicted to reach US$4.7 trillion by 2025, Bain and Company (2019) and the Organisation for Economic Co-operation and Development (OECD) (2019) mentioned that SEA represents one of the world's largest and fastest-growing regions. ASEAN Secretariat (2020b) noted this region is the seventh-largest economy in the world and is predicted to become the fourth largest by 2050.

However, more than 70% of the adult population in SEA is either underbanked or unbanked with limited access to financial services. Even though millions of MSMEs play a crucial role in contributing to employment and inclusive growth in this region, in fact, they still face funding gaps. On the other hand, utilization of digital services and applications in SEA also have grown speedily with the quick spreading of broadband. Table 11.1 shows the growth of digital financial services, which is indicated by the projected growth of the compound annual growth rate (CAGR) from 2019 to 2025.

Furthermore, Indonesia deserves to represent the SEA region and ASEAN in implementing the financial inclusion agenda. Besides the geographical factor that requires the presence of digital technology to reach it, Indonesia presents significant opportunities in the fintech sector based on its standing as the largest economy in SEA and the fourth-most populous nation in the world. Referring to Soejachmoen (2016), the high cost of opening branches in remote areas and the high penetration of mobile phones even among the poor make the digital payment system and branchless banking the most appropriate strategy to be adopted in

Table 11.1 The growth of digital financial services in SEA

Countries	*The growth of CAGR (2019–2025)*				
	Digital payments	*Digital remittance*	*Digital lending*	*Digital insurance*	*Digital investment*
Vietnam	10%	31%	83%	45%	80%
Indonesia	13%	36%	61%	50%	90%
Philippines	13%	18%	83%	50%	78%
Thailand	9%	33%	42%	24%	53%
Malaysia	10%	20%	21%	27%	60%
Singapore	3%	7%	17%	29%	26%
SEA	10%	17%	29%	30%	41%

Source: Euromonitor; GlobalData; Bain and Temasek; in Bain and Company (2019)

Indonesia to boost financial inclusion. Table 11.2 shows some key indicators of the socio-demography, economy, and connectivity of Indonesia in 2019.

Referring to the OJK (2020a), the level of financial literacy and inclusion in Indonesia has continued to move positively over the past five years. Based on the results of the National Financial Literacy Survey conducted by OJK in 2019, the financial literacy index reached 38.03% and financial inclusion index reached 76.19%. By gender, the literacy index and financial inclusion improved equally for men and women. Although it is still below the rise in conventional financial literacy, the *sharia* financial literacy index also rose to 8.93% in 2019 from 8.1% in 2016. Musari (2020) highlighted that the high levels of financial inclusion is not accompanied by high levels of financial literacy, which explains why people often fall victim to delusive investments or get trapped by digital moneylenders. Overall, the index of financial literacy and inclusion in Indonesia, by gender and type of industry, is shown Table 11.3.

Regarding the existence of fintech industry, the Indonesia FinTech Association (AFTECH) (2020) reported that the fintech industry in Indonesia is on the rise and should thrive, as indicated by growing number of licensed players, the variety of financial services solutions offered, as well as adoption in the market. The number of fintech start-ups registered as AFTECH members has increased from 24 to 275 (end of 2019), and by the end of Q2–2020, it has reached 362. The kind of fintech solutions ready for use in the market has also diversified from only digital payment and online lending to include project financing, financial planning, equity crowdfunding (ECF), innovative credit scoring, aggregation, as well as around 16 other solutions.

According to OJK (2020b), as of October 2020, there were 119 registered fintech P2P lending operators and 36 licensed. A total of 155 operators cover 144 conventional, 11 *sharia*, 102 local, and 53 foreign investments. The total assets of P2P

Table 11.2 Key indicators of the socio-demography, economic, and connectivity of Indonesia in 2019

Socio-demography	
– Land area (sq km)	1,916,862.2
– Population (000)	266,911.9
– Unemployment rate (%)	5.3
– Adult literacy rate (%)	95.9
Economic	
– GDP at current price (USD million)	1,121,298.3
– GDP per capita (USD)	4,201.0
– GDP growth at constant price (%)	5.0
– Inflation rate (%), end of period	2.7
Connectivity	
– Internet subscribers per 100 persons	47.7
– Cellular phone users per 100 persons	127.5

Source: ASEAN Secretariat (2020a)

Table 11.3 Level of financial literacy and inclusion based on gender and type of financial industry in Indonesia

Aspect	*Financial literacy (%)*		*Financial inclusion (%)*	
	2016	*2019*	*2016*	*2019*
National Index	29.70	38.03	67.80	76.19
Gender				
– Men	33.2	39.94	69.6	77.24
– Women	25.5	36.13	66.2	75.15
Type of Industry				
– Conventional	65.6	75.28	29.5	37.72
– *Sharia*	8.10	8.93	11.1	9.10

Source: OJK (2020a)

lending operators reached IDR3.42 trillion. The progress of registered fintech P2P lending platforms in Indonesia or commonly mentioned information technology-based lending services (LPMUBTI) in 2019–2020 is shown in Table 11.4. The overall data shows that fintech P2P lending is moving towards a new business model in Indonesia.

In regard to the existence of philanthropy platform, Hartnell (2020) wrote that a more open and democratic society in Indonesia today provides fertile ground for the growth of philanthropy. She collected the currently existing terms of philanthropy in Indonesia and grouped them into six clusters as shown in Table 11.5.

Hartnell (2020) mentioned that a national platform on philanthropy today originates from the initiative of a number of individuals and institutions/non-profit organizations. It includes high-value institutions, media organizations, and a few social justice/rights-based grantmaking organizations as most of the main players. Then, the key organization for philanthropy ecosystem support in Indonesia is Filantropi Indonesia. Filantopi Indonesia (2020) classified philanthropy in Indonesia into seven clusters that are successfully developed in Indonesia. In the beginning there were six clusters, but after the Covid-19 pandemic, a new cluster appeared in the health sector so that by 2020 there are seven philanthropic clusters. The seven philanthropy clusters are shown in Table 11.6.

One of the cluster coordinators in Indonesia is the National Board of Zakat Republic of Indonesia (BAZNAS), which represents a faith-based philanthropy institution. Based on the report by CAF (2019) and Hartnell (2020), *zakat*, as one of the Islamic philanthropy instruments, has boosted Indonesia's ranking in the World Giving Index to make it the most generous country in the world. Buana (2019) also confirmed a high encouragement from the government of Indonesia in partnership with the UN to link *zakat* to the SDGs. Table 11.7 shows the growth of Islamic philanthropy through *zakat*, *infaq*, *sadaqa*, and other social-religious funds (Dana Sosial Keagamaan Lainnya/DSKL) in Indonesia, which surpasses the growth of GDP.

As mentioned by Masters et al. (2021), Indonesia today is working towards mainstreaming Islamic social finance. The studies of Haji-Othman et al. (2020),

Table 11.4 Progress of registered fintech P2P lending platforms in Indonesia (2019–2020)

Description	*December 31*		
	2019	*2020*	*% Δ*
Accumulation of Loan Distribution (IDR)			
Aggregate (Total)	81,497,510,828,317	155,902,554,218,280	91.30%
Monthly Loan Distribution (IDR)			
Aggregate (Total)	6,952,811,986,388	9,651,764,080,376	38.82%
Loan Outstanding (IDR)			
Aggregate (Total)	13,157,156,009,827	15,319,085,394,949	16.43%
Success Rate/Loan Quality			
Repayment Success Rate (90 Days)	96.35%	95.22%	−1.17%
Rate of Non-Performance Return (90 Days)	3.65%	4.78%	30.83%
Accumulation of Lender Accounts (Unit of Account)			
Aggregate (Total)	605,935	716,963	18.32%
Accumulation of Borrower Accounts (Unit of Account)			
Aggregate (Total)	18,569,123	43,561,362	134.59%
Accumulation of Lender Transactions (Unit of Account)			
Aggregate (Total)	60,418,211	136,602,879	126.10%
Accumulation of Borrower Transactions (Unit of Account)			
Aggregate (Total)	81,876,033	248,407,423	203.39%
Loan Characteristics			
Lowest Loan Value (IDR)	1,020	1,000	−1.96%
The Average Value of Loans (IDR)	99,708,028	113,761,116	14.09%
Asset			
Conventional Provider	2,985,645,653,280	3,636,486,269,415	21.80%
Islamic Provider	50,618,571,149	74,677,072,107	47.53%
Total of Provider	3,036,264,224,429	3,711,163,341,522	22.23%

Source: OJK (2020b)

Hidayat et al. (2020), and Hassan et al. (2021) proved that Islamic social finance contributes to reviving the economy during the Covid-19 pandemic crisis. Islamic social finance helps those affected by the crisis as well as augments economic activities. Extending debt can generate economic growth, but too much will carry risks to the economy because it leads to larger borrowing costs. The alternative is to optimize the role of Islamic social finance as well as Islamic investment

Table 11.5 Clusters of currently exist in terms of philanthropy in Indonesia

No.	*Cluster*	*Types*
1	Secular institutional philanthropy	– Corporate philanthropy. – Media philanthropy. – Family philanthropy.
2	Faith-based philanthropy	– Traditional Islamic philanthropy. – Modernization of faith-based philanthropy. – State-based *zakat* management agencies. – Non state *zakat* management agencies (LAZs). – Non *zakat* Islamic charitable institutions.
3	Social justice philanthropy	Philanthropy organizations which support rights-based.
4	Social enterprise	Social enterprise.
5	Individual giving	– Crowdfunding and online giving. – Fundraising from the public.
6	Philanthropy infrastructure	Infrastructure organizations.

Source: Hartnell (2020)

Table 11.6 Philanthropy clusters in Indonesia

No.	*Cluster*	*Coordinator*
1	Cluster of *zakat* philanthropy for SDGs. *Zakat* on SDGs	BAZNAS
2	Cluster of urban and residential philanthropy	Habitat for Humanity
3	Cluster of arts and cultural philanthropy	Koalisi Seni
4	Cluster of educational philanthropy	Tanoto Foundation
5	Cluster of food and nutrition security philanthropic	Dompet Dhuafa
6	Cluster of environmental and conservation philanthropy	Yayasan Konservasi Alam Nusantara
7	Cluster of health philanthropy	Center for Policy and Health Management (PKMK) Gadjah Mada University and Tahija Foundation

Source: Filantopi Indonesia (2020)

Table 11.7 Comparison of the growth of GDP and Islamic philanthropy in Indonesia (2010–2025)

Year	*GDP current*	*Growth (%)*	*Islamic philanthropy (zakat, infaq, sadaqa) and DSKL*	*Growth (%)*
	(IDR trillion)		*(IDR trillion)*	
2010	6,864.1	-	1.500	–
2011	7,831.7	14.10	1.729	15.27

(*Continued*)

Table 11.7 (Continued)

Year	*GDP current* (*IDR trillion*)	*Growth (%)*	*Islamic philanthropy* (zakat, infaq, sadaqa) *and DSKL* (*IDR trillion*)	*Growth (%)*
2012	8,615.7	10.01	2.212	27.94
2013	9,546.1	10.80	2.639	19.30
2014	10,569.7	10.72	3.300	25.05
2015	11,526.3	9.05	3.650	10.61
2016	12,401.7	7.59	5.017	37.45
2017	13,589.8	9.56	6.224	24.06
2018	14,838.3	9.20	8.117	30.42
2019	15,833.9	10.11	10.227	26.00
2020*	17,122.1	8.14	12.241	22.41
2025*	22,252.5	3.97	24.580	11.18

**Forecasting*
Source: Puskas BAZNAS (2021), BPS – Statistics Indonesia (2015, 2020), Processed

instruments. *Zakat*, *infaq*, *sadaqa*, *waqf*, crowdfunding, and *sukuk* can be options; also, as mentioned by Musari (2019a, 2019b, 2021), *esham* as a fiscal instrument in the Islamic civilization era, which was proven capable to overcome the crisis, could also be explored.

The presence of Islamic social finance is actually a representation of faith-based philanthropy. Referring to Hartnell (2020), philanthropy in Indonesia has practised giving in various ways, and giving has always been driven primarily by religion. Through digitalization, Bensar and Rodríguez (2018) emphasize that Islamic social finance provides experiences for *sharia* fintech through charitable initiatives that have an impact on a paradigm shift in the financial landscape. The current experience of Islamic fintech can also be found in the areas of crowd-funding platforms, Islamic wealth management, and blockchain technology applications.

Discussion

Entry barriers

A study by Kikkawa and Xing (2014) reported four major factors that affect the demand of the targeted groups for financial services in Indonesia: education level, low marginal propensity to save, migration, and geographic location. To boost financial inclusion for these targets, digital technology has been developed by authorities to overcome the physical constraint of conventional financial institutions in serving poor people living in remote areas.

However, Ayyagari and Beck (2015) emphasized the importance of understanding not only the actual use of and access to financial services but also the barriers to financial inclusion to better enable policymakers to design policies to close the gaps. Oliver Wyman et al. (2017) have identified barriers to financial inclusion in Indonesia into three categories, namely (1) entry barriers; (2) product design and delivery of solutions; and (3) regulatory oversight. Entry barriers mean demand-side constraints that obstruct individuals from entering the digital financial service and supply-side constraints that curtail suppliers from serving excluded and underserved people. Table 11.8 summarizes the entry barriers for digital financial inclusion for P2P lending and philanthropy platforms in Indonesia through literature review, observation, and following discourses/discussions/interviews with informants as the representatives of stakeholders.

Table 11.8 Entry barriers for digital financial inclusion through demand/supply-side constraint

Demand-side constraint	
Financial literacy	Unable to manage finances well; undisciplined in separating finance for consumption and business; unable to make financial reports; do not understand financial products.
Digital literacy	Most people still consume information functionally, still at a low level to consume critically, have skills in producing and critical processing skills.
Behavioural economic	Community groups that are targeted by P2P lending and philanthropic platforms in general are groups of people who do not access higher education, are often marginalized, do not have assets, are prone to falling into poverty, and the business fields they are involved in are non-formal. With this character, there is a mindset that tends to be irrational and often includes an emotional element in making economic decisions.
Internet usage	Internet usage is highest amongst younger consumers and declines with age. The largest group of internet users were between the ages of 17 to 25 years old. This age group is generally still a student or has just graduated from college and is still exploring job opportunities. They do not have work experience and still have minimal savings/investment.
Cost of digital access	Although the data price in Indonesia was the lowest compared to the neighbouring countries like Singapore and Malaysia, for some people, especially community groups who are the target of P2P lending and the philanthropy platform, the cost of digital access (data cost) is expensive and can reduce the income that should be used to meet the basic needs of the family.
Quality of digital access	Due to geographic and demographic factors, causing weak network coverage and slow connection.
Security and data-privacy risk	Security, information security, compliance and data-privacy risks and related issues.

(*Continued*)

Table 11.8 (Continued)

Demand-side constraint		
The dark side of unregistered digital lender		The emergence of digital moneylenders and debt collectors who open bad loan data to family, friends, and colleagues.
Others		Do not know how to access internet on a mobile; no access to internet-enabled phone; handset cost; reading/writing difficulties; not sufficient support in learning how to use internet; do not know how to use a mobile; too expensive; lack of documentation; and lack of trust.
Supply-side constraint		
Regulation	P2P Lending	Regulation is limiting the ability to implement the right solutions; difficulty to conform to local regulations for fintech; the rigid financial regulations hinder the further expansion for the platform provider; law enforcement by the Indonesian regulators that may create an uneven level of playing field between the local and global platform providers; international agreements which cause more import technology products so as weaken the local technology providers.
	Philanthropy platform	The existing legal framework, the Law of Societal Organizations/Law on Community Organization (Ormas), gives the Ministry of Home Affairs considerable powers to control civil society. It threatens the operational independence of NGOs and burdens them with cumbersome bureaucratic requirements.
Digital literacy		Leadership lacks understanding of the fintech benefits.
Lack of funding		Convincing investors of start-up potential; a minimum number of investors or individual fund providers; access to private funding/investors.
Marketing and networking		Establishing relationships and channels to market; establishing partnerships with banks and other financial intermediaries.
Lack of organizational capacity		Limited organizational capacity; the current culture does not support innovation; lack of understanding about the division of roles and managerial skills; workforce does not have the relevant skills and experience; trouble to hire qualified employees and attracting the right talent.
Problems for impact investing		Investment unreadiness of social enterprises; most funding is still coming from overseas, and smaller-scale SMEs and social enterprises currently cannot receive funding from overseas because they must be PMA entities, which involves securing a certain amount of capital.
Know your customer (KYC) policy		To combat money laundering and financing of terrorism, KYC becomes a requirements that are essential for obtaining licenses for money remittance. KYC policy has become a barrier to the underserved, underbanked and unbanked, the BoP, and MSMEs to open accounts.

Demand-side constraint	
Infrastructure	Data-management practices and data landscape do not support fintech; insufficient infrastructure also limits the digitization towards digitalization.
Innovation and strategy	Product development to market fit; fintech strategy lacks clarity; business model viability.
Risk	New systems risk adding complexity.
Others	Regulator and public policy equivalence in treatment of different players; consumer protection; maintain high performance culture; creating suitable systems and process, etc.

Source: Kikkawa and Xing (2014), Ayyagari and Beck (2015), Oliver Wyman et al. (2017), PwC Indonesia (2019), Groupe Speciale Mobile Association (GSMA) (2020), Musari (2020), Hartnell (2020), Hakam (2020), Statista (2018a, 2018b, 2021), and informants

Regarding the achievement of Indonesia as the most generous country, Hartnell (2020) compared the report by the Centre for Asian Philanthropy and Society's Doing Good Index 2018, which looked at 15 countries in Asia and ranked them in terms of conduciveness for philanthropy, especially focusing on the legal framework. One of the bottom countries was Indonesia. The two highly different rankings contemplate the reality that most philanthropy in Indonesia is still unstructured and ad hoc, based on faith and personal preferences rather than on objective reasoning of societal necessities. Institutional philanthropy covers only a small segment of the larger philanthropy.

Developing a digital financial inclusion ecosystem

Digital financial services open a range of opportunities. Klapper (2016), Soejachmoen (2016), ADB (2016, 2017), and Yang and Zhang (2020) confirmed that digital technology contributes to financial inclusion and achieving the SDGs. Digital technology is quickly embracing economic innovation, competition, and growth in the world. Although many people have been kept out from the digital economy, many opportunities exist for obtaining financial inclusion for sustainable economic development.

In order to promote and boost financial inclusion policies through digital technology, Oliver Wyman et al. (2017) mention that a digital financial inclusion ecosystem must be developed by recognizing key stakeholders and regulatory default and by looking at the crucial elements required to establish the ecosystem go forward. This is also intended to guide regulators in addressing issues that appear in data governance and customer protection.

The International Telecommunication Union (ITU) (2016) also conveyed that identifying all key stakeholders must be done in developing a digital financial services ecosystem. Then, the critical elements necessary for encouraging and enabling financial inclusion policies must be found. Oseni and Ali (2019) mentioned that the key players in the complex fintech ecosystem include financial institutions, technology companies, infrastructure players, start-ups, regulators and governments, consumers and users as well as investors/incubators/accelerators. For Islamic fintech, there needs to be additional things related to supervision, regulations, and applicable considerations for principles of *sharia*.

Furthermore, DinarStandard and Elipses (2021) reported that the Global Islamic Fintech (GIFT) Index of 64 countries ranks Indonesia as one of the top five strongest ecosystems. It is a composite index of 32 indicators covering five categories: Islamic fintech market and ecosystem, talent, regulation, infrastructure, and capital. In Indonesia, BAZNAS, as one of the leading institution for philanthropy platforms, also develops a digital-based ecosystem. Mainly in the aspect of collection, BAZNAS has digitized *zakat* collection in various ways to increase coverage and donor networks and make it easier for them to distribute *zakat* in collaboration with fintech companies, develop smartphone-based applications and websites, and offer quick response (QR) codes to collect *zakat* funds. Table 11.9 shows digitalization of *zakat* by BAZNAS.

Regarding the digital financial inclusion ecosystems, developed from DinarStandard and Elipses (2021), International Telecommunication Union Telecommunication Standardization Sector (ITU-T) (2016), and by the results of observation and following discourses/discussions/interviews with informants as the representatives of stakeholders, Table 11.10 shows Indonesia's fintech ecosystem with P2P lending and philanthropy platform within it. As digital transformation accelerates across financial ecosystems around the world, P2P lending and philanthropy platforms in Indonesia are also establishing the ecosystem. The pandemic has accelerated the process given the excluded and

Table 11.9 Digitalization in managing *zakat* by BAZNAS

Collecting zakat		*Distributing* zakat		Zakat *management*		
Internal platform – Website – Application	External platform – E-wallet – Ride hailing – Crowdfunding – E-commerce	Automated teller machine (ATM) for rice	Integrated social welfare data	BAZNAS Information Management System (SIMBA)	Blockchain (i-zakat)	Application-based muzaki service

Source: Puskas BAZNAS (2020)

Table 11.10 Digital financial inclusion ecosystem in Indonesia

Digital financial inclusion users	Customers (excluded and underserved, unbanked and underbanked, the BoP, and MSME segments), merchant, businesses, philanthropy institutions, governments, non-profit groups.	
Digital financial inclusion operations	Back office	Information technology, human resources, accounting, and sharia compliance.
	Middle office	Risk, treasury, supply chain, customer service.
	Business intelligence	Market research, decision-making tools, dashboards.

Digital financial inclusion services	Giving and protecting	– Philanthropy/social finance/donate. – Insurance.
	Saving and investment	– Wealth management. – Deposit and lending. – Transaction accounts. – Saving accounts. – Investment accounts.
	Financing	– Raising fund: P2P lending, crowdfunding. – Payments: digital payments, remittance, foreign exchange. – Capital market: investment, trading, sukuk, shares. – Digital assets: platform & exchange, wallet & custodians, token issuers. – Alternative finance.
Digital financial inclusion provider and enablers	Advisory	– Consultant/nongovernmental organizations (NGOs). – Companion volunteers. – Sharia scholars.
	Legal and regulatory enablers	– International: multilateral institutions/industry organizations. – Regional: communities/ organizations. – National: authorities/regulators.
	Financial institutions	– Conventional/Islamic banks. – Conventional/Islamic microfinance or nanofinance institutions. – Cooperation/*baitul mal wat tamwil*. – Venture capital firms. – Sovereign wealth fund. – Other financial institutions.
	Technology firms	– Fintech firms. – Fintech associations.
	Supporting institutions	– Industry associations. – Research and development institutions. – University/Higher education institution. – Education & training institutes. – Licensed nonbanks. – Agents. – Processors. – Accelerators.
Enabling technologies	Artificial intelligence	Big data, data & analytics, machine learning.
	Distributed ledger technology	Blockchain, crypto, tokenization.
	Security	Cybersecurity, biometrics, identity verification.
	Cloud	Cloud and software.

Source: DinarStandard and Elipses (2021), ITU-T (2016), and informants

underserved, unbanked and underbanked, BoP, and MSMEs were the groups in society that were the hardest hit.

Social and economic impacts

The pandemic has propelled an unprecedented acceleration in the process of financial digitalization and shows P2P lending and philanthropy platforms as the new face of digital financial inclusion. The existence of P2P lending and philanthropy platforms has social and economic impacts. Apart from adding to diversify investment for investors, it also facilitates access and provides several allocation options for philanthropist or donor in making donations. However, how far might digital finance influence the social and economic impacts of digital financial inclusion?

Certainly, not all financial exclusion can be addressed through digital initiatives. But most people would agree that technology brings digital transformation to financial services and makes a major contribution to the achievement of financial inclusion. UNSGSA, the Better Than Cash Alliance, UNCDF, and the World Bank (2018) made sure that sufficient evidence is presented on how digital financial inclusion may boost program progress towards the SDGs. Digital financial inclusion also has a socially and economically resilient impact on millions of people around the world. Digital financial services help families economize money, survive from shocks, secure assets over risk, and enable pensions, wages, and government transfers to efficiently attain people and stimulate start-up business models which have opportunities to access the low-cost financial services.

The social impact of philanthropic platforms in Indonesia is shown by the results of the study by Nurdiyanti and Suryadi (2019), among others,. The study indicated that digital philanthropy by Aksi Cepat Tanggap (ACT) can develop a more participatory culture of digital citizenship. Through new media as a digital citizenship infrastructure, this civil culture becomes a digital-based social movement that encourages community commitment for improving their living standard, including efforts to resolve various social and injustice problems. Through digital philanthropy, Musari and Fathorrazi (2021) also noted that ACT initiates Warung Wakaf, an empowering program through *waqf*-based retail businesses in agriculture, livestock, and entrepreneurship by involving community groups. Warung Wakaf provides employment opportunities and a series of social activities to meet their basic needs for the surrounding communities. There is also Warung Wakaf Mobile by ACT as a combination of *waqf* and productive economy by presenting a lifestyle, technology, and mobility.

Regarding digital technology, in addition to utilizing digital media to conduct education and socialization, Filantopi Indonesia (2020) also provides a digital sustainability reporting platform to help philanthropic and non-profit organizations store data, compile and complete the required information based on a reporting structure and framework. Overall, even though in the previous year digital promotions had been carried out, digital activities and interactions of Filantropi Indonesia and the public in 2020 have increased in all platforms of social media.

When digital technology begins to rule social and economic life, Hartnell (2020) confirmed that one of the achievements is that the youth generation has emerged in the field of philanthropy. They introduce innovative ways of doing philanthropy, combining passion, concern for environmental and social issues, and social entrepreneurship. Likewise, a study by Niswah et al. (2019) indicated a generation of Indonesian Muslim millennials pays attention to the development of fintech in Indonesia, including in the donation service. However, their intentions are not always realized by donating through fintech. The perception of the ease and usefulness of fintech also does not make them comfortable and think that donating using fintech is good to do.

As a faith-based philanthropy institution, BAZNAS (Puskas BAZNAS, 2021) also acknowledged that the massive *zakat* digitalization has also encouraged fundraising. The result of their survey showed that the use of online donation channels during the pandemic increased from 48.31% to 78.57%. From March to June 2020, the collection of *zakat*, *infaq*, and *sadaqa* funds increased by 69.29% compared to the previous year in the same period. Another increase also occurred in other *zakat* philanthropic groups. To support economic activity during a pandemic, the allocation and distribution of *zakat* funds are directed and developed to empower new *mustahiqs* due to the weakening economy because of the pandemic. Interestingly, the score of Literacy *Zakat* Index 2020, for basic knowledge, showed *Zakat* digital payment literacy scored the highest than the *Zakat* program literacy, *Zakat* impact literacy, *Zakat* regulation literacy, and *Zakat* institution literacy as shown Table 11.11.

Furthermore, Oliver Wyman et al. (2017) estimated that regulatory initiatives to support digital finance applications could generate more than USD50 billion in additional electronic payment flows, more than USD11 billion in additional credit uptake, and more than USD13 billion in savings mobilization. Tapping these opportunities would lead to an increase of about 2% in Indonesia's GDP and of about 10% in the incomes of the population segment earning less than USD2 per day. Table 11.12 shows the impact of digital application in financial inclusion on GDP growth, target segment income level, and volume increases as percentage of total market supply.

Meanwhile, PwC Indonesia (2019) forecasted the potency of P2P lending to apply IDR19.4 trillion to the MSMEs financing gap or the equivalent to

Table 11.11 Score of literacy *zakat* index 2020 for basic knowledge

Zakat *literacy for basic knowledge*	*Index scores*
Zakat institution literacy	56.54
Zakat regulation literacy	60.85
Zakat impact literacy	81.29
Zakat program literacy	74.10
Zakat digital payment literacy	84.38

Source: Puskas BAZNAS (2020)

Table 11.12 Impact of digital applications on GDP growth and the growth of the financial services market

Impact of digital applications on GDP growth and target segment income level	
Total GDP growth potential	9%
GDP growth impact of digital applications	2%
Target segment income level	10%
Impact of digital applications on the growth of the financial services market	
Payments	54 million (15%) *Large government to person, person to business, person to government, and person to person untapped opportunity*
Savings	13 million (5%)
Credit	11 million (7%) *Opportunity in digital delivery of credit*

Source: Oliver Wyman et al. (2017)

Table 11.13 Potential impact of fintech lending to close the MSME financing gap and individual credit access

	2018	*2019*	*2020*
Estimated additional credit access to MSMEs from fintech lending.	IDR4.3 trillion	IDR7.5 trillion	IDR19.4 trillion
Accumulative contribution to individual credit access.	2.4%	4.9%	12.4%

Source: Global Findex 2018, OJK, PwC Customer Survey, in PwC Indonesia (2019)

increasing credit access for individuals by 12.4% by 2020. Then, Statista (2021) predicted that the transaction value in the crowdlending (business) segment would reach USD39.3 million in 2021. Transaction value is expected to reach an annual growth rate (CAGR 2021–2025) of 11.22% resulting in a projected total amount of USD60.2 million by 2025. The average funding per campaign in the crowdlending (business) segment amounts to USD3,905 in 2021. Table 11.13 shows the P2P lending potential impact to close the MSME financing gap and individual credit access. Overall, this indicates strongly that digitalization has the potency to extend and scale up access to financial services. Through digital financial inclusion, it is expected to help accelerate swiftly toward the achievement of the SDGs.

Therefore, summarizing the information already conveyed, supported by the results of observation and following discourses/discussions/interviews with informants as the representatives of stakeholders, the social and economic impacts of digital financial inclusion, in this case the P2P lending and philanthropy platform, can be compiled as shown in Table 11.14. Basically, its social and economic impact is not much different from instruments that are not based on digital technology. However, it must be admitted that digitalization has accelerated and

Table 11.14 Social and economic impact

Social impact	*Economic impact*
– Wealth distribution; – Reducing inequality; – Reducing low-income trap rigidity; – Improving community welfare; – Alleviating poverty; – Elevating the Human Development Index (HDI); – Preventing over-leveraged debt behaviour; – Preventing crime; – Preventing and reducing unemployment; – Community empowerment, particularly for women; – Growing awareness to caring by sharing; – Maintaining the dignity of the nation and state by not expanding to debt.	– Increasing economic efficiency; – Maintaining economic growth; – Supporting financial system stability; – Supporting financial market deepening; – Serving the large "financing invisible"; – Collaborating for sustainable platform; – Developing a typical fintech lending ecosystem; – Looking at the potential for impactful growth; – Providing potential new markets for the banking industry; – Reducing shadow banking and irresponsible finance; – Contributing to sustainable local and national economic growth; – Controlling inflation by encouraging money velocity rather than money creation.

Source: PwC (2019), informants, developed

offers easier access to people with various levels of financial inclusion, especially during the pandemic crisis, which worsened the situations of the excluded and underserved, unbanked and underbanked, BoP, and MSME segments. In line with the recommendation from the study by Nuryakin et al. (2019), strengthening the fintech landscape must be one of the focal points going forward.

Although digital financial inclusion brings positive social and economic impacts, the paradox that occurs at the implementation level is a challenge that should not be ignored. Referring to Rumata and Sastrosubroto (2020), there are at least two paradoxes of digital economic development that have occurred in Indonesia. They are the regulation paradox and the productivity paradox. The major implication of these paradoxes is law enforcement by the Indonesian regulators that may inflict an unfair and rough level of playing field between the global and local platform providers.

However, it can not be denied, digital financial inclusion enables coverage towards the excluded and underserved, unbanked and underbanked, BoP, and MSME markets that results in an end-to-end impact towards society. Through digitalization and through evidence by Indonesia, Asia can drive economic growth through financial inclusion not only through P2P lending but also through philanthropy platforms, which are low-cost funds oriented to help these community groups. In this case, Asia can also encourage faith-based philanthropy, especially from traditional Islamic philanthropy, by considering that Asia is home to 65% of the world's Muslims.

Conclusion

This chapter documented the progress of digital financial inclusion across developing Asia by using the case study of Indonesia. The country is a representation of several emerging market economies in Asia which employ financial inclusion as an integral component of development to achieve inclusive growth. As one of East Asia Pacific's most eager democracies, with the third-largest population in Asia and Southeast Asia's biggest economy, Indonesia has evidenced that digitalization has accelerated the attainment of financial inclusion works through P2P lending and philanthropy platforms.

Furthermore, the main findings of entry barriers for P2P lending and philanthropy platform in demand-side constraint includes financial literacy, digital literacy, behavioural economic, internet usage, cost of digital access, quality of digital access, security and data-privacy risk, the dark side of unregistered digital lending. Other barriers to demand-side constraint are not knowing how to access the internet on a mobile, no access to an internet-enabled phone, handset cost, reading/writing difficulties, insufficient support in learning how to use the internet, not knowing how to use a mobile, too expensive, lack of documentation, and lack of trust.

In supply-side constraint, the entry barriers for P2P lending and philanthropy platforms include regulation, digital literacy, lack of funding, marketing and networking, lack of organizational capacity, problems for impact investing, KYC policy, infrastructure, innovation and strategy, and risk. Other barriers in supply-side constraint are regulator and public policy equivalence in treatment of different players, consumer protection, maintaining high performance culture, and creating suitable systems and process.

In developing a digital financial inclusion ecosystem, the key stakeholders which must be involved include (1) digital financial inclusion users – customers (excluded and underserved, unbanked and underbanked, the BoP, and MSME segments), merchant, businesses, philanthropy institutions, governments, non-profit groups; (2) digital financial inclusion operations – back office, middle office, and business intelligence; (3) digital financial inclusion services – giving and protecting, saving and investment, and financing; (4) digital financial inclusion provider and enablers – advisory, legal and regulatory enablers, financial institutions, technology firms, and supporting institutions; and (5) enabling technologies – artificial intelligence, distributed ledger technology, security, and cloud.

Then, regarding the social and economic impacts, many can be identified. The interesting thing that emerged from the social impacts are the growing awareness of caring by sharing and maintaining the dignity of the nation and state by not expanding to debt. Highlights from the economic impacts are reducing shadow banking and irresponsible finance, contributing to sustainable local and national economic growth, and controlling inflation by encouraging money velocity rather than money creation.

Last but not least, by using the Indonesian case study, this chapter highlights that digital financial inclusion can drive inclusive growth in Asia. Through digital technology, both fintech and enabling technologies and P2P lending and philanthropy platforms can invite public involvement in supporting the financial inclusion agenda. Besides being able to help the emerging countries avoid a deep debt trap, these platforms can be a source of low-cost funds for helping the excluded and underserved, unbanked and underbanked, the BoP, and MSME segments to become empowered and able to reach a better living standard.

References

Book/Journal/Proceeding/Working Paper/Report

ADB – Asian Development Bank. (2016). *Financial inclusion in the digital economy*. Asian Development Bank (ADB).

ADB – Asian Development Bank. (2017, January). *Financial inclusion in the digital economy*. ADB Briefs No. 75. Asian Development Bank (ADB).

ADBI – Asian Development Bank Institute. (2014). *Financial inclusion in Asia: Country surveys*. Asian Development Bank Institute (ADBI).

AFTECH – Indonesia FinTech Association. (2020). *Annual member survey 2019/2020*. Indonesia FinTech Association (AFTECH).

ASEAN Secretariat – Association of Southeast Asian Nations Secretariat. (2020a). *ASEAN statistical leaflet 2020*. ASEAN Secretariat.

ASEAN Secretariat – Association of Southeast Asian Nations Secretariat. (2020b). *ASEAN sustainable development goals indicators baseline report 2020*. ASEAN Secretariat.

Athoillah. (2020). *Fintech contribution to Indonesia's economic growth*. Munich Personal RePEc Archive (MPRA) Paper No. 97884. MPRA.

Ayyagari, M., & Beck, T. (2015). *Financial inclusion in Asia: An overview*. ADB Economics Working Paper Series No. 449. Asian Development Bank (ADB).

Bain & Company. (2019). *Fulfilling its promise, the future Southeast's Asia digital financial services*. Bain & Company.

Bensar, F. Z., & Rodríguez, G. (2018). Islamic fintech and the paradigm shift in the financial landscape. In V. Cattelan (Ed.), *Islamic social finance: Entrepreneurship, cooperation and the sharing economy* (pp. 129–143). Routledge.

Bhowmik, S. K., & Saha, D. (2013). *Financial inclusion of the marginalised: Street vendors in the urban economy*. Springer.

BPS – Statistics Indonesia. (2015). *Gross domestic product of Indonesia by expenditure 2010–2014*. Statistics Indonesia (Badan Pusat Statistik/BPS).

BPS – Statistics Indonesia. (2020). *Gross domestic product of Indonesia by expenditure 2015–2019*. Statistics Indonesia (Badan Pusat Statistik/BPS).

Charities Aid Foundation. (2019). *CAF world giving index* (10th ed.). Charities Aid Foundation (CAF).

DinarStandard, & Elipses. (2021). *Global Islamic fintech report 2021*. DinarStandard, Elipses, and Salam Gateway.

Filantopi Indonesia. (2020). *Laporan program 2020 filantropi Indonesia*. Filantopi Indonesia.

Gopalan, S., & Kikuchi, T. (Eds.). (2016). *Financial inclusion in Asia: Issues and policy concerns*. Palgrave Macmillan.

GSMA – Groupe Speciale Mobile Association. (2020). *Connected women, the mobile gender gap report 2020*. Groupe Speciale Mobile Association (GSMA).

Haji-Othman, Y., Abd Latib, M. F., Ahmad, M. N., & Hasnan, R. (2020, November). The role of islamic social finance in reviving the economy during COVID19 pandemic crisis. *International Journal of Muamalat*, *4*(1), 147–152.

Hartnell, C. (2020). *Philanthropy in Indonesia*. A Working paper of Philanthropy for Social Justice and Peace in association with Alliance, Filantropi Indonesia, Indonesia for Humanity and WINGS. https://globalfundcommunityfoundations.org/wp-content/uploads/2020/02/Philanthropy-in-Indonesia-Feb-2020.pdf

Hassan, M. K., Muneeza, A., & Sarea, A. M. (Eds.). (2021). *COVID-19 and islamic social finance*. Routledge.

Hidayat, S. E., Farooq, M. O., & Alim, E. A. (Eds.). (2020). *Impacts of the COVID-19 outbreak on islamic finance in the OIC countries*. The National Committee for Islamic Economy & Finance (KNEKS) and Supported by DinarStandard and Salaam Gateway.

ITU – International Telecommunication Union. (2016, July). *Digital financial inclusion*. Issue Briefs Series Inter-Agency Task Force of Financing for Development ITU.

ITU-T – International Telecommunication Union Telecommunication Standardization Sector. (2016, May). *The digital financial services ecosystem*. ITU-T Focus Group Digital Financial Services.

Kikkawa, K., & Xing, Y. (2014). Financial inclusion in Indonesia: A poverty alleviation strategy. In ADBI – Asian Development Bank Institute. In *Financial inclusion in Asia: Country surveys* (pp. 45–61). Asian Development Bank Institute (ADBI).

MGI – McKinsey Global Institute. (2016, September). *Digital finance for all: Powering inclusive growth in emerging economies*. Executive summary, McKinsey & Company.

Musari, K. (2019a, August 28–29). *Esham for fiscal sustainability, an alternative to sukuk in islamic finance perspective: Historical experience*. A paper was presented at Researcher Day 2019 The 2019 International Conference on Fiscal Policy and Input-Output Modeling at Auditorium of Fiscal Policy Agency Building, Ministry of Finance.

Musari, K. (2021). Esham, the origin of sukuk for facing the crisis: Historical experience. *Iqtishoduna: Jurnal Ekonomi Islam*, *10*(1), 45–58.

Musari, K., & Fathorrazi, M. (2021). Islamic helix approach, the islamic social finance partnership models for MSMEs: Lesson learned from Indonesia. In T. Azid, M. Mukhlisin, N. Akbar, & M. Tahir (Eds.), *Monetary policy, Islamic finance, and Islamic corporate governance: An international overview*. Emerald Publishing Limited.

Niswah, F. M., Mutmainah, L., & Legowati, D. A. (2019). Muslim millennial's intention of donating for charity using fintech platform. *Journal of Islamic Monetary Economics and Finance*, *5*(3), 623–644.

Nurdiyanti, A., & Suryadi, K. (2019). Digital philanthropy in Indonesia: Strengthening civic virtue for digital citizens. *Advances in Social Science, Education and Humanities Research*, *317*, 139–143.

Nuryakin, C., Aisha, L., & Massie, N. W. G. (2019, May). *Financial technology in Indonesia: A fragmented instrument for financial inclusion?* Working Paper 036. Institute for Economic and Social Research, Faculty of Economics and Business, Universitas Indonesia (LPEM-FEB UI).

OJK – Indonesia Financial Services Authority. (2020a). *The indonesian financial services sector master plan 2021–2025*. Indonesia Financial Services Authority (OJK).

OJK – Indonesia Financial Services Authority. (2020b). *Perkembangan fintech lending – December 2020*. Deputy Commissioner for Supervision of IKNB II, Department of Supervision of IKNB 2A, Directorate of Fintech for Regulation, Licensing, and Supervision, Indonesia Financial Services Authority (OJK).

Oliver Wyman, MicroSave, & Asian Development Bank. (2017). *Accelerating financial inclusion in South-East Asia with digital finance*. Asian Development Bank (ADB).
Osafo-Kwaako, P., Singer, M., White, O., & Zouaoui, Y. (2018, March). *Mobile money in emerging markets: The business case for financial inclusion*. Global Banking Practice, McKinsey & Company.
Oseni, U. A., & Ali, S. N. (Eds.). (2019). *Fintech in islamic finance*. Routledge.
Puskas BAZNAS. (2020). *Indonesia zakat outlook 2020*. Center of Strategic Studies, The National Board of Zakat Republic of Indonesia (Puskas BAZNAS).
Puskas BAZNAS. (2021). *Indonesia zakat outlook 2021*. Center of Strategic Studies, The National Board of Zakat Republic of Indonesia (Puskas BAZNAS).
PwC – PricewaterhouseCoopers (2019). *Global fintech report 2019*. Pricewaterhouse-Coopers (PwC).
PwC – PricewaterhouseCoopers Indonesia (2019). *Indonesia's fintech lending: Driving economic growth through financial inclusion*. PricewaterhouseCoopers (PwC) Indonesia.
Rumata, V. M., & Sastrosubroto, A. S. (2020). *The paradox of Indonesian digital economy development*. IntechOpen. https://doi.org/10.5772/intechopen.92140
Soejachmoen, M. P. (2016). Financial inclusion in Indonesia: Moving towards a digital payment system. In S. Gopalan & T. Kikuchi (Eds.), *Financial inclusion in Asia: Issues and policy concerns*. Palgrave Studies in Impact Finance. https://doi.org/10.1057/978-1-137-58337-6_5
Statista. (2018a, January). *Internal challenges for fintech companies in ASEAN countries 2018*. https://www.statista.com/statistics/884830/asean-internal-challenges-for-fintechs/
Statista. (2018b, January). *External challenges for fintech companies in ASEAN countries 2018*. https://www.statista.com/statistics/884848/asean-external-challenges-for-fintechs/
Statista. (2021, January). *Alternative lending report 2021, statista digital market outlook*. https://www.statista.com/outlook/dmo/fintech/alternative-lending/crowdlending-business/indonesia
United Nations Secretary-General's Special Advocate for Inclusive Finance for Development (UNSGSA), the Better Than Cash Alliance, the United Nations Capital Development (UNCDF), and the World Bank. (2018). *Igniting SDG progress through digital financial inclusion*. UNSGSA.
Yang, L., & Zhang, Y. (2020). Digital financial inclusion and sustainable growth of small and micro enterprises – evidence based on China's new third board market listed companies. *Sustainability, MDPI, Open Access Journal*, *12*(9), 3733. https://doi.org/10.3390/su12093733

Newspapers/Magazines/Internet

Buana, G. K. (2019, February 12). *Indonesia is giving proof of a zakat paradigm shift*. https://worldfinancialreview.com/indonesia-is-giving-proof-of-a-zakat-paradigm-shift/
Hakam. (2020, September 9). *Digital literacy competency of indonesian society's begins to develop*. www.ugm.ac.id/en/news/20028-digital-literacy-competency-of-indonesian-society-s-begins-to-develop
Klapper, L. (2016, August 11). *Financial inclusion has a big role to play in reaching the SDGS*. www.cgap.org/blog/financial-inclusion-has-big-role-play-reaching-sdgs
Masters, A., Junaidi, E., & Ishak, M. (2021, February 27). Indonesia, in the midst of mainstreaming islamic social finance. *The World Financial Review*. https://worldfinancialreview.com/indonesia-in-the-midst-of-mainstreaming-islamic-social-finance/

Mulyani, E. (2020, February 28). Let's talk hand-in-hand financial inclusion and literacy . . . before P2P. *Jakarta Post*. www.thejakartapost.com/academia /2020/02/28/lets-talk-hand-in-hand-financial-inclusion-and-literacy-before-p2p.html

Musari, K. (2019b, September 6). Perpetual sukuk untuk biaya ibu kota baru. *Jawa Pos Daily Newspaper, Opini*, p. 4.

Musari, K. (2020, February). QRIS, behavioral economics, dan literasi keuangan digital. *Buletin Strategi Nasional Keuangan Inklusif (SNKI), Edisi XXV*, 6–8.

OECD – The Organisation for Economic Co-operation and Development. (2019). *Southeast Asia going digital: Connecting SMEs*. www.oecd.org/going-digital/southeast-asia-connecting-SMEs.pdf

12 Antecedents of user acceptance of digital banking service

A qualitative study in Vietnam

Bình Nghiêm-Phú and Thành Hưng Nguyễn

Introduction

The earliest form of a bank might have appeared more than 3,000 years ago (Davies, 2002). However, the current banking systems could only be developed and sustained with the help of modern communication technologies, including the Internet and personal equipment. Internet banking, for example, was facilitated by the widespread use of the World Wide Web (the second and third generations, or 2G and 3G) and private computers. Later on, mobile banking was promoted, undoubtedly, by the Internet (the third and fourth generations, or 3G and 4G) and the boom in the use of mobile computer-like devices, such as phones and tablets. Throughout this development, user acceptance or adoption has been a prominent topic in research on such modern banking services (Hanafizadeh et al., 2014; Shaikh & Karjaluoto, 2015). As a result, many factors have been found to be significant antecedents of user adoption. Shaikh and Karjaluoto (2015), for example, identified 84 different factors when reviewing 55 academic papers published between 2005 and 2012, including self-efficacy, need for interaction, uncertainty avoidance, technology anxiety, perceived ease of use, perceived usefulness, social influence, and perceived risks, among others. However, a differentiation of groups of impacting factors is largely missing in research, which is mostly structured and quantitative, on user adoption of Internet and mobile banking (Baabdullah et al., 2019; Hassan & Wood, 2020; Malaquias & Hwang, 2019; Shankar et al., 2020). As a consequence, bank managers and administrative agents may have to deal with an overload of uncategorized information about the antecedents of users' behavioural intentions.

After mobile banking, digital banking is the next generation of online banking (Ananda et al., 2020; Nel & Boshoff, 2021). Different from Internet or mobile banking, digital banks are totally virtual units where all products and services are carried out online. The Internet environment is also advanced to the fifth generation or 5G. Digital banks are expected to start their operations soon in many countries and territories, for example, Hong Kong, Israel, Singapore, and Thailand (Bick et al., 2021; Iwamoto, 2020). After that, this system may be adopted in lagging markets. An understanding of the factors which may affect user adoption behaviour at this early stage will provide important insights for both bank

DOI: 10.4324/9781003224532-12

managers and administrative agents when designing and delivering their products and services.

The purpose of the study reported in this chapter, therefore, is to examine the antecedents of user acceptance of digital banking services. However, different from previous studies on Internet and mobile banking, this study aims to separate the impacting factors using a qualitative method. This study, thus, will expand the current knowledge about online banking services by investigating the future generation of digital banking, which has not received enough academic attention due to its novelty and future-ness. In addition, it will help identify the actual factors, not the theory-based ones, which can affect customers' adoption of the new banking products and services.

This study chooses Vietnam as its setting. According to Statista (2021), the amount of digital payment implemented in this market is expected to be around 15 million USD in 2021. The number of users of mobile POS (point-of-sale) payments is projected to be around 34.9 million in 2025. Approximately one third of the market consists people aged between 25 and 34 (as of 2020). Given the market size and power, the potential of online banking, in general, and of digital banking, in particular, in Vietnam in the future is great. This study, as a result, will provide practical implications for the management of online banking in Vietnam in the upcoming years. It should be noted that several banks in Vietnam have already initiated their digital banking products and services, for example, Military Bank, Techcombank, Tienphong Bank, and VP Bank (Fintechnews Vietnam, 2020; Nguyen, 2021). However, their operations are still simple and meagre. The existing products and services, such as automated transaction booths, actually are extensions of the current Internet and mobile banking ones. They serve as transiting or bridging products and services (digital-like pseudonym), not the digital banking products and services in their truest forms (digital only). Therefore, the authentic digital banking products and services still are the future ones, and the current banking users are potential customers of these products and services.

Literature review

Online banking or electronic/e-banking is an Internet-based delivery channel of retail banking (Aladwani, 2001). Thanks to online banking, users do not have to go to banks to do certain common transactions, such as money transfer and balance check. Instead, they can stay at home or anywhere, and use their private computers (Internet banking) or other mobile communication devices (mobile banking) to do these activities. Convenience, thus, is a prominent feature of online banking in general (Chong et al., 2010; Sikdar & Makkad, 2015). However, given the ambivalence of the Internet environment, safety and security are other characteristics of online banking about which users often worry (Casaló et al., 2007; Lim et al., 2010).

In recent years, several studies have been carried out to understand Vietnamese users' adoption of Internet and mobile banking products and services in particular. Pham and Doan (2014), for example, surveyed a sample of 168 potential users of e-banking. Employing theory of planned behaviour (TPB), theory of reasoned action (TRA), technology acceptance model (TAM), and decomposed theory of planned behaviour (DTPB), these researchers found that bank customers' intention to use is significantly affected by subjective norms, perceived ease of use, trust, and perceived benefits. The effects of these four factors were found to be in this descending order. It should be noted that the aforementioned theories (Ajzen, 1991; Davis, 1989; Fishbein, 1979; Taylor & Todd, 1995) were originally developed for other fields of study, both business and non-business, then later adopted by researchers in the banking sector. These theories have been proved to be able to explain bank users' perceptions of and behaviours toward different banking products and services.

In another study, Lin et al. (2015) developed a theoretical model based on TAM and TPB, and tested that model on a sample of 350 Vietnamese respondents. Their findings confirmed that subjective norms are a direct antecedent of intention to use. In addition, they revealed that attitudes toward Internet banking and perceived behavioural control are the other significant influencers. The effect of subjective norms still was the largest, followed by those of perceived behavioural control and attitude toward Internet banking.

From a different perspective, Le et al. (2017) collected data from a sample of 272 respondents in the central area of Vietnam and found that customer satisfaction with electronic banking is indeed a strong predictor of intention to retain. Customer satisfaction might be structured by four main elements: accuracy, convenience, privacy, and customer service (Liang & Nguyen, 2018). It is significantly influenced by several website-related factors, including information quality, security, response time, and visual appeal (Le et al., 2017).

The outcomes of previous research on Internet and mobile banking in Vietnam in particular, interestingly, are somewhat similar to those on retail banking in the country in general. For example, Dinh and Pickler (2012) observed that customer satisfaction in the latter setting is determined by a group of five factors: tangibility (physical facilities and operating hours), reliability (e.g., do as promised and error-free), responsiveness (e.g., willingness to help and response to requests), assurance (e.g., trustworthiness and safety), and empathy (e.g., individual attention and personal assistance). Phan and Ghantous (2013) added that Vietnamese banks' customer loyalty is significantly controlled by trust and perceived brand associations (e.g., bank reputation, location, and personnel). As a consequence, the findings of previous studies in the Internet and mobile context could not identify the factors that are peculiar to the Vietnamese banking sector. In other words, these outcomes can also be observed elsewhere (Baabdullah et al., 2019; Hanafizadeh et al., 2014; Hassan & Wood, 2020; Li et al., 2021; Malaquias & Hwang, 2019; Shaikh & Karjaluoto, 2015; Shankar et al., 2020).

The structured method employed by previous studies may be the main reason behind this situation. As all the factors under examination were predetermined based on the existing literature, there may be an overemphasis on some factors, in addition to an overlooking of other ones. It should be noted that some differences could be expected from one market to another. For example, in a comparative research between Taiwan and Vietnam, Lin and Nguyen (2011) discovered that customers in these two markets differ, either marginally or significantly, in their perceptions of ease of use, usefulness, risks, information, personal innovativeness in technology, and e-payment use.

Method

This study aims to identify the factors that may promote or block the acceptance of digital banking in Vietnam. Considering the limitations of quantitative methods, this study adopted a qualitative approach. Specifically, focus group discussion was selected as the data collection method for the following reasons. First, as a qualitative method, focus group discussion is effective for the gathering of in-depth information about customers' opinions, which suited the purpose of this study (Neuman, 2014; Seal et al., 1998). Second, as digital banking is regarded as a potential service, the participation of two or more participants in one session helped create a friendly atmosphere to facilitate the discussion on this novel topic (Colucci, 2007).

A total of five discussions were implemented both online (group 4 via Zoom) and onsite (the remaining groups) over a one-year period (March 2020–February 2021) in Hanoi, the capital city of Vietnam. Participants ($n = 22$) were purposefully selected among the acquaintances of the second researcher, who is currently located in the country (Palinkas et al., 2015). These participants, as experienced customers of the current Internet and mobile banking services (some of them are even using or aware of the digital-like products and services), are more likely to become customers of digital banking, the next generation of online banking (Table 12.1). In a sense, they can be considered early users of the new products and services compared to late adopters (Ngugi et al., 2010). It should be noted that one participant (P2) unintentionally joined two discussions (group 1 and group 2). Since he accidentally made his appearance at the site of the second discussion and greeted the group, he was invited to join in.

The discussions started with the participants explaining their past and current experiences with Internet and mobile banking. They then moved on to the participants giving their opinions about future digital banking. The second researcher, who served as the local moderator, asked both direct and indirect questions during the discussions to uncover information about the participants' behaviours toward and perceptions of the related banking services. After each discussion, the two researchers exchanged opinions and came up with further questions and directions for the next one. This process was repeated until the fifth and last discussion, when the researchers realized that little new information was being extracted. In other words, the point of data saturation was reached (Saumure & Given, 2008).

The discussions were recorded and then the content was inductively analysed (Elo & Kyngäs, 2008). The two researchers worked together to identify the factors that would facilitate and encourage or hinder and discourage the potential use of future digital banking from the perspectives of these potential users in Vietnam. In this process, one researcher identified a factor, and the other agreed

Table 12.1 Profile of participants

Group	*Time and method*	*Participant*	*Age*	*Sex*	*Job*
1	March 2020 Onsite	P1	40	Male	University lecturer (Faculty head)
		P2	33	Male	University lecturer
		P3	34	Male	Office worker
		P4	29	Male	Office worker
2	May 2020 Onsite	P5	27	Male	Marketing director
		P6	26	Male	Bank staff
		P7	24	Female	Bank staff
		P8	24	Male	Accountant
		P9	25	Male	Accountant
		P2	33	Male	University lecturer
3	December 2020 Onsite	P10	31	Male	Head accountant
		P11	33	Male	Businessman
		P12	32	Male	Accountant
		P13	33	Male	University lecturer
		P14	33	Male	Head accountant
4	February 2021 Online	P15	38	Male	Software company director
		P16	37	Female	Software company deputy director
		P17	25	Male	Marketing staff
		P18	24	Male	Accountant
5	February 2021 Onsite	P19	29	Male	Accountant
		P20	32	Female	Accountant
		P21	26	Female	Accountant
		P22	38	Male	Head accountant

or disagreed with the proposal based on the information found in the discussions. A factor was retained when agreement was reached between the two researchers. These agreements served as the reliability criteria of the results of the analysis (Kassarjian, 1977).

After all the factors were identified, the researchers separated them into groups to report in this chapter (Braun & Clarke, 2006). The similarity or dissimilarity between one factor and the remaining served as the criterion of the categorization process. In addition, business marketing theory, particularly the part about the marketing environment (Kotler & Armstrong, 2018), was adopted as the guiding principle of the grouping procedure. The coding was manually managed in a Microsoft Excel file.

It should be noted that the researchers used the raw audio recording files (Fasick, 1977) instead of transcribed texts in the analysis for two reasons. First, the transcriptions separated the texts from the contexts and eliminated all non-verbal cues contributed by the participants (Wellard & McKenna, 2002). Thus, important parts of the discussion, the atmosphere and the emotions, for example, could also be wiped out. Second, unlike one-to-one interviews, two or more participants in discussions can state their opinions simultaneously. Transcriptions, unfortunately, cannot convey such simultaneity, and thus, the importance of the point being made. However, when necessary, parts of the discussions were transcribed to use as quotes in this chapter.

The quotations taken from the original materials in Vietnamese were initially translated into English by DeepL Translate and Google Translate. The first researcher then compared the two versions, identified errors where they existed, and then selected or created the most suitable version to be presented here.

Findings

Facilitators of digital banking acceptance

The analysis of the discussions revealed 39 factors that may facilitate the use of digital banking by Vietnamese customers. These factors were grouped into nine subcategories and three main categories (Table 12.2).

The first category of facilitators involves the banks themselves. Accordingly, the prominent characteristics of digital banking products and services, such as

Table 12.2 Facilitating factors

Category	*Subcategory*	*Item*
Banks	Product and service characteristics	No time limit (24/7 service)
		No need to go outside
		No need to keep and carry physical cards
		Short wait for transaction
		Quick transaction speed
		Cheap transaction fee
		Quick confirmation speed
		Automatic confirmation
		Good safety and security measures
		Interconnected products and services (between a bank and the providers)
		Intraconnected products and services (within a bank)
		Products and services peculiar for digital banking
		Reduced human-to-human transaction risks
		Reduced errors intentionally or unintentionally caused by humans
	Bank characteristics	Large intrabank and interbank networks
		Reputation of bank
		Reputation of bank staff
	Promotional activities	Advertisement and promotion
		Special treatments for digital banking customers
	Connectivity	Payment channels diversity
		Reduced transaction intermediaries
		Connection between bank and payment acceptance units

Category	*Subcategory*	*Item*
Customers	Socio-demographic characteristics	Age
		Experience with banking products and services
		Customer status (borrower)
	Psychological characteristics	Customer optimism
		Customer trust
		Customer risk negligence
		Customer technology sensitivity
		Digital banking needs
Environment	Eco-techno environment	Natural development of banking products and services
		Development of e-commerce
		Widespread Internet network
		Large number of Internet users
	Legal environment	Role of governmental administration entities
		Regulation on traditional banking
	Medical environment	Transmittable diseases (e.g., Covid-19)

convenience (no time and geographical limits), quickness, cheapness, automation, safety and security, and reduced risks and errors, are doubtlessly the points that attract potential customers. In addition, several characteristics of the banks, including their networks and reputation, can also quicken customers' adoption of the new products and services. Moreover, promotional initiatives carried out by banks, and connections between/among banks and their partners, are other factors that can encourage the adoption process.

P13: "Currently there is no problem with bank safety and security, especially with the apps. There are at least three levels of security: log-in password, OTP (One-Time Pin) code, and security password."

P10: "Bank apps provide different levels of safety and security measures. If the amount of the transaction is small, the security level can be low and simple."

The second category of facilitators concerns the potential customers. On the one hand, customer age (young) and experiences with Internet and mobile banking are some positive socio-demographic features that can help facilitate the adoption process. On the other hand, customers' needs, optimism and trust, knowledge of technology, and even their neglecting of the risks are important psychological features that can help generate similar positive impacts on digital banking.

P2: "Stock and financial investors and money exchangers will be the very first customers of digital banking."

P15: "There is a risk of leaking personal information. However, we customers do not care much about this issue. We think that it is normal and not very serious."

Finally, the third category reflects the impacts of the outside environment on customers' intentions. The economic and technological environment, for example, shows the level of readiness of e-commerce and Internet facilities and users as the significant facilitator of digital banking. Additionally, the legal environment presents the preparedness of digital banking laws and related administrative organizations. Moreover, since the discussions were implemented during the Covid-19 pandemic (2020–2021), the participants also mentioned the role of transmittable diseases as another potential encourager of digital banking use.

> P5: "Due to Covid-19, customers choose to use e-commerce and online banking products and services more often."

Constraints on digital banking acceptance

In addition to the facilitators, the analysis of the discussions also identified 40 factors that can limit the adoption of digital banking in Vietnam. These factors were further classified in eight subcategories and three major categories (Table 12.3).

Table 12.3 Constraining factors

Category	*Subcategory*	
Banks	Product and service characteristics	Limited products and services at the early stage
		Product and service quality
		Lack of physical evidence (e.g., cards, bank books)
		Risk of personal information leaks
		Weak safety and security measures
		Repetition of procedures
		Inability to reverse a transaction
		Unknown methods of money transaction
		Unlawful treatments for customers
		Lack of direct consultation with bank staff
		Customer complaints management
		Transaction fee
	Bank characteristics	Human resources
		Degree of standardization
	Promotional activities	Lack of information about banking products and services
		Lack of brand identifiers
		Lack of physical existence (e.g., office, branch)
	Connectivity	Intrabank system errors
		Interbank system errors
		Interbank connectivity (e.g., technological platform, transaction fee/time)
		Gap between point of transaction and point of confirmation

Category	*Subcategory*	
Customers	Socio-demographic characteristics	Age
		Experience with banking products and services
		Knowledge about existing banking products and services
		Knowledge about technologies
		Customer status (lender)
		Customer status (individual vs. organizational)
	Psychological characteristics	Customer needs
		Customer habits
		Levels of resistance to change of customers
		Levels of trend setting or following
		Customer carelessness
Environment	Eco-techno environment	Levels of resistance to change of banking sector
		Digital banking transformation speed
		Digitalization transformation speed
		Digital banking infrastructure (e.g., Internet, database)
		Unhealthy competition among banks
		Peer customers
	Legal environment	Role of governmental administration entities
		Regulation on digital banking

The first category, "banks," includes four subcategories: "product and service characteristics," "bank characteristics," "promotional activities," and "connectivity." More specifically, product quality, digital-environment-related risks, the lack of physical evidence and human contact, and the transaction fee are some of the concerns that the participants had about potential digital banking products and services. The participants were also dissuaded by the quality of the current bank staff, as well as the level of standardization of banks. They might not have had enough information about the potential products and services due to the ineffectiveness of the information and promotional materials provision. Errors inside and between/among banks were other factors that added to the worries of participants.

P17: "Interbank money transfer is quite slow."
P16: "But there is 24/7 service."
P17: "Yeah. 24/7 service is faster, but some banks require a fee."
P16: "Sure. The 24/7 service is more expensive. But there are few banks providing this type of service for free."

The second category, "customers," consists of two subcategories: "socio-demographic characteristics" and "psychological characteristics." Customer age (old), lack of experience, and status (e.g., lender) may slow down the adoption of digital banking products and services. Customers' needs, habits, resistance level, and even their carelessness may additionally restrain their willingness to use these services.

P2: "Younger people are quick adopters of information technology, unlike those born before the 1970s. It may take the former one or two days to get familiar with a new technology, while it takes more time and it's harder for the latter to change their habits."

The third and final category, "environment," is made up of two subcategories: "eco-techno environment" and "legal environment." More specifically, the slow speed of digitalization of banks in particular and of the economy in general and the lack of readiness of the legal and administrative frameworks were mentioned by the participants as the major constraints on digital banking development and adoption.

P2: "To facilitate the use of digital banking, it is necessary to create and promote an eco-system of advanced products and services. If banks only provide traditional and ordinary products and services, it may be difficult to persuade customers to change their habits."

Discussion

In a recent study, Ananda et al. (2020) found that awareness of the service, web features, and perceived usefulness have a positive influence on digital banking acceptance. In another study, Nel and Boshoff (2021) observed that lack of acceptance of digital banking is enhanced by a customer's negative attitude. This negative attitude is significantly controlled by perceived barriers related to image, value, risk, and tradition. Similar observations can also be found in other attempts, for example, Jünger and Mietzner's (2020) and Valsamidis et al.'s (2020).

This research agrees with the aforementioned studies in several ways. First, customers' awareness of the digital banking products and services is very important for their intention to use them. Without this knowledge, customers have no choice but to use the older and more traditional banking products and services, such as retail banking, Internet banking, and mobile banking. Therefore, the importance of promotional and branding activities, such as the creation and maintenance of brand associations (e.g., name, logo, themed colours) and advertisements, should be thoroughly acknowledged (Gartner, 1993; Maulan et al., 2016; Pinar et al., 2012).

Second, customers' perceptions of digital banking product and service characteristics, such as usefulness, convenience, and risk, can also affect their intentions. This point in particular is strongly supported by findings of previous studies on the earlier generations of online banking, including Internet and mobile banking (Liang & Nguyen, 2018; Lin et al., 2015; Pham & Doan, 2014), as well as these of recent studies on digital banking (Ananda et al., 2020; Jünger & Mietzner, 2020; Nel & Boshoff, 2021; Valsamidis et al., 2020).

Third, although digital banking is a virtual concept, certain tangible features, such as websites, cannot be neglected. Obviously, the role of a website in the performance of a bank has been previously confirmed (Casaló et al., 2008; Waite et al., 2011).

Finally, customers' habits of monetary payment and transfer are a personal antecedent of their intention to use banking products and services, including digital ones. Thus, promotion of banking habits, especially in developing economies, has been strongly advocated (Dadzie et al., 2021). Eventually, a new social norm can be established and later can display its role in impacting customers' behaviours (Lin et al., 2015; Pham & Doan, 2014).

On the other hand, this research adds some new observations to the literature. First, certain characteristics of banks, such as their personnel and reputation, are necessarily considered by customers. In a sense, the quality of the staff and the existence or lack of human contact with the staff can either encourage and facilitate or discourage and limit the use of digital banking products and services. The impact of this factor has been demonstrated in findings of previous studies on earlier manifestations of banking (Durkin, 2007; Phan & Ghantous, 2013). It has also been acknowledged by bank executives (Kaur et al., 2021). The assurance provided by the staff is a major determinant of this factor's importance (Durkin, 2007).

Second, the interconnectivity of products and services of a bank with those of payment acceptance, escrow service, and digital wallet companies and other partners is another essential factor regarded by customers. Unsurprisingly, Internet of Things (IoT) is an outstanding feature of the digital economy, in general, and of the digital banking sector, in particular (Boumlik & Bahaj, 2017; Suseendran et al., 2019).

Third, customers' personal characteristics also are important in their intentions to participate in digital banking or not. For example, younger, experienced, and financially educated customers are more likely to become earlier adopters of digital banking compared to those who are older, inexperienced, and somewhat financially uneducated (Jünger & Mietzner, 2020; Nel & Boshoff, 2021). This can be indirectly inferred from the findings of Nel and Boshoff (2021) as the negative attitudes toward digital banking were contributed by a sample of which two-thirds of the respondents were aged 40 years or above. In addition, customers' optimism and tendency to trust, to lead or follow – especially technological – trends, to neglect or notice risks, and to resist changes or not cannot be ignored. Evidence of the importance of these factors can be found in the consumer psychology and marketing literature (Othman et al., 2020; Roy et al., 2018; Tseng & Teng, 2016; Zhang et al., 2019).

Finally, the role of the economic, technological, legal, and even medical environment cannot be overlooked. Specifically, digital banking can only be facilitated when there are a variety of necessary supporters, for example, a good Internet network, a decent number of smart and mobile devices, a proper pool of big data, a significant number of Internet users, and an observable group of peer customers (Al-Somali et al., 2009; Hassani et al., 2018; Pigni et al., 2002; Valsamidis et al., 2020). The development of digital banking, therefore, must be in tandem with that of the digital economy as a whole (Youssef et al., 2021). In this process, the administrative bodies and the legal frameworks must be prepared and ready to use in a timely manner. If not, slow adoption or stagnation in the roll-out of these services cannot be avoided. Restrictions related to transmittable diseases, such as the Covid-19 pandemic, can help quicken the digitalization process of the economy, in general, and of the banking sector, in particular (Nicola et al., 2020).

Theoretical implications

Digital banking is not a brand-new product but the next level of online banking. Therefore, it is unsurprising if the factors that encourage and facilitate or hinder and discourage customer adoption of digital banking are similar to those of traditional retail banking, Internet banking, and mobile banking (Dinh & Pickler, 2012; Le et al., 2017; Liang & Nguyen, 2018; Lin et al., 2015; Pham & Doan, 2014; Phan & Ghantous, 2013). However, since digital banking is the most virtual product so far, the existence of the Internet of Things and the absence of bank staff and other physical brand associations seem to be some of the major factors that can differentiate digital banking from its predecessors as well as impact customers' intentions concerning this particular product.

The impacting factors are numerous (Shaikh & Karjaluoto, 2015). However, regardless of their effects (facilitating or discouraging), these factors can be grouped in three large categories: one involving the banks, one involving the customers, and one involving the environment in which both the banks and the customers exist. Figure 12.1 displays some main factors to demonstrate the association among them and customer intentions. This selection, however, is only representative.

With the Vietnamese market in particular, customers seem to specifically care about transaction confirmation, including its speed of completion and its automation. Interestingly, this desire of Vietnamese customers is the same as it was/is for

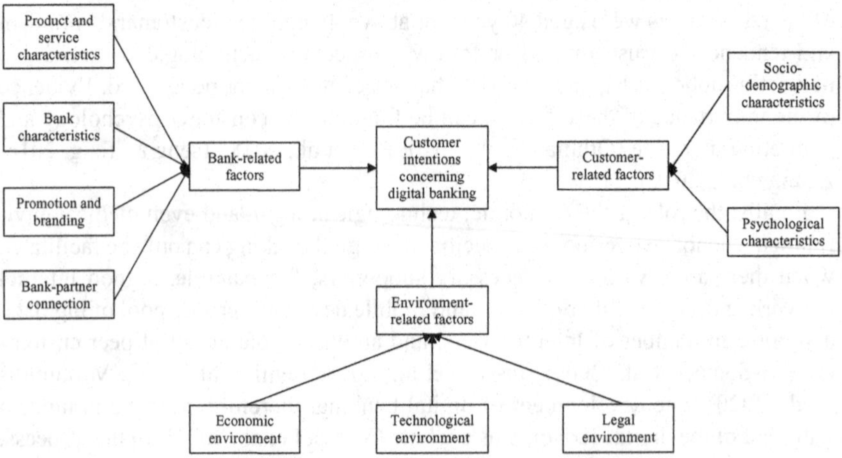

Figure 12.1 Factors affecting customer adoption of digital banking

earlier generations of banking, such as telephone banking, and the current digital financial products, such as digital money (Erdin et al., 2020; Peevers et al., 2011). This, however, has largely been neglected by previous studies on online banking, in general, and on Vietnamese bank customers, in particular.

Practical implications

The findings of this study suggest that banks should adopt a focused strategy when expanding the digital customer market. Specifically, they should try to introduce the new products and services to the existing customers' portfolios rather than to explore new territories (e.g., customers of other banks or new banking customers). Among the existing customers, it seems that focusing on the younger ones would initially be more likely to succeed since they have better knowledge about the economy and technology and thus a greater tendency to try new things (Khare et al., 2010; Valsamidis et al., 2020). After this, a new generation of digital banking customers can be fostered, and these early customers (as trend setters) will lead the next generation to follow the same ways. The psychological characteristics of future customers should also be referred to when designing and offering new products and services to some degree. However, a total reliance on these characteristics is not strongly recommended since the psychological features of customers are personal and subjective and thus are difficult to measure and meet.

In addition, digital banks should be fully aware of their invisibility. The identification and differentiation of one digital bank from the others, although this is not easy to do in the Internet environment (Pigni et al., 2002), must be carried out with utmost care. Websites, apps, and virtual human contacts need to be decided as they are the key points to deal with this particular issue. These modern platforms or channels will further assist banks in their advertisement and promotion campaigns to spread the information about their new products and services to potential customers in a fashionable and attractive way.

Bank initiatives and practices, however, cannot be successful if governmental organizations do not perform their duties properly. Specifically, the development of digital banking must be ensured by an adequate development of the Internet-related infrastructure of the economy as a whole. This must also be secured by the necessary development of a supportive legal framework and administrative system. These essential conditions are doubtlessly in the preparing hands of the central government and affiliated organizations. In the case of a developing country like Vietnam, the pledge of the tectonic government (Tran, 2020) about the digitalization of the economy must be kept and even quickened when and where applicable.

Methodological implications

Quantitative methods are robust in identifying the relative importance of each impacting factor of customers' intentions toward banking products and services (Lin et al., 2015; Pham & Doan, 2014). Nonetheless, such theory-based determinations often lead to both the overemphasis of certain factors and the negligence of others.

The qualitative method adopted in this study, on the other hand, helped in a practical way to discover the factors that bank customers really care about. The number of factors is not small, as the literature has been suggesting (Shaikh & Karjaluoto, 2015). However, a careful thematic analysis of the discussions suggests that these factors belong to three large categories: banks, customers, and environment. From here, implications for each and every related stakeholder can be correctly proposed. Therefore, the use of the qualitative methods should be further promoted in research about customer opinions, in general, and in the banking sector, in particular.

Conclusion

Despite it being the early stages of the digital banking concept, especially in developing countries, this study identified three categories (banks, customers, and environment) and eight main subcategories (product and service characteristics, bank characteristics, promotional activities and connectivity; personal characteristics and psychological characteristics; and eco-techno environment and legal environment) of factors that can affect customers' decision to use the new products and services or not. Although there may be certain differences, these factors can either encourage and facilitate or discourage and inhibit customers in adopting digital banking products and services, depending on who the customers are and what stage of development the digital banks are in.

Based on these observations, implications for banks and administrative bodies are proposed to further assist the development of digital banking. In a sense, banks should be realistic and focused in choosing the right segment of their current customers (e.g., young and experienced with technology) at which to aim their efforts to promote digital banking. It takes time to nurture a new generation of customers, but the benefits can be optimistically foreseen. In another sense, administrative entities, especially the central government, should exhibit their readiness to support and promote digital banking by preparing and providing the necessary economic, technological, and legal conditions to allow for the natural and irreversible evolution of digital banking. With these things in mind, a bright prospect can be predicted for digital banks in the very near future.

Limitation and future directions

This study, due to its exploratory and qualitative nature, could not avoid some limitations. First, the discussions were dominated by male participants (18 out of 22). Two of the five discussions were even male-only (group 2 and group 3). As a result, differences between male and female customers' opinions about digital banking, if there are any, could not be detected. Second, the discussions were implemented in Hanoi. The situations with customers in other parts of Vietnam and in other countries, therefore, could not be identified. Third, the structure of the impacting factors was revealed through a thematic analysis. As a consequence, the correlations among the subcategories and categories could not be inspected.

To address these issues, future studies may expand the context and scale of this research to include customers in other cities in Vietnam and more females. This effort will help identify intracultural differences (Bagwell, 2006) among bank customers and provide more implications for the localization of digital banks. In addition, by extending such research to other countries, intercultural differences (Heslop et al., 1998) may also be revealed that could support the globalization or glocalization of digital banking products and services. Last, but not least, a quantitative study may be useful to confirm the proposed structure of the factors impacting customers' decisions. A thorough understanding of the associations among the factors and the relative importance of each factor will become helpful information for the further development of digital banking, not only in Vietnam, but also in other countries.

References

Ajzen, I. (1991). The theory of planned behavior. *Organizational Behavior and Human Decision Processes*, *50*(2), 179–211. https://doi.org/10.1016/0749-5978(91)90020-T

Aladwani, A. M. (2001). Online banking: A field study of drivers, development challenges, and expectations. *International Journal of Information Management*, *21*(3), 213–225. https://doi.org/10.1016/S0268-4012(01)00011-1

Al-Somali, S. A., Gholami, R., & Clegg, B. (2009). An investigation into the acceptance of online banking in Saudi Arabia. *Technovation*, *29*(2), 130–141. https://doi.org/10.1016/j.technovation.2008.07.004

Ananda, S., Devesh, S., & Al Lawati, A. M. (2020). What factors drive the adoption of digital banking? An empirical study from the perspective of Omani retail banking. *Journal of Financial Services Marketing*, *25*, 14–24. https://doi.org/10.1057/s41264-020-00072-y

Baabdullah, A. M., Alalwan, A. A., Rana, N. P., Kizgin, H., & Patil, P. (2019). Consumer use of mobile banking (M-Banking) in Saudi Arabia: Towards an integrated model. *International Journal of Information Management*, *44*, 38–52. https://doi.org/10.1016/j.ijinfomgt.2018.09.002

Bagwell, S. (2006). UK Vietnamese businesses: Cultural influences and intracultural differences. *Environment and Planning C: Government and Policy*, *24*(1), 51–69. https://doi.org/10.1068/c058

Bick, R., Bugrov, D., Gerson, H., McFaull, A., & Pariyskiy, A. (2021, January 26). *Joining the next generation of digital banks in Asia*. McKinsey. www.mckinsey.com/industries/financial-services/our-insights/joining-the-next-generation-of-digital-banks-in-asia#

Boumlik, A., & Bahaj, M. (2017). Big data and IoT: A prime opportunity for banking industry. In M. Ezziyyani, M. Bahaj, & F. Khoukhi (Eds.), *Advanced information technology, services and systems. AIT2S 2017: Lecture notes in networks and systems* (Vol. 25, pp. 396–407). Springer.

Braun, V., & Clarke, V. (2006). Using thematic analysis in psychology. *Qualitative Research in Psychology*, *3*(2), 77–101. https://doi.org/10.1191/1478088706qp063oa

Casaló, L. V., Flavián, C., & Guinalíu, M. (2007). The role of security, privacy, usability and reputation in the development of online banking. *Online Information Review*, *31*(5), 583–603. https://doi.org/10.1108/14684520710832315

Casaló, L. V., Flavián, C., & Guinalíu, M. (2008). The role of satisfaction and website usability in developing customer loyalty and positive word-of-mouth in the e-banking services. *International Journal of Bank Marketing, 26*(6), 399–417. https://doi.org/10.1108/02652320810902433

Chong, A. Y. L., Ooi, K. B., Lin, B., & Tan, B. I. (2010). Online banking adoption: An empirical analysis. *International Journal of Bank Marketing, 28*(4), 267–287. https://doi.org/10.1108/02652321011054963

Colucci, E. (2007). "Focus groups can be fun": The use of activity-oriented questions in focus group discussions. *Qualitative Health Research, 17*(10), 1422–1433. https://doi.org/10.1177/1049732307308129

Dadzie, C. A., Winston, E. M., Williams, A. J., & Dadzie, K. Q. (2021). Promoting bank usage habits in Africa's savings mobilization programs: A strategic marketing perspective. *Journal of Macromarketing, 41*(2), 391–410. https://doi.org/10.1177/0276146720958063

Davies, G. (2002). *A history of money*. University of Wales Press.

Davis, F. D. (1989). Perceived usefulness, perceived ease of use, and user acceptance of information technology. *MIS Quarterly, 13*(3), 319–340. https://doi.org/10.2307/249008

Dinh, V., & Pickler, L. (2012). Examining service quality and customer satisfaction in the retail banking sector in Vietnam. *Journal of Relationship Marketing, 11*(4), 199–214. https://doi.org/10.1080/15332667.2012.741022

Durkin, M. (2007). On the role of bank staff in online customer purchase. *Marketing Intelligence & Planning, 25*(1), 82–97. https://doi.org/10.1108/02634500710722416

Elo, S., & Kyngäs, H. (2008). The qualitative content analysis process. *Journal of Advanced Nursing, 62*(1), 107–115. https://doi.org/10.1111/j.1365-2648.2007.04569.x

Erdin, E., Cebe, M., Akkaya, K., Solak, S., Bulut, E., & Uluagac, S. (2020). A bitcoin payment network with reduced transaction fees and confirmation times. *Computer Networks, 172*, 107098. https://doi.org/10.1016/j.comnet.2020.107098

Fasick, F. A. (1977). Some uses of untranscribed tape recordings in survey research. *Public Opinion Quarterly, 41*(4), 549–552. https://doi.org/10.1086/268415

Fintechnews Vietnam. (2020, November 18). Digital banking heats up in Vietnam amid COVID-19, booming e-commerce sector. *Fintechnews* https://fintechnews.sg/44097/vietnam/digital-banking-heats-up-in-vietnam-amid-covid-19-booming-e-commerce-sector/

Fishbein, M. (1979). A theory of reasoned action: Some applications and implications. *Nebraska Symposium on Motivation, 27*, 65–116.

Gartner, W. (1993). Image formation process. *Journal of Travel and Tourism Marketing, 2*(2–3), 191–215. https://doi.org/10.1300/J073v02n02_12

Hanafizadeh, P., Keating, B. W., & Khedmatgozar, H. R. (2014). A systematic review of Internet banking adoption. *Telematics and Informatics, 31*(3), 492–510. http://doi.org/10.1016/j.tele.2013.04.003

Hassan, H. E., & Wood, V. R. (2020). Does country culture influence consumers' perceptions toward mobile banking? A comparison between Egypt and the United States. *Telematics and Informatics, 46*, 101312. https://doi.org/10.1016/j.tele.2019.101312

Hassani, H., Huang, X., & Silva, E. (2018). Banking with blockchain-ed big data. *Journal of Management Analytics, 5*(4), 256–275. https://doi.org/10.1080/23270012.2018.1528900

Heslop, L. A., Papadopoulos, N., & Bourk, M. (1998). An interregional and intercultural perspective on subcultural differences in product evaluations. *Canadian Journal of Administrative Sciences, 15*(2), 113–127. https://doi.org/10.1111/j.1936-4490.1998.tb00156.x

Iwamoto, K. (2020, December 11). *Singapore ushers ASEAN into new digital banking era*. Nikkei Asia. https://asia.nikkei.com/Business/Business-Spotlight/Singapore-ushers-ASEAN-into-new-digital-banking-era

Jünger, M., & Mietzner, M. (2020). Banking goes digital: The adoption of FinTech services by German households. *Finance Research Letters*, *34*, 101260. https://doi.org/10.1016/j.frl.2019.08.008

Kassarjian, H. H. (1977). Content analysis in consumer research. *Journal of Consumer Research*, *4*(1), 8–18. https://doi.org/10.1086/208674

Kaur, S. J., Ali, L., Hassan, M. K., & Al-Emran, M. (2021). Adoption of digital banking channels in an emerging economy: Exploring the role of in-branch efforts. *Journal of Financial Services Marketing*, *26*, 107–121. https://doi.org/10.1057/s41264-020-00082-w

Khare, A., Singh, S., & Khare, A. (2010). Innovativeness/novelty-seeking behavior as determinants of online shopping behavior among Indian youth. *Journal of Internet Commerce*, *9*(3–4), 164–185. https://doi.org/10.1080/15332861.2010.529054

Kotler, P., & Armstrong, G. (2018). *Principles of marketing* (17th ed.). Pearson.

Le, V. H., Pham, L., O'Connor, A., & Pham, D. T. (2017). The development and measurement of a customer satisfaction index (E-CSI) in electronic banking: An application to the central Vietnam region. *International Journal of Strategic Decision Sciences*, *8*(3), 45–58. https://doi.org/10.4018/IJSDS.2017070102

Li, F., Lu, H., Hou, M., Cui, K., & Darbandi, M. (2021). Customer satisfaction with bank services: The role of cloud services, security, e-learning and service quality. *Technology in Society*, *64*, 101487. https://doi.org/10.1016/j.techsoc.2020.101487

Liang, C. C., & Nguyen, N. L. (2018). Marketing strategy of internet-banking service based on perceptions of service quality in Vietnam. *Electronic Commerce Research*, *18*, 629–646. https://doi.org/10.1007/s10660-017-9261-z

Lim, N., Yeow, P. H. P., & Yuen, Y. Y. (2010). An online banking security framework and a cross-cultural comparison. *Journal of Global Information Technology Management*, *13*(3), 39–62. https://doi.org/10.1080/1097198X.2010.10856519

Lin, C., & Nguyen, C. (2011). Exploring e-payment adoption in Vietnam and Taiwan. *Journal of Computer Information Systems*, *51*(4), 41–52. https://doi.org/10.1080/08874417.2011.11645500

Lin, F. T., Wu, H. Y., & Tran, T. N. N. (2015). Internet banking adoption in a developing country: An empirical study in Vietnam. *Information System and e-Business Management*, *13*, 267–287. https://doi.org/10.1007/s10257-014-0268-x

Malaquias, R. F., & Hwang, Y. (2019). Mobile banking use: A comparative study with Brazilian and U.S. participants. *International Journal of Information Management*, *44*, 132–140. https://doi.org/10.1016/j.ijinfomgt.2018.10.004

Maulan, S., Omar, N. A., & Ahmad, M. (2016). Measuring halal brand association (HalBA) for Islamic banks. *Journal of Islamic Marketing*, *7*(3), 331–354. https://doi.org/10.1108/JIMA-09-2014-0058

Nel, J., & Boshoff, C. (2021). "I just don't like digital-only banks, and you should not use them either": Traditional-bank customers' opposition to using digital-only banks. *Journal of Retailing and Consumer Services*, *59*, 102368. https://doi.org/10.1016/j.jretconser.2020.102368

Neuman, W. L. (2014). *Social research methods: Qualitative and quantitative approaches*. Pearson.

Ngugi, B., Pelowski, M., & Ogembo, J. G. (2010). M-pesa: A case study of the critical early adopters' role in the rapid adoption of mobile money banking in Kenya. *The Electronic Journal of Information Systems in Developing Countries*, *43*(1), 1–16. https://doi.org/10.1002/j.1681-4835.2010.tb00307.x

Nguyen, T. B. N. (2021, January 16). *Vietnamese ride-hailer launches digital bank with VPBank*. Nikkei Asia. https://asia.nikkei.com/Spotlight/DealStreetAsia/Vietnamese-ride-hailer-launches-digital-bank-with-VPBank

Nicola, M., Alsafi, Z., Sohrabi, C., Kerwan, A., Al-Jabir, A., Iosifidis, C., Agha, M., & Agha, R. (2020). The socio-economic implications of the coronavirus pandemic (COVID-19): A review. *International Journal of Surgery*, *78*, 185–193. https://doi.org/10.1016/j.ijsu.2020.04.018

Othman, A. K., Hamzah, M. I., & Abu Hassan, L. F. (2020). Modeling the contingent role of technological optimism on customer satisfaction with self-service technologies: A case of cash-recycling ATMs. *Journal of Enterprise Information Management*, *33*(3), 559–578. https://doi.org/10.1108/JEIM-09-2019-0295

Palinkas, L. A., Horwitz, S. M., Green, C. A., Wisdom, J. P., Duan, N., & Hoagwood, K. (2015). Purposeful sampling for qualitative data collection and analysis in mixed method implementation research. *Administration and Policy in Mental Health and Mental Health Services Research*, *42*, 533–544. https://doi.org/10.1007/s10488-013-0528-y

Peevers, G., Douglas, G., Marshall, D., & Jack, M. A. (2011). On the role of SMS for transaction confirmation with IVR telephone banking. *International Journal of Bank Marketing*, *29*(3), 206–223. https://doi.org/10.1108/02652321111117494

Pham, L., & Doan, N. P. A. (2014). Intention to use e-banking in a newly emerging country: Vietnamese customer's perspective. *International Journal of Enterprise Information Systems*, *10*(2), 103–120. https://doi.org/10.4018/ijeis.2014040106

Phan, K. N., & Ghantous, N. (2013). Managing brand associations to drive customers' trust and loyalty in Vietnamese banking. *International Journal of Bank Marketing*, *31*(6), 456–480. https://doi.org/10.1108/IJBM-04-2013-0038

Pigni, F., Ravarini, A., Tagliavini, M., & Vitari, C. (2002). Bank strategies and the internet: An interpretation of the banking industry based on the Italian retail market. *Journal of Information Technology Case and Application Research*, *4*(3), 8–37. https://doi.org/10.1080/15228053.2002.10856002

Pinar, M., Girard, T., & Eser, Z. (2012). Consumer-based brand equity in banking industry: A comparison of local and global banks in Turkey. *International Journal of Bank Marketing*, *30*(5), 359–375. https://doi.org/10.1108/02652321211247417

Roy, S. K., Balaji, M. S., Quazi, A., & Quaddus, M. (2018). Predictors of customer acceptance of and resistance to smart technologies in the retail sector. *Journal of Retailing and Consumer Services*, *42*, 147–160. https://doi.org/10.1016/j.jretconser.2018.02.005

Saumure, K., & Given, L. M. (2008). Data saturation. In L. M. Given (Ed.), *The Sage encyclopedia of qualitative research methods* (pp. 195–196). Sage.

Seal, D. W., Bogart, L. M., & Ehrhardt, A. A. (1998). Small group dynamics: The utility of focus group discussions as a research method. *Group Dynamics: Theory, Research, and Practice*, *2*(4), 253–266. https://doi.org/10.1037/1089-2699.2.4.253

Shaikh, A. A., & Karjaluoto, H. (2015). Mobile banking adoption: A literature review. *Telematics and Informatics*, *32*(1), 129–142. http://dx.doi.org/10.1016/j.tele.2014.05.003

Shankar, A., Jebarajakirthy, C., & Ashaduzzaman, M. (2020). How do electronic word of mouth practices contribute to mobile banking adoption? *Journal of Retailing and Consumer Services*, *52*, 101920. https://doi.org/10.1016/j.jretconser.2019.101920

Sikdar, P., & Makkad, M. (2015). Online banking adoption: A factor validation and satisfaction causation study in the context of Indian banking customers. *International Journal of Bank Marketing*, *33*(6), 760–785. https://doi.org/10.1108/IJBM-11-2014-0161

Statista. (2021). *Digital payments – Vietnam*. Statista. www.statista.com/outlook/296/127/digital-payments/vietnam#market-users

Suseendran, G., Chandrasekaran, E., Akila, D., & Kumar, A. S. (2019). Banking and FinTech (Financial Technology) embraced with IoT device. In N. Sharma, A. Chakrabarti, & V. Balas (eds.), *Data management, analytics and innovation: Advances in intelligent systems and computing* (Vol. 1042, pp. 197–211). Springer.

Taylor, S., & Todd, P. (1995). Decomposition and crossover effects in the theory of planned behavior: A study of consumer adoption intentions. *International Journal of Research in Marketing*, *12*(2), 137–155. https://doi.org/10.1016/0167-8116(94)00019-K

Tran, Q. V. (2020). Fulfill the responsibility to ensure the civil rights – the policy implications for tectonic government in Vietnam today. *VNU Journal of Science: Policy and Management Studies*, *36*(3), 12–18. https://doi.org/10.25073/2588-1116/vnupam.4232

Tseng, F. C., & Teng, C.-I. (2016). Carefulness matters: Consumer responses to short message service advertising. *International Journal of Electronic Commerce*, *20*(4), 525–550. https://doi.org/10.1080/10864415.2016.1171976

Valsamidis, S., Tsourgiannis, L., Pappas, D., & Mosxou, E. (2020). Digital banking in the new era: Exploring customers' attitudes. In A. Horobet, P. Polychronidou, & A. Karasavvoglou (Eds.), *Business performance and financial institutions in Europe: Contributions to economics* (pp. 91–104). Springer.

Waite, K., Harrison, T., & Hunter, G. (2011). Exploring bank website expectations across two task scenarios. *Journal of Financial Services Marketing*, *16*, 76–85. https://doi.org/10.1057/fsm.2011.6

Wellard, S. J., & McKenna, L. (2002). Turning tapes into text: Issues surrounding the transcription of interviews. *Contemporary Nurse: A Journal for the Australian Nursing Profession*, *11*(2–3), 180–186. https://doi.org/10.5172/conu.11.2-3.180

Youssef, A. B., Boubaker, S., Dedaj, B., & Carabregu-Vokshi, M. (2021). Digitalization of the economy and entrepreneurship intention. *Technological Forecasting and Social Change*, *164*, 120043. https://doi.org/10.1016/j.techfore.2020.120043

Zhang, X., Wu, Y., & Li, Y. (2019). The tendency of trust in a distrustful environment: The mediation role of contextual perceptions in eWOM. *Journal of Marketing Development & Competitiveness*, *13*(5), 46–64. https://doi.org/10.33423/jmdc.v13i5.2641

13 The role of usability in business-to-customer digital transactions on multiservice platforms of Indonesian e-money providers

Dian Palupi Restuputri, Ilyas Masudin and Alfina Damayanti

Introduction

In a country's economy, information technology seems to have an essential role because its advancement will increase the industrial world's productivity, especially from the information technology-based creative industry (Gomes et al., 2018; Zeng & Koutny, 2019). This also applies to developing countries such as Indonesia (Musa, 2006). It can be seen from many mobile applications in Indonesia, both local and foreign products, which show significant growth every year. The rapid development of internet technology has also led to social changes (Lopez-Sintas et al., 2020; Zhu et al., 2020). Many businesses have started to appear by taking advantage of these developments in information technology, one of which is the emergence of application-based service providers. Gojek and Grab are transportation application providers operating in Indonesia. Initially, these two technology companies only provided transportation services through taxi bikes. After that, the two companies innovated by developing the features offered in addition to transportation services, fulfilling both lifestyle and logistics needs in one application. For example, Gojek adds services other than taxi bikes, namely Go-Car (transportation by car), Go-Food (food purchasing services), Go-Shop (goods purchasing service), and Go-Send (goods delivery service), as well as payment features such as Go-Pulsa (credit purchases), Go-Bill (bill payment), Go-Give (donation), and Go-Sure (insurance). Meanwhile, in addition to providing a taxi bike transportation service called GrabBike, Grab is also innovating by adding services such as GrabCar (transportation by car), GrabExpress (goods delivery service), GrabFood (food purchasing service), GrabMart (goods purchasing service), as well as payment features, such as credit purchases, insurance, health, groceries, billing, tickets, hotels, and attractions. Both of these companies have a feature to make non-cash payments using electronic money. Gojek uses Gopay while Grab collaborates with OVO (rOVOlution) for its electronic money.

Currently, e-payment is growing and increasingly being used by Indonesians to make transactions, in the form of both cards (e-money) and applications (e-wallets) (Mulyana & Wijaya, 2018; Summers et al., 2020). Electronic money has

DOI: 10.4324/9781003224532-13

experienced rapid development, which is now in the form of applications stored on smartphones (Gichuki & Mulu-Mutuku, 2018; Kiconco et al., 2020; Usman, 2017). Electronic payments are rapidly growing because they provide various benefits and convenience in transactions, so that many people are interested in using non-cash payment methods. Based on the results of Bank Indonesia data in 2019, there has been an increase in the use of electronic payments every year (Shufi, 2019). It is known that there were 2.9 billion electronic money users in 2018, with 577.3 million debit card users and 330.1 million credit card users. Meanwhile, in 2019, the number of electronic money users is 10 million Gopay and T-Cash users, 7 million PayPro users, 6.5 million OVO users, 5.5 million Mandiri eCash users, 1.9 million XL Tunai users, and 1 million Sakuku users (Wang et al., 2019).

Based on the approach to human-computer interaction and combining it with psychology, the technology acceptance model (TAM) was born (Scherer et al., 2019). It suggests that three factors can explain user motivation: perceived usefulness, perceived ease of use, and attitudes toward system use (Dulloo et al., 2015). According to TAM, perceived ease of use has a dual effect, directly and indirectly, on consumers' intentions to shop online. The indirect effect occurs through the perception of its usefulness because the more comfortable a technology is to use, the more it is used (Dabholkar, 1996; Davis et al., 1989; Venkatesh, 2000). Ease of use is one of the main factors in accepting electronic banking (Daniel, 1999; Rahman et al., 2017; Simon & Thomas, 2016). Ease of use (ease to use) is the main usability concept (Bevana et al., 1991). Usability consists of all user experience elements related to the ease of learning, finding content, and doing a lot with a design/product (Bevan, 1995). People at the Centre of Mobile Application Development (PADMAC) is a usability measurement method that takes the Nielsen usability concept by adding three new variables: memorability, error, and cognitive workload (Baharuddin et al., 2013). The PADMAC method is designed to overcome the limitations of existing usability models when applied to mobile devices (Nahum-Shani et al., 2018; Shitkova et al., 2015). Based on this, the method is suitable for assessing ease of use, especially in the use of payments using electronic money on mobile phone applications (Jake-Schoffman et al., 2017; Kortum & Sorber, 2015). The objective of this study is to compare the usability of two main e-money providers in Indonesia: Gopay by Gojek and OVO by Grab.

Literature review

International Organization for Standardization (ISO) 1998 interprets usability as the level at which specific users can use a product to achieve their needs more effectively, efficiently, and satisfactorily within the scope of its users (Bevan et al., 2015). PACMAD is a model developed by Harrison et al. (2013) from the collaboration of Nielsen's usability model (Nielsen, 1994) and ISO (Bevan, 2001) by affixing a cognitive load variable. According to Harrison et al. (2013) the PACMAD is a model designed to overcome the limitations of the existing usability model when applied to mobile devices. The PACMAD model collaborates with different previous usability models' significant attributes to create a more comprehensive model (Harrison et al., 2013). The usability of the PACMAD model consists of seven subvariables: effectiveness, efficiency, satisfaction, learnability, memorability, errors, and cognitive load (Baharuddin et al., 2013; Harrison et al., 2013), as shown in Figure 13.1.

a Effectiveness is the user's ability to complete tasks in a specific context (Harrison et al., 2013).
b Efficiency is the user's ability to complete their tasks with speed and accuracy. This attribute reflects the productivity of the user when using the application (Harrison et al., 2013).
c Satisfaction is the perceived threshold of comfort and enjoyment provided to users through the use of the software. It is reflected in the user's attitude towards the software (Harrison et al., 2013).
d Learnability refers to the threshold of convenience where users gain the ability to use the application within a certain time. Learnability is the ease with which proficient users can understand an application. It usually reflects how long somebody takes to use the application effectively (Harrison et al., 2013; Nielsen, 2012b).
e Memorability is the user's ability to memorize how to use the application effectively. Any software may not be used regularly and sometimes only sporadically.

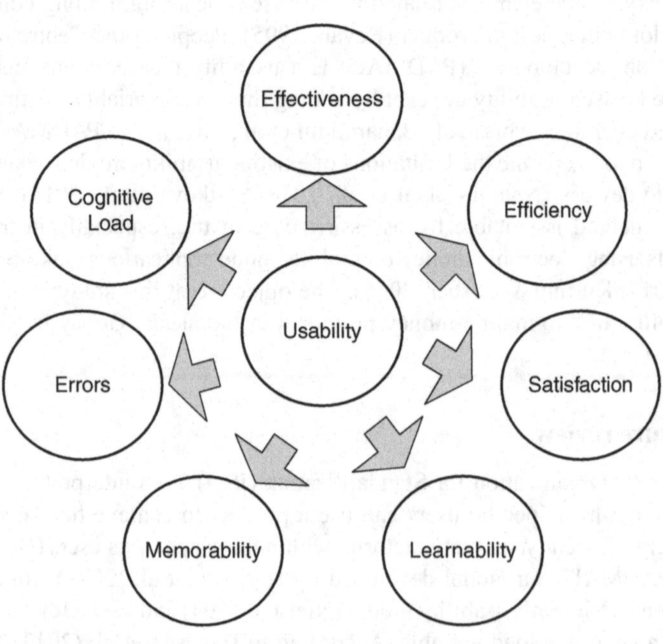

Figure 13.1 Subvariables in PACMAD model usability

Therefore, the user must remember how to use the software without relearning it after a period of inactivity (Harrison et al., 2013; Nielsen, 2012b).

f Errors entails how the software works regardless of user error and how quickly a problem that occurs can be solved. This attribute is used to reflect how well the user can complete the desired task without error. The user's error rate can be used to infer the simplicity of the system. Understanding the nature of these errors makes it possible to prevent them from occurring in future versions of the application (Harrison et al., 2013; Nielsen, 2012b).

g Cognitive load refers to the amount of cognitive processing required by the user to use an application. The main contribution of the PACMAD model is the cognitive load attribute in measuring usability. By using a mobile phone, users can use the cognitive load method to assess the usability of an application (Harrison et al., 2013)

Methodology

The data were collected through survey interviews or questionnaires with 32 respondents. In this study, data collection techniques are divided into three types: performance measurements, system usability scale (SUS), and retrospective think-aloud (RTA). The criteria for respondents in this study are users who can use mobile applications; with the standard, the users must have an Android smartphone to support their daily activities. Gojek and Grab consumers have used the e-payment method –Gojek uses Gopay, and Grab uses OVO as the payment method. Performance measurement techniques are used to produce quantitative data about the respondent's performance in completing a task on a test to measure the Gojek and Grab application system pages' usability. The performance measurement technique is conducted by recording the smartphone screen into a video when the respondent takes the test. After that, the respondent's processing time is calculated based on the video. The RTA technique can measure the usability of the Gojek and Grab application pages based on satisfaction aspects. This technique is combined with filling out the system usability, which is performed after taking performance measurement data. The variables and measurement methods used in this study are shown in Table 13.1.

Table 13.1 Research variables and measurement

Variable	*Measurement method*
Effectiveness (Harrison et al., 2013)	The level of effectiveness can be obtained from the percentage of user success in completing all tasks. Efficiency will reach a value of 100% if the respondent completes a task.
Efficiency (Harrison et al., 2013)	Measuring the efficiency of the task is carried out using performance measurement techniques using time-based efficiency.

(*Continued*)

Table 13.1 (Continued)

Variable	*Measurement method*
Satisfaction (Harrison et al., 2013)	After the respondent has finished interacting with the Gojek and Grab applications, the respondent is then given a SUS questionnaire to gauge satisfaction. The calculation is conducted by calculating the score for each questionnaire. The questionnaire uses a Likert scale for calculations.
Learnability (Harrison et al., 2013; Nielsen, 2012b)	The measurement of memorability is conducted using a combination of effectiveness values and overall relative efficiency.
Memorability (Harrison et al., 2013; Nielsen, 2012b)	The data used in measuring this attribute is a task that participants can complete correctly.
Errors (Harrison et al., 2013; Nielsen, 2012b)	Measuring error requires data in the form of the number of errors or trials conducted more than once by participants. Before measuring this component, an opportunity to make errors on the task is created, with an assumption that participants have a chance to make mistakes while doing the task.
Cognitive load (Harrison et al., 2013)	Measuring the cognitive load is conducted by comparing the number of complaints, the number of completed tasks, the number of clicks, the duration of processing time, the number of errors, the duration of the request for assistance time, and the duration of help time used by users to seek assistance in related applications during testing the usability of the Gojek and Grab applications.

Findings

Respondents are users of OVO and Gopay e-money with a minimum period of one year. Respondents were given scenarios to carry out several tasks and then observed based on the tasks' results. Respondents were also given a survey interview and questionnaire after completing the scenario given. The 32 respondents are given tasks to complete. In each task, the respondent will have processing time. After the respondent has completed the task, the respondent will tap on the cellphone. If a respondent fails to do it, the respondent is considered to have failed in completing the task. In this study, there are two types of tasks, namely informational tasks and navigational tasks. In this study, the informational task respondents are given duties that contain information in the Gojek and Grab applications, especially when using e-money transactions on Gopay (Gojek) and OVO (Grab). Meanwhile, in the navigational task, respondents are given a task to search for specific things in the application. Table 13.2 describes the task statement in which there are five tasks in this study.

Table 13.2 Task and research description

	Task	*Description*
Navigational task	Login	Respondents look for a login button so they can log into their account.
	Top-up	Respondents are asked to fill in the e-money balance top-up.
	Money transfer	Respondents are asked to send an e-money balance.
Informational task	Payments	Respondents are asked to find information about payments.
	Review	Respondents are asked to review the results of transactions that have been carried out.

Effectiveness

The level of effectiveness can be obtained from the percentage of user success in completing all tasks. According to ISO/IEC 9126–4, if a respondent succeeds in completing a task, he/she would get a score of 1, while if the respondent failed to complete the task, he/she would get a value of 0 (Al-Kilidar et al., 2005). In finding out the percentage of successful completion of a respondent's task, the following formula can be used. Effectiveness can therefore be defined as a percentage by utilizing the simple equation represented as follows (Alturki et al., 2017):

$$Percentage\ of\ Success = \frac{the\ number\ of\ tasks\ completed}{the\ total\ number\ of\ tasks} x\, 100\% \quad (1)$$

In Table 13.3, it can be seen that the percentage of successful respondents to log in is 100%, both on OVO and Gopay. While for top-up, Gopay gets a value of 72% while OVO is 84%. OVO gets a lower value for money transfer than Gopay, which is 78% for OVO and 84% for Gopay. Gopay gets a lower value of 78% for the payment feature, while OVO is 94%. Meanwhile, for giving a review after a successful transaction, OVO gets lower scores, namely 78% compared to Gopay's 94%.

Efficiency

Measuring the task's efficiency is done by using performance measurement techniques and comparing the respondents' work duration in the first test and time-based efficiency in the last one. This test's results can represent the users' speed level in finding the information needed in the application; that is, to measure efficiency, it can be done in several ways, namely the time needed to do the task and the time needed to complete the task. The duration data used is the first test data

Table 13.3 Data of successful respondents

Type of task	*Percentage of success*	
	Grab (OVO)	*Gojek (Gopay)*
Login	100%	100%
Top-up	84%	72%
Money transfer	78%	84%
Payment	94%	78%
Review	78%	94%
Average	87%	86%

Table 13.4 Data of successful tasks and work duration

OVO testing (5 tasks)			*Gopay testing (5 tasks)*		
Respondent	*Successful tasks*	*Duration*	*Respondent*	*Successful tasks*	*Duration*
Total	82	**26,674**	Total	74	**28,759**
Result		0.0144	Result		0.0125

and the last one of each application. The task is calculated in seconds based on the analysis while on the screen record.

The calculation of time-based efficiency uses:

$$Time\ based\ efficiency = \frac{\sum_{j=1}^{R}\sum_{i=1}^{N}\frac{nij}{tij}}{NR} \quad (2)$$

Where:
N = The total number of tasks (goals)
R = The number of users
n_{ij} = The result of task i by user j; if the user completes the task, then $N_{ij} = 1$; if not, then $N_{ij} = 0$
t_{ij} = The time spent by user j to complete task i. If the task is not completed, then time is measured until the moment the user quits the task.

From Table 13.4, the calculation of the time-based efficiency obtained for the OVO application is 0.0144, while the Gopay application is 0.0125. Thus, more respondents can complete tasks in a shorter time with the OVO application. The time-based efficiency comparison for OVO and Gopay users, as seen in Figure 13.2, shows that respondents' login for the Gopay application is faster than OVO. OVO top-up is faster than Gopay. For money transfers, OVO is also faster than Gopay. The payment process of OVO is faster than Gopay. Meanwhile, Gopay's review is higher than OVO's.

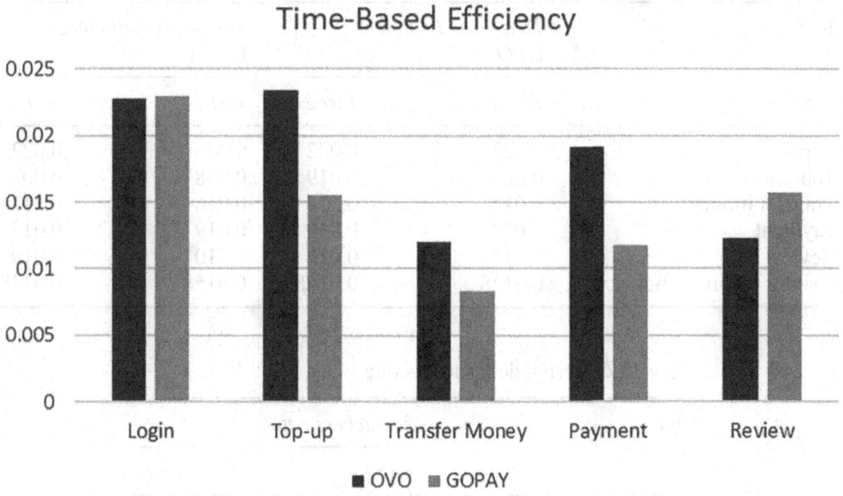

Figure 13.2 Time-based efficiency for OVO and Gopay

Learnability

The data used in measuring learnability represent a task that can be completed by the respondent correctly, while the data used are the final test data. Calculating learnability is done with a combination of effectiveness values and overall relative efficiency. Table 13.5 shows the success of each respondent in doing the task.

The *learnability* component is calculated by comparing the overall relative efficiency score based on the tasks per second of the test results. Lewis and Sauro (2009) stated that learnability could be measured by the user's ability to complete a task. Respondents were asked to do a pre-test and a final test for all five assignments. The time effectiveness of these five tasks was calculated using the time-based efficiency formula. The results obtained in the first experiment are OVO got a time-based efficiency value of 0.0178, while for the second test, it got a score of 0.0168%. Meanwhile, the first test of the Gopay application resulted in a time-based efficiency value of 0.0158, while the second test resulted in a score of 0.0138. Both OVO and Gopay got an increase in the second test. Harrison et al. (2013) stated that an application must be easy to learn so that users can quickly complete tasks using the application.

Memorability

Memorability is the level of ease with which users can remember how to use the application effectively. It is measured by asking the user to perform a series of tasks after becoming proficient at using the app and then asking them to perform a similar task after a break. To determine how easy the app is to remember, a comparison is made between two result sets.

Table 13.5 Overall relative efficiency

Task	*Time-based efficiency OVO*		*Time-based efficiency Gopay*	
	Test 1	*Test 2*	*Test 1*	*Test 2*
Login	0.023	0.022	0.026	0.022
Top-up	0.020	0.019	0.008	0.008
Transfer money	0.014	0.012	0.016	0.012
Payment	0.019	0.019	0.019	0.017
Review	0.013	0.012	0.010	0.010
Overall relative efficiency	0.0178	0.0168	0.0158	0.0138

Table 13.6 Respondent success rate

Task	*% Success rate*	
	OVO	*Gopay*
Login	100%	78%
Top-up	100%	88%
Transfer money	91%	56%
Payment	100%	44%
Review	38%	50%
Success rate	**51.2%**	**46.2%**

The data used in measuring memorability is a task that can be completed by the respondent correctly, while the data used is the final test data. Table 13.6 shows the success of each respondent's task. The memorability component is calculated using the *success rate* calculation. The success rate is the percentage of correct users' tasks (Nielsen & Tahir, 2001). The success rate represents the level of ease with which the user can complete the task. The success rate calculation uses the formula:

$$Success\ Rate = \frac{success\ task + \left(particial\ successx0,5\right)}{Total\ Task} \times 100 \quad (3)$$

From Table 13.6 it can be seen that the success rate obtained for OVO is 51.2%, and for Gopay as a whole 46.2%. According to Nielsen in Harrison et al. (2013), to have good memorability a system in an application must be easy to remember so that users can repeat the operation process that was previously used in a certain period without relearning it.

Errors

In measuring errors, data are needed in the number of errors or trials that the user has made more than once. Before measuring the components, the an opportunity to make mistakes should be formulated for the participants if there is a chance they will make mistakes while doing the task. The *error rate* component represents the error level of respondents when using the application, in which calculating the errors can be done by using the number of errors made by the respondents, the number of errors during the overall task, and the number of activities done correctly. It can be calculated with the formula:

$$Error\ rate = \frac{Total\ error}{Total\ Opportunities} \quad (4)$$

$$OVO\ Testing\ Error\ Rate = \frac{Total\ error}{Total\ Opportunities} = \frac{78}{32\ x\ 5} = 0.488$$

$$GoPay\ Testing\ Error\ Rate = \frac{Total\ error}{Total\ Opportunities} = \frac{86}{32\ x\ 5} = 0.538$$

Satisfaction

The calculation of satisfaction in this study uses the SUS scale. The SUS is a questionnaire with ten items, each with a five-step scale. Odd-numbered items have a positive tone; the tone of even-numbered items is negative. According to Brooke (2013), participants must complete the SUS after using the system under evaluation but before debriefing or other discussions. Instructions to participants should include asking them to record their immediate responses for each item rather than overthinking it. The core SUS method requires participants to stop responding to all items. For some reason, participants cannot respond to an item; they must choose a scale center point. The score contribution will range from 0 to 4. For items with positive words (odd number), the score contribution is the scale position minus 1 (xi−1). For items with negative words (even numbers), the score's contribution is five minus the scale position (5−xi). To get an overall SUS score, multiply the number of contribution items by 2.5. Thus, the overall SUS score ranges from 0 to 100 in 2.5-point increments.

After the respondents have finished interacting with OVO and Gopay, they fill out a questionnaire to see the respondents' satisfaction. The calculation is done by calculating the score for each questionnaire. Table 13.7 shows the results of the SUS questionnaire:

Cognitive load

Cognitive load has been identified as a measure of mental activity on working memory in each particular sample (De Jong, 2010). To determine the application's cognitive load, we will use the National Aeronautics and Space Administration (NASA) Task Load Index (TLX) test. NASA-TLX allows users to evaluate the workload situation after the testing is complete. It measures the overall task

Table 13.7 System usability scale mean scores

System usability scale	*OVO*		*Gopay*	
	Mean	*SD*	*Mean*	*SD*
I think that I would like to use the system frequently.	7.97	0.86	6.17	0.98
I found the system unnecessarily complex.	8.83	0.57	6.95	0.97
I thought the system was easy to use.	7.73	1.09	6.41	0.95
I think that I would need the support of a technical person to be able to use the system.	7.58	0.93	6.17	1.11
I found the various functions in the system were well-integrated.	7.5	0.88	6.41	0.88
I thought there was too much inconsistency in the system.	7.97	0.78	6.41	1.01
I would imagine that most people would learn to use the system very quickly.	8.28	0.86	6.64	0.97
I found the system very cumbersome (awkward) to use.	7.58	0.86	6.72	1.06
I felt very confident using the system.	7.73	0.93	6.64	0.94
I needed to learn many things before I could get going with the system.	7.73	0.89	5.23	1.03
Total	78.91		63.75	

demands by identifying three scales, namely related to task, behavior, and subject. The task-related scale includes mental, physical, and temporal demands. Behavior-related scales include performance and effort. The subject-related scale includes frustration. A user needs to have a description for each of the factors as shown by the following (Alturki et al., 2017):

Mental demand: to what extent did you need to perform mental and perceptual activities (such as thinking and calculating)?
Physical demand: to what extent did you need to perform physical activities (such as pushing and pulling)?
Temporal demand: to what extent did you feel time pressure while performing tasks?
Effort: how hard did you have to work hard (mentally and physically) to perform tasks?
Performance: how satisfied are you with your performance?
Frustration level: how stressed or annoyed did you feel while performing these tasks?

The NASA-TLX test contains two stages, namely weights and ratings. In the weighting procedure, the user will be asked to evaluate the effect of each task-related factor. Fifteen pairs of potential factors will be used to make comparisons. A user will give 15 cards. Each card contains a factor pair, and the user is asked to choose the most relevant factor related to the task. Each time the user selects from a pair, the tester counts them. The factor scale for each user can range from 0 to 15. The total comparison for all factors must equal 15. In the

Table 13.8 NASA-TLX score element comparison

Factor	*Percentage (%)*
Mental demand	23.62
Physical demand	6.34
Temporal demand	16.24
Performance	24.93
Effort	18.89
Frustration level	9.98

second stage, the users need to rate each of the aforementioned factors on a scale divided into 20 equal intervals and each interval equal to 5 points totaling 100 on the scale. The performance aspect shows the success rate that respondents have achieved in completing the work under predetermined goals. The mental demand aspect shows how much mental and perceptual activity it takes, such as controlling, counting, remembering, thinking, deciding, and seeing or monitoring. The effort aspect shows how much physical and mental activity it takes to achieve the desired performance. Then the temporal demand aspect shows the time it takes to complete the task. The frustration aspect shows the conditions experienced by a respondent while doing his/her task, such as confusion, fear, and work stress. Then the physical demand aspect shows how much physical activity is used to complete the work being done. Cognitive load is measured by comparing the number of complaints, the number of tasks completed, the duration of processing time, and the number of errors related to usability testing of the OVO and GOPAY applications.

Table 13.8 presents a comparison of the cognitive load aspects, which shows each user's rank for each subscale in cognitive load. Based on the indicators as a whole, it can be seen that the most significant part is the mental burden when compared to other indicators. Mental indicators and performance indicators scored the highest among all subscales. On the other hand, physical demand and frustration get the lowest score.

Discussions

Usability is a quality attribute that assesses how easy it is to use a graphical user interface (GUI). The word "usability" also refers to methods for increasing the ease of use during the design process (Nielsen, 2012a). Usability evaluation (UE) is a set of methodologies for measuring and evaluating the usability aspects of a system user interface (UI) and identifying interface design problems (Weichbroth, 2020). UE usually takes a subset of the user's actions; thus, it is suggested to use several different evaluation techniques (Rodden et al., 1998). As mentioned earlier, Harrison et al. (2013) introduced a new usability model called PACMAD to overcome existing limitations. Currently, the usability model is used to measure the usability of mobile applications. Research on mobile applications' usability is reviewed in which most of the usability models are generally based on three attributes: effectiveness, efficiency, and satisfaction. The PACMAD usability model, however, identifies three major dimensions affecting the overall usability of a mobile application: the user, the task, and the context of use (Weichbroth, 2020). PACMAD also proposes a model by adding four attributes besides these three: learnability, memorability, error, and cognitive load. The PACMAD model introduced is based on user, task, and usage context, which can overcome the limitations of the current usability model in parallel (Zahra et al., 2017). According to Kim et al. (2014), user characteristics will affect the consumer's ability to adapt, one of which is the technology contained in a product. In this study, the authors used the Gopay and OVO application usability tests.

Effectiveness can be calculated by measuring the level of completion (Hvannberg et al., 2007). Based on ISO/IEC 9126–4, it is stated that a system is said to be effective if the percentage of success when completing a task is 78% or more (Jung et al., 2004). Of the five types of tasks that have been assessed, only one is considered ineffective, namely top-up on Gopay, which is 72%. Respondents felt that finding information on how to fill in the top-up on Gopay is not easy. When respondents have to fill in a certain amount of money, they will be directed to another application called OneKlik. The respondent has to fill in the card number and daily limit for the process instantly. There is information for filling in the top-up using other methods on the next page if closely looked at. Respondents felt this was not very clear, so they found this information difficult to find and understand. The respondents' average percentage of task completion was 87% on the OVO application and 86% on the Gopay application. The results of this calculation indicate that both applications have achieved a high level of effectiveness (Az-zahra et al., 2019). Following the opinion of Harrison et al. (2013), an application's effectiveness can be measured by evaluating whether the user can complete a given set of tasks. Both Gopay and OVO get good scores for effectiveness. This means that Indonesians are familiar with the use of e-money for making payments and top-ups. But users also feel uncomfortable if things related to payments are linked to bank accounts or other applications. This indicates that they do not feel secure with this step and may also be worried about phishing on their bank account.

Efficiency is the user's ability to complete a task in a specific context. It is measured by the number of successful completion of the task, the number of steps required to complete the task, the number of taps/clicks that are not related to the application's operation, and the number of times the mobile device uses the back button. Efficiency is often measured in terms of the task's timing, that is, the time (in seconds or minutes) participants take to complete the task successfully. The time taken to complete the task can then be calculated by subtracting the start time from the end time. This study uses time as a measure of efficiency. From the obtained time-based efficiency, the OVO application's score is 0.0144, and the Gopay application's is 0.0125. Thus, more respondents can complete tasks in a shorter time with the OVO application even though the difference is not much different. The comparison of time-based efficiency for OVO and Gopay users shows that the respondents' login for the Gopay application is faster than OVO's. This is because OVO still asks for a verification code when logging in, while Gopay only needs to log in based on the SMS verification from the cellphone number. To top-up, OVO is faster than Gopay because the choice of nominal money has appeared on the screen, for example 10,000, 50,000, 100,000, etc., making it easier for us to top-up. Moreover, on Gopay, respondents are directed to enter their debit card number first to top-up; if we click "skip," then another procedure appears for topping up. Meanwhile, other top-up methods on Gopay are on the next page and are considered less informative. Likewise, for money transfers, OVO is also faster than Gopay. It is because the transfer menu is visible in the application.

In contrast to Gopay, for transfer, the word "pay" instead of "transfer" is the information that appears. It causes respondents to feel confused when they are required to transfer money. The OVO payment process is faster than Gopay's, because, in OVO, users usually enter the cellphone number for payment, while Gopay requires scanning the QR payment. As for the Gopay review, it gets more value than OVO as after the transaction is complete, Gopay immediately raises a review of the transaction. If users have not reviewed it, the transaction review appears on the start page, waiting for the user to complete a review. Meanwhile, OVO still waits for a while before a review appears, and if we do not review it immediately, we have to look in the history column, which is confusing for the respondent. Overall, it can be concluded that OVO is faster at doing its job than Gopay is. This may be because of the more straightforward display of OVO, which does not have too many menus, and tasks to be carried out are listed on the application's start page. With a lower Gopay efficiency value than OVO's, it shows that some words in English may not be understood by Indonesian people. Indonesians also do not like steps that require a lot of clicks, which makes the task completion time longer.

Learnability is the ease with which users can acquire proficiency with an application. To measure learning ability, researchers can look at participants' performance over a series of assignments and measure how long it takes for them to reach a predetermined proficiency level (Linja-aho, 2006). Learnability is measured by comparing the time taken by first-time users to complete a task on the first and second tests (Alturki et al., 2017; Saleh et al., 2015). We calculated learning ability by comparing overall relative efficiency scores based on assignments per second of test results. The result obtained in the first experiment showed that OVO got a time-based efficiency of 0.0178, and for the second test, it got a value of 0.0168%. Meanwhile, the Gopay application got a time-based efficiency value of 0.0158 on the first test and a value of 0.0138 on the second test. Both OVO and Gopay got an increase in the second test. It shows that the respondents learn quickly about using this application based on the assignment given so that there is a learning process for the respondent. Harrison et al. (2013) state that an application must be easy to learn so that users can quickly complete tasks using the application. The learnability of mobile applications is also affected by mobile applications' user-interface designs, which are generally not designed for older adults (Leung et al., 2008). Learnability studies have often concentrated on user-interface design's effect on learnability (Lin et al., 1997; Linja-aho, 2006). In ISO

9241 (1998), learnability is also defined through the three attributes of efficiency, effectiveness, and satisfaction. Dix et al. (2000) define learnability as the ease with which new users can begin effective interaction and achieve maximal performance. Some researchers have also emphasized that the term learnability should also cover expert users' ability to learn new functions (Kiili, 2002). Lin et al. (1997) found that learnability is correlated with user satisfaction. Both OVO and Gopay have a good learnability value. This indicates that they are old users who already understand the e-money application. It can also be seen that the number of e-money users is increasing in Indonesia every year.

Harrison et al. (2013) believe that to have good memorability, a system in an application must be easy to remember so that users can repeat the previously used operation process in a certain period without relearning it. Based on calculations using the OVO application, it is obtained that the memorability result is 0.5584 in the last test, which is higher than for Gopay, whose value is 0.4826. Thus, it can be concluded that the level of OVO memorability is better than Gopay's. It shows that it is easier for respondents to remember what to do in performing tasks in the OVO application. There are not many icons in the OVO application, and there are not many menus to click compared to Gopay. Memorability is the user's ability to know how to use the application effectively. The software may not be used regularly and sometimes can only be used a limited number of times. Therefore, users need to remember how to use the software without relearning it after a period of inactivity (Alturki et al., 2017). Memory can be measured by asking participants to perform a series of tasks after becoming proficient with the software and then asking them to perform a similar task after a period of inactivity. A comparison can then be made between the two sets of results to determine how easy it is to remember the application. If an application is easy to learn, the user may be willing to relearn how to use the application, and therefore, memorability may not be significant. On the other hand, some applications have a high learning curve, taking much time to learn, so according to Harrison et al. (2013), it is an important attribute in an application. The memorability value on OVO has a better value. This can be caused by the appearance of their application, which is much simpler, has a bigger font, and is not too colorful with its use of just two colors, purple and white. Indonesians prefer simple user interfaces.

Errors are mistakes made by users, and they can be resolved. The system should have a low error rate so that users make few mistakes during system use, and if they do, they can easily recover from them. Furthermore, catastrophic errors should not occur. Harrison et al. (2013) said that a mobile application must have a low error rate, and through the help of information, the users can quickly recover from the error. Errors can be measured by the number of mistakes made by the users during an activity. The error rate results can represent the level of errors made by the user. The error rate is calculated by counting the number of errors made by the participants during completion of the task (Alturki et al., 2017). The error rate made by each participant in each task was calculated to get the general error. The error rate is obtained from the total number divided by the number of tasks performed (Saleh et al., 2015). The result of the error rate calculation for OVO is 0.488 and for Gopay is 0.538.

The errors found are classified into three types: (1) input errors, (2) navigation errors, and (3) comprehension errors (Liu & Zhu, 2012). Input errors appear because the input filled in by the participant does not match what was ordered in the task description. Navigation errors also arise because participants either clicked the wrong button or skipped to fill in the required fields until the error message appeared. Comprehension errors occur when participants misinterpret the task or information in the application. OVO gets a lower error rate compared to Gopay. It happens because the information provided is clearly stated in the application. It is different from Gopay as there is much information displayed so that the participants are confused, and mistakes occur when doing the task. Compared with the average number of errors per task, which is 0.70 (Az-zahra et al., 2019), test participants' error rate using the Gopay and OVO applications falls in the small or reasonable category. The error rate on OVO also has a small value since the information listed on the OVO application is easy to understand. So that may be what makes e-money users in Indonesia comfortable because the Indonesian words and icons are easy to understand.

Satisfaction is the perceived level of comfort and enjoyment provided to users through software, which is reflected in user attitudes towards software (Harrison et al., 2013). It is reflected in the user's attitude towards the software. These are usually measured subjectively and vary among individual users. Questionnaires and other qualitative techniques are commonly used to measure user attitudes towards software applications. The SUS has become a very popular questionnaire for assessing perceived usability, both in usability studies and in surveys (Erdinç & Lewis, 2013; Grier et al., 2013; Lewis, 2018). SUS scores were then analyzed according to the original developer's scoring criteria to determine an overall satisfaction score (Wakefield et al., 2015). The feeling of satisfaction felt by respondents when using the OVO application is 78.91% and is included in the category with grade A–, whereas the Gopay application scored 63.75% and is included in the grade C category based on the SUS curved grading scale (CGS) table Sauro and Lewis (2016). This means that the Gopay application needs to increase the comfort in its use. Satisfaction is mostly influenced by how users perceive the usability of these services, more specifically their efficiency (De Oliveira et al., 2012). Satisfaction is related to effectiveness and efficiency. Therefore, if the value of effectiveness and efficiency is high, of course the value of satisfaction will also be high as well.

According to Harrison et al. (2013), cognitive load refers to the ability to use mobile applications in conjunction with user mobility. The main contribution of PACMAD is the inclusion of cognitive load as a usability attribute (Zahra et al., 2017). If seen from the indicators as a whole, the most significant part is the mental burden when compared to other indicators. Mental indicators and performance indicators scored the highest among all subscales. On the other hand, physical demand and frustration get the lowest score. Performance and mental demand are considered the most dominant in influencing the mental workload in their work. Performance is the success of a person in completing his/her job; it is related to how much success the respondent has in completing the task. Respondents may feel under pressure or fear not completing assigned tasks quickly and correctly, resulting in low performance scores. While the mental demand is how much mental activity is used at work, it is related to decision-making, thinking, and monitoring, leading to work stress. Mental demand also gets low scores because respondents feel that all the tasks given are related to thought processes and decision-making so that if they are wrong, they will fail to complete their assignments. Basically, users may feel afraid if they failed during the tasks, especially those related to a certain amount of money to burden their mental load. There are worries such as top-up tasks. They worry about losing their money if they cannot complete the task. Therefore, assurance is needed that shows safety and a solution if there is a problem.

Managerial implication

This section discusses managerial implications for management practice, with the aim of providing a theoretical contribution. The purpose of this managerial implication is solely to have a positive influence on all parties involved with e-money providers. The following are suggestions given by the researchers.

Effectiveness can be increased, for example, by finding information on how to fill in the top-up easily. This is consistent with Harrison et al. (2013), who said that effectiveness means the user can complete tasks successfully. Efficiency can be increased, for example, by making the transfer menu visible in the application. Efficiency is often measured in terms of the task's timing, that is, the time (in seconds or minutes) participants take to complete the task successfully. This means that the simpler it is and, if possible, provides options that users often use, the faster users complete tasks. Harrison et al. (2013) state that an application must be easy to learn so that users can quickly complete tasks using the application. The level of learnability can be increased by reducing the number of icons in the application and reducing the menu that must be clicked. The system should have a low error rate so that users make few mistakes during system use, and if they do, they can easily recover from them. The way to lower the error rate is to reduce the information displayed. When participants are confused, they make mistakes when doing the task. Satisfaction is the perceived level of comfort and enjoyment provided to users through software, which is reflected in user attitudes towards software (Harrison et al., 2013). Increase satisfaction by increasing the effectiveness and efficiency of the application. Mental demand is how much mental activity is used at work; it is related to decision-making, thinking, and monitoring, leading to work stress. Mental demand also gets low scores because respondents feel that all the tasks given are related to thought processes and decision-making so that if they are wrong, they will fail to complete their assignments. Mental demands can be reduced if respondents feel that all tasks related to thinking processes and decision-making are easy to do so they do not feel overwhelmed.

Conclusions

This study reviewed current usability measurement practices and found that the basic usability dimensions represented in the PACMAD model can assist mobile application developers in application evaluation. This chapter's main objective is to examine the use of existing e-money applications in Indonesia, namely Gopay and OVO. This study presents a methodology and procedures for testing applications using seven useful attributes: effectiveness, efficiency, satisfaction, memory, errors, learning abilities, and cognitive load. Based on the usability metric calculation results, it can be seen that OVO always scores higher than Gopay. OVO excels in the effective factor with a value of 87%, efficiency (0.0144), memorability with a value of 51%, error with a value of 48%, satisfaction with 79%, and cognitive load with a value of 76. Gopay's usability value for the learnability aspect is better, with a value of 0.002, while OVO's is 0.001. Overall, OVO's usability calculation results scored better than Gopay even though the difference is small, except for the satisfaction factor. The contribution of this research is to be able to determine the level of usability of the two e-money providers in Indonesia. By knowing the level of usability of these two providers, it is hoped that they will be able to understand the ease of using electronic money in consumers' applications so that the number of e-money users in Indonesia will increase. The limitation of this study is that we did not map the demographic data of the respondents; it would be better if the respondents were mapped based on certain criteria so that it would be seen whether there was a gap between one criterion and another, such as age, gender, and so forth. The number of respondents we used was also only 32 people; increasing the number of respondents could improve further research. It is necessary to conduct further research, namely the relationship between the overall usability factor value and user satisfaction. Satisfaction can change as a function of severe usability problems in the context of achieving a specific goal. It is also necessary to conduct further research on displaying an exemplary user interface to get good usability assessment results.

References

Al-Kilidar, H., Cox, K., & Kitchenham, B. (2005). *The use and usefulness of the ISO/IEC 9126 quality standard.* Paper presented at the 2005 International Symposium on Empirical Software Engineering.

Alturki, R., Gay, V., & Alturki, R. (2017). *Usability testing of fitness mobile application: Methodology and quantitative results.* Paper presented at the 7th International Conference on Computer Science, Engineering & Applications.

Az-zahra, H. M., Fauzi, N., & Kharisma, A. P. (2019). *Evaluating e-marketplace mobile application based on people at the center of mobile application development (PACMAD) usability model.* Paper presented at the 2019 International Conference on Sustainable Information Engineering and Technology (SIET).

Baharuddin, R., Singh, D., & Razali, R. (2013). Usability dimensions for mobile applications-a review. *Research Journal of Applied Sciences, Engineering and Technology, 5*(6), 2225–2231.

Bevan, N. (1995). Usability is quality of use. In *Advances in human factors/ergonomics* (Vol. 20, pp. 349–354). Elsevier.

Bevan, N. (2001). International standards for HCI and usability. *International Journal of Human-Computer Studies, 55*(4), 533–552.

Bevan, N., Carter, J., & Harker, S. (2015). *ISO 9241–11 revised: What have we learnt about usability since 1998?* Paper presented at the International Conference on Human-Computer Interaction.

Bevana, N., Kirakowskib, J., & Maissela, J. (1991). *What is usability*. Paper presented at the Proceedings of the 4th International Conference on HCI.

Brooke, J. (2013). SUS: A retrospective. *Journal of Usability Studies, 8*(2), 29–40.

Dabholkar, P. A. (1996). Consumer evaluations of new technology-based self-service options: An investigation of alternative models of service quality. *International Journal of Research in Marketing, 13*(1), 29–51.

Daniel, E. (1999). Provision of electronic banking in the UK and the Republic of Ireland. *International Journal of Bank Marketing, 17*.

Davis, F. D., Bagozzi, R. P., & Warshaw, P. R. (1989). User acceptance of computer technology: A comparison of two theoretical models. *Management Science, 35*(8), 982–1003.

De Jong, T. (2010). Cognitive load theory, educational research, and instructional design: Some food for thought. *Instructional Science, 38*(2), 105–134.

De Oliveira, R., Cherubini, M., & Oliver, N. (2012). *Influence of usability on customer satisfaction: A case study on mobile phone services*. Paper presented at the I-UxSED.

Dix, A., Finlay, J., Abowd, G. D., & Beale, R. (2000). Human-computer interaction. *Harlow ua*.

Dulloo, R., Mokashi, J., & Puri, M. (2015). Exploring technology acceptance theories and models-a comparative analysis. *KHOJ: Journal of Indian Management Research and Practices*, 308–317.

Erdinç, O., & Lewis, J. R. (2013). Psychometric evaluation of the T-CSUQ: The Turkish version of the computer system usability questionnaire. *International Journal of Human-Computer Interaction, 29*(5), 319–326.

Gichuki, C. N., & Mulu-Mutuku, M. (2018). *Determinants of awareness and adoption of mobile money technologies: Evidence from women micro entrepreneurs in Kenya*. Paper presented at the Women's Studies International Forum.

Gomes, A. O., Alves, S. T., & Silva, J. T. (2018). Effects of investment in information and communication technologies on productivity of courts in Brazil. *Government Information Quarterly, 35*(3), 480–490.

Grier, R. A., Bangor, A., Kortum, P., & Peres, S. C. (2013). *The system usability scale: Beyond standard usability testing*. Paper presented at the Proceedings of the Human Factors and Ergonomics Society Annual Meeting.

Harrison, R., Flood, D., & Duce, D. (2013). Usability of mobile applications: Literature review and rationale for a new usability model. *Journal of Interaction Science, 1*(1), 1–16.

Hvannberg, E. T., Law, E. L. C., & Lérusdóttir, M. K. (2007). Heuristic evaluation: Comparing ways of finding and reporting usability problems. *Interacting with Computers, 19*(2), 225–240.

Iso, W. (1998). 9241–11, ergonomic requirements for office work with visual display terminals (VDTs). *The International Organization for Standardization, 45*(9).

Jake-Schoffman, D. E., Silfee, V. J., Waring, M. E., Boudreaux, E. D., Sadasivam, R. S., Mullen, S. P., . . . Bennett, G. G. (2017). Methods for evaluating the content, usability, and efficacy of commercial mobile health apps. *JMIR mHealth and uHealth, 5*(12), e190.

Jung, H. W., Kim, S. G., & Chung, C. S. (2004). Measuring software product quality: A survey of ISO/IEC 9126. *IEEE Software, 21*(5), 88–92.

Kiconco, R. I., Rooks, G., & Snijders, C. (2020). Learning mobile money in social networks: Comparing a rural and urban region in Uganda. *Computers in Human Behavior, 103*, 214–225.

Kiili, K. (2002). *Evaluating WAP usability: "What usability?"*. Paper presented at the Proceedings. IEEE International Workshop on Wireless and Mobile Technologies in Education.

Kim, H., Kwon, S., Heo, J., Lee, H., & Chung, M. K. (2014). The effect of touch-key size on the usability of In-vehicle information systems and driving safety during simulated driving. *Applied Ergonomics, 45*(3), 379–388.

Kortum, P., & Sorber, M. (2015). Measuring the usability of mobile applications for phones and tablets. *International Journal of Human-Computer Interaction, 31*(8), 518–529.

Leung, R., McGrenere, J., & Graf, P. (2008). *The learnability of mobile application interfaces needs improvement.* Paper presented at the Proceedings of British HCI Workshop on HCI and the Older Population.

Lewis, J. R. (2018). Measuring perceived usability: The CSUQ, SUS, and UMUX. *International Journal of Human – Computer Interaction, 34*(12), 1148–1156.

Lewis, J. R., & Sauro, J. (2009). *The factor structure of the system usability scale.* Paper presented at the International conference on human centered design.

Lin, H. X., Choong, Y. Y., & Salvendy, G. (1997). A proposed index of usability: A method for comparing the relative usability of different software systems. *Behaviour & Information Technology, 16*(4–5), 267–277.

Linja-aho, M. (2006). Creating a framework for improving the learnability of a complex system. *Human Technology: An Interdisciplinary Journal on Humans in ICT Environments, 2.*

Liu, M., & Zhu, Z. (2012). A case study of using eye tracking techniques to evaluate the usability of e-learning courses. *International Journal of Learning Technology, 7*(2), 154–171.

Lopez-Sintas, J., Lamberti, G., & Sukphan, J. (2020). The social structuring of the digital gap in a developing country: The impact of computer and internet access opportunities on internet use in Thailand. *Technology in Society, 63*, 101433.

Mulyana, A., & Wijaya, H. (2018). Perancangan e-payment system pada e-wallet Menggunakan kode QR berbasis android. *Komputika: Jurnal Sistem Komputer, 7*(2), 63–69.

Musa, P. F. (2006). Making a case for modifying the technology acceptance model to account for limited accessibility in developing countries. *Information Technology for Development, 12*(3), 213–224.

Nahum-Shani, I., Smith, S. N., Spring, B. J., Collins, L. M., Witkiewitz, K., Tewari, A., & Murphy, S. A. (2018). Just-in-time adaptive interventions (JITAIs) in mobile health: Key components and design principles for ongoing health behavior support. *Annals of Behavioral Medicine, 52*(6), 446–462.

Nielsen, J. (1994). *Usability inspection methods.* Paper presented at the Conference companion on Human factors in computing systems.

Nielsen, J. (2012a). *Usability 101: Introduction to usability.* Nielsen Norman Group.

Nielsen, J. (2012b). *Usability 101: Introduction to usability.* Nielsen Norman Group. Recuperado Octubre 27, 2014, de www. nngroup. com/articles/usability-101-introduction-to-usability/

Nielsen, J., & Tahir, M. (2001). *Homepage usability: 50 websites deconstructed.* New Riders Publishing.

Rahman, M., Saha, N. K., Sarker, M. N. I., Sultana, A., & Prodhan, A. (2017). Problems and prospects of electronic banking in Bangladesh: A case study on Dutch-Bangla bank limited. *American Journal of Operations Management and Information Systems, 2*(1), 42–53.

Rodden, T., Cheverst, K., Davies, K., & Dix, A. (1998). *Exploiting context in HCI design for mobile systems.* Paper presented at the Workshop on human computer interaction with mobile devices.

Saleh, A., Isamil, R. B., & Fabil, N. B. (2015). Extension of pacmad model for usability evaluation metrics using goal question metrics (GQM) approach. *Journal of Theoretical & Applied Information Technology*, *79*(1).

Sauro, J., & Lewis, J. R. (2016). *Quantifying the user experience: Practical statistics for user research*. Morgan Kaufmann.

Scherer, R., Siddiq, F., & Tondeur, J. (2019). The technology acceptance model (TAM): A meta-analytic structural equation modeling approach to explaining teachers' adoption of digital technology in education. *Computers & Education*, *128*, 13–35.

Shitkova, M., Holler, J., Heide, T., Clever, N., & Becker, J. (2015). *Towards usability guidelines for mobile websites and applications*. Paper presented at the Wirtschaftsinformatik.

Shufi, F. A. (2019). *Analisis bauran pemasaran pada produk e-money studi pada mahasiswa universitas airlangga*. Universitas Airlangga.

Simon, V. T., & Thomas, A. (2016). Effect of electronic banking on customer satisfaction in selected commercial banks, Kenya. *International Academic Journal of Human Resource and Business Administration*, *2*(2), 41–63.

Summers, K. H., Baird, T. D., Woodhouse, E., Christie, M. E., McCabe, J. T., Terta, F., & Peter, N. (2020). Mobile phones and women's empowerment in Maasai communities: How men shape women's social relations and access to phones. *Journal of Rural Studies*, *77*.

Usman, R. (2017). Karakteristik uang elektronik dalam sistem pembayaran. *Yuridika*, *32*(1), 134–166.

Venkatesh, V. (2000). Determinants of perceived ease of use: Integrating control, intrinsic motivation, and emotion into the technology acceptance model. *Information Systems Research*, *11*(4), 342–365.

Wakefield, B., Pham, K., & Scherubel, M. (2015). Usability evaluation of a Web-based symptom monitoring application for heart failure. *Western Journal of Nursing Research*, *37*(7), 922–934.

Wang, G., Putri, N. M., & Christianto, A. (2019). An empirical examination of characteristics of mobile payment users in Indonesia. *Journal of Theoretical and Applied Information Technology*, *96*(1).

Weichbroth, P. (2020). Usability of mobile applications: A systematic literature study. *IEEE Access*, *8*, 55563–55577.

Zahra, F., Hussain, A., & Mohd, H. (2017). *Usability evaluation of mobile applications; where do we stand?* Paper presented at the AIP Conference Proceedings.

Zeng, W., & Koutny, M. (2019). Modelling and analysis of corporate efficiency and productivity loss associated with enterprise information security technologies. *Journal of Information Security and Applications*, *49*, 102385.

Zhu, Z., Ma, W., Sousa-Poza, A., & Leng, C. (2020). The effect of internet usage on perceptions of social fairness: Evidence from rural China. *China Economic Review*, *62*, 101508.

14 The next frontier towards Digital Sarawak

Advancing into the future

Chai Lee Goi

Introduction

The total world population by 2050 will be 9.7 billion and will continue to increase to 11 billion by 2100 (United Nations, n.d.). More than half of the total population lives in major urban areas. As urbanisation speeds up, particularly in Asian and African countries, five of the biggest challenges confronting the future of cities are environmental threats, resources, inequality, technology, and governance (World Economic Forum, 2018). Digital transformation is the answer for helping to solve some of the current and future challenges of urbanisation (Zhou et al., 2018).

In Southeast Asia, the COVID-19 pandemic has led to massive permanent digital services adoption. More than a third of digital consumers are new users, out of which 90% intend to continue using digital services (German-Indonesian Chamber of Industry and Commerce, 2020). Malaysia is one of the countries in Southeast Asia that responds to digital and technological change challenges. Malaysia aspires to move towards a technology-driven and high-tech production-based pattern of development and thus replicate the experience of the newly industrialising economies (NIEs) of Asia (Lai & Yap, 2014). Not only has this development benefited Malaysia as a country, but the digital transformation and innovation have also spilled over to other states in Malaysia, including Sarawak. The Sarawak government embarked on a journey towards digital transformation and developed a state with the concept of "Digital Sarawak".

Currently, not much research has been conducted regarding the implementation and development of digitalisation in Sarawak. Thus, the objectives of this book chapter are as follows:

- To provide the first step in Malaysia's digital transformation.
- To provide an overview of the implementation and development of Digital Sarawak.
- To analyse the process of advancing into the digital era in Sarawak.
- To analyse the opportunity and challenges of Digital Sarawak.

DOI: 10.4324/9781003224532-14

Methodology

In completing this chapter, the first process was to identify the articles in the database such as directory of open access journals, Web of Science, Scopus, Elsevier/ScienceDirect, Springer, and Taylor & Francis. Searching for articles using freely accessible web search engines such as Google and Google Scholar was also used. In addition, printed materials such as newspapers and reports published by government and private agencies were also used to prepare this chapter. The articles search and selection process can be referred to in Figure 14.1.

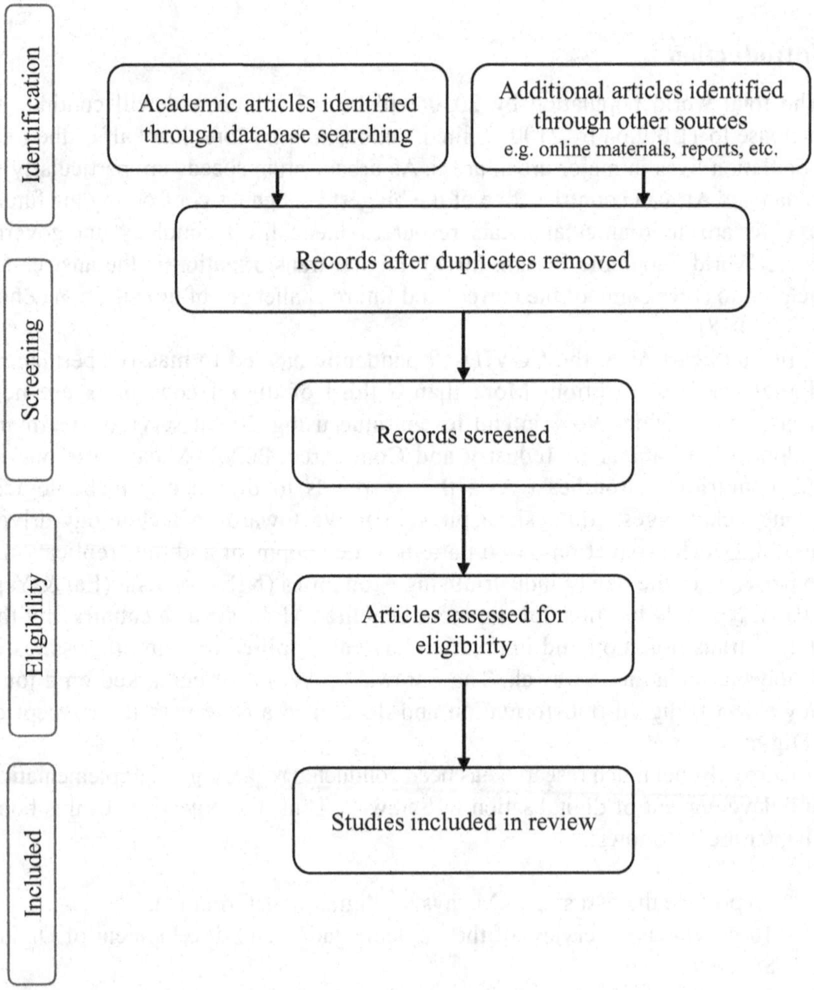

Figure 14.1 Articles search and selection process

The first step in Malaysia's digital transformation

The communication revolution began when Perak became the forerunner of telephone services when the hand-operated Magneto-operated device was first introduced in 1880. Kuala Lumpur only saw its first telephone about ten years later in 1891 (Teh, 2017). In 1967, the South East Asia Commonwealth Cable (SEACOM) was introduced to connect Peninsular Malaysia to Sarawak via the South China Sea (Trove, n.d.).

Malaysian Institute of Microelectronic Systems (MIMOS) was established in 1985 to provide critical infrastructure for the development of the local electronics industry and later started internet services in 1987. In 1992, the Joint Advanced Research Integrated Network (JARING) was conceived by MIMOS as part of the Sixth Malaysia Plan to provide internet services to the nation. More than 27 organisations and government agencies had become JARING's members with more than 200 users in early 1992.

The government has seen the potential and growth in the telecommunications industry. To increase efficiency, productivity, and competition in the market, the Telecommunications Department was privatised to Telekom Malaysia Berhad (TM), which was later listed on the Stock Exchange in 1990. In 2000, Telekom Malaysia had the largest fixed-line market share accumulated to 96.7%. Subsequent growth led to the separation of its mobile and fixed services in 2008, which allowed the company to focus more on its core business of internet and multimedia, data, and fixed-line services (Ramadass & Osman, 2012). In 1995, TM was given a license to be the second internet service provider (ISP). Initially, they introduced TM Net. TM has transformed into an integrated telecommunications service provider, with the introduction of COINS in 1997, a multimedia networking solution based on asynchronous transfer mode (ATM) technology (TM, n.d.). It is one of the prerequisites for the successful implementation of the Multimedia Super Corridor (MSC). Telekom Malaysia Berhad launched Streamyx, a broadband service in 2001 and later UNIFI, a combination of internet, voice and IPTV services in 2010 (TM, 2010). The development of the internet and broadband is growing rapidly with the participation of more private companies. Apart from Celcom, Unifi, and Streamyx (TM subsidiary companies), other companies such as Maxis, Digi, U-Mobile, YES 4G, Time, ViewQwest, and Y5Zone also provide internet and broadband services.

According to a report released by DataReportal in January 2021 (Kemp, 2021), there has been an increase in internet and social media usage. There are 27.43 million internet users in Malaysia, which means a rise of 2.8% compared to 2020. Internet penetration in Malaysia reached 84.2%, and there are 28 million social media users in Malaysia, an increase of 7.7% compared to 2020. It is equivalent to 86% of the total population. Meanwhile, there are 39.99 million mobile connections in Malaysia, equivalent to 122.8% of the total population (Kemp, 2021). The rapid growth and use of digital technologies have led to the growth of Malaysia's digital economy. From 2010 to 2016, the digital economy grew by 9% per year,

GDP, and approached 20% of the economy by 2020. E-commerce grew rapidly, generating Malaysia ringgit (RM) 110 billion by 2020, which will cover almost 40% of the digital economy (World Bank, 2018).

To achieve the goal of digital transformation, the government was and is in the process of implementing a digital transformation action plan (refer to Figure 14.2) (Malaysian Administrative Modernisation and Management Planning Unit, 2016). Policies, roadmaps, initiatives, and frameworks have been formulated to support and achieve these digital transformation aspirations. Among them are National Industry 4WRD Policy, National eCommerce Roadmap, National BDA Framework, National DFTZ Initiative, National AI Framework, and National AI Framework (Malaysia Digital Economy Corporation, n.d.).

- National Industry 4WRD Policy is a national policy which aims to transform the manufacturing sector and related services within the period from 2018 to 2025.
- National eCommerce Roadmap is to accelerate e-commerce growth based on six thrust areas – to accelerate seller adoption of e-commerce, to increase adoption of e-procurement by businesses, to lift non-tariff barriers (domestic e-fulfilment, cross-border e-commerce, e-payment, and consumer protection), to realign existing economic incentives, to make strategic investments in select e-commerce player(s), and to promote national brand to boost cross-border e-commerce.
- National BDA Framework is aiming for two major objectives – to create a national big data analytics (BDA) ecosystem, and to make BDA a catalyst for further economic growth in all sectors.
- National DFTZ Initiative is a strategic national initiative, spearheaded by the Malaysia Digital Economy Corporation (MDEC) to drive seamless

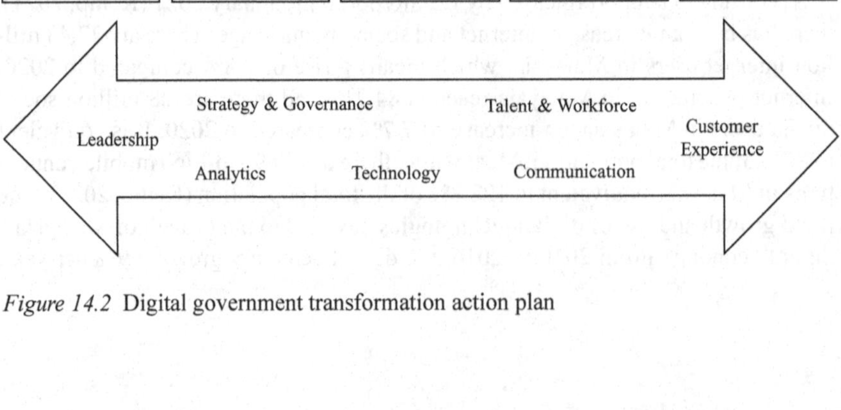

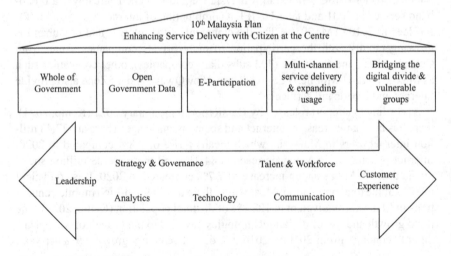

Figure 14.2 Digital government transformation action plan

cross-border trade through digitalisation and to facilitate access of local SMEs to vast opportunities in the global markets via e-commerce.

- National AI Framework is an expansion of its existing National Big Data Analytics Framework in October 2017, with the aim to drive Malaysia's AI ecosystem. This includes transforming the nation to become an AI hub and laying foundation frameworks and policies related to the main pillar of Industry 4.0 by continuously engaging and encouraging the private sector and related agencies to play a vital role in this digital transformation.
- National IoT Framework aims to realise the vision of Malaysia as the premier regional IoT development hub with the mission of creating a national ecosystem to enable the proliferation of use and industrialisation of IoT as a new source of growth for the national economy.

Malaysia's ambition is to be the digital heart of ASEAN. To achieve this aspiration, a government agency under the Ministry of Communications and Multimedia Malaysia has been established, Malaysia Digital Economy Corporation, a regional digital powerhouse launching global champions to lead the Fourth Industrial Revolution, ensuring our digital economy will drive shared prosperity for all Malaysians. MDEC plays a leading role in catalysing the transition to Malaysia 5.0 as a new narrative for the nation. This includes introducing and using emerging technologies that are now considered as essential tools in the new Malaysia 5.0 digital economy (Hussin, 2020).

The report released by the World Bank (2018) highlighted that the strategy for developing cutting-edge technologies is still in its infancy in Malaysia. In terms of digital connectivity, Malaysia underperforms in providing high-quality infrastructure, and regional disparities are likely to continue in the near term. The rapid growth of digital technologies has not yet been fully translated into digital dividends even as access to the internet by businesses tripled during 2010–2015. Digital technologies have not yet fully made a commensurate impact on business practices. The Sarawak government has carried out new efforts to address these gaps through a major paradigm shift in the development of Sarawak Digital.

An overview of the implementation and development of Digital Sarawak

The Telecommunications Department in Sarawak was established in 1946 (Sarawak Government, 2010). Throughout the 1950s, thousands of miles of cable and telecommunication infrastructure destroyed during World War II were rebuilt and repaired (Idrus & Zainol, 2007). In 1956, $12 million was spent on telecommunications development. In 1960, the establishment of a trunk telephone system between Kuching, Sibu, Bintulu, and Miri allowed international calls to be made. Telecommunication services were administered under the Department of Posts and Telecommunications until 1967, when the separation of the two services took place. On January 1, 1968, the Malaysian Telecommunications Department was established after the merger of the Telecommunication Departments between Sabah, Sarawak, and Peninsular Malaysia (Sarawak Government, 2010). Since then, the Telecommunications Department, later Telekom Malaysia Berhad, played an important role in the development of telecommunication networks in Sarawak.

JARING was opened for public connectivity using dial-up modems and became more popular with the introduction of Gopher and the World Wide Web (WWW). The usage of these two applications resulted in the congestion of JARING's backbone, which operated at 64 kbps. The backbone was then upgraded to 1.5 Mbps in 1994 to cope with the dramatic increase in data transmission within JARING. Later that year, JARING was accessible throughout the nation, where its nodes were placed in 16 major cities in Malaysia, including Kuching. This effort enabled even more users to access JARING/internet services using fixed-line telephones (Ramadass & Osman, 2012).

In a challenging era, marketers face significant global challenges. Moreover, during the COVID-19pandemic situation, it has undoubtedly had severe economic and social effects that have affected social interaction and community life. Marketers are no longer able to do business as usual (Kong, 2020). Sarawak has begun to transform the state into a digital economy superpower. With the advent of new disruptive technologies, the digital economy will be a strong platform and the catalyst for Sarawak to reach out to the global business community as well as to forge international collaborations (Povera & Rasid, 2017).

The process of advancing into the digital era in Sarawak

Malaysia is among the countries in Southeast Asia with high internet penetration. The penetration of internet usage in 2019 was 90.1% (Department of Statistics Malaysia, 2020) and is expected to increase to 97.5% (Nurhayati-Wolff, 2020). The summary of the use and access of ICT and internet in Malaysia can be referred to in Figure 14.3.

However, internet connectivity, especially in Sarawak's rural areas, is still low, and some parts do not have any connectivity at all (The Star, 2019). According to Horn and Rennie (2018), better access and increased potential use of ICT and the internet will facilitate development and reduce marginalisation in Sarawak's remote areas. But there are various problems such as lack of reliable, high-quality and affordable internet access in remote areas. Another study conducted by Jalli (2020) in Sabah and Sarawak from April 15 until May 30, 2020, showed that 67.1% of respondents expressed dissatisfaction with an internet connection. The major problems were poor connection, slow and unstable internet connection, and no internet access.

According to Sarawak Chief Minister Datuk Patinggi Abang Johari Tun Openg, Sarawak cannot rely solely on funds from the federal government to expedite the implementation of several utility and infrastructure projects, especially for the rural community (Dayak Daily, 2018). During an opening address at the official launch of the International Digital Economy Conference Sarawak 2019 (IDECS), Datuk Patinggi Abang Johari Tun Openg mentioned that Sarawak cannot afford

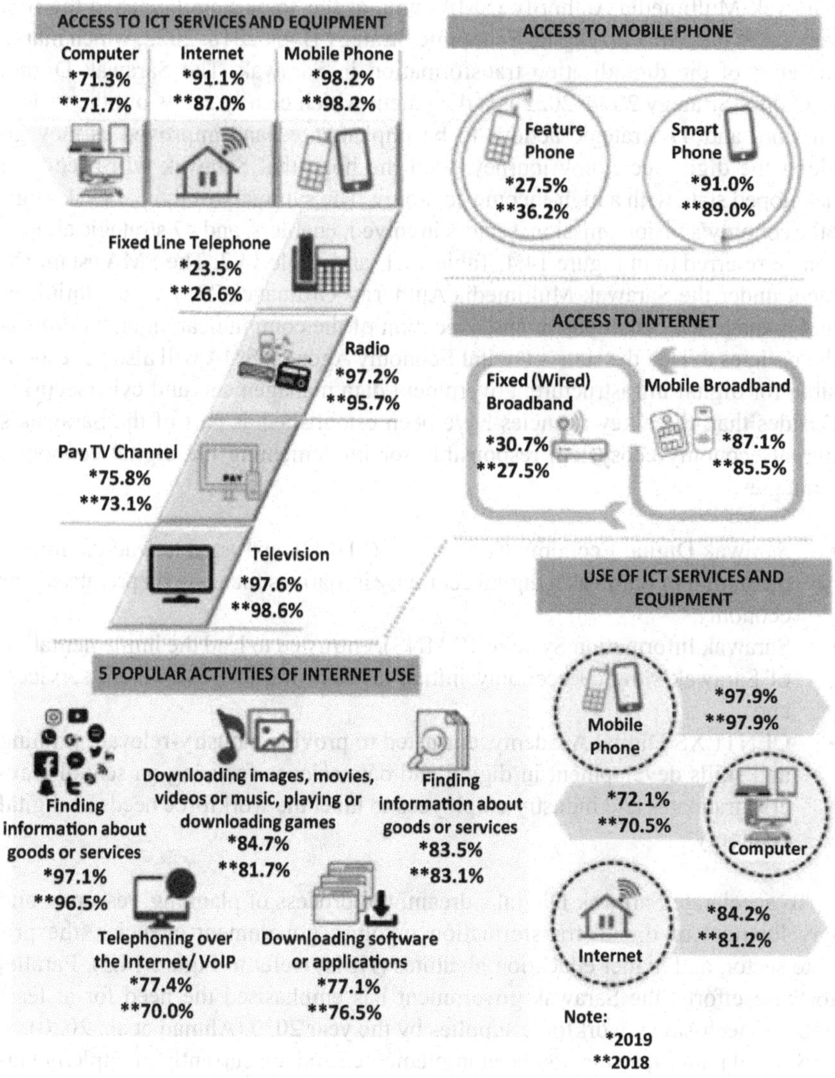

Figure 14.3 ICT and internet use and access in Malaysia (*Source*: Department of Statistics Malaysia, 2020)

to be left behind in terms of digital technology adoption and digital economic growth, which can benefit the people. He also wanted Sarawak to be on the same par with developed countries in this digital journey, which saw the world experiencing more intricate and complex technological terms, including 5G telecommunications, Internet of Things (IoT), artificial intelligence (AI), voice recognition, and virtual and augmented reality (VR/AR).

In December 13, 2017, Datuk Patinggi Abang Johari Tun Openg launched the Sarawak Multimedia Authority (SMA) and, at the same time launched the first version of the Sarawak Digital Economic Strategy Book 2018–2022, which marks the start of the digitalisation transformation in Sarawak. The Sarawak Digital Economy Strategy 2018–2022 is a document which clearly spells out the vision, mission, and 47 strategic actions to be implemented and improved as they go along the digital economy journey, with the hope that Sarawak will become a developed state with a high-income economy. The summary of the Sarawak Digital Economy's vision, mission, sectors involved, enablers, and 47 strategic actions can be referred to in Figure 14.4, Table 14.1, and Table 14.2. The SMA establishment under the Sarawak Multimedia Authority Ordinance 2017 is to administer and manage the development and execution of the communication and multimedia policies to lead the state's Digital Economy Agenda. SMA will also be responsible for digital infrastructure, government data management, and cybersecurity. Besides that, three key agencies have been established as part of the Sarawak's digital economy ecosystem responsible for implementing the digital economic strategies.

- Sarawak Digital Economy Corporation (SDEC), entrusted to lead the implementation of Sarawak's digital economy initiatives focusing on private sector economy.
- Sarawak Information Systems (SAINS), entrusted to lead the implementation of Sarawak's digital economy initiatives focusing on government services; and
- CENTEXS Digital Academy, entrusted to provide industry-relevant training and skills development in digital and data science focusing on school leavers, graduates and industry employees to meet the workforce needs of digital economy.

To accelerate Sarawak Digital's dream, the process of planning, research, and development of digital transformation involves government agencies, the private sector, and higher education institutes (HEIs) (refer to Figure 14.5). Parallel to these efforts, the Sarawak government has emphasised the need for at least 350,000 tech-savvy workforce supplies by the year 2030 (Ahmad et al., 2020).

Several plans have already been implemented and are currently in implementation. Among them are as follows (Sarawak Multimedia Authority, n.d.):

- Sarawak Multimedia Authority and Malaysian Communications and Multimedia Commission (MCMC) have worked together to increase broadband connectivity to underserved areas in Sarawak. Sarawak Multimedia Authority Rural Telecommunication (SMART) is a flagship project under the SMA that aims to build 600 telecommunication towers throughout Sarawak as one of the foundations to realise the Digital Economy Strategy 2018–2022 for Sarawak. SMA has also announced the deployment of very small aperture terminals (VSAT) under the Sarawak Multimedia Authority Linking Urban, Rural, and Nation (SALURAN) 200 plan as an interim connectivity solution to targeted areas.

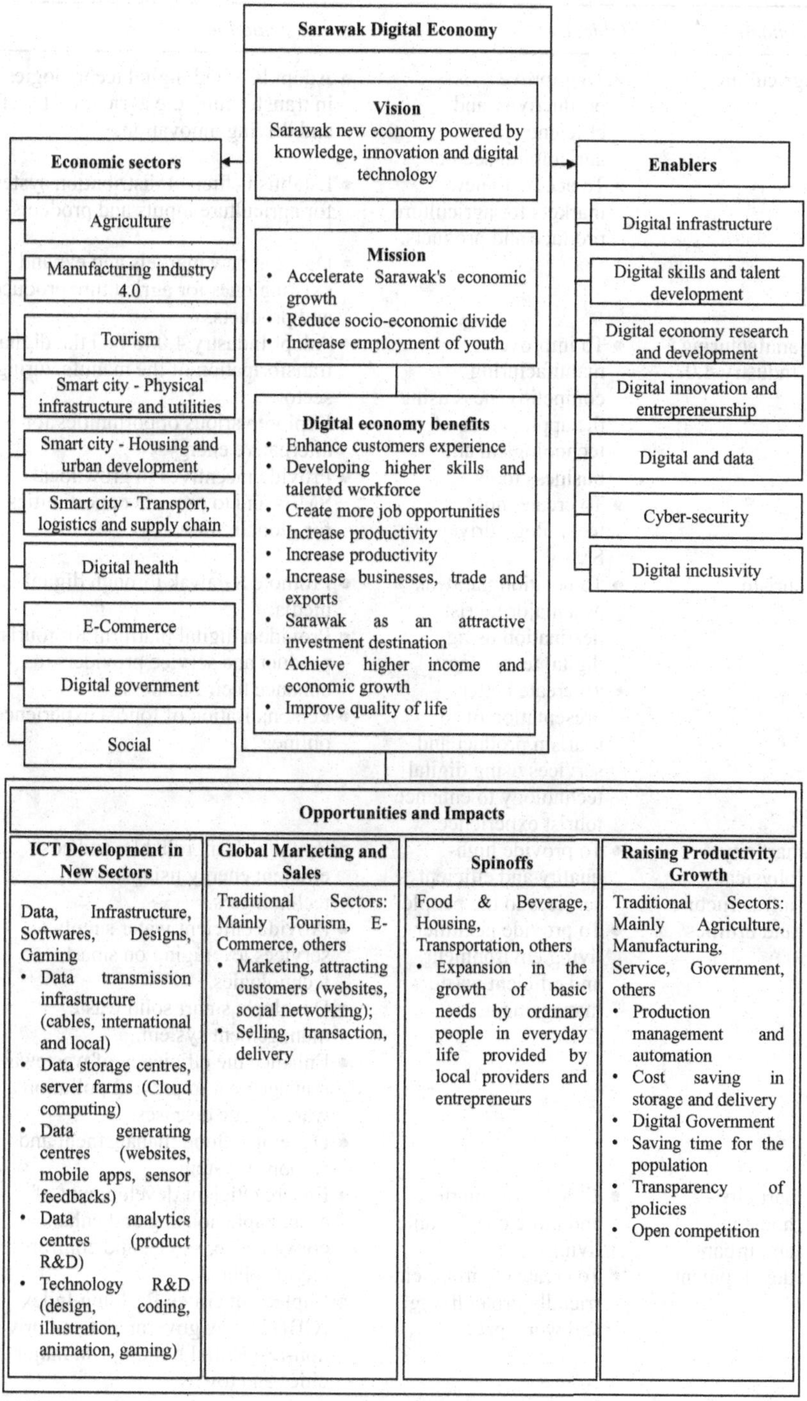

Figure 14.4 Sarawak digital economy (*Source*: Sarawak Multimedia Authority, n.d.)

Table 14.1 The anchor sectors of Sarawak Digital Economy

Economic sector	*Objective*	*Strategic action*
Agriculture	• To improve productivity and efficiency of agricultural sector. • To access to new markets for agriculture produce and products.	• Adopt ICT and digital technologies in transforming the agricultural sector and driving innovation. • Establish efficient distribution system for agriculture inputs and products. • Develop new markets and expand existing ones for agriculture produce and products.
Manufacturing Industry 4.0	• To improve manufacturing competitiveness using the applications of technological and business tools. • To create more technology driven SMEs.	• Adopt Industry 4.0 to fuel the digital transformation of the manufacturing sector. • Explore various opportunities for alternative energy. • Provide incentives to grow local SMEs and to provide opportunities for globalisation.
Tourism	• To position Sarawak as a major tourist destination using digital technology. • To create better presentation of tourism product and services using digital technology to enhance tourist experience.	• Promote Sarawak through digital media. • Provide a digital platform for tourism product and service providers to enhance their business. • Personalisation of tourist experience online.
Smart city – physical infrastructure and utilities	• To provide high-quality and efficient services to the people. • To provide healthier living environment and efficient waste management.	• Provide clean, reliable, and cost-efficient energy using smart technologies. • Provide efficient water supply services leveraging on smart technologies. • Develop a smart solid waste management system. • Enhance the efficiency of wastewater management to prevent pollution and water-borne diseases. • Develop a flood management and response system.
Smart city – housing and urban development	• To achieve smarter and more comfortable living. • To create environment-friendly urban living and workspace.	• Ensure efficient development of sustainable housing and enhance convenience, safety, and comfort for city dwellers. • Implement Green Building Index (GBI) in new government and private non-residential buildings in major cities and towns.

Economic sector	*Objective*	*Strategic action*
Smart city – transport, logistics and supply chain	• To improve mobility and user experience in transport service. • To develop more efficient logistics support for digital economy activity.	• Establish a comfortable and safe mobility for commuters using smart technologies. • Develop integrated logistics solutions to support e-commerce.
Digital health	• To improve the accessibility, efficiency, and quality of medical and health services for everyone, everywhere. • To improve the management of communicable diseases. • To achieve higher revenue from health tourism in Sarawak.	• Increase accessibility and improve level of medical and health services. • Safeguard the health of people who are living, staying, and working in Sarawak. • Provide world-class specialist healthcare services and grow health tourism in Sarawak.
E-commerce	• To increase sales and revenue from export of Sarawak products globally. • To improve the marketing of local products via e-commerce strategies and platform.	• Improve the Sarawak e-commerce and services ecosystem. • Increase awareness of Sarawak products and services through digital platform. • Increase e-commerce adoption. • Create a fintech platform that provides technological and business tools to secure a competitive advantage in current and future markets.
Digital government	• To create an open and seamless digital government. • To innovate and improve government service delivery.	Initiate digital government based on five principles: • Open government • Data-centric government • Innovative government • Excellent service delivery • Excellent digital governance
Social	• To improve social well-being of Sarawakians. • To preserve Sarawak's culture and heritage.	• Sports: roll out smart digital technology in sports to enhance spectator experience and attendance at the stadium. To foster game development, e-sports, marketing, and sport science. • Arts and culture: preserve the value of our heritage and culture physically and digitally to enhance tourism in Sarawak. • Social: accelerate the social development support to disadvantaged communities through the use of digital and data technologies.

Source: Sarawak Multimedia Authority, n.d.

Table 14.2 The enablers of Sarawak digital economy

Enabler	*Objectives*	*Strategic action*
Digital infrastructure	• To increase the broadband coverage and upgrade its speed and reliability. • To optimise the utilisation of existing and new telecommunication and network infrastructure. • To achieve higher investment inflow in digital businesses.	• Develop the infrastructure in more cost-effective way using hub-and-spoke development concept in all towns in Sarawak by end of 2020. • Develop an international internet gateway in Sarawak and a new submarine cable system to connect directly to international internet gateway. • Liberalise the infrastructure sector to attract foreign digital businesses to set up their operation in Sarawak. • Provide affordable and high-speed internet access for the masses through carrier-independent backhaul and backbone data transmission services.
Digital skills and talent development	• To develop human resources for Sarawak's digital economy; • To enhance our education system and infrastructure especially in STEM.	• Build, develop, and head hunt a workforce that is agile, digital-savvy, and industry-ready. • Strengthen current STEM and ICT education in primary, secondary, and tertiary institutions.
Digital economy research and development	• To develop and congregate knowledge and research capabilities to support digital economy in Sarawak.	• Establish a Centre of Excellence (CoE) to engage in fundamental and translational research in core areas of digital economy and other economic sectors in partnership with universities, industry, governments, and community.
Digital innovation and entrepreneurship	• To inculcate the culture of innovation. • To increase the number of successful technopreneurs including spin-offs and start-ups. • To achieve continuous technology transfer and commercialisation.	• To establish one innovation centre in each division and facilitate others (private sectors, universities, and communities). • Establish Digital Village to facilitate technology transfer and commercialisation and accelerate the maturity of the start-ups through global accelerator partnership. • Establish "Launch Sarawak" Programme at Digital Village to provide a transformative pathway to support innovation, intellectual property creation, and spin-offs.

Enabler	*Objectives*	*Strategic action*
		• Setup "Digital Landing Pads" overseas to promote Sarawak as a destination for high-tech innovation and entrepreneurship like Silicon Valley or Shanghai, etc. and to encourage both domestic and foreign investment.
Digital and data	• To use data analysis for better decision-making. • To develop and use data as our "next oil".	• Collect data from current and future digital services to support data-driven decision-making. • Monetise big data. • Develop an open data ecosystem.
Cyber-security	• To increase the awareness and knowledge among individuals and organisations on cyber-security. • To improve resilience against cyber-security threats.	• Develop a cyber-security code of practice to improve awareness about cyber-security. • Create an effective legal framework to tackle cyber risks in Sarawak. • Protect the state's critical information infrastructure.
Digital inclusivity	• To enhance the competency and readiness of all communities for digital economy.	• Establish a digital-ready community through developing digital skills and competencies and promoting inclusive digital participation.

Source: Sarawak Multimedia Authority, n.d.

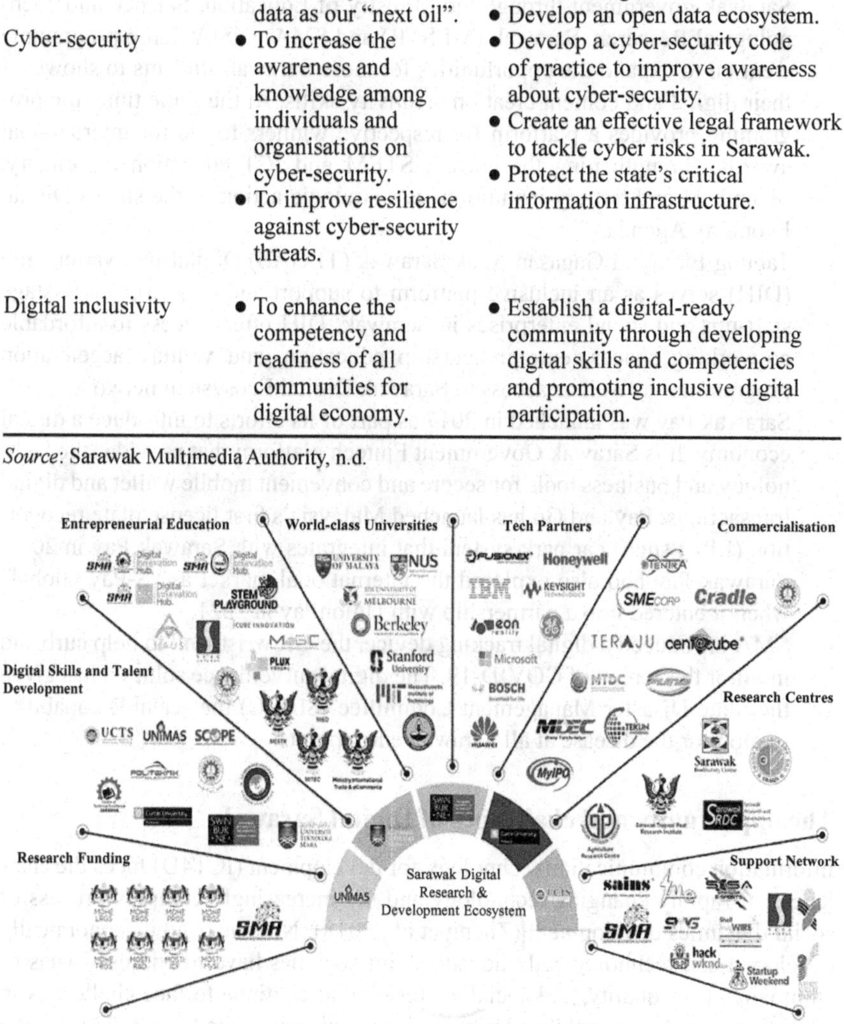

Figure 14.5 Sarawak Digital research and development ecosystem (*Source*: Sarawak Multimedia Authority, n.d.)

- Making a strong emphasis in the rural areas, the Sarawak portion of Jalinan Digital Negara (JENDELA) initiative with 636 new sites, makes up 38.3% of the total 1,661 sites allocated nationally. This initiative covers mobile broadband, satellite broadband, high-speed broadband, and fixed wireless access (FWA). SMART will contribute 600 towers to JENDELA in the form of the First300 and Next300 projects.
- Ministry of Local Government and Housing, in collaboration with SMA, has started the installation of 800 CCTVs at 200 websites in Greater Kuching under the Smart City digital economy sector agenda. This initiative aims to accelerate Sarawak's economic growth through the Smart City concept while improving the quality of life amidst a sustainable green environment.
- Sarawak government through the Ministry of Education, Science and Technological Research, Sarawak (MESTR) and SMA, DiStA Camp programme went on to expand the opportunities for more Sarawak students to showcase their digital and content creation creativity skills. At the same time, the programme provides a platform for respective winners to vie for international awards. Strengthening the current STEM and ICT education in primary, secondary, and tertiary institutions is a strategic action of the state's Digital Economy Agenda.
- Tabung Ekonomi Gagasan Anak Sarawak (TEGAS) Digital Innovation Hub (DIH) serves as an inclusive platform to support and empower early-stage start-ups and social enterprises in Sarawak. DIH offers access to affordable co-working spaces, entrepreneurship education, and venture acceleration programmes as well as access to Sarawak Digital Ecosystem network.
- Sarawak Pay was launched in 2017 as part of its efforts to introduce a digital economy. It is Sarawak Government Fintech platform that provides the technology and business tools for secure and convenient mobile wallet and digital transactions. Pay and Go has launched Malaysia's first license plate recognition (LPR) smart car park system that integrates with Sarawak Pay in 2020. Sarawak Pay had also explored the international market as "S-Pay Global" when it entered into a partnership with UnionPay in 2021.
- SMA introduced a digital tracking device, the QR wristband to help curb and monitor the spread of COVID-19. The digital surveillance solution has given the State Disaster Management Committee (SDMC) the scalable capability to monitor the disease at all Sarawak entry points.

The opportunity and challenges of Digital Sarawak

Information communication technology for development (ICT4D) faces the challenges of rapidly changing technology and the increasingly complex process of social dynamics development (Zheng et al., 2018). No matter how economically developed and technologically advanced, all societies have to address issues of employment, inequality, and social exclusion and continue to face challenges in education, healthcare, public administration, civil society, and so on. This notion implies a primary interest in the ICT artefact rather than its transformative potential to make a better world (Walsham & Sahay, 2006).

In a world where almost everything from social to industrial is disrupted by technology, moreover building a sustainable state, Sarawak's move is to focus on and accelerate digital transformation. "Digital transformation is no longer an option – it's a requirement" (Polemitis, 2019). The emphasis on the development of the proper infrastructure system for the development of the digital economy or Digital Sarawak is to create new jobs for young people in urban and rural areas and change the way people live and do business. This will create a whole new dimension of development and growth for the state. In addition, the digital economy will challenge the traditional model of doing business in Sarawak and enable new entrepreneurs to move forward (Sarawak Tribune, 2017). Following the launch of the Sarawak Multimedia Authority and the first version of the Sarawak Digital Economic Strategy 2018–2022, other important initiatives that have been and are being implemented in the digital economy in the state include the establishment of the Development Bank of Sarawak (DBOS), the Sarawak Digital Economy Corporation, and the Digital Village, as well as improving and promoting of ICT infrastructure, e-learning, data hosting, and big data and organising the Digital Economy Laboratory. While opportunities are available as a result of rapid digital development, there are still some major challenges. Digital infrastructure is one of the main challenges of the Sarawak government to achieve its target as a developed state by 2030 based on the digital economy. In fact, the basic thing that needs to be addressed is whether the mentality of society is ready for the digital revolution and moving at the same pace with Industrial Revolution 4.0.

Success requires bringing together and coordinating a far greater range of effort with digital transformation, which requires talent. Assembling the right team of technology, data, and process people who can work together, with a strong leader who can bring about the change, may be the important step in contemplating digital transformation. Technology is the engine of digital transformation, data is the fuel, process is the guidance system, and organisational change capability is the landing gear. All must function well together (Davenport & Redman, 2020). Nadkarni and Prügl (2020) addressed different technological and organisational aspects of digital transformation (refer to Figure 14.6). Meanwhile, Gong and

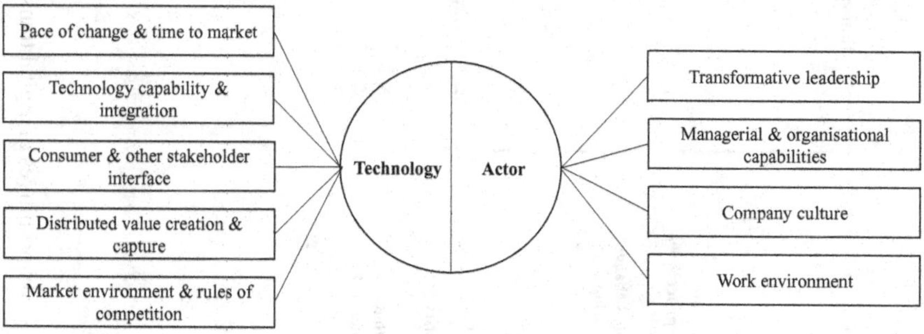

Figure 14.6 Digital transformation

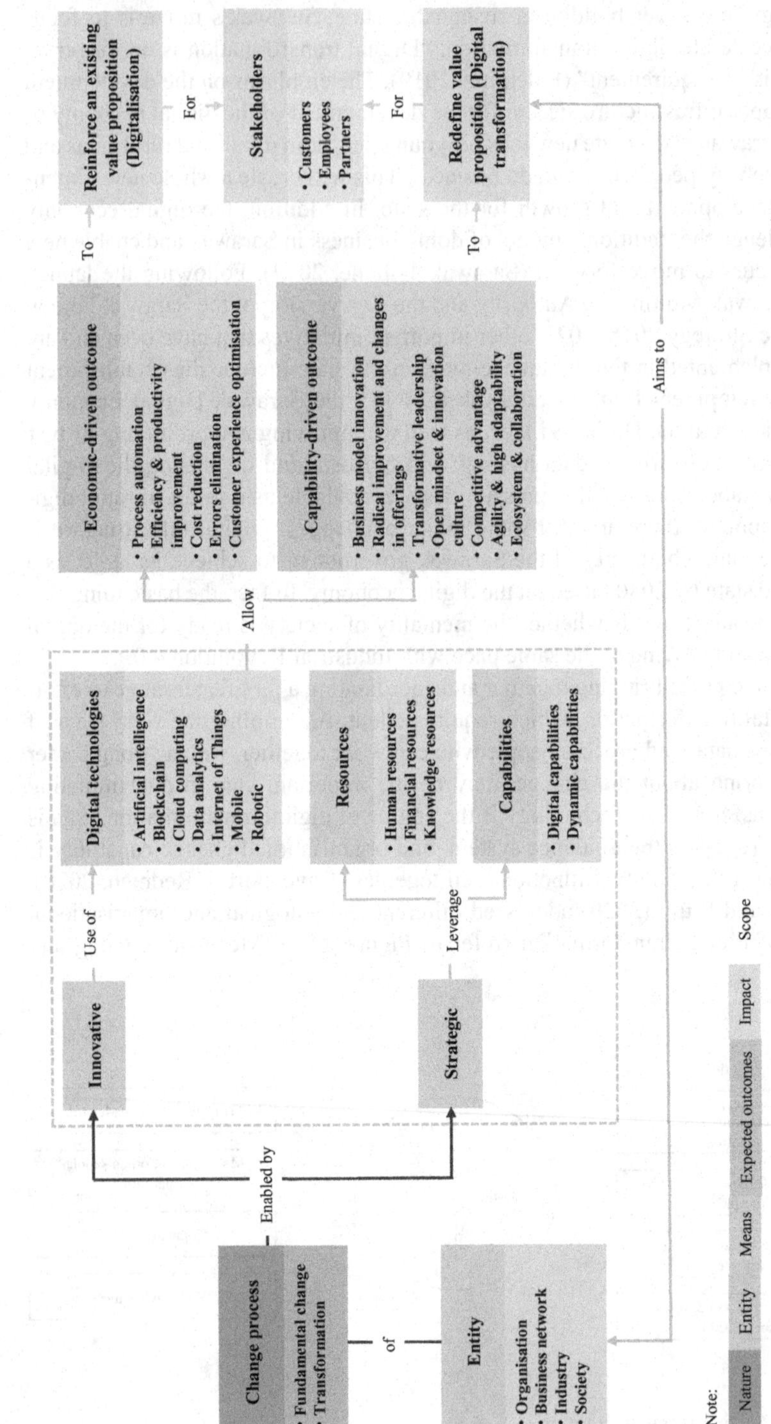

Figure 14.7 Six primitives of digital transformation

Ribiere (2020) divided digital transformation into six primitives (nature, entity, means, expected outcome, impact, and scope) that emerged from the most frequent defining attributes in each primitive (refer to Figure 14.7).

Conclusion

Sarawak Digital started more vigorously after the announcement of Sarawak's chief minister, Datuk Patinggi Abang Johari Tun Openg, with the launch of the Sarawak Digital Economy in 2017. To help make this plan a success, the state government has set up SMA with the support of several other agencies such as the Sarawak Digital Economy Corporation, the Sarawak Information Systems, and the CENTEXS Digital Academy. The planning and implementation of Sarawak Digital Economy involves ten economic sectors as well as seven enablers and 47 strategic actions.

To achieve Sarawak Digital Economy's vision, there are some significant challenges. Implementing digital infrastructure is one of the challenges to achieve its target as a developed country by 2030. Most Sarawak areas need time to receive development due to logistical, climate, and physical aspects, especially the mountainous interior, which makes communication difficult. The essential thing to note is whether the community mentality is ready for the digital revolution and moving at the same pace as the Industrial Revolution 4.0.

To secure the benefits from and minimise digitalisation risks, the government should take a holistic approach that involves multi-stakeholder dialogue and involvement. Also, policies and strategies should focus on harnessing digital data for development by developing relevant infrastructure, skills, and regulations. Finally, it is important in human capital development to create an environment where people can learn better and apply innovative ideas, acquire new competencies, and develop skills, behaviours, and attitudes.

References

Ahmad, D. A. M. A., Ahmad, J., & Saad, S. (2020). Sarawak digital economy and the organisational sensemaking process of CSR: A conceptual view. *Jurnal Komunikasi: Malaysian Journal of Communication, 36*(1), 205–223.

Davenport, T. H., & Redman, T. C. (2020). Digital transformation comes down to talent in 4 key areas. *Harvard Business Review*. https://hbr.org/2020/05/digital-transformation-is-about-talent-not-technology

Dayak Daily. (2018). *Sarawak to get busy implementing major infrastructure and utilities projects*. https://dayakdaily.com/sarawak-to-get-busy-implementing-major-infrastructure-and-utilities-projects

Department of Statistics Malaysia. (2020). *ICT use and access by individuals and households survey report, Malaysia, 2019*. www.dosm.gov.my/v1/index.php?r=column/cthemeByCat&cat=395&bul_id=SFRacTRUMEVRUFo1Ulc4Y1JlLzBqUT09&menu_id=amVoWU54UTl0a21NWmdhMjFMMWcyZz09

German-Indonesian Chamber of Industry and Commerce. (2020). *Southeast Asia digital market continues to surge*. https://indonesien.ahk.de/en/infocenter/news/news-details/southeast-asia-digital-market-continues-to-surge

Gong, C., & Ribiere, V. (2020). Developing a unified definition of digital transformation. *Technovation, 102*, 102217.

Horn, C., & Rennie, E. (2018). Digital access, choice and agency in remote Sarawak. *Telematics and Informatics, 35*(7), 1935–1948.

Hussin, R. (2020). *Malaysia 5.0 – digital transformation for Malaysian businesses*. www.digitalnewsasia.com/insights/malaysia-50-%E2%80%93-digital-transformation-malaysian-businesses

Idrus, S. M., & Zainol, K. A. (2007). History of communication in Malaysia (1940–2008). In A. B. M. Supaat, S. M. Idrus, & F. Mohamad (Eds.), *Wireless communication tech in Malaysia* (pp. 1–16). UTM.

Jalli, N. (2020). *In East Malaysia, Internet connection is still a privilege*. www.theborneopost.com/2020/07/19/grouses-over-poor-internet-access

Kemp, S. (2021). *Digital 2021: Malaysia*. https://datareportal.com/reports/digital-2021-malaysia

Kong, S. (2020). *The next frontier towards digital sarawak*. www.theborneopost.com/2020/10/11/the-next-frontier-towards-digital-sarawak

Lai, M. C., & Yap, S. F. (2014). Technology development in Malaysia and the newly industrializing economies: A comparative analysis. *Asia-Pacific Development Journal, 11*(2), 53–80.

Malaysia Digital Economy Corporation (MDEC). (n.d.). *Government, public policy, and sustainable business*. https://mdec.my/about-malaysia/government-policies

Malaysian Administrative Modernisation and Management Planning Unit. (2016). *Digital government transformation action plan*. www.malaysia.gov.my/media/uploads/1d510df1-a212-4e36-9c29-ef477daca172.pdf

Nadkarni, S., & Prügl, R. (2020). Digital transformation: A review, synthesis and opportunities for future research. *Management Review Quarterly, 71*, 233–341.

Nurhayati-Wolff, H. (2020). *Internet user penetration Malaysia 2015–2025*. www.statista.com/statistics/975058/internet-penetration-rate-in-malaysia/#:~:text=In%202019%2C%20about%2091%20percent,to%20grow%20to%2097.5%20percent

Polemitis, M. I. (2019). *Digital transformation is no longer an option – it's a requirement*. https://monica-ioannidou.medium.com/digital-transformation-is-no-longer-a-choice-94a45cbe6c4f

Povera, A., & Rasid, A. H. (2017). *Sarawak going all out to transform itself into digital economy powerhouse: CM at 13th WIEF*. www.nst.com.my/news/nation/2017/11/305588/sarawak-going-all-out-transform-itself-digital-economy-powerhouse-cm-13th

Ramadass, S., & Osman, A. (2012). *Malaysia: Snapshot of the Internet around 1990*. https://sites.google.com/site/internethistoryasia/book1/Malaysia-snapshot

Sarawak Multimedia Authority. (n.d.). www.sma.gov.my

Sarawak Government. (2010). *Telecommunications*. www.ictu.tmp.sarawak.gov.my/seg.php?recordID=M0001&sscontent=SSM0081

Sarawak Tribune. (2017). *Sarawak to leap-frog in ICT development*. www.newsarawaktribune.com.my/sarawak-to-leap-frog-in-ict-development

The Star. (2019). G*? Parts of Sarawak don't have Internet at all*. www.thestar.com.my/news/nation/2019/07/04/5g-parts-of-sarawak-dont-have-internet-at-all

Teh, A. L. (2017). *Hello . . . Malaya calling*. www.nst.com.my/lifestyle/sunday-vibes/2017/05/241149/hello-malaya-calling

TM. (2010). *Annual report 2010*. www.tm.com.my/annualreport-m/images/pdf/pyr/ar/ar2010.pdf

TM. (n.d.). *Milestones*. www.tm.com.my/AboutTM/AwardsandMilestones/Pages/Milestones.aspx

Trove. (n.d.). *Chronological history of Cairns*. https://webarchive.nla.gov.au/awa/20080111045209/http://pandora.nla.gov.au/pan/80208/20080111-1146/www.cairns.qld.gov.au/heritage/History/Timeline4.html

United Nations. (n.d.). *Population*. www.un.org/en/sections/issues-depth/population

Walsham, G., & Sahay, S. (2006). Research on information systems in developing countries: Current landscape and future prospects. *Information Technology for Development*, *12*(1), 7–24.

World Bank. (2018). *Malaysia's digital economy – a new driver of development*. https://openknowledge.worldbank.org/bitstream/handle/10986/30383/129777.pdf?sequence=1&isAllowed=y

World Economic Forum. (2018). *5 big challenges facing big cities of the future*. www.weforum.org/agenda/2018/10/the-5-biggest-challenges-cities-will-face-in-the-future

Zheng, Y., Hatakka, M., Sahay, S., & Andersson, A. (2018). Conceptualising development in information and communication technology for development (ICT4D). *Information Technology for Development*, *24*(1), 1–14.

Zhou, Y., Lohr, A., Subudhi, S., & Liu, Y. (2018). *Is digital the answer to urbanisation's biggest problems? The city of the future*. www.bcg.com/en-sea/publications/2018/digital-answer-urbanization-biggest-problems

Index

Note: Page numbers in *italics* indicates figures and page numbers in **bold** indicates tables.

Printed in the United States
by Baker & Taylor Publisher Services